D1525428

Technocracy and the Politics of Expertise

Technocracy and the Politics of Expertise

Frank Fischer

SAGE PUBLICATIONS
The Publishers of Professional Social Science
Newbury Park   London   New Delhi

For information address:

SAGE Publications, Inc.
2111 West Hillcrest Drive
Newbury Park, California 91320

SAGE Publications, Ltd.
28 Banner Street
London, ECIY 8QE
England

SAGE Publications India Pvt. Ltd.
M-32 Market
Greater Kailash I
New Delhi 110 048 India

Printed in the United States of America

Library of Congress Cataloging-in-Publication Data

Fischer, Frank, 1942–
      Technocracy and the politics of expertise / Frank Fischer.
          p.   cm.
      Includes bibliographical references.
      ISBN 0-8039-3379-7.
      1. Democracy.   2. Technocracy.   3. Decision-making.
   4. Expertise.   5. Policy sciences.   I. Title.
   JC423.F565   1990   89-37649
   321.8—dc20   CIP

FIRST PRINTING, 1990

Contents

Preface

This book ventures into contested terrains: postindustrialism, technocracy, and the politics of expertise. Focusing on the United States, it is concerned in particular with the role of two technocratic disciplines—the managerial and policy sciences—in the planning and guidance of increasingly elitist and undemocractic decision processes, both in the political system and in the workplace. Emphasizing the tensions between expertise and participation, the first half of the book delves into the technocratic politics and practices of managerial and policy expertise and their forms of decision making. It explores the history and political agenda of the technocratic project, examines the functions of the "technostructure," explicates its central importance to a postindustrial society, provides illustrations of technocractic policy and managerial decision strategies, and outlines an emergent "technocorporate" ideology in contemporary postindustrial politics.

The second half of the study turns from political critique to methodological reconstruction. Committed to the emancipatory ideals of participation and empowerment, these chapters sketch out the contours of an alternative political and methodological approach to organizational and policy expertise. They examine the postpositivist challenge to the managerial and policy sciences, illustrating its implications for policy discourse, and offer a political reconceptualization of organization theory that counters the managerial bias of the technobureaucratic model.

The importance of a political perspective, for experts as well as managers and workers, is explored in the practical context of the computerized postindustrial workplace. In the concluding section, the book advances a model of "participatory expertise" designed to pull together the methodological elements of a more democratic set of expert practices.

Normative and theoretical in approach, the primary objective of this work is to bring the implications of the critique of technocracy to bear on the pragmatic task of reconstructing the methodologies and practices of these professions. While social and political theorists have developed sophisticated critiques of technocracy, most of this literature moves in lofty theoretical and epistemological realms. Except in the most general ways, it remains far removed from actual organizational and policy processes. In fact, expertise in such matters is frequently written off as an ideological manifestation of the corporate-bureaucratic state. Moreover, theorists all too often conflate expertise and technocracy. Professional expertise in general thus tends to be denigrated as a hindrance—structural and ideological—to genuine social and political reform.

On the other hand, the practitioners of the empirically oriented managerial and policy sciences—planners, policy analysts, and organizational specialists—have mainly been oblivious to or disinterested in the social and political implications of their practices. For the most part, they have merely complained of being maligned by philosophers who fail to understand their role. This complacency has serious consequences; it is basic to the "crisis of the professions."

This study takes a different theoretical tack. Concerned with the interrelations of theory and practice, it proceeds from a specific conviction—the belief that the future of democratic institutions in the postindustrial age depends as much on the redesign of organizational and policy expertise as it does on the critique and rejection of technocratic practices. The fact that professional practices have been structured institutionally and methodologically to serve a specific mode of governance in no way vitiates the need for expertise in organizational and policy decision processes. Unfortunately, the task of reconstructing the practices of expertise has largely been ignored by democratic theorists, especially radical theorists. Expertise is not, so to say, a matter for "after the revolution." What is required is a *different kind* of expertise, one committed to the democratic redesign of hierarchical, bureaucratic institutions. To be sure, such fundamental change depends on political struggles external to the dominant institutions. But given the complexities of Western society, the effectiveness of major political change also depends on the ability to alter institutional cultures, structures, and practices. Such change must, in short, take place *through* the institutions.

Most of these issues have scarcely been explored. In such uncharted territories, it is often difficult to follow a straight and narrow path. One problem is the fact that in this middle realm between theory and practice the empirical and normative dimensions of organization and policy are difficult to separate, and even then only at a cost to both theoretical understanding and practical relevance. Moreover, as with normative analysis generally, the discussion is concerned as much with the questions that *should be asked* as with their answers. (Indeed, empirical answers to many questions raised here are at present simply beyond reach.) Such factors tend to conspire against analytical rigor, at least in the standard sense of the term. To some extent, this is reflected in a mosaic of themes that weave throughout the chapters. Rather than a tight construction from beginning to end, the reader will find particular definitions, themes, and problems restated at various points throughout the book. In an interpretive approach to complex themes, where ways of seeing are as important as conclusions, a constant return to basic themes need not be a liability. It is my hope that this is one of those cases.

Most of this book was written during the past three years, although parts of it extend back much further. Along the way, many people provided me with helpful comments on various parts of the manuscript. No one was more helpful than Alan Mandell. From beginning to end, he offered invaluable advice and criticism on both the conceptualization of the project and the written text. I benefited enormously from our discussions of these matters; they must be counted among the most rewarding experiences of the project. I am thus profoundly indebted to this good friend.

Special thanks also go to Jerry Mitchell. He carefully read—and reread—many of the chapters of the book and supplied a steady stream of critical and constructive comments that illuminated a number of stubborn theoretical problems. His efforts greatly contributed to the improvement of the manuscript, for which I remain deeply appreciative.

Many others were helpful as well. In particular, I must express my gratitude to Peter Wagner, John Forester, Rob Hoppe, Susan Fainstein, Paul Shrivastava, Carmen Sirianni, Duncan MacRae, Leslie Pal, Björn Wittrock, Tim Luke, Steven Maynard-Moody, Peter deLeon, Rita Mae Kelly, Andreas Knie, Wolf Heydebrand, Ralph Hummel, Michel Quéré, Dirk Rabe, Giovanna Procacci, Henk Verhoog, and Ken Fox. All generously provided helpful comments on various segments of the project.

And, of course, the standard disclaimer applies: None of the aforementioned bears any responsibility for the limitations of the final product.

My colleagues in political science at Rutgers University kindly helped to ease my academic responsibilities at important junctures along the way. It would be difficult to find a more sympathetic departmental chairperson than Yale Ferguson. I extend my appreciation to the department as a whole and to Yale in particular.

Thanks must also go to Meinolf Dierkes and the *Wissenschaftszentrum Berlin für Sozialforschung* for supplying me with a comfortable and stimulating environment in which to complete the final chapters of the book.

Finally, I express my personal gratitude to Hanna Trautmann. *Ihre persönliche Unterstützung war für mich im letzten Jahr dieser Arbeit äußerst wichtig, und dafür danke ich ihr sehr.*

PART I

INTRODUCTION

We shall understand "democracy" to mean the institutionally secured forms of general and public communication that deal with the practical question of how men can and want to live under the objective conditions of their ever-expanding power of control. Our problem can then be stated as one of the relation of technology and democracy: how can the power of technical control be brought within the range of the consensus of acting and transacting citizens.

—JÜRGEN HABERMAS

The language and icongraphy of democracy dominates all the politics of our time, but political power is no less elitist for all that. So too the technocracy continues to respect the formal surface of democratic politics; it is another, and this time extraordinarily potent means of subverting democracy from within its own ideals and institutions. It is a citadel of expertise dominating the high ground of urban-industrial society.

—THEODORE ROSZAK

1

Technocracy and Expertise:
The Basic Political Questions

It is commonplace today to say that we live in the age of expertise. Expert knowledge is indeed one of the most distinctive features of modern society; it is tightly woven into the very fabric of our existence. Yet recognition of this fact scarcely elucidates the full significance of the deeper phenomenon that it reflects. Our reliance on experts is now nothing less than a central component of a deep-seated transformation of the very form and content of advanced industrial society itself.

It has never been easy to define major social and economic transformations. The industrial revolution, for example, was long under way before it was widely recognized and described as a major societal transformation. Similarly, theorists today search for adequate terminology to describe the phenomenon unfolding before us. While there is still much disagreement on the exact shape and implications of the emerging societal transformation, in economic terms it is variously described with phrases such as "postindustrialism," the "information economy," and the "technetronic society." In political and institutional terms, writers speak of "Organizational America," the "Administrative State," and the "Techno-Corporate Complex." James Bendiger has identified 75 terms coined since 1950 to name this emerging world.[1]

Although it is difficult to define this new postindustrial system precisely, most commentators acknowledge its primary features to include the central importance of science and technology for economic growth, large-scale technological complexity, a high degree of organizational interdependence, increasingly centralized forms of economic and political decision making, greater reliance on technical experts, and rapid rates of economic and technological change. Enthusiasts of this new social system describe a framework of socioeconomic relationships that differ dramatically from those of the past and argue that it constitutes nothing less than a new historical "stage." While there is reason to doubt the demise of the extant economic form, it is nonetheless widely agreed that fundamental changes in the structure, institutions, and behavior of corporate capitalism are indeed appearing on the economic scene and are, moreover, reshaping social and political life as well.[2]

It is in the context of this transformation that the study of technocracy takes on special importance. In the chapters that follow, we examine its influence at the level of both the state and the organization. Indeed, we argue that technocratic theory and practices are largely shaped at the level of the organization and that much of postindustrial politics can be understood as an attempt to extend such technocratic managerial practices to the state. In this chapter, we focus on its manifestations at the level of the state, turning more to its organizational and methodological implications in the next chapter. Although much of what follows pertains to changes occurring in advanced industrial societies generally, the specific focus is on the United States.

It is also important to offer a disclaimer. No attempt is made to present a rigorous theory of technocracy or technocratic power. While this must be a goal for future studies of postindustrial technocracy, here we only seek to illuminate in critical perspective an interrelated set of technocratic themes that have yet to receive sufficient attention, especially in the managerial and policy sciences. Most important among these themes are the ways in which expert knowledge and technocratic practices have become key political resources sustaining increasingly undemocratic forms of decision making. The objective is to expand a much needed discussion of technocratic theory and practices in the hope of stimulating further investigation into this contemporary political phenomenon, both empirically and theoretically. We begin the exploration with the key element of the postindustrial equation: knowledge or information.

The Information Society:
Expertise and the Decline of Politics

Although there has been a good deal of disagreement about the
nature of the postindustrial transformation, one theme is invariant: the
idea that we are becoming a "knowledge" or "information" society.
Daniel Bell, for example, tells us that the fundamental principle organizing this new system is the "codification of theoretical knowledge."[3]
Such knowledge is now shaping not only innovation in science and
technology but developments in social policy as well. The production of
"information value" rather than "material value" is seen to be the driving
force of the postindustrial system.[4] Information value has given rise to
industries based on the computer sciences, telecommunication,
robotics, and biotechnology (concerned with breaking the information
codes of life itself). These burgeoning "information industries" are
widely recognized as transforming the very economic and social fabric
of society, a topic to which we turn in the latter half of Chapter 4.

While many celebrate the economic potentials of this information
society, others see very worrisome social and political problems.[5] Most
troublesome are the implications for democratic government. In sharp
contrast to the interest-group politics that have defined American democratic theory, this new societal formation dramatically extends a much
more monolithic system of large interlocking economic and political
institutions. At the level of both the state and the enterprise, the technological and organizational commitments of this system tend to generate
goals and problems (economic priorities, technical uncertainties, and
political requirements) that result in the curtailment of policy options
and choices. Governance essentially devolves to a consideration of what
is "feasible" given the constraints of the system. Little room is left for
meaningful debate, let alone the free play of political interests.[6]

For those who worry about the future of American politics, the pros-
pects are disturbing. The postindustrial scenario portrays an apolitical
decision-making system that often appears to have a life of its own. Political actors—both inside and outside the government—more and more
find themselves faced with a difficult reality: Even when deliberate guidance of change is a possibility, the opportunity is often fraught with
risky, potentially destabilizing consequences.

In this context, governance becomes less a matter of determining the

appropriate direction for society than one of adjusting its institutions
and policies to the flows of economic and technological development.[7]
Politics, in short, is increasingly reduced to the technically oriented task
of "keeping the machine running." Economic and political guidance
becomes more a problem of planning and management than an issue for
public deliberation and, as such, is seen as a job for which only the
experts are uniquely equipped. It is a process that opens the door to an
unprecedented extension of increasingly sophisticated forms of technocratic politics.

What happens to the prospect of a democratic politics in the course
of this enduring transformation? For many of postindustrialism's proponents, the question is essentially unproblematic. In a highly technological society, the pivotal roles of public opinion and citizen participation
are seen as artifacts of an earlier time (see Parts II and III). In a governance system geared to mediating between technological and organizational imperatives and the demands of the citizenry, politics must be
administratively centralized, much more technocratic, and largely elitist.
Democratic government, as conventionally understood, must inevitably
wither under these arrangements, a process well under way. Democracy
is, in short, taken to be an inappropriate and inferior decision-making
system for the emerging postindustrial society. Anchored to a long-
standing and deep-seated animosity toward politics itself, this view (as
we see in the first half of the book), is basic to the technocratic project.
In Chapter 5, we identify it as the core belief of a powerful new political
ideology, "technocorporatism."

On the other side of the issue are the partisans of democracy. For
them, the challenge posed by technological realities is seen as the
impending political tragedy of contemporary society. Portending a
highly centralized technological economy and large-scale bureaucratic
networks of power, postindustrialism leaves little room for traditional
concepts of democracy, particularly the concept of individual participation. Bertram Gross has defined the emergent new system as a form of
"friendly fascism."[8] Paul Goodman has called it the "metaphysical emergency" of our time.[9]

The outcome of the struggle between these political orientations is
difficult to predict. However, the imposing power of postindustrialism's
large-scale organizational and technological systems does not encourage
confidence in the future of democratic political processes, already long
in trouble in the United States and other Western nations. Clearly one
manifestation will be a greater tension between experts and laypersons,

predicted by many to be the characteristic form of conflict in the postindustrial era. It is a concern that underlies our examination of technocracy; it punctuates the discussion throughout the ensuing chapters.

Technocracy: The Basic Concepts

There is nothing new about the concept of technocracy in the social sciences, but it has never had the kind of central importance that postindustrialism is now conferring upon it. Contemporary social and political theory, however, has yet to devote to postindustrial technocracy the kind of serious attention it requires. The purpose in this section is to help rectify this shortcoming. The focus is on the broad definition of the concept and its implications.

Technocracy, in classical political terms, refers to a system of governance in which technically trained experts rule by virtue of their specialized knowledge and position in dominant political and economic institutions.[10] Dating back at least to the seventeenth century, as we see in Chapter 3, the concept of a knowledge elite has continued to gain political significance. During the past century, in fact, technocratic themes have become prominent features of many important theories of political transformation in advanced industrial societies. One observer captures the political significance of contemporary technocratic themes in these words: "If the dominant figures of the past hundred years have been the entrepreneur, the businessman, and the industrial executive, the 'new men' are the scientists, the mathematicians, the economists, and the engineers of the new intellectual technology."[11]

Historically, the theory and practice of technocracy have been political and ideological responses to industrialization and technological progress. Indeed, as we shall see in Chapters 4 through 8, the evolution of technocracy remains intricately associated with basic economic transformations. Today, technocratic planners are quite busy "adjusting" decision-making processes to the emerging realities of the "high-technology" era.[12]

Like industrial development in general, technocracy has taken numerous forms. Even within particular countries it has varied in different institutional settings. For this reason, there has been no single theory of technocracy. Numerous theories have stressed various aspects of the phenomenon and explained it somewhat differently. Among these theories, however, there has been a remarkable degree of consensus over what constitutes the basic elements of technocracy itself. The main agreement is on use of "technical expertise." Although in conventional usage technical expertise can denote a wide range of specialized skills (from automobile maintenance to medical surgery), in the theory of technocracy it refers primarily to trained expertise in the "applied sciences," particularly engineering, applied mathematics and computer sciences, economics, and the managerially and policy-oriented social sciences (or the managerial and policy sciences, as they have come to be called). Within these disciplines, expertise pertains especially to knowledge and skills that further the development of modern "decision technologies."

But technocracy is more than expertise per se. Expertise can be organized to serve a variety of social functions and interests. Technocracy, in this respect, refers to the adaptation of expertise to the tasks of governance. It gives rise to a theory of governmental decision making designed to promote technical solutions to political problems. The theory, in turn, supports a political project that advocates experts as the dominant basis for organizing political power. Technocracy, in short, pertains to the use of experts and their technical disciplinary knowledge in the pursuit of political power and the "good society," in the spheres of both the state and the economy.

In a pure technocracy, technical knowledge would serve as the base of power, with education and training providing credentials for access to it. Those who rule would justify themselves by appeal only to technical expertise grounded in scientific forms of knowledge. Such a project, of course, remains utopian. But this must not overshadow the fact that technocratic trends more and more shape contemporary society. In various ways, technocrats everywhere now share important decision-making functions with traditional economic and political elites. In a few cases, it is even possible to point to full-fledged instances of technocratic control.[13]

In terms of formal organizational structures, both public and private, experts still remain subordinate to top-level political and administrative elites. This reality, however, tends to obscure very important changes in the ways decisions are actually made in such organizations. Writers such as Skocpol, Heclo, and Hall have identified the evolution of a fundamentally different kind of policy making process in the modern bureaucratic state.[14] In the decision processes of these systems, the traditional roles of political parties and politicians have largely given way to administratively based cadres of policy experts. Examination of a range of policy domains shows that, during specific periods, policy decisions are better understood as the outcomes of evolving "learning processes" among experts within the governmental institutions than as the struggles of external political forces. In short, technically trained administrative and policy experts, at least for significant periods of time, often determine the direction and development of economic and social policy.

The influence of such experts, moreover, is in important ways increasingly independent of the politicians and political administrators they formally serve. In large part, their influence is anchored to the professional communities to which they belong. Such communities have come to be identified as "policy communities," that is, networks of experts, administrators, and constituencies geared to shaping policy in a particular domain.[15] Aptly described as "hidden hierarchies," such policy communities have a disproportionate influence not only over the definitions of specific public issues but also over decisions regarding both the advisability and the feasibility of the various solutions.

Similarly, others have identified the appearance of policy "discourse coalitions" that form between experts and political leaders.[16] Such discourse coalitions formulate and advance policy strategies very differently than do traditional party coalitions. While party elites retain formal authority in the goverance process, as we see in Chapter 6, they themselves increasingly justify decisions by appeal to the technical analyses of their coalition experts. In the face of the escalating complexities of advanced technological societies, it is appropriate to assume that both the ideologies and the practices of technocracy will continue to expand, often at the expense of traditional elites and assuredly at the expense of the broader public.

The Quiet Revolution

The specific nature of technocratic practices at the operational level of decision making is not always easy to identify, thus making it difficult to study the actual workings of technocratic power and influence. For one thing, technocratic decision making largely takes place in administrative settings where it is typically shielded from public scrutiny. But even more important is its emphasis on knowledge and information technologies. Technocratic politics, based on uses of information and analytical techniques, easily escapes conventional political categories. Unlike traditional political activity, it displays neither leaders nor barricades. Instead, it moves quietly—even facelessly at times—through the administrative hierarchies of the political and economic systems. Portrayed as the "quiet revolution," it subtly manifests itself as a transformation in the very nature and terrain of politics.[17] Working through technical methodologies and their forms of arguments, its machinations are opaquely hidden in discussions over decision criteria rather than in policy decisions per se. Politicians still choose one policy option over another, but it is increasingly the experts who shape the deliberative framework within which they must choose. More and more, they structure the processes of political deliberation by illuminating and defining the problems that politicians are compelled to consider, as well as detailing the options from which they can choose. At this more fundamental "meta-level" of political deliberation, the role of these "unelected representatives" constitutes a *basic* challenge to values that have traditionally organized the political system itself. In short, technocracy shapes, if not subverts, the very ways we think about and understand politics.

This hidden dimension of technocratic politics poses thorny problems for political theory. Although technocracy is clearly associated with specific groups of people, its emphasis on criteria and techniques rather than on a shared agenda of policies and programs makes it difficult to identify technocracy as a political movement in the ordinary sense of the term (i.e., as an organized set of activities held together both by a commonly accepted programmatic ideology and by identifiable leaders). The problem is exacerbated by the fact that technocrats tend to eschew the label. To be called a technocrat today tends to imply pejorative connotations.[18] For this reason, few contemporary technocratic theorists readily acknowledge an intellectual and ideological allegiance to the creed. Thus the critique of technocracy must focus more on implicit assumptions than explicit statements.

Further complicating the conceptualization of technocratic politics is the fact that technocrats are found across the political spectrum. In both conventional ideological and progammatic terms, they can as a group disagree on almost everything. An examination of the technocratic professions reveals numerous factors that work to divide their members. Included among them is the general scarcity of "hard" research evidence, making it possible to interpret many issues in conflicting ways. Another reason is owed to the result of differences in training across the disciplines, fostering competition between scientific approaches. A third has to do with the experts' desires to ingratiate themselves with those who financially support them—money-granting agencies and employers. And not least among the reasons are the experts' own personal convictions and ideological commitments. Like the rest of us, and for many of the same reasons, technocrats are quite divided on the pressing value issues that confront modern society.[19]

How then can we characterize a political phenomenon with no apparent political leaders or program? The answer is to be found on a deeper level of social reality, that of epistemology. If technocrats do not agree on specific policy solutions, what they do agree on are the *methods* to be used to resolve policy differences. Essentially, as we demonstrate in Chapter 8, they are identified by their common call for a greater role of experts in the political decision-making processes and the use of scientifically based decision methodologies. As an epistemological orientation, technocracy can be, and has been, adapted by peoples and countries pursuing remarkably differing political goals. In Moscow as well as in Washington the technocratic worldview is a prominent feature of the political landscape.

Technocracy, then, is fundamentally an intellectual ethos and worldview. In political terms, it is a "meta-phenomenon" geared more to the *shape* or *form* of governance than a specific content per se. In theoretical terms, it is more properly interpreted as a "project" than as a "movement." As such, it refers "to the goals and strategies pursued by a group, but does not take them to be entirely clear or deliberate for all the members nor even for the most determined and articulate among them."[20] Applied to the historical results of a specific course of action, the term pertains to the consistency and coherence that can only be uncovered or ascribed to a sequence of events with the assistance of analytical and historical hindsight.

We turn at this point to the ideology that has historically linked together this otherwise disparate group of technocrats as an identifiable political project.

Apolitical Ideology

The historical coherence that defines technocratic thought is a deep-seated animosity toward politics—particularly democratic politics—coupled with an unswerving commitment to scientific decision making. As Stone puts it, the common mission of this "rationality project" is to rescue "public policy from the irrationalities and indignities of politics, hoping to conduct it instead with rational, analytical, and scientific methods."[21] Putnam has explicated from the technocratic literature six fundamental tenets basic to this ideology and the "mentality" it shapes.

(1) Technocrats believe "that 'technics' must replace 'politics'" and define their own tasks in "apolitical" terms. (2) They are "skeptical and even hostile toward politicians and political institutions." (3) They are "fundamentally unsympathetic to the openness and equality of political democracy." (4) They believe that social and political conflict is, at best, judged to be "misguided, and at worst, contrived." (5) They "reject ideological or moralistic criteria, preferring to debate policy in practical, 'programmatic terms.'" (6) They are "strongly committed to technological progress and material productivity" and are "less concerned about the distribution questions of social justice." From Saint-Simon forward, politics is seen as a process that "can and ought to be reduced to a matter of technique, that is . . . political decisions should be made on the basis of technical knowledge, not the parochial interests of untutored value preferences of politicians."[22]

Thus for technocrats the solution is to replace the "irrational" decision processes of democratic politics (group competition, bargaining, and compromise, in particular) with "rational" empirical/analytical methodologies of scientific decision making, or what has been aptly called "methodological decision-making." Nothing is more irrational to technocratic theorists than the disjointed, incremental forms of decision making (typically described as "muddling through") that result from a political commitment to democratic bargaining and compromise. Whereas many democratic political theorists have long celebrated these features as the marks of a well-functioning and politically legitimate government (indeed, for some the highest achievement in political history), technocratic writers see them as a nightmare of irrationality—a system of government perpetually generating ineffective policies that mainly compound the very problems they seek to solve. Such processes, they argue, have no place in a complex technological society. In the era of "high tech," they are seen as the height of folly.

To put it pointedly, technocrats see politics as a *problem* rather than a *solution*. In the Western context, this view is manifested in a belief that the contemporary malaise—budgetary crises, inflation, pollution, poverty, energy shortages, educational decline, crime, and so on—is largely attributable to the way decision making is organized in democratically structured governments. Political systems governed by bargaining and compromise are seen to be out of place in the exacting world of technology. To ask a politician, let alone the person on the street, to make decisions about complex issues like nuclear power is said to be archaic. Neither the politician nor the everyday citizen has the information and sophistication to deal with such decisions. Albeit unpalatable to many, the technocratic solution is seen to be foreordained: political issues must be redefined in scientific and technical terms. This is the job of experts. They must be brought to the fore.

It is not an argument without elements of cogency. Western democratic regimes are rampant with contradictory, if not irrational, policies (many of which either simply do not work or operate at cross-purposes). Democracy would indeed seem to be in trouble; with this it is difficult to take issue. What is far less clear, however, is whether the turn to technocratic strategies offers a *better* alternative? This question is fundamental to the book as a whole.

Although the importance of the question has traditionally been limited to the theoretical realm, today it takes on a very practical dimension. Experts in every area of economic and social life are now asked to play larger and larger decision-making roles and, as a consequence, technocratic strategies abound. Two of the most significant contemporary illustrations are the "Star Wars" program (the Reagan administration's Strategic Defense Initiative) and the search for a solution to the AIDS (Acquired Immune Deficiency Syndrome) epidemic. In both cases, the primary responses of the relevant professional communities and governmental officials have been to search for *technical* solutions that sidestep the problematic social and political questions raised by these issues. In the case of Star Wars, the federal government has sought a technological space shield to deal with the problem of nuclear weapons. This is promoted by technocrats as preferable to the political alternative of sitting down with the Soviet Union and negotiating a mutual security treaty. Similarly, in the case of AIDS, technocratic decision makers have placed emphasis on finding a vaccine "to make the problem go away" rather than dealing with the very difficult social and human issues that it raises for society, particularly those of homosexuality and the civil liberties issues associated with the testing and screening of potential AIDS carriers.

This is not to argue that everyone supporting the search for a vaccine for AIDS is technocratic in mentality. Such a position would surely err in the opposite direction. Rather, it is to specify the feature distinguishing technocratic thought as the attempt to avoid the political and social dimensions of these problems through the search for scientific and technological solutions. In short, "the way out" is through the "technological fix."[23]

Technocracy, then, is clearly a deep-seated challenge to democracy and its political form of decision making. But it is interesting that it is not always easy to catch technocrats directly criticizing the democratic ideal. Although American democracy is frequently honored in the breach, it remains the country's most hallowed tradition. Those who criticize it often find *themselves* criticized. To sidestep such counterattacks, technocrats most frequently present their argument somewhat obliquely. Using terms like "systems overload" and "governance crisis," as we make clear in Chapter 7, they typically speak of a need to "readjust" political institutions to contemporary economic and social realities. Dr. John Kemeny, former chairperson of the presidential commission appointed to investigate the Three Mile Island nuclear disaster, offered this assessment to an audience at Massachusetts Institute of Technology:

> I've heard many times that although democracy is an imperfect system, we somehow always muddle through. The message I want to give you, after long and hard reflection, is that . . . it is no longer possible to muddle through. The issues we deal with do not lend themselves to that kind of treatment. . . . Jeffersonian democracy cannot work in the year 1980—the world has become too complex.[24]

At the root of the problem is the political interest group. For technocrats, competing interest groups are the *virtual enemy* of rational social organization. The solution is to replace politicians and interest group leaders with technically trained experts who "stand above" the political process. Only through the adoption of rational decision-making techniques based on the objective principles of scientific planning and management can effective prescriptions be found to the complex problems confronting contemporary society. Moreover, from this point of view, only those "above the political fray" can genuinely represent the public interest in the search for solutions. The public interest is said to be safeguarded by the "impartial conscience" and "neutral competence" of the technical expert.[25]

How then does technocratic theory prescribe the public interest? The answer, as we see in Chapter 8, is to be found in the pursuit of material progress. Toward this end, the efficient and effective utilization of scarce resources become the primary decision criteria. Politically and managerially, this involves the continuous monitoring and adjustment of institutional structures and processes to the functional criteria of economic and technological development. The public interest is thus defined in instrumental and functional terms. As instrumental techniques replace political substance, the "means" of policy become the "ends."[26] In the process, the essential political question—production for what?— is at best relegated to secondary status. At worst, it is simply ignored.

Technocracy's emphasis on the rational coordination of institutional processes to the functional requirements of the productive system gives rise to a uniquely administrative or managerial conception of the state. Historically, technocrats have viewed the state as a positive instrument in the pursuit of economic and social progress. The reason for this stems from the state's central position in society. Essentially, the state is the only institution capable of engaging in comprehensive systemwide planning and management. Insofar as political conflict is the principal impediment to such planning, the state is seen as the institution that can stand above the destructive play of competing interests and thus only the state is potentially capable of providing the coordinated leadership needed to oversee a complex technological society.[27] Toward this end, the liberal democratic state must be replaced with an "administrative state" designed for technocratic governance.

In practice, the technocratic concept of the administrative state has been most influential in the socialist world of planned economies.[28] Given their emphasis on comprehensive economic and social planning, technocratic theory is ready-made both to guide and to legitimate the centralized bureaucratic decision-making systems that direct most socialist regimes. Easily aligned with the ideas and techniques of scientific planning, particularly those shaped by Marxist economists, technocratic concepts have played an important role in the evolution of socialist theory and practice.

But technocratic strategies have by no means been limited to socialist systems. They have been fashionable under fascist and liberal governments as well. In the case of corporate-liberal states, such as the United States, technocratic theories and practices have played important roles in the rationalization of industrial and corporate workplaces, the shaping of economic and regulatory policies, and, more recently, the development of science and technology policy. In the case of the workplace, the father of American management, Frederick Taylor, fashioned one of the most famous of all technocratic theories, "scientific management." Explored in Chapters 4 and 12, scientific management has at times been elevated to a basic American ideology.

While most technocratic thinking in the United States has been shaped by theorists of a liberal persusasion, neoconservatives as well have embraced technocratic practices, particulary in recent years. Indeed, conservatives have promoted a technocratic conception of cost-benefit analysis to serve as the primary criterion for governmental decision making. Steeped in modern utilitarianism and its theories of rational choice, conservative economists and political scientists have touted the "objective" calculation of costs and benefits as the essence of rationality in the realm of action, social as well as economic (a topic we take up in Chapter 8). During the Reagan years, in fact, cost-benefit analysis played an unprecedented practical and ideological role in the formulation and review of governmental and regulatory policy. Not without irony, as we show in Chapter 6, the adaptation of technocratic decision techniques to the pursuit of the conservative agenda proved to be a key strategy of the "Reagan Revolution."

But no policy area has in recent years had a larger impact on the evolution of technocratic strategies than that of science and technology. As we enter the so-called high-tech postindustrial era, the worldviews of scientific and technical experts have increasingly moved toward the center of the political stage. In the face of the "governance crisis" said to emerge with the economic and political woes facing the United States, the "technocratic paradigm" is advanced as a response to the country's deteriorating situation. As a direct challenge to liberal democracy, "technocorporate" ideology is put forward in both liberal and conservative quarters as the foundation of a new and seductive form of technocratic politics.

Technocorporate Ideology and the Politics of Expertise

In Chapters 7 and 8 we argue that it is possible to identify on the contemporary political scene the emergence of a powerful political ideology that elevates the technocratic project to a new plateau in its evolution. A variant of corporate liberalism, this new form of technocratic politics can be called "technocorporate liberalism," or more simply "technocorporatism." At the level of the state, stated simplistically, it is a strategy to reshape the political arena through the centralization of governance and the depoliticizing of the mass public. It seeks to refortify, both structurally and ideologically through greater reliance on expertise, a political transformation that first began to appear in the United States with the rise of corporate liberalism.

Although technocorporate government is only in its formative stages, the ideology makes clear the primary features of the system. It can be understood in terms of three spheres: a top echelon of political and economic elites, a technocratic strata of experts and specialized administrators (identified here as the "technostructure"), and a largely depoliticized mass public.[29] At the top of the political system, a small number of competing elites make the basic governing decisions. Typically, the governing coalition at any particular time includes the executive branch, key members of the legislature, and the private establishment (including leaders of the key economic sectors). Making political decisions in a manner increasingly described as corporatist (see Chapter 7), these groups are relatively free to shape the policy agenda in ways that favor elite interests and ends. Dealing mainly with the broad economic and political priorities of central governance, they neither possess nor require highly specialized technical competencies and skills. In technical matters they rely on access to—and the allegiances of—the policy and administrative experts directly below them. Given their primary decision-making powers, coupled with their access to the technical experts, the members of this sphere constitute the ruling elites of society.

In the second sphere are the experts, technical and managerial. Technical knowledge and skills provide this "technostructure" with a privileged position in society. While technostructure experts do not rule per se, their position in the political structure can be described as one of "relative autonomy." Ensconced in the upper echelons of the governance structure, they serve in powerful decision-making positions (e.g., as influential advisers on the staffs of the politically powerful or as top-level administrators with expert knowledge). From such positions they mediate the policy decisions made by top elites as well as direct their implementation. In some cases, subject to elite oversight, they make the actual policy decisions.

The politics of this technocratic sphere is a pivotal dimension of technocorporatism. Here the most basic issue is the technocrats' political allegiances. By and large, the experts of the technostructure are well enough rewarded, both politically and monetarily, to remain firmly committed to the existing political structure of society. With the understanding—both formal and informal—that their technical information is to serve the needs of elite decision makers, technostructure experts are granted a comfortable position in the system. As a consequence of this bargain, such experts often withhold from the rest of society the kinds of information necessary to play a meaningful role in the governance processes. Both wittingly and unwittingly, it is a commitment subtly encoded in various norms of their professional associations, particularly those pertaining to client privilege, anonymity, and confidentiality.

But to recognize this stabilizing influence of experts is not to overlook the very important "politics of expertise" that takes shape *within* this second sphere. While experts remain committed to the basic system of governance, the political struggle between liberal and conservative elites now includes competition for the allegiances of the experts. The result, exacerbated by the political differences among technocrats themselves, has been both the promotion and the sharpening of political conflicts among experts and their policy communities. Although most policy experts still try to stand behind the ideologies of apolitical (or neutral) analysis and decision making, at times (as we see in Chapter 6) this politicization of expertise manifests itself in the competing methodological orientations of particular disciplines.

Under such political arrangements effective opposition is more and more limited to those who have access to their own experts. Basically, this means competing elites who seek out advice that supports their own policy choices and overlook counsel which does not. Political controversy, as a result, is increasingly restricted to powerful elites and interest groups operating at the top echelons of society. Their cadres of experts generate technical reports, cost-benefit studies, computer simulations, impact statements, surveys, and other forms of analysis used to elaborate and legitimate the arguments advanced by the competing sides of an issue. The outcome is a process of "counter policy expertise," also the focus of Chapter 6.

Technical experts, then, are not in political control, but their information becomes a key resource in the governance of modern society. It is access to this technical knowledge and skill that sustains the power of the top-level political and economic elites. And, conversely, it is the lack of access to such knowledge that hinders the possibility of an active and meaningful involvement in the political decision processes for the large majority of the public. Thus the technostructure's allegiances to the top elites—liberal or conservative—is one of the critically important features of the emerging political-economic structure.

We take the dynamics of this policy process to be a primary thrust of contemporary technocratic politics. Many have criticized the technocracy thesis as a "straw man" standing on thin propositions. More often than not, the thesis is rejected because technocrats remain subordinate to governing elites. Given the conventional definition of technocracy as the rise to power of a technical or knowledge elite, the conclusion is easy to understand.[30] Unfortunately, however, this interpretation overlooks the other important dimension of the technocratic phenomenon. As Laird makes clear, the function of technocracy, at least at this stage of its development, rests not so much on its assent to power (in the traditional sense of the term) as on the fact that technocracy's growing influence shields the elites from political pressure from below.[31]

Pressure from below brings us to the third sphere of this society, the public, and the role of interest groups. Basic to technocorporate ideology is the belief that interest-group politics and social movements are "out of control" in the United States, a situation said to constitute a contemporary "crisis of governance." To the degree that such groups can politically activate members of the public, they are seen to be worrisome threats to the agendas of political and corporate elites, particularly those geared to the high-technology postindustrial agenda.[32] The technocorporate solution, as we make clear in Chapter 7, is the depoliticization of the public sphere.

Such depoliticization is now a widely recognized phenomenon. Years ago C. Wright Mills could already sum it up in these words: American citizens feel they are "living in a time of big decisions; they know they are not making any."[33] Today no more than 5% of the population as a whole fully participates in political matters.[34] Another 60% to 75% are basically uninvolved but can potentially be aroused around certain issues (with a smaller number among them sometimes mobilizable to action). The remainder of the population, about 20%, is never interested or involved in the political process in any form. Lacking the kinds of knowledge, competencies, and access needed to participate in decision-making processes, the vast majority of the public is thus cut off from a meaningful role in ongoing political activities. Public participation is largely restricted to general elections that, more often than not, offer only narrowly proscribed choices between competing political elites. During such contests, moreover, the public's information is generally trivialized, if not distorted, by the mass media and the bevy of public relations specialists and communications experts who filter and shape its messages. The situation obviously breeds alienation and apathy. Perceiving a sharp disjunction between politics and life generally, many among the main body of the population become more and more disaffected with their political institutions: occasionally there is active hostility toward them; more often only passive indifference.[35]

Against this contemporary political reality, one might ask how postindustrialism can substantially exacerbate the situation? Indeed, what is at stake here would appear to be less the depoliticization of the public than the structural solidification of the existing depoliticized configuration. In this respect, the target of technocorporate strategy is the 60% of the public who are *potentially* attentive to political issues. It is through the periodic activation of members of this segment that interest groups and social movements have had an impact on the political process. Technocorporatism's attempt to structure decision processes technocratically is interpreted here as a strategy to impede this process of political activation. It is, in short, designed to facilitate the maintenance of a depoliticized mass public.

While the technostructure, then, is not the political theorist's much prophesied ruling elite, the technocorporate politics of expertise is clearly a new political dynamic that requires attention. In Chapters 7 and 8, we examine in some detail the technocratic politics underlying the technocorporate strategy.

Technocracy and the Democratic Prospect

Finally, what are democracy's chances in the face of this technocratic threat? If technocratic planning and managerial strategies are important for the growth and stability of the modern postindustrial economy, at least as presently structured, few will rush to embrace ideas portrayed as the products of a bygone era. Indeed, the fact that technocratic strategies violate democratic principles will pose few immediate problems for postindustrial planners. Throughout American history the general populous has consistently preferred economic prosperity to ideological purity. In the face of economic decline, there is no reason to believe that such preferences will suddenly change.

This is not to suggest that democratic principles are unimportant to the American public. Even though frequently slighted in practice, such principles are never publicly rejected. Thus, despite the technostructure's aversion to democratic politics, democratic ideas present a political barrier that technocrats cannot altogether ignore. Not only must they remain sensitive to the public and its opinions, technocrats must also conceal their indifference to them. This has led writers such as Offe, Heydebrand, and Wolfe to argue that, while technocracy is a system of guidance, it must not appear to be one. Because, as Heydebrand puts it, "the split between those who guide and those who are guided can never be totally concealed . . . technocratic strategies tend to run into simple political opposition or resistance . . . which can activate latent structural contradictions."[36] Technocratic governance thus potentially suffers from an inherent instability.

But the technostructure's need to at least pay lip service to democratic practices does not threaten the validity of the larger and more difficult question: Can democracy *work* in a complex technological society? In part, this depends on what we mean by democracy. Specifically, we must confront the issue of political participation: To what degree is it possible for large numbers of citizens to meaningfully participate in postindustrial politics?

We do not suggest that everyone must—or even can—participate in all matters. In a complex technological world, this is as impossible as it is undesirable. More practically, we seek only to address the widely recognized challenge confronting American democracy: How can we begin to *lessen* the very substantial gap between elite decision-making centers and the generally undifferentiated mass of citizens altogether left out of the process?

Stated more specifically: Can we build participatory institutions that establish and mediate procedural and discursive relationships between elite decision makers and the public?[37] Can we design political structures at the organizational and community levels of a technological society that can, in turn, be authentically linked up with top-level decision processes? Is it, in short, possible to establish a public community capable of engendering a political conversation between the rulers and the ruled?

The questions are scarcely new. They have, in fact, generated a substantial literature from both ends of the political spectrum.[38] At the level of the state, political theorists define the problem as a fundamental tension between expertise and democracy; at the organizational level it is conceptualized as the conflict between efficiency and participation. For those on the political left, the call has been for more democracy and participation; for those on the right, more expertise and efficiency. This study sides with the advocates of participation, though somewhat cautiously. Rather than positing democracy and expertise as a choice of "either/or," we recognize the possibility of an irreducible tension between them. Even though it may never be completely eliminated, we contend here that it can nonetheless be significantly mitigated by alternative methodologies and practices.

The following chapters engage these pragmatic questions of organization, participation, and policymaking from a normative theoretical perspective. Although grounded in the ideals of political emancipation, the discussion attempts to remain practical. Focusing on applied sciences, it seeks only to point in the direction of the possible. In this respect, our position keenly recognizes the necessity of technical knowledge and efficiency. The fact that efficiency has often been misused to further the interests of particular groups over others (especially management over labor) does not vitiate its fundamental importance in the realms of organization and policy. Rather than rejecting it as an ideological ploy in the struggle for control, as is too often the case in radical literature, the critical task from the perspective here is to restrict it to its proper realm in the organization and analysis of action.

But what is the proper realm? We make no attempt to say how much efficiency or participation should exist in a particular society or situation. This we leave to the relevant participants to work out among themselves in the context of their own pragmatic political experiences. It is a question that must in part be determined empirically in the context of the technical structures of society and, in part, through the processes of democracy itself. Citizens and workers, in fact, must decide their own relationships to technology and its uses. Our principal concern, in this regard, is the need to open and extend the processes that make such democratic determinations possible.

We also acknowledge that a serious discussion concerned with expanding democratic practices must concede a basic political reality: Throughout the history of the idea, democracy has remained as much a vision as a reality. Indeed, in today's complex society such concepts as "town hall democracy" are still largely utopian dreams. To say this, however, is not to overlook their important function in the critically important realm of political discourse. The virtue of democratic theory is to be found in the legacy of the standards it has bequeathed. Although political theorists will continue to debate the proper application of such standards, they nonetheless provide valuable criteria against which political practices can be discussed and judged. Indeed, the very purpose of democracy is to establish a framework for engaging in open discourse and, in turn, for judging its quality. As a public ideology, democratic standards are essential to the processes of honest and open discussion of public affairs. On this the record is clear.

To worry about language and standards of judgment in the face of power is not necessarily to fall into the trap of idealism. That is, such a concern need not confuse political discourse with political power itself. Discourse has a subtle and complex relationship to power. While it is not power per se, political discourse produces and transmits power. In this respect, it can serve as a tool of either domination or liberation. To use Foucault's words, discourse can "be a hindrance, a stumbling block, a point of resistance and a starting point for an opposing strategy." Not only can it produce and reinforce power, it can "render it fragile and make it possible to thwart it."[39] The long history of democratic struggles is in very large part a story of the liberating functions of political discourse.[40]

In an emerging "knowledge society," where politics moves toward a politics of expertise, the role of discourse becomes increasingly evident. As Gouldner makes clear, it is a "culture of discourse" that defines and unites the technical intelligentsia itself.[41] Underlying the disciplinary languages of the various professions, technical experts—like experts in general—are committed to the art and science of their discourses, albeit technical discourses. Thus their own preoccupation with standards and criteria makes it difficult for the technostructure to steer altogether clear of other discourses, especially democratic discourse. Democracy's privileged status in American political discourse is, moreover, a particular liability for technocrats. As an instrumental theory of governance, technocracy is poorly equipped to defend itself openly in the public sphere. Essentially, it can offer little more than functional arguments based on pragmatic considerations (i.e., it is geared to the goverance problems of the existing system and can thus provide the necessary "fixes"). In democratic discourse, however, the efficiency or efficacy of a policy or program is, in and of itself, insufficient grounds for political acceptance. Instrumental proposals can thus never be democratically legitimated in terms of the technostructure's own instrumental and technical criteria alone.

While such argumentation over criteria and standards seldom erupts in the political sphere (especially in methodological terms), the matter is frequently a source of contention in the academy, where discourse is the central activity. To the degree that technocrats can be engaged in such methodological discussions, the issue of criteria opens the door to a "politics of methodology," a topic we turn to in the next chapter. Such a politics can take on particular significance in the university. Insofar as the professional schools of the university are the primary sites for technocratic training, such strife is at times a major source of concern for those charged with furthering professional ideologies and their technocratic models of governance.[42]

A common strategy of mainstream professionals in such discussions is to portray the search for nontechnocratic alternatives as impractical and ill-suited for a modern technological economy. There is, however, much evidence that paints a different picture. Numerous experiments (particularly in cooperative communities, worker-managed enterprises, and alternative technology projects) make clear that citizens and workers can effectively balance the tensions between expertise and participation.[43] Their decisions, to be sure, tend to be different from those made by managers in large corporate enterprises and governmental bureaucracies, but this is more the point than the problem. How such decisions will, or should, be made in a democratic setting is a central question for empirical and theoretical explanation. It is the kind of question to which these pages hope to call attention.

The most powerful force behind the search for alternatives has been the "new social movements." Even though their power and significance have diminished during the 1980s, largely due to the conservative trends that have swept Western nations, new social movements still represent the most significant struggles to take seriously "grass-roots democracy." As such, they clearly indicate the struggle for participatory democracy to be very much alive in contemporary Western societies, particularly in Europe.

The struggles of these movements are often direct responses to the technostructure and its strategic interventions into social and political life. Grounded in the human desire for self-determination, they seek alternative ways of life free of social and ideological manipulation. Many of them, in fact, are explicitly organized around the demand for participatory democracy; they emphasize direct political participation in the decisions that affect the lives of their own members. Advocating empowerment and self-help, their opposition to technocratic rule centers on a demand for participation in decision making.[44] Their struggle is as "countercultural" as it is political in form.[45]

In response to the alienation bred by technocratic strategies, these participatory movements have sought to "problematize" human needs. Where technocratic modes of reason have eroded the very languages of decision making in the political sphere, social movements have sought to reestablish the priority of normative discourse in the pursuit of human needs and individual autonomy. As such, these movements are potentially a powerful challenge to the technocratic paradigm. They are, moreover, the source of important efforts to reconstruct the practices of expertise per se, a topic we turn to in the final chapter.

In the theoretical sphere there are also positive signs. Democratic theory, at least in the academic world, is alive and thriving. In reality, however, most of it fails to genuinely grapple with the basic question posed by contemporary technocratic theorists: Will democracy *work* in a complex technological world? Few technocrats openly argue that democracy per se is wrongheaded; rather, they merely contend that it must be dramatically redefined in hierarchical, elitist terms. Democracy, as traditionally understood, is believed to be simply incompatible with the realities of a complex postindustrial society.

In confronting the technocratic challenge, democratic theorists can, for this reason, no longer comfortably limit themselves to the tasks of theoretical critique. To undermine the technocratic position adequately, they must also show the ways in which democracy can be made compatible with technological complexity. Toward this end, democratic theorists must take up what one writer has called "the nuts and bolts of democracy."[46] It is at this level that the "real-world" clash between democratic and technocratic paradigms will ultimately play itself out. Democratic theorists must turn from their preoccupation with the history of ideas to the analysis of operant political theories that underlie contemporary institutional practices.[47] What we need, to paraphrase Heilbroner, is a cadre of "worldly theorists" capable of moving from democratic critique to social reconstruction.[48]

Committed to democratic principles, this new breed of theorists must also be knowledgeable in the intricacies of how organizations, policy processes, and in some cases even technologies actually work. We need something like the new discipline Winner calls "political ergonomics."[49] In this respect, nothing is more basic to the challenge than the question of the relation of expertise to democratic politics. It is the essence of a politics of expertise. Can we, in short, build a meaningful system of participatory decision processes in the age of technology and expertise? All we can say with certainty is that the answer is not yet in. It is also clear that time is getting short. Unless the challenge is taken up soon, it is likely that the partisans of democracy will lose by default.[50]

Notes

1. James R. Bendiger, *The Control Revolution: Technological and Economic Origins of the Information Society* (Cambridge, MA: Harvard University, 1986), pp. 4–5.
2. Robert L. Heilbroner, "Economic Problems of a 'Postindustrial' Society," *Dissent*, Spring 1973, pp. 163–76.
3. Daniel Bell, "The Social Framework of the Information Society," in *The Computer Age*, ed. by Michael L. Dertouzos and Joel Moses (Cambridge: MIT Press, 1980), pp. 163–211; and Bell, "The Third Technological Revolution," *Dissent*, Spring 1989, pp. 164–76.
4. Yoneji Masuda, "Computopia," in *The Information Technology Revolution*, ed. Tom Forester (Cambridge: MIT Press, 1985), pp. 620–34; Wilson P. Dizard, Jr., *The Coming Information Age* (New York: Longman, 1985); and Frederick Williams, ed., *Measuring the Information Society* (Newbury Park, CA: Sage, 1988).
5. For an interesting review of this literature, see Kevin Robins and Frank Webster, "Athens Without Slaves . . . Or Slaves Without Athens?" *Science as Culture*, no. 3 (1988): 7–53.
6. For the classic statement, see Jacques Ellul, *The Technological Society* (New York: Vintage, 1964). Also, see Victor C. Ferkiss, *Technological Man* (New York: George Brazillier, 1969); and Langdon Winner, *Autonomous Technology: Technics-Out-of-Control as a Theme in Political Thought* (Cambridge: MIT Press, 1977).
7. Jürgen Habermas, *Legitimation Crisis* (Boston: Beacon, 1973).
8. Bertram Gross, *Friendly Fascism* (New York: Evans, 1980).
9. Paul Goodman, *New Reformation: Notes of a Neolithic Conservative* (New York: Random House, 1970).
10. Jean Meynaud, *Technocracy* (New York: Free Press, 1969).
11. Bell, "The Social Framework," p. 344.
12. For example, see Simon Nora and Alain Minc, *The Computerization of Society* (Cambridge: MIT Press, 1980).
13. The most significant examples tend to be in policy areas that draw heavily on the physical sciences. For a classic example, see Herbert York, *The Advisors: Oppenheimer, Teller and the Superbomb* (San Francisco: Freeman, 1976).
14. See Theda Skocpol, "Bringing the State Back in: Strategies of Analysis in Current Research," in *Bringing the State Back in*, ed. Peter Rueschemeyer and Theda Skocpol (New York: Cambridge University Press, 1985), pp. 3–43; Margret Weir and Theda Skocpol, "State Structures and the Possibility for 'Keynesian' Responses to the Great Depression in Sweden, Britain and the United States," in Rueschemeyer and Skocpol, *Bringing the State Back in*, pp. 107–68; H. Heclo, *Modern Social Politics in Britain and Sweden* (New Haven, CT: Yale University Press, 1974); Heclo, "Conclusion: Policy Dynamics" in *The Dynamics of Public Policy*, ed. Richard Rose (London: Sage, 1976), pp. 237–66; and Peter A. Hall, "Policy Learning and the State: The Evolution of British Macroeconomic Policy, 1970–1988" (Paper prepared for delivery at the XIVth World Congress of the International Political Science Association, September 1, 1988, Washington, DC). This role of policy experts is strongest in economic affairs, particularly in the regulation of fiscal and monetary policy. But it can also be seen in areas of social policy as well. Educational policy is an important example. With

specific regard to the role of administrative experts in the state bureaucracies, see Joel D. Aberbach, Robert D. Putman, and Bert A. Rockman, *Bureaucrats and Politicians in Western Democracies* (Cambridge, MA: Harvard University Press, 1981).

15. See, for example, Jerry Mitchell, "Policy Community Politics: Explaining Inconsistencies in Disability Policy" (Ph.D. diss., University of Kansas, Division of Government, 1987).

16. Peter Wagner and Björn Wittrock, "Discourse Coalitions and State Developments: Toward a Realist Theory of Argumentation and Power" (Paper delivered at the 84th Annual Meeting of the American Political Science Association, September 1–4, 1988, Washington, DC).

17. Bernd Marin, "Die Stille Revolution der Technokratie," *Die Paritaetische Kommmission: Aufgeklaeter Technokorporatismus in Oesterreich* (Wien: Internationale Publicationen Gessellschaft m.b.H., 1982), pp. 265–300. For an interesting case study that illustrates this hidden dimension of technocratic politics, see Michael J. Malbin, *Unelected Representatives: Congressional Staff and the Future of Representative Government* (New York: Basic Books, 1980).

18. Although the term *technocracy* is generally pejorative, it has begun in recent years in the popular press to be used to mean pragmatic managerial competence. During his bid for the presidency, for example, Governor Dukakis was described as a "technocrat." Referring to the need for managerial competence in the White House, writers often ascribed the term approvingly.

19. For more examples, see Dorothy Nelkin, *Controversy: The Politics of Technical Decisions* (Beverly Hills, CA: Sage, 1984).

20. Magali Sarfatti Larson, *The Rise of Professionalism* (Berkeley: University of California Press, 1977), p. 6.

21. Deborah A. Stone, *Policy Paradox and Political Reason* (Glenview, IL: Scott, Foresman, 1988), p. 4.

22. Robert D. Putnam, "Elite Transformation in Advanced Industrial Societies: An Empirical Assessment of the Theory of Technocracy," *Comparative Political Studies* 10, no. 3 (October 1977): 385–87.

23. On the concept of the "technological fix," see Rudi Volti, *Society and Technological Change* (New York: St. Martin's, 1988), p. 23. Volti also offers other interesting examples. One is the use of the drug Methadone to combat heroin addiction. As Volti puts it, "Beset by the epidemic spread of heroin addiction, the U. S. government has engaged in a large-scale program to eliminate the addict's craving through the administration of Methadone" (itself an addictive drug). Another is the case of highway safety: "As highway accidents continue to result in tens of thousands of deaths and hundreds of injuries each year, efforts have been mounted to develop and manufacture cars capable of protecting their passengers from the consequences of incompetent driving." In the case of environmental pollution, some scientists see the solution to lie in the newly emerging biotechnological sciences. They point to the genetic engineering of microbes that live off of air pollution; and, hopefully more facetiously, the possibility of genetically redesigning humans to better breathe polluted air has also been mentioned.

24. Quoted in David Dickson, "Limiting Democracy: Technocrats and the Liberal State," *Democracy* 1, no. 1 (January 1981): 62–63. Also see John Kemeny, "Saving American Democracy: The Lessons of Three Mile Island," *Technology Review* 83, no. 7 (June–July 1980): 10.

25. For a classic statement, see Karl Mannheim, *Man and Society in an Age of Reconstruction* (New York: Harcourt, Brace and World, 1967). For a contemporary discussion of the issue, see Anthony Lukas, "Harvard's Kennedy School: Is Competence Enough?" *The New York Times Magazine*, March 12, 1989, p. 36.

26. Ellul, *The Technological Society*.

27. On this point, see F. F. Ridley, "French Technocracy and Comparative Government," *Political Studies* 14 (February 1966): 44.

28. See, for example, Erik P. Hoffmann and Robbin F. Laird, *Technocratic Socialism* (Durham, NC: Duke University Press, 1985); and Stanley Aronowitz, *Science as Power* (Minneapolis: University of Minnesota Press, 1988) for a discussion of science and technology in socialist theory.

29. Jürgen Habermas, "The Scientization of Politics and Public Opinion," in *Toward a Rational Society* (Boston: Beacon, 1970), pp. 62–80; and Barry Barnes, "Expertise in Society," *About Science* (Oxford: Basil Blackwell, 1985), pp. 90–112.

30. For an example of this argument, see Samuel C. Forman, *Blaming Technology: The Irrational Search for Scapegoats* (New York: St. Martin's, 1981), chaps. 3 and 4; Daniel S. Greenberg, "The Myth of the Scientific Elite," *The Public Interest*, no 1 (Fall 1965): 51–62.

31. Frank N. Laird, "Technocracy Revisited: Knowledge and Power in Technical Decisions" (Paper delivered at the annual meeting of the American Political Science Association, Washington, DC, September 1, 1988).

32. Mary Douglas and Aaron Wildavsky, *Risk and Culture* (Berkeley: University of California Press, 1982).

33. C. Wright Mills, *The Power Elite* (New York: Oxford University Press, 1959), p. 5.

34. See W. Russell Neuman, *The Paradox of Mass Public: Knowledge and Opinion in the American Electorate* (Cambridge, MA: Harvard University Press, 1986); and Benjamin Ginsberg, *The Consequences of Consent: Elections, Citizen Control and Popular Acquiescence* (Reading, MA: Addison-Wesley, 1982).

35. The literatures of political science and sociology are filled with examples of such apathy and indifference in the United States. They range from low voter turnouts to widespread ignorance among citizens about political affairs.

36. Wolf V. Heydebrand, "Technocratic Corporatism: Toward a Theory of Occupational and Organizational Transformation," in *Organization Theory and Public Policy*, ed. Richard H. Hall and Robert E. Quinn (Beverly Hills, CA: Sage, 1983), p. 102; Alan Wolfe, *The Limits of Legitimacy* (New York: Free Press, 1977); and Claus Offe, "Das politische Dilemma der Technokratie," in *Strukturprobleme des kapitalistischen Staates* (Frankfurt: Suhrkamp, 1973).

37. Peter L. Berger and Richard J. Neuhaus, *To Empower People: The Role of Mediating Structures in Public Policy* (Washington, DC: American Enterprise Institute for Public Policy Research, 1977).

38. Task Force on Science Policy, Committee on Science and Technology, U.S. House of Representatives, 99th Congress, 2nd Session, *Expertise and Democratic Decisionmaking: A Reader*, Background Report no. 7, (Washington DC: Government Printing Office, 1987).

39. Michel Foucault, *The History of Sexuality, I* (New York: Random House, 1980), p. 101: also see Kathy Ferguson, "Elements of a Feminist Discourse," in *The*

Feminist Case Against Bureaucracy (Philadelphia: Temple University Press, 1984), chap. 5.

40. Richard Flacks, *Making History: The American Left and the American Mind* (New York: Columbia University Press, 1988).

41. Alvin W. Gouldner, *The Future of Intellectuals and the Rise of the New Class* (New York: Oxford University Press, 1979).

42. The university is of critical importance to the technostructure. The home of science and the professional schools, the university is the source of technocracy's own reproduction. In recent years, moreover, universities have become top-heavy with technocratic training programs, particularly attributable to the growth of management education. Largely occurring at the expense of the nontechnocratic liberal arts, technocratically oriented programs have generated tensions that today run throughout university politics. Many see the dominance of technocratic thought in the modern university to be at the root of what is today widely accepted as the "educational crisis" in higher education.

43. For a guide to this literature, see John Case and Rosemary C. R. Taylor, eds., *Coops, Communes and Collectives* (New York: Pantheon, 1979). Experience shows that workers in democratic settings are quite capable of choosing efficient arrangements over participatory structures when they better suit specific tasks. In the case of scientific and technological projects, the experience of the Cambridge Experimentation Review Board (established by the Cambridge City Council) testifies to the fact that citizens can responsibly grapple with complex technical questions pertaining to the regulation of science and technology. For a guide to the literature of this experiment, see Sheldon Krimsky, "Beyond Technocracy: New Routes for Citizen Involvement in Social Risk," in *Citizen Participation in Science Policy*, ed. James C. Peterson (Amherst: University of Massachusetts Press, 1984), pp. 43–61.

44. Anthony Giddens, *The Class Structure of the Advanced Societies* (New York: Harper & Row, 1975), pp. 253–64.

45. Theodore Roszak, *Where the Wasteland Ends* (New York: Doubleday, 1972).

46. Richard Sclove, "Democratic Theory and Technological Design: The Nuts and Bolts of Democracy" (Paper delivered at the American Political Science Association Meetings, Chicago, September 3–6, 1987).

47. This idea is adapted from John Gunnell's remarks at the Columbia University Seminar on Political and Social Thought, September 1983.

48. Robert L. Heilbroner has called the great economic thinkers "the worldly philosophers." See his book *The Worldly Philosophers* (New York: Simon & Schuster, 1980).

49. Langdon Winner, "Political Ergonomics" (Paper for delivery at the 1987 Annual Meeting of the American Political Science Association, Chicago, September 30, 1987). For his examples, see Martin Carnoy and Derek Shearer, "A Democratic Technology," *Economic Democracy* (Armonk, NY: M. E. Sharpe, 1980), pp. 195–232.

50. For an interesting discussion related to this point, see Albert Borgmann, "Technology and Democracy," in *Technology and Politics*, ed. Michael E. Kraft and Norman J. Vig (Durham, NC: Duke University Press, 1988), pp. 54–72.

2

The Neglect of Normative Reason:
Technical Rationality and the
Politics of Methodology

It is not always easy, as we argued in the preceding chapter, to identify technocratic politics. A significant part of this problem must be attributed to the seemingly innocuous character of the technocrats' basic concerns. Typically, their efforts appear to be limited to the important but politically mundane task of providing decision makers with better information—for example, through a call for more analytically sophisticated staffs, or the formation of research projects and study commissions. In the age of complexity, such proposals generally seem entirely reasonable. On general principle, few of us are apt to oppose efforts to obtain more information or knowledge. Wherein, then, lies our concern? It is, as we make clear in Chapters 8 and 9, hidden in a more subtle misunderstanding of the uses and values of particular types of knowledge. Fundamental to the critique of technocratic expertise is the argument that experts have overrelied on and misused scientific and technical knowledge. This critique has given rise to a vigorous—and at times strident—debate over the political implications of specific methodological practices, or what we call here the "politics of methodology."

The problem basically stems from the technical intelligentsia's adherence to a positivistic conception of knowledge and the technological and material values that such knowledge sustains. It is a commitment that has been shaped to a set of professional theories and practices that fundamentally neglect the full range of human and social values. Failing to attend sufficiently to the social and political value questions that give meaning and direction to our lives, scientific and technical experts have played a major role in setting us on a dramatic technological trajectory with little thought as to where it is taking us. This "metaphysical neglect" cannot be understated: It has been portrayed as the coming crisis of Western society.[1] As we witness the unanticipated consequences of technological progress—environmental crisis, industrial disasters, the depletion of our natural resources, social alienation and the decline of community, among others—the question of *where* we are headed more and more becomes the central concern. We find ourselves, on the one hand, mesmerized by the belief that a magnificent future lies before us, and fearful, on the other, that the very destruction of our species may lie just down the road. Our very expertise propels us into directions that we are unable to grasp intellectually. Or, as Norman Mailer eloquently put it, "The itch [is] to accelerate—the metaphysical direction unknown."[2]

How is it that we find ourselves in such a predicament? The answer is to be found in the technocratic "mentality" or "consciousness" that is deeply lodged in the basic economic, administrative, and institutional processes governing advanced industrial societies. To grasp the origins of this "normative crisis," we turn first to the nature of technocratic reason.

Technocratic Consciousness: The Basic Mode of Thought

The technocratic challenge is rooted much more in a way of thinking than in a specific set of political activities. This way of thinking, or "technocratic consciousness," rests on a set of beliefs about how the world works, a conception of the way it should work, and a set of tactics for changing it. As Giddens puts it, "Technocracy is not just the application of technical modes to the solution of defined problems, but a pervading ethos, a world-view which subsumes aesthetics, religion, and accustomary thought to the rationalistic mode."[3]

Technocratic consciousness is organized around a unique configuration of ideas and practices that emerged in the West during the past several hundred years. Originating with the eighteenth-century Enlightenment ideology, taken up in Chapter 3, technocratic theory is fundamentally founded on an unswerving belief in the power of the rational mind to control societal change in constructive directions. In epistemological terms, the "rationalist" orientation is based on the principles of positivism, or today "neopositivism."

Intellectual "rationalism" is the pattern of thought that differentiates technocratic consciousness from other worldviews and cultural orientations. Empirical and analytical in epistemological form, rationalism is technocracy's basic intellectual strategy for taking control of the natural and social worlds. As a positivistic thought form, it relies on empirical measurement, analytical precision, and a concept of "system," which provides the foundation of a worldview. As a methodological calculus, it constitutes a "logical, practical, problem-solving, instrumental, orderly and disciplined approach to objectives."[4]

Basic to neopositivism and its rationalistic worldview has been a fairly ambitious, if not arrogant, epistemological assumption: The neopositivist method is believed to be the only valid means of obtaining "true knowledge."[5] Still today it is said that modern neopositivism will in time subordinate all other modes of thought to its principles. Moreover, rigorous adherence to the methodology is believed to eventually pay off in the discovery of valid empirical regularities, if not the "laws" of society. Not only is such knowledge seen to make possible the resolution of many of our economic and social problems, it also claims to facilitate the rational design of social systems in ways that enable us to better predict and manage, if not altogether eliminate, the persistent conflicts and crises that now plague modern society.

In concrete terms, then, neopositivist theory gives shape to an abstract and technical formulation of society and its problems. Social problems, conceptualized in technical terms, are freed from the cultural, psychological, and linguistic contexts that constitute the lens of social tradition. Breaking the "recipes of tradition" and "ordinary knowledge" through the power of its unique abstract language, the neopositivist form of thought creates an illusion of cultural and historical transcendence, which, in turn, sustains a sense of political, cultural, and moral neutrality. In pursuit of the most efficient problem-solving strategies, typically expressed in the precise but abstract symbols of mathematics, experts appear to objectively transcend partisan interests. Their technical methodologies and modes of decision making are said to be "value-free."

Basic to this process of abstraction is the translation of "experience into theory." As Bowers puts it, the technocratic "pattern of thought understands the phenomenological world in terms of component parts that allow for abstracting the part from the whole, as well as an increasingly specialized knowledge of each component part."[6] The result of this "logic of componential thinking" is a view of the world as a system (social as well as physical) that can be technically redesigned in ways that make it more efficient and controllable.

A critically important dimension of this componential thinking is the tendency to see technical solutions as applicable to various social and cultural situations. Technical problem solving, in short, is reduced to a matter of plugging solutions into different social contexts. Writing about education, Bowers offers the following illustration: "Reading programs, learning packages, and management systems . . . created by experts [are] imposed on schools and communities without regard for local and cultural differences." If the technocratic planner "has demonstrated through a process of measurement a degree of reliability and efficiency, the rationally designed response to problems cannot effectively be resisted by those at the bottom who are often the unwilling recipients of expert knowledge."[7] Because of the fundamental differences in the legitimacy and power of their respective languages—technical versus everyday language—the interaction between the educational planners and the other members of the local school community gives shape to an unequal communicative relationship, or what Habermas calls "systematically distorted communication."[8] When expert knowledge, as Bowers puts it, "can be legitimated in terms of being rational, efficient, educated, progressive, modern, and enlightened, what metaphors can members of other speech communities use to challenge them?"[9]

This technical ("value-neutral") understanding of social action is manifested through an administrative conceptualization of problem solving and policy formation. Basic to managerial strategy, the objective is to move as many political and social decisions as possible into the realm of administrative decision making, where they can be redefined and processed in technical terms. Vexing economic and social problems are thus interpreted as issues in need of improved administrative design; their solutions are to be found through the application of managerial techniques, including policy science.[10] It is a conviction fundamental to contemporary technocratic strategy.

Inherent in this strategy is a subtle, and sometimes not so subtle, form of authoritarianism. Once the idea that we can empirically calculate and administratively design "the right way" to accomplish our goals is accepted, there is little reason to engage in the exploration of other views. The "rational" person is the one who agrees to submit to the properly derived technical and administrative knowledge of the experts. The authority of the expert, from this perspective, must take precedence over the democratic exchange of opinions.[11]

Basic to the hubris of this position is an anthropocentric view of the world. With no small arrogance, "technocratic man" has managed to construe humankind's unique powers of the mind as legitimation for his own rapacious appropriation of the physical world.[12] Nature, in short, is tamed and subordinated to serve man's own economic ends. Emphasizing what is seen as the mechanistic character of the physical laws governing nature, the technocratic worldview takes nature's creator—much like the technocrat himself—to be something of an engineer. Organized according to the laws of nature, human as well as physical nature, the everyday world can thus be conceptualized as a configuration of "problems" to be technically and administratively engineered by experts.

The repercussions of this worldview today are readily apparent. The most striking example is no doubt the ecological crisis. What began several hundred years ago as the technocratic exploitation of nature's resources for unlimited industrial progress today constitutes a serious ecological problem. Although substantial amounts of research and development monies are being poured into the search for solutions, much of this effort appears to miss the point. By and large, it is governed by the same kind of technocratic thinking that gave rise to the problem in the first place. Rather than looking for new relationships between technology and nature (emphasizing conservation and a more efficient planning and control of economic growth), experts plunge forward on the premise that future technological and administrative innovations will themselves get us out of our present fix. Ignoring the need for a new "existential balance" among the factors of production—technology, nature, and human purposes, in particular—the technocratic response to the ecological crisis is proving to be the paradigmatic example of metaphysical crisis. We turn next to a more systematic look at the neglect of normative reason.

Technical Rationality and the Neglect of Normative Reason

Max Weber was the first to systematically examine the use of technical and administrative strategies to rationalize the social spheres of contemporary life. The increasing domination of technical reason in the decision processes of social and political institutions, as Weber's classic work makes clear, is a deeper by-product of economic and technological progress and its bureaucratic organizational forms.[13] As Larson puts it, Weber recognized that "the concentration of power in the modern state apparatus and in the large productive units of mature industrial capitalism sets in motion a dialectic of growing size and complexity, which feeds the demand for rational techniques of control and decision-making." Writing at the turn of the century, he could already identify "the bureaucratic mode of domination" to be "the first rational response of centralized political power to large-scale administrative problems." Moreover, he saw this mode of domination to represent "an organizational matrix within which rational techniques of control are further developed and applied, while the control of knowledge and information is deliberately transformed into a power resource in organizational struggles."[14]

One of the most deep-seated and troublesome social phenomena of our time, this continuing process of societal rationalization has given rise to what Herbert Marcuse called the "one-dimensionality" of modern society.[15] Fundamental to technocratic consciousness, it is best understood as a failure to identify and maintain a clear distinction between two basic modes of reason, one technical and the other normative. Each of these forms of reason, as Habermas makes clear, pertains to a different and autonomous sphere of human activity.[16] Whereas the sphere of economic production (including work) is governed by technical criteria, the world of everyday social life (including the family, culture, religion, and politics) is negotiated through normative reason. Although in reality each sphere is deeply intertwined with the other, as we see in Chapter 9, analytically they must be conceptualized as separate spheres governed by different modes of reason.

For example, where the world of work is governed by the empirical-analytical logic of technical rationality (specifically the laws of cause and effect and the principles of efficient action), the social "life-world" is normatively constructed through mutually established intersubjective understandings between the members of a community or social group. In contrast to an empirical orientation (concerned with how things function), such agreements (concerned with how things *ought* to work) are the products of normative/hermeneutic discourses. They result, in short, from distinctive epistemological rules.

Throughout most of history the social life-world has taken precedence over the technical realm. New technologies were integrated into the life-world on terms dictated by social criteria. But with the dramatic rise of industrial and material progress in this century, supported by an unswerving adulation of technology, the relation between the two spheres has gradually been reversing. More and more, the technical criteria of the productive sphere have begun to determine the shaping of our social institutions. Technical rationality has thus penetrated the social life-world and the processes that constitute it. In the context of Western liberal societies, this has meant an erosion of the two most fundamental values organizing the liberal social life-world, individual autonomy and self-determination.

The basic force behind this rationalizing process is the tendency of technologically driven industrial development to concentrate wealth, power, and benefits. Demanding the accumulation of large amounts of capital, as well as sophisticated organizational structures and managerial techniques, advanced industrial development and its large-scale technological systems require extensive coordination and planning to overcome the uncertainties, risks, and interferences inherent in their development.[17] Such projects are typically carried out by the corporate sector in conjunction with the state. Only the centralized agencies of the state can coordinate planning on the appropriate scale. This leads to the expansion of administrative planning systems and the innovation of new state-corporate structures designed to facilitate the development and accommodation of such technologies. In Chapters 7 and 8, we identify these planning instrumentalities and point to the emergence of a "technocorporate" conceptualization of the state geared to systemwide planning. These structures constitute the further extension of a depoliticized mass society guided by a small number of centrally organized political and economic elites and their technocratic planners.

But state-level coordination alone is not enough to ensure the success of such efforts. In the context of technological risk, as well as uncertain (and sometimes hostile) social and political circumstances, the technostructure often finds it necessary to expand planning beyond the boundaries of the economic and technological systems themselves.[18] In the interest of facilitating larger system objectives (both organizational and technical), planners increasingly attempt to accommodate social subsystems to the instrumental criteria governing the technical sphere. The result is the technical rationalization of more and more aspects of society as a whole.

There are many examples of this instrumental process. In the name of technological progress and economic growth, schools—universities as well as high schools—have been transformed from institutions for general enlightenment into job training centers designed to supply industry with a technically educated work force (history and literature are replaced with business management and computer programming).[19] The family socialization function has increasingly been transformed into an exercise in consumer training.[20] The mass media have become an instrument for advertising and marketing strategies. Psychotherapy now focuses on how to emotionally adjust people to the existing socioeconomic system rather than dealing with their personal needs for autonomy. People's attitudes about such technological issues as nuclear power, toxic waste, and genetic engineering have been manipulated by political and economic leaders to secure support. The political process has more and more been relegated to the role of a legitimating mechanism for state-corporate decisions. In sum, people are subtly molded into instrumental means for the achievement of larger systems goals. In the words of Paul Goodman, "people" are turned into "personnel."[21]

The point here is not to deny the importance of material progress. Rather, it is to recognize the boundaries appropriate to the application of technical criteria in society as a whole. The technocratic intelligentsia, through its unquestioned belief in technological and material progress, obscures an underlying epistemological concatenation of the two separate realms of human activity. Specifically, planners and managers blur the distinction between the worlds of economic production and social interaction, thus making it difficult for many to distinguish between the priorities of the economic system and those of their own lives. It is not that people should reject economic and technological progress, but rather that they should establish their own relationships to it through the processes of intersubjective discourse.[22] Traditionally, the political community is the basic collective arena for the intersubjective discussion of the "way of life" itself. It is just such discourse that technocratic strategies suppress.

At the most basic level, this "colonization" of the life-world promotes the instrumentalization of human life itself: Human beings are largely treated as "means" for the achievement of economic and technological imperatives. As technical issues overshadow all others, attention increasingly turns to complex debates among experts. In the process, discussion is diverted away from the *value* issues underlying economic and technological progress itself. Barnes offers a classic example:

Think of the way in which the introduction of a new weapons system is now considered and appraised at the "higher levels" of society. Nearly all the appraisal will deal with the weapon as a *means*, with the question, for example, of how cost effective it is in killing people, and how long it is likely to retain its capacity to kill people. Debate about ends, about whether it is right to possess the capability to kill, or to kill the particular people involved, civilians say rather than military personnel, will be far less extensive, to say the least, and less visible.[23]

Typically, such debate among policy specialists and decision makers, whether concerned with production costs or weapon performance, is couched in the technical and quantitative languages of expertise.[24] This imbues the debate with an aura of authority and reputability that normative discussion about goals or ends, at least on the surface of the matter, does not seem to match. Lacking experts in ethics, morals, and general human decency (in the sense that we recognize technical experts), we acknowledge no privileged methodological rules capable of deciding the normative issues that confront us. For this reason, such discussions are merely written off as "just matters of opinion." Those involved in decision making increasingly turn away from such discussion, devoting their attention to technical problems that lend themselves to "rational" formulation.[25]

As a result of this "scientization" of social and political life, people begin to lose their intellectual and emotional capacities to criticall discuss their social needs and political interests. Questions concerning the origins and qualities of social needs, as well as the art of reflecting on them, have simply been swept away by the utilitarian criteria of technocratic theory. In the place of such questions, we find only technical languages that substitute such techniques as risk and liability assessment for a genuine discussion of human needs and values.[26]

This failure to examine the fundamental value questions raised by economic and technological progress presents a deep-seated paradox: as technologically based affluence increases in advanced industrial societies, so does the sense of goallessness, drift, and insecurity among the citizens who benefit from it.[27] The basic values that influence and shape the decisions of those who guide and manage our technological society remain unarticulated and unexamined. We plunge forth without any clear sense of goals, other than technological progress and economic production for their own sake. The qualitative question of "production for what?" is lost in the feverish pursuit of quantity.[28] This is perhaps the most fundamental crisis of our time.

Emphasis on technical criteria at the expense of everyday moral concerns thus causes people to lose confidence in both their institutions and themselves (particularly in their own common sense ways of talking together and in their ability to agree upon notions of right and wrong). And with this loss of confidence, they are increasingly compelled to fall back on the opinions of experts, which concern only the amoral and instrumental aspects of social and political problems. In a nutshell, the crisis of normative neglect is truly a fundamental crisis of democracy.

Redesigning Expertise: The Managerial and Policy Sciences

The expertise problem clearly poses a dilemma. We live in a world utterly dependent on expert knowledge but find ourselves unable to comfortably put our trust in professional experts. Among the various manifestations of this dilemma is a remarkable loss of confidence in expertise per se.[29] Such worries stem from a variety of sources. The most significant among them have surely been the technological catastrophes that have occurred in recent years—such as Three Mile Island, Bhopal, Chernobyl, and the Space Shuttle *Challenger.* Writing after the Bhopal accident, for instance, the *New Yorker* magazine observed that even in the face of some 2,000 deaths, for many the most profoundly troublesome dimension of the tragedy was the stark realization that our technical and managerial systems of expertise had failed.[30]

Evidence of the failures of experts is hardly limited to large-scale technologies. They are apparent in economic and social policy as well. One of the most prominent examples is the failure of the economics profession. Once considered the "new priests" of modern society, economists today flounder over the guidance of the American economy. Another case in point is the management profession. Although management skills were long considered the source of America's economic prowess, today it is widely believed that management's neglect and misguidance of our primary economic institutions is a basic source of the country's current economic difficulties (see Chapter 11). Or consider the educational experts. Educational specialists, administrators in particular, are seen to have merely stood by while our school systems degenerated to a national "crisis." Throughout these cases, as well as many more that could be cited, one finds a growing awareness of the technocratic underpinnings of such failures. Leading authorities on the professions, in fact, now trace the "crisis of the professions" to their overreliance on technical orientations. While the problem is becoming increasingly clear, then, the question of what to do about it begins to loom as one of the most sophisticated political and methodological issues confronting our age of expertise.

Some, like Gouldner, argue that expertise, even though "flawed," remains our best hope for the future.[31] If the choice is between guidance by technical specialists and the uncontrolled processes of capitalist markets, so the argument goes, it is best to accept technocracy and struggle to democratize the planning process. An argument with a long history in the left wing of the political spectrum, it is not without its appeal.

But is such a strategy viable? The history of socialism, punctuated with authoritarian practices justified in the name of science and rationality, often testifies to the precarious nature of this argument. Seldom have its advocates fully confronted the deeper political and methodological questions that underlie the design of a more "convivial" set of practices and techniques.[32] Can we, in fact, restructure expert planning and decision processes to make them better serve social and democratic purposes? In methodological terms, as we see in Part V, it is a question of how to integrate technical and normative rationality into the analytical and deliberative processes of the technocratic disciplines. That is, how can we rationally include the substantive content of social values and political ends as well as particular cultural orientations toward life itself? In political terms, it is a question of how to break the experts away from their allegiances to the elites.

In the context of the emerging postindustrial society, such questions raise profoundly difficult issues. The depoliticizing tendencies accompanying postindustrialism's technocratic practices, whether in the form of scientifically based decision making or merely as legitimation for elite decisions, represent a serious threat to the future of the political community. In this study we only attempt to single out one piece of the threat, namely, the role of two primary technocratic disciplines. Specifically, we focus on the two disciplines most concerned with the elaboration of modern organizational structures and their decision processes: the managerial and policy sciences. (It is important to clarify the linguistic convention employed here. Some writers speak of the "policy sciences" and the "managerial sciences," emphasizing the diverse and interdisciplinary character of the techniques that constitute them. Others refer to "policy science" and "managerial science," stressing more the intellectual orientation or concept rather than the contributing disciplines. Here we shall use the latter singular form, except, of course, when speaking of the two disciplines together.[33])

Why focus on the managerial and policy sciences? As the embodiment of technical rationality, these two applied sciences are the quintessential technocratic disciplines. They are the two intellectual endeavors primarily concerned with the application of technical decision criteria in the social life-world.

Both disciplines are products of the technocratic worldview that first appeared in the United States with the Progressive movement. Modern managerial science has its roots in Frederick Taylor's "scientific management." (We distinguish here between "managerial" and "management" science. The former is used to refer to the management discipline generally, whereas the latter is reserved for a specific set of techniques in the discipline.) Although policy science came somewhat later as a response to a different set of political circumstances, the contemporary discipline is in very large part a functional outgrowth of the managerial orientation. In practice, if not always in theory, policy science has evolved as a tool for managerial rationalization.

Both sciences are largely American in origin. At times, their narrowly conceived commitments to the rationalization of organizational and political processes have, in fact, taken the form of a basic American value system, or what has beeen called an "American Ideology."[34] Management, or "managerialism," emerged in the second decade of this century as "a philosophy, a science, and a pervasive metaphor which would dominate the way Americans viewed themselves and their institutions for the next fifty years." It provided the country with "a set of organizing principles at precisely the time when many . . . sensed a need for greater organization." These principles were to shape "every dominant American institution precisely as they helped those institutions become dominant."[35] Recognizing the deeper social significance of management, Peter Drucker contends that "scientific management" is arguably "the most powerful as well as the most lasting contribution America has made to Western thought since the Federalist Papers."[36]

Drucker's claim is perhaps a bit hyperbolic, but it does underscore the philosophical and ideological contribution of these disciplines. During the second half of this century, administrative theory has gradually supplanted democratic theory as the "real" or "operative" political theory of American institutions.[37] One manifestation of this significant change is the subtle but unmistakable "instrumentalization" of the social sciences.

Initially addressed to the broad questions of social and political life—
questions concerning ideology, social class, power, bureaucracy, and
alienation—much of contemporary social science has devolved into a
narrowly empirical discipline designed to supply policy-oriented
answers to managerial decision makers.

What we are observing, then, is as much a worldview as a set of scientific techniques. Not only do these sciences supply pragmatic answers
to economic and administrative problems, they have also created and
sought to perpetuate a technocratic philosophy about the relations of
such expertise to society itself. Indeed, some see this philosophy as the
professional ideology of a "new class."[38]

As both an ideology and a set of practices, the managerial and policy
sciences provide the theory and techniques of what Saint-Simon was the
first to call the "Administrative State." They are primarily geared, in this
respect, to the decision and planning requirements of complex large-
scale administrative organizations, both public and private. As the disciplines responsible for the development, organization, and implementation of the "information and decision technologies," they are essential to
the management of modern bureaucratic institutions. Most fundamentally, their tasks are to adjust corporate and governmental bureaucracies
to the flow of technical imperatives and their administrative requirements.[39] Such adjustment is a function basic to the central guidance of
the emerging postindustrial system.

The ensuing examination of these disciplines has two interrelated
foci. In the first part of the book, Chapter 3 through 8, the discussion
broadly underscores the dominance of technocratic ideas in the social
sciences, largely manifested in the rise of the managerial and policy
sciences themselves. More specifically, we also explore the ways the
managerial and policy sciences have functioned to technocratically
design and manage the governance of American institutions. They are
seen to have evolved to serve a particular twentieth-century model of
political and organizational governance, namely, the elitist practices of
the corporate state. Examining the theory and methods of these two
applied sciences, we illustrate how the decision criteria of the extant
governance processes have been functionally embedded in their
intellectual technologies.

In the case of managerial science, for example, we detail these patterns as they evolve in human relations psychology and later again in the
case of the contemporary computerized factory. Using the case of the
human relations movement, we describe how technocratic strategies

have helped to prestructure the managerial control of particular organizational practices. Organizational psychology is shown to be biased toward *managerial* solutions to workplace conflicts. The discipline has in large part committed itself to producing solutions that ensure a managerially dominated governance structure.

The second part of the book asks what these disciplines might look like under a different political structure, one that replaces elitist decision structures with a more participatory set of institutional arrangements. In Chapters 9 through 14, the emphasis shifts from an examination of the ways in which these disciplines supported elitist practices to a much more challenging question: Can the social sciences transcend their narrow managerial biases to help facilitate a broadly conceived political dialogue in American governmental and organizational life? Here we consider how the managerial and policy sciences might be reconstructed to promote a more authentic, democratic dialogue between experts and clients, as well as the kinds of participatory organizations and institutions needed to sustain such collaborative decision processes.[40]

While most organizational and policy experts continue to plod forward with the established technical methodologies, a small but growing number of theorists have begun to rethink the theories and practices of policy expertise. By and large, their work can be characterized as an effort to democratize the organizational and policy sciences. They seek for the practice of policy expertise a political and methodological orientation appropriate to participatory democracy. Working within the framework of this commitment, we explore ways of redesigning the practices of expertise that not only help to bring research closer to the relevant issues that confront the society as a whole but also facilitate movements that seek to bring people into the decision-making processes that govern their own lives. The task is both methodological and political. It is political in the fundamental sense that experts have to be weaned away from their dedication to the interests and problems of the elites. It is methodological in the sense that the actual practices of expertise have to be redevised to bring the full array of pertinent interests into the process. In the final chapter, we specify this as a process of "participatory expertise."

Notes

1. See Jacques Ellul, *The Technological Society* (New York: Knopf, 1964); and William G. Scott and David K. Hart, "Administrative Crisis: The Neglect of Metaphysical

Speculation," *Public Administration Review* 33 (September–October 1973), pp. 415–22; and Murry Bookchin, *The Ecology of Freedom* (Palo Alto, CA: Cheshire, 1982).

2. Norman Mailer, *Of a Fire on the Moon* (Boston: Little, Brown, 1970), pp. 51–52.

3. Anthony Giddens, *The Class Structure of Advanced Societies* (New York: Harper & Row, 1973), p. 258.

4. Daniel Bell, "Technocracy and Politics," *Survey* 16 (1971), p. 10.

5. See Brian Fay, *Social Theory and Political Practice* (New York: Holmes and Meyers, 1975).

6. C. A. Bowers, "The Reproduction of Technological Consciousness: Locating the Ideological Foundations of a Radical Pedagogy," *Teachers College Record* 83, no. 4 (Summer 1982), p. 531; and Alvin W. Gouldner, *The Dialectic of Ideology and Technology* (New York: Seabury, 1976).

7. Bowers, *ibid*.

8. Jürgen Habermas, "On Systematically Distorted Communication," *Inquiry* 13 (1970): 205–18.

9. Bowers, "The Reproduction of Technological Consciousness," pp. 531–32.

10. For an example of this argument, see John Platt, "What We Must Do," *Science* 28 (November 1969): 1117.

11. See Thomas L. Haskell, *The Authority of Experts* (Bloomington: Indiana University Press, 1984).

12. William Leiss, *The Domination of Nature* (Boston: Beacon, 1974).

13. Max Weber, *Max Weber: Selections in Translation*, ed. W. G. Runciman (Cambridge: Cambridge University Press, 1978), chap. 11.

14. Magali Sarfatti Larson, "The Production of Expertise and the Constitution of Expert Power," in Haskell, *The Authority of Experts*, p. 38.

15. Herbert Marcuse, *One-Dimensional Man* (Boston: Beacon, 1964).

16. See Jürgen Habermas, *Knowledge and Human Interests* (Boston: Beacon, 1971). For a related argument in the context of organization theory, see Alberto G. Ramos, *The New Science of Organization* (Toronto: University of Toronto Press, 1981).

17. Edward Wenk, Jr., "Political Limits in Steering Technology," in *Technology and Man's Future*, ed. Albert H. Teich (New York: St. Martin's, 1988), pp. 256–69.

18. For an interesting discussion of this phenomenon, see Kathy Ferguson, *The Feminist Case Against Bureaucracy* (Philadelphia: Temple University Press, 1984).

19. Frank Fischer and Alan Mandell, "Relegitimating Meritocracy: Educational Policy as Technocratic Strategy," *Telos*, no. 76 (Summer 1988): 50–64.

20. Christopher Lasch, *Haven in a Heartless World* (New York: Basic Books, 1977).

21. Paul Goodman, *People or Personnel* (New York: Random House, 1965).

22. For an interesting discussion related to this point, see Leroy C. Gould, et al., *Perceptions of Technological Risks and Benefits* (New York: Russell Sage, 1988).

23. Barry Barnes, *About Science* (Oxford: Basil Blackwell, 1985), p. 101.

24. On the role of language in politics, see Murray Edelman, *Political Language* (New York: Academic Press, 1977).

25. Barnes, *About Science*, pp. 101–2; and Alan Mandell, "Language, Power and Legitimation: The World of Nuclear Defense Intellectuals" (An interview with Carol Cohn), *Kairos* 2, no. 2 (1988): 57–68.

26. For example, a broad ecological focus in environmental policy is replaced by

"pollution risk analysis." Stephen L. Esquith, "Professional Authority and State Power," *Theory and Society* 16 (1987): 237–67.

27. Philip Slater, *The Pursuit of Loneliness* (Boston: Beacon, 1970).

28. Walter A. Weisskopf, *Alienation and Economics* (New York: Dell, 1972).

29. Robert Kanigel, "Angry at Our Gods," *Columbia*, October 1988, pp. 23–35.

30. "The Talk of the Town," *The New Yorker*, February 18, 1985, p. 29.

31. Alvin W. Gouldner, *The Future of the Intellectuals and the Rise of the New Class* (New York: Oxford University Press, 1979), pp. 7–8.

32. See Ivan Illich, *Tools for Conviviality* (New York: Harper & Row, 1973).

33. With reference to this interpretation of policy *science*, see Yeheskel Dror, *Ventures in Policy Sciences* (New York: American Elsevier, 1971), p. 13. The analytical techniques and methodologies that constitute the policy *sciences* are primarily drawn from the disciplines of economics, political science, and sociology. They are essentially the methodologies these disciplines have brought to bear on the analysis of public policy. Similarly, the managerial *sciences* are made up of techniques borrowed from a range of disciplines, including managerial economics, operations research, computer science, organizational sociology, and psychology.

34. T. H. Wilson, *The American Ideology* (London: Routledge, 1977).

35. Robert B. Reich, *The Next American Frontier* (New York: New York Times Books, 1983), p. 49.

36. Peter F. Drucker, *The Practice of Management* (New York: Harper & Row, 1954), p. 280.

37. On administrative theory as political philosophy, see Sheldon S. Wolin, "A Critique of Organizational Theories," in *A Sociological Reader in Complex Organizations*, ed. Amitai Etzioni (New York: Holt, Rinehart & Winston, 1969), pp. 133–49; and David K. Hart and William G. Scott, "The Philosophy of American Management," *Southern Review of Public Administration* 6, no. 2 (Summer 1982): 240–52.

38. Gouldner, *The Future of the Intellectuals*. Although we take up a piece of the "new class" issue in Chapter 6, the subject is too complex to deal with here in any detail.

39. On this point, see John McDermott, "Technology: The Opiate of the Intellectuals," in *Technology and the Future*, ed. Albert Teich (New York: St. Martin's, 1986), pp. 98–99.

40. See H. T. Wilson, *Political Management* (Berlin: Walter de Gruyter, 1985).

PART II

THE TECHNOCRATIC PROJECT: ITS HISTORY AND AGENDA

The people's trust in their new intellectual leadership is, by its very nature, totally different from that which they once placed in their theological leaders. Trust in the opinions of experts has a completely different character. The fear that there will be one day established a despotism based on science is a ridiculous and absurd fantasy. Such a thing could only arise in minds wholly alien to the positivist idea.

—CLAUDE HENRI SAINT-SIMON

A comfortable, smooth, reasonable, democratic unfreedom prevails in advanced industrial society, a token of technical progress. . . . [T]he technological society is a system of domination which operates already in the concepts and constructs of techniques. . . . In the medium of technology, culture, politics, and the economy merge into an omnipresent system which swallows up or repulses all alternatives. . . . Technological rationality has become political rationality.

—HERBERT MARCUSE

Part II outlines the basic tenets of the technocratic project, from Francis Bacon to Daniel Bell. Both chapters provide the historical and political context for the chapters that follow. Chapter 3, "Technocratic Theory: The Basic Themes in Historical Perspective," presents the theoretical concepts of the early technocratic writers, particularly Saint-Simon and Auguste Comte. The discussion focuses on the idea that technical elites should rule, the concept of a "new class," positivism, the central importance of technology, the purportedly "apolitical" character of expertise, the administrative state, organization theory, and state planning. Chapter 4, "Technocratic Theory in America: From the Progressives to the Postindustrialists," shifts to the adoption and adaptation of these ideas in the Progressive era in the United States and traces them to the present. Ideas that emerged as eighteenth-century utopian prophecies are increasingly seen to correspond to twentieth-century American realities.

Even though technocracy has yet to arrive as the governing system, the issues posed by the project are now seen to be critical concerns in contemporary political and social theory. Everywhere there are experts and their functions in society are recognized to be among the most fundamental social and political issues of our time. There is, however, an important difference between early and modern theories of technocratic development. Whereas earlier technocratic writers saw knowledge replacing politics in governance processes, leading contemporary theorists no longer necessarily see the ascent of experts ushering in the demise of politics per se. Some postindustrial writers maintain that technocratic strategies only lead to a *new type* of politics, much more technical in nature. Indeed, it is from this premise that the book draws its primary theme, "the politics of expertise." The study as a whole is an effort to take seriously this contemporary dimension of expert decision making and to examine its implications for the managerial and policy sciences, the key technocratic disciplines of modern society.

3

Technocratic Theory:
The Basic Themes in Historical Perspective

This chapter outlines the basic themes in the history of technocratic theory. Beginning with the concept of modernity, it sketches the rise of technical rationality as a primary social force in Western society. Focusing in particular on the European origins of technocratic thought, the discussion centers on the most persistent technocratic conviction: the idea that science is superior to politics. This chapter seeks to draw out and clarify the basic ideological dimensions of this idea, especially the ways in which it supports and justifies a specific set of social forces and interests. The purpose is to lay the groundwork for the analysis that follows.

Modernity and the Rise of
Technical Rationality

Technocracy has roots deeply embedded in our cultural past, particularly the scientific and technological worldviews of the modern Western tradition. Technocratic thought, in this respect, is the product of a period called "modernity," an age beginning in about the seventeenth century. Essentially, it refers to the emergence in Europe of a Western form of life increasingly shaped by science and technology. As Langdon

Winner puts it, modernity denotes the "astonishing increase in the scope, variety, sophistication, and effectiveness of man's scientific and technological activity" during the past two or three hundred years. Its impact is reflected in almost every aspect of modern life. "As the knowledge of physical reality has expanded, men have been able to exploit immense new sources of energy and materials and to devise larger, more complex, more productive forms of manufacturing, agriculture, transportation, communication, medicine and warfare." In conjunction "with these developments have come a vast array of social, economic, demographic, and political changes that bring a whole new character to civilized life—increased per capita income, longer life expectancy, rapid expansion of the world population, rise in literacy, proliferation of social roles, and so on." [1]

By the twentieth century, especially during its latter half, it was no longer sufficient merely to chronicle science and technology's impact on society. Indeed, the worldview underlying scientific and technological progress had begun literally to challenge the long-standing ideological hegemony of capitalism in the West. Some writers, in fact, argue that in the not-too-distant future the emerging institutions of science and technology will dominate the capitalist system. Few have underscored this historical ascent of science and technology more vividly than Robert Heilbroner. "Like the first manifestations of the market in the medieval era," he explains, "science and its technology emerge as a great underground river whose tortuous course has finally reached the surface during the age of capitalism." And like the earlier forces of market capitalism, "the river of scientific change, having now surfaced, must cut its own channel through the existing landscape." It is a channel that has profoundly altered the existing societal terrain. Heilbroner himself suggests that the alteration may portend the demise of capitalism. He poses the question this way:

> If we ask what force in our day might in time be strong enough to undercut the bastions of privilege and function of capitalism and to create its own institutions and social structures in their place, the answer must surely be the one force that dominates our age—the power of science and scientific technology. [2]

Modern society, simply stated, cannot be understood apart from the influences of science and its technologies. So central is our fundamental commitment to technologically induced growth that it has come to shape other basic societal processes. "What is involved," Moore writes, "is a 'total' transformation of a traditional or pre-modern society into the types of technology and associated social organization that characterizes the 'advanced' economically prosperous, and relatively politically stable nations of the Western world."[3] Another writer explains modern political development as consisting of "the elaboration of new and more complex forms of politics and government as societies restructure themselves to absorb progressively the stock and flow of modern technology."[4]

It is customary to think of technologies as material objects, particularly as machines. Such a conception, however, fails to capture the full significance of modern technology. In the broadest sense, the term today refers to the totality of rational methods designed to efficiently organize human activities in general, both material and social activities. The word *technology* now properly refers to a "systematic, disciplined, approach to objectives." It involves the use of a concept of system and a calculus of precision and measurement to order efficiently the means to specific ends.[5] Some, in this sense, use the term synonymously with *technique*.[6]

Increasingly structured around the imperatives of technology and its techniques, the basic institutions of society have been gradually but systematically organized around technically oriented modes of reason and action. Organizations designed to guide and implement the flow of technological innovations were themselves structured to conform to the criteria of technology. In the language of organization theory, such institutions have been steadily restructured around the principles of "technical rationality." A technically rational institution is one strictly governed by the rules of efficient action. Efficiency became *the* standard of organizational action.

The theory and practice of modern technocracy is a response to these technical and organizational forces. Modern technocrats must be considered both the products and the agents of these technologically oriented institutions. As agents, they monitor, guide, and restructure organizations to conform with evolving requirements of contemporary technologies. Their tools and strategies in the language of methodology are guided by the logic of technical rationality.

No social theorist has contributed more to our understanding of the rise and evolution of technical rationality than Max Weber, the great German sociologist. Weber identifies the critical force in the rise of technical rationality and the modern technocratic worldview as the appearance in

Western European culture of a specific form of knowledge, scientific reason, and instrumental rationality. Between the sixteenth and eighteenth centuries, scientific and technical reason were broadly institutionalized as underlying forces of society as a whole. In Weber's view, this became the specific feature of the secularization of the modern society, which he variously described as the "intellectualization" or "rationalization" of the world. This new mode of reason included the following characteristics: (1) a progressive mathematization of knowledge and experience, social as well as natural; (2) an insistence on rational—generally experimental—proofs in the origination of both scientific knowledge and the conduct of social life; and (3) the appearance and evolution of a technically trained organization of expert officials. These experts, both technological and managerial, have become the "absolutely inescapable condition of our entire existence."[7]

The distinguishing feature of this new emphasis on scientific and technical reason is the "formalization" of its knowledge. Emerging in sharp opposition to the other types of knowledge dominating human affairs for centuries, particularly religious and craft knowledge, scientific and technological knowledge was rapidly accorded the status of "superior" or "higher" knowledge. As Freidson explains, "In the West, higher knowledge was formalized into theories, and other abstractions, on efforts at systematic reasoned explanation, and on justification of the facts and activities believed to constitute the world." Such "formal knowledge," as it came to be called, "remains separate from both common, everyday knowledge and nonformal specialized knowledge."[8]

Basic to this formalization of knowledge is Weber's concept of rationalization. Rationalization, as Freidson explains, pertains to "the pervasive use of reason, sustained where possible by measurement, to gain the end of functional efficiency." Applied to the social as well as the material world, "rational action is manifested most obviously in technology but also in law, the management of institutions, the economy, indeed, the entire institutional realm of modern society." It first clearly emerged "with the accounting and management methods that developed with capitalism and the administrative methods of developing predictable social order" that arose with the modern state in the form of "rational-legal bureaucracy." Later it became identified more generally with the rise of modern science, in particular "the application of the scientific method to technical and social problems."[9] In fact, the formal knowledge generated in the universities during the past century has increasingly been geared to such applications. Parallel to the rapid expansion of such knowledge has also been the dramatic growth of the professional disciplines, especially those with technocratic orientations.

The question as to why technical rationality emerged as a basic organizing principle of economic and social life is still the subject of debate, particularly between Marxists and Weberian scholars. Indeed, the issue between these two groups dates back to Weber himself. One of Weber's purposes was to refute the Marxist argument that the spread of technical rationality was a direct manifestation of the development of capitalistic productive forces. For Weber, this rationalizing tendency possessed a larger universal-historical character and capitalism was only the form it took in the Occidental world at the societal level in a specific historic period. The emergence of technical rationality as a dominant social force, he argued, must be traced to a confluence of ideas and modes of life—institutional, religious, and personal tendencies—that existed prior to the development of industrial capitalism. Particularly important in his formulation was the role of the Reformation and the rise of the Protestant ethic.[10] Weber also pointed to the same rationalizing tendencies in socialist countries undergoing institutionalization, a reality that has caused Marxists a good deal of embarrassment.

In this discussion, we sidestep the long-standing debate between Marxists and Weberians. For present purposes, we merely accept the fact that capitalist development, whether it initiated this rationalizing mode or not, has served as a primary vehicle for its expansion. Under capitalism, economic enterprises and government institutions were from the outset increasingly organized in a "purposive-rational" form. Economic behavior, first that of the entrepreneurs and officials but later also that of workers, was obliged to conform to the principles of technical or instrumental rationality. Characteristic of both capitalist enterprise and modern state administration was "the concentration of the material means of administration" in the hands of the rationally calculating entrepreneur or political leader.[11]

The search for technical rationality and the growth of bureaucratic administration have occurred together. Bringing technical knowledge to bear on organizational performance requires the systematic division and subdivision of tasks, typically the identifying character of bureaucracy. It is, moreover, the unfolding of this system of intellectual and organizational rationality that brought the technocratic project to the fore. In a social system where "the methodological attainment of a . . . given . . . political end . . . by the use of an increasingly precise calculation of means" becomes a central dynamic, it is inevitable that the technical expert will emerge as an important person.[12] The technocrat, in short, is assigned the central task of fitting the bureaucratic organization to the technological mission of modern society.

Today society is dominated by an interlocking network of bureaucratic institutions that are functionally geared—directly and indirectly—to the processes of economic and technological change. No one has more clearly outlined the primary features of this network than Strasser:

- The development of our technology inevitably has led, apart from the specific capitalist tendencies toward concentration and centralization, to an ever greater accumulation of power in a few centers, thereby increasing the chance of the use of that power to thwart democratic decisions.

- The same process furthers and accelerates centralization in political systems that are increasingly distant from the citizenry, given that executives strive to adapt their sphere of action to economic realities.

Because of the increasing scope of technological requirements, as well as their extensive "social externalities," or "spillovers" into other areas of modern social life, the costs of large-scale technologies "create immense demands that dramatically narrow the room for democratic decision-making." The development of these projects thus works to exclude alternative policy goals and options.

- The hierarchical structure of the technological apparatus, the radical separation of labor between planners and executors, and the division within the labor process lead to one-sidedness and atrophy, and demand subordinate behavior.

- To the extent that new segments of life are constantly being opened up by the marketing strategies of large corporations and taken into the grip of the technological apparatus, and to the extent that new occupations are becoming professionalized, the dependence of people on external services grows, while their ability to help themselves diminishes.

- The questions that are added to the political agenda become ever more complicated; the scope of relevant data, ever more overpowering; and the process of shaping popular will and decision, ever more inscrutable. Despite all education efforts in this area, the political competence of the layman, one of the buttresses of democracy, is undermined. We are moving toward an expertocracy.[13]

The dominant institutions that structure this dynamic are the corporation and the state, especially its bureaucratic administrative agencies.

Guided, if not governed, by technocratic decision rules, these primary institutions—both separately and together—have emerged as the dominant carriers of modern technological development and societal change.[14]

In the interests of systems maintenance, the dominant institutions have necessitated the development of a unique set of secondary and cultural institutions functionally geared to a technologically based society. Among the most important of these institutions are the urban city and its forms of sociopolitical pluralism; a mobile system of social stratification; a "private sphere" as the context of industrial social life; mass education; and the various institutions for scientific and technological innovation, including the great national universities. Each of these institutions has, to one degree or another, been rationalized to support the imperatives of the primary institutions. They provide basic systems supports: institutions for socializing the population to accept specific value systems, the provisions of procedures for conflict resolution, the establishment of efficient spatial relations, the supply of basic infrastructure for economic stability, the development of technical research, education for the work force, and so on. All of these activities must be rationally coordinated to facilitate the mission of the primary institutions. The rationalization of secondary institutions is never simple, as these institutions can at times acquire considerable autonomy. Bringing them in line with the requirements of the primary institutions can be the source of major political conflicts.[15]

This gradual but steady extension of technical rationality and its bureaucratic system is an enormously complex phenomenon that has long been the subject of a great deal of writing. Technology's advocates generally emphasize a self-evident premise: Technological progress has brought unprecedented wealth to the Western world. Despite extensive celebration of this reality, however, those committed to the forces of technology and bureaucracy have never been able to shake off some very fundamental worries about their impact on our way of life.

Included among those who have worried about the impact of technical rationality on social life was Weber himself. Weber expressed very mixed feelings about this mode of reason and warned of its potentially malevolent consequences. In particular, he worried about the technical expert's continuous extension of the bureaucratic form to more and more "departments" of social life. For Weber, the advance of bureaucratic administration brought about the "disenchantment of the world." Modern life was becoming an "iron cage." As he put it:

No one knows who will live in this cage, or whether at end of this tremendous development entirely new prophets arise, or there will be a great rebirth of old ideals, or, if neither, mechanized petrification, embellished with a sort of convulsive self-importance. For, of the last stage of this cultural development, it might be truly said: "specialists without spirit, sensualists without hearts; this nullity imagines that it has attained a level of civilization never before achieved."[16]

For some, the culmination of this process is the ultimate bureaucratic system, the totalitarian society. Short of totalitarianism, life under the rule of technical expertise is seen as becoming more and more impersonal and alienated. As Goodman put it, people feel "powerless in immense social organizations; desperately relying on technological means to solve problems caused by previous technological means."[17] One need only think of the alienation bred by large bureaucratic workplaces, urban cities that are technically and fiscally unmanageable, the disaster of Three Mile Island, the pollution from toxic wastes in the environment, the explosion of the spaceship Challenger, or the irrationality of the nuclear arms race. Such realities often leave us with the feeling that nothing can be done. Our fate appears to be hopelessly tied to the bureaucratic world of the experts and their seemingly autonomous technologies.

The pressing question then is this: Have we become bureaucratically subjugated to the blind forces of technology? Will it be possible in the future to take control of events and infuse new technological developments with humanistic values? Although we do not have the answer to this question, some of the problems that must be addressed are clear. Technocracy is one of those problems. Technocrats are the principal agents of these trends; it is their values and methods that guide—if not set—the course of technological progress. It is for this reason that we must begin to rethink the nature of expert knowledge and the processes by which it is employed. As the next step toward this end, we turn to the technocratic theorists themselves. We begin with the origin of the technocratic idea.

Technocracy and the Enlightenment

Although the term *technocracy* was first used in 1919 by an American engineer, William Henry Smyth, the idea is generally traced back to Francis Bacon in the seventeenth century.[18] For Bacon, the defining feature of history was rapidly becoming the rise and growth of science and technology. Where Plato had envisioned a society governed by "Philosopher-kings," men who could perceive the "forms" of social justice, Bacon sought a technical elite who would rule in the name of efficiency and technical order. Indeed, Bacon's purpose in *The New Atlantis* (1622) was an explicit attempt to replace the philosopher with the research scientist as the ruler of the utopian future. New Atlantis was a pure technocratic society. Replete with research institutions aimed at advancing technological progress, scientific rationality was located at the very core of the community. Its research institutes were described as "the very eye of the kingdom."[19]

Bacon was much more than an English utopian visionary. He also bore a major role in promoting modern science. Though he only experimented himself in a somewhat random and unproductive fashion, he was the tireless proponent of the essential elements of scientific research—particularly the observation of phenomena and the accumulation of data. His writings, in this respect, represent a major seventeenth-century continuation of the earlier Renaissance attack on the abstract and the deductive methods of medieval philosophy, especially that of the Ecclesiastics. As such, he was a leading ideologue for the rise of scientific progress.

Beyond Bacon, the idea of a technocracy continued to grow with the rise of the newly emerging industrial order.[20] Specifically, it was elaborated as the ideology of the eighteenth-century Enlightenment theorists seeking to explain and legitimate the coming of industrial society.[21] Originating as a response to the crumbling of the "Old Regime," the Enlightenment was an intellectual and cultural search for a new order that culminated in the French Revolution. Fundamental to this search was the optimistic creed of the *philosophes*. While few of these intellectuals were philosophers in the strict sense of the term, and by no means were all French, they all shared a dedication to the ideals of reason, natural law, and progress. Enlightenment thinkers—in large part publicists, economists, political theorists, and social reformers—derived their principles from their intellectual predecessors of the two preceding centuries, particularly the empiricists such as Newton and Locke. Fundamentally, they believed that human reason could free mankind from the errors and misfortunes of the past and lead to perpetual peace, perfect government, and a utopian society. For many, the French Revolution was a manifestation of this dream. It has been described as "the Heavenly City" of the eighteenth-century *philosophes*.

Highly influenced by Newton's mathematical laws and principles, the *philosophes* believed they could find the underlying order and logic governing human affairs. Indeed, they frequently portrayed themselves as the Newtons of statecraft, justice, and economics. The ultimate goal was to translate—or, perhaps more accurately, "reduce"—our understanding of societal institutions to empirical formulas as rigorous as those put forth by Newton himself. The course of society was to be understood no differently than the movement of the planets or the gravitational fall of a physical object.

Underlying their formulations was a powerful metaphor borrowed from Newtonian physics and the emerging industrial order, namely, that of mechanics and the machine. For most of history, according to the *philosophes*, men had hampered the operations of the social machine largely because they failed to grasp its principles. Once in possession of these fundamental laws, however, mankind would finally allow the "world-machine" to function smoothly and efficiently for "the greater good." The optimism of the age was expressed by Condorcet. In *The Progress of the Human Mind* (1974) he asked his readers to consider the following:

> If men can predict, with almost complete assurance, the phenomena whose laws are known to them . . . , why should it be regarded as a vain enterprise to chart, with some degree of probability, the course of the future destiny of mankind by studying the results of human history? Since the only basis of belief in the natural sciences is the idea that the general laws, known or unknown, regulating the phenomena of the universe are regular and constant, why should this principle be any less true for the development of the intellectual and moral faculties of man than for other operations of nature.[22]

Condorcet's argument had a profound influence on Enlightenment thinkers. Among them were Saint-Simon and August Comte. No other writers were to have more influence on the development of technocratic thinking than these two social theorists. Saint-Simon, in fact, is generally considered the "father of technocracy."

Saint-Simon and Comte: The Positivist State

It is difficult to convey adequately the full impact of Saint-Simon's contribution to the technocratic project. He was one of the most popular utopian thinkers of the nineteenth century, attracting followers throughout the Western world. One reason for his influence was surely the fact that his work harbored a number of diverse theoretical implications. E. H. Carr has captured this point by describing him as "the precursor of socialism, the precursor of the technocrats, and the precursor of totalitarianism."[23]

Saint-Simon's utopian vision was a response to the social crises erupting in the wake of the industrial and political revolutions in France. Fundamentally, his writings represented an attempt to spell out a new European social order. Segal has outlined the main themes of the vision: Science and technology were "to solve major social as well as technical problems"; technical experts would be needed "to run society"; the "unenlightened masses" would have to be controlled "in order to effect these changes"; there would be a need to establish a new European hierarchy "based not on social origins" but on "natural talent and society's requirements"; and a "need to abandon mass democracy and, in turn, politics."[24]

For Saint-Simon, the political, intellectual, and cultural unity that had once defined Europe had collapsed under the assault of various movements and creeds. Numerous competing forces—Protestant, capitalist, and nationalistic among them—had connived to unravel the foundations of the old culture. In his view, a new unity based upon an all-encompassing ideology had to be forged. Only a belief in science and technology could replace the divisive ideologies prevalent at the time, particularly those of the church. In short, priests and politicians—the old rulers of Europe—had to be supplanted by scientists and technicians.[25] As one writer put it, Saint-Simon's work can be interpreted as a prescription for Bacon's prophecy.[26]

True progress, according to Saint-Simon, was only to be found in a society free of competing political interests. This was to be achieved through the introduction of a new system of "expert management" in industry and government. The new state, in fact, was called the "Administrative State." Initially, Saint-Simon argued that governance of the new system was to be carried out by scientists and technicians. In his later writings, he modified this position by calling for a triumvirate of scientists and technicians, industrial managers, and philosophers and artists to head the dominant institutions.[27]

No other topic was more important to Saint-Simon than the precise organization of these governing institutions. Even though science in all its forms held a privileged position in his philosophy, he proclaimed one science to transcend all others, namely, the "science of organization." The essence of his approach to organization was a system of bureaucratic power directed by a hierarchy of experts. Appealing to the common interest of all, he counseled the working classes to accept authority from the top of the organization in proportion to the expert's enlightenment. Knowledge was stressed as the prerequisite for upward mobility in the organizational hierarchy, although individuals could only be invited to join the technocratic elites by those groups themselves. It was an idea clearly popular among newly emerging professional groups.

We can begin to see here some of the class implications of Saint-Simon's system. Written in a period of turbulent class struggle, key aspects of his work can be interpreted as expressions of the aspirations of the new middle classes. Like the rising middle classes in general, the scientists and technicians of his new order were seeking a secure place in the postrevolutionary class structure. To advance their interests, Saint-Simon devoted considerable time to selling technocracy to both the emerging industrial elites and the working classes, both of whom were generally suspicious. Nowhere is his effort more apparent than in his famous "parable of the idlers." Basically an attack on the classes of the "Old Regime," he asked his fellow countrymen to consider the impact of losing 3,000 of the country's best scientists, technicians, and artisans with losing 30,000 of the old guard: nobles, hierarchs of the church, officers of the crown, magistrates, marshals, and "ten thousand of the richest proprietors who live in the style of the nobles." The scientists and technicians, he argued, were virtually indispensible, whereas society would find it easy to manage without the others. Such realities, he maintained, "show that society is a world which is upside down."[28]

Saint-Simon's principal disciple was Auguste Comte. In his famous *Course of Positive Philosophy*, Comte set out a synthesis of "positive knowledge," which Saint-Simon himself had failed to develop. In the six volumes of this study Comte emphasized that *real* knowledge (defined as empirical knowledge) is obtainable only by the use of the "positivist method."[29] Based on the epistemological canons of the physical sciences, the positivist method spells out the rules and evaluative criteria for assessing the empirical dimensions of human experience.[30] Principally, such rules pertain to the conduct of scientific observation, experimentation, and empirical analysis (including the strict separation of factual and empirical premises). The underlying objective of positivist research is the discovery of the general "scientific laws" of society. Comte himself had little interest in such empirical research; his primary purpose was to locate the unity of science—both physical and social—in the adoption of a common *method* rather than in a specific set of empirical discoveries or laws per se. The methodological principles of his positivist epistemology constituted the common method. They remain deeply entrenched in contemporary technocratic thinking.

To explain the gradual realization of his positivist philosophical system, Comte divided history into several stages, beginning with the imminent positive revolution in philosophy and science and culminating in the "Positive State." To persuade the "ignorant masses" of the virtues of the positive state (largely understood as the hegemony of science and industry), Comte envisioned the need for an interim revolutionary dictatorship. Although he described the dictatorship as "transitional," the ideals of liberty and equality would eventually be supplanted by the technocratic values of order and progress. Disappointed by the "antiprogressive" sentiments that characterized the later phase of the French Revolution, he gradually became intolerant of individual liberties. In the end, Comte turned politically to conservatism and sought to align his philosophy of social change with a conservative theory of history.

Along with this conservative turn, Comte began to worry that the emergence of science and industry (even when coupled with higher levels of education) would be insufficient to ensure the future of the Positive State. To shore up these concerns he advocated the development of a surrogate religion, an idea that Saint-Simon also contemplated. Toward this end, Comte advanced the concept of a "sociocracy," defined as a new "religion of humanity." Sociologists were to identify the principles of this new faith and to implement them through a "sociolatry." The sociolatry was to entail a system of festivals, devotional practices, and rites designed to fix the new social ethics in the minds of the people. In the process, men and women would devote themselves not to God (deemed an outmoded concept) but to "Humanity" as symbolized in the "Grand Being" and rendered incarnate in the great men of history.[31]

To be sure, Comte's theory of a sociolatry has been the source of considerable amusement. By and large, his modern-day defenders have sought to dissociate his theory of positive knowledge from his idea of a sociolatry. For these writers, positivism is at once a theory of knowledge, a philosophy of history, *and* a political program (some would even say a way of life and thought). In either case, Comte's new "science of mankind," variously called "Positivism" or the "New Social System," proved to be very influential in the rise of modern sociology. Many call him the father of the discipline, a fact that also underscores the technocratic origins of modern social science itself.

Positivism and Utilitarianism:
Bridging the Fact-Value Separation

Although the theoretical writings of Saint-Simon and Comte shaped the development of the nineteenth-century technocratic thought, it is also important, before closing this chapter, to mention the influence of utilitarian economic and moral theory. Utilitarians are typically not theorists of technocracy in the usual sense of the term, but their principles have played a fundamental role in the theory and practice of the project. Such influence can perhaps first be traced back to the reform movement inspired by Jeremy Bentham's utilitarian moral theory in the second half of nineteenth-century Victorian England.[32] During this period organized groups of reformers sought to measure the utility of almost every aspect of economic and social life and to bring their findings to bear on parliamentary lawmaking. They were in large part zealots who idolized Bentham and his work. One can identify interesting parallels between this movement and twentieth-century technocratic reform movements, especially that of scientific management, which we take up in the next chapter. Here we must content ourselves with a brief outline of the principles of utilitarianism and their relationship to the positivist theory of decision making.

Most technocrats are utilitarians of one form or another. Nowhere is the emphasis on utilitarianism—both manifest and latent—stronger than in the managerial and policy sciences.[33] The general principles of utility, common to the several theoretical variants of utilitarianism, underlie the major decision techniques of the managerial and policy sciences, particularly cost-benefit analysis. (In explicit theoretical terms, the principles of utility supply the normative foundations of conventional economic analysis generally.)

Often the technocratic social sciences are described as "amoral," but this judgment only represents the rejection of a specific moral theory, namely, utilitarian ethics. Indeed, utilitarianism connects these disciplines to a well-established, sophisticated moral theory. Its theoretical function is to supply positivist decision techniques with a normative decision criterion.[34] Essentially, it provides positivists with a normative rule capable of bridging the fact-value dichotomy in practical matters of decision making.

To understand the way in which utilitarian decision-making theory can serve positivist social science, it is essential to grasp the tenets of "value noncognitivism," the meta-theoretical foundation of the fact-value dichotomy.[35] According to this theory, value judgments are essentially emotional responses to life conditions. As subjective commitments, they contain no verifiable truth content. To qualify as objective knowledge, statements must be verified by formal scientific methods. Although important aspects of value statements can be investigated scientifically, particularly statements about the conditions that lead to the adoption of specific values or statements about consequences that result from the acceptance of value positions, there is no way of scientifically establishing the categorical truth of a value judgment. Thus, in the final analysis, value judgments must fall beyond the rational methods and procedures of science. Even though frequently violated in practice, at the methodological level, the fact-value dichotomy remains a dominant governing principle in the social sciences, especially the managerial and policy sciences. To be judged as proper, all research must—at least officially—pay its respects to this principle.

According to positivism, then, facts and values have different epistemological statuses. Where facts refer to "real things" in the world "out there," and thus can be established by empirical investigation, values are interpreted as subjective responses to the existing world. As such, they are considered merely relative to existing conditions. They can be studied empirically, but it is impossible to "prove" the validity or superiority of one set of values (or value systems) over another. This poses a thorny question: How does one judge which course of action is best? Utilitarianism offers an answer.

For utilitarians, the solution is to be found in an empirical emphasis on the preferences and desires of individuals and groups. Although there are a variety of theories of utilitarianism, all fundamentally take the presence of specific values (preferences and interests) as established and, therefore, "given." Sidestepping the passing of judgments on competing values, utilitarians seek to maximize values in whatever way that yields the greatest amount of satisfaction in the society as a whole (or, in its classic formulation, it seeks to maximize "the greatest good for the largest number of people"). It attempts to do this by rationally calculating the most efficient and effective distribution of resources to achieve the given ends. Decision makers, in this view, should not be in the business of making value judgments. Rather, their function is merely to apply "objectively" and "neutrally" the principles of utility—that is, to identify the existing distribution of values and to select the most efficient means for maximizing these values.

In the language of moral theory, the strategy of utilitarianism has been described as an attempt to derive an "ought" (i.e., a statement about what should constitute the "greatest good") from an "is" (i.e., the existing preferences of individuals and groups), a practice long considered by many to be a violation of ethical principles. By stressing the verifiability of facts about what people want, while saying nothing about the relative importance of different value orientations, utility theory suggests in effect that established concepts of right and justice—for example, those of capitalism or socialism—cannot be subjected to rigorous and decisive critiques. Insofar as the moral principles of one political system cannot be judged to be more rational than those of another, utilitarian decision making conveniently serves to deflect political criticisms of existing social arrangements and the ruling value systems that govern them.

It does this in two ways. It insulates elite value systems from political critique based on "counterfactual" values and ideals: If value judgments are ultimately a matter of personal predilections, then the ruling value system must be as valid as an oppositional value system. Second, it turns inherently normative political questions about what "ought" to be the end goals of social action into pragmatic empirical questions about the efficiency of specific means to given ends. As such, it provides an inherently functional normative foundation for the managerial and policy sciences, largely invented to serve the informational needs of policies determined at higher levels in the decision hierarchy. In short, political issues are restructured to conform to the requirements of technical decision making, thus paving the way for the development and expansion of the Administrative State.[36]

It is sufficient for present purposes to rest our discussion of the theoretical origins of technocracy here. The theories discussed in this section, particularly those of Saint-Simon and Comte, supply the essential concepts and principles that have come to define the technocratic movement. Present in their writings is the idea of a scientific/technical elite as a new class, an emphasis on positivism and its methodologies, the central role of social engineering through planning, the beginnings of organization theory, and the concept of the Administrative State. Even more important than these concepts are the principles that tie them together. In Saint-Simon and Comte we find a hostility to politicians; the idea that democracy is the root of political and social conflict; the belief that class struggle should be replaced with technical decision making; and the deep-seated convictions that technological progress and material productivity are the defining characteristics of the good society. These themes, echoing Bacon's earlier arguments, underlie their deep-seated conviction that politicians should be replaced by scientific and technical elites. These ideas, as we shall see in the following chapters, occur again and again throughout technocratic writings. Only the historical circumstances change; the ideas themselves remain remarkably constant.

Notes

1. Langdon Winner, *Autonomous Technology: Technics-out-of-Control as a Theme in Political Thought* (Cambridge: MIT Press, 1977), p. 47.

2. Robert Heilbroner, *The Limits of American Capitalism* (New York: Harper & Row, 1966), p. 115.

3. Wilbert E. Moore, *Social Change* (Englewood Cliffs, NJ: Prentice-Hall, 1963), p. 89.

4. Walter E. Rostow, *Politics and the Stages of Growth* (New York: Cambridge University Press, 1971), p. 56.

5. Daniel Bell, *The Coming of Post-Industrial Society* (New York: Basic Books, 1973), p. 349.

6. Jacques Ellul, *The Technological Society* (New York: Knopf, 1964), p. xxv.

7. Cited in Herbert Marcuse, "Industrialization and Capitalism in the Work of Max Weber," in *Negations* (Boston: Beacon, 1968), p. 204.

8. Elliot Freidson, *Professional Power* (Chicago: University of Chicago Press, 1986), p. 3.

9. Ibid.

10. Max Weber, *The Protestant Ethic and the Spirit of Capitalism* (New York: Scribner, 1958).

11. Hans Gerth and C. Wright Mills, *From Max Weber* (New York: Oxford University Press, 1958), p. 221.

12. Ibid.

13. Johanno Strasser, "1984: Decade of the Experts?" in *1984 Revisited* ed. Irving Howe (New York: Harper & Row, 1984), pp. 162–63.

14. Peter Berger, Brigitte Berger, and Hansfried Kellner, *The Homeless Mind: Modernization and Consciousness* (New York: Vintage, 1973), pp. 97–115.

15. Ibid.

16. Weber, *The Protestant Ethic*, p. 182.

17. Paul Goodman, *New Reformation: Notes of a Neolithic Conservative* (New York: Random House, 1970), pp. 192–93.

18. William H. Smyth, "Technocracy: Definitions and Origin," *Nation* 125 (December 28, 1932), p. 646.

19. Francis Bacon, *The Great Instauration and the New Atlantis*, ed. J. Weinberger (Arlington Heights, IL: AHM, 1980).

20. See William Leiss, *The Domination of Nature* (Boston: Beacon, 1972).

21. Peter Gay, *The Enlightenment: An Interpretation*, 2 vols. (New York: Knopf, 1966–69).

22. Marquis de Condorcet, *Sketch for a Historical Picture of the Progress of the Human Mind* (New York: Noonday, 1955).

23. E. H. Carr, *Studies in Revolution* (New York: Grossett and Dunlap, 1964), p. 2.

24. Howard P. Segal, *Technological Utopianism in American Cultural* (Chicago: University of Chicago Press, 1985), pp. 62–63.

25. Ibid., p. 47.

26. Bell, *The Coming of Post-Industrial Society*.

27. Henri de Saint-Simon, *Social Organization, the Science of Man and Other Writings* (New York: Harper Torch, 1964), pp. 1–27.

28. This parable is in Saint-Simon's book, *L'Organisateur* (1819). It appears in English in Felix M. H. Markham, ed., *Henri Comte de Saint-Simon: Selected Writings* (Oxford: Blackwell, 1952), pp. 72–75.

29. Auguste Comte, *Cours de philosophie positive*, vol. 6 (Paris: Bachelier, 1830).

30. Positivism, according to Kolakowski, refers to "a collection of rules and evaluative criteria for referring to human knowledge," and as "a normative attitude, regulating how we use such terms as 'knowledge,' 'science,' 'cognition,' and 'information.'" He specifies four primary rules that govern what constitutes positive knowledge. They are the following: (1) data collection must be restricted to facts manifested in concrete experience; (2) insights formulated in general terms have no referents other than specific facts; (3) value assumptions are not discoverable in the same way empirical knowledge is generated; and (4) there is an essential unity of the scientific method. See Leszek Kolakowski, *Positivist Philosophy* (Harmondsworth: Penguin, 1972).

31. Auguste Comte, *System of Positive Polity: Treatise on Sociology Instituting the Religion of Humanity*, 4 vols. (London: Longman's Green, 1851).

32. G. M. Young, *Victorian England: Portrait of an Age* (Oxford: Oxford University Press, 1964), pp. 32–33.

33. Laurence Tribe, "Policy Science: Analysis or Ideology," *Philosophy and Public Affairs* 2 (1972): 66–110; and Alasdair MacIntyre, "Utilitarianism and Cost/Benefit Analysis: An Essay on the Relevance of Moral Philosophy to Bureaucratic Theory," in *Ethical Theory and Business*, ed. Tom Beauchamp and Norman Bowie (Englewood Cliffs, NJ: Prentice-Hall, 1979).

34. For an excellent discussion of this point, see Peter Steinberger, *Ideology and the Urban Crisis* (Albany: State University of New York Press, 1985), pp. 40–62.

35. On the fact-value dichotomy and value noncognitivism, see M. E. Hawkesworth, *Theoretical Issues in Policy Analysis* (Albany: State University of New York Press, 1988), pp. 36–72.

36. John Byrne, "Policy Science and the Administrative State: The Political Economy of Cost-Benefit Analysis," in *Confronting Values in Policy Analysis*, ed. Frank Fischer and John Forester (Newbury Park, CA: Sage, 1987), pp. 70–93.

4

Technocratic Theory in America:
From the Progressives to
the Postindustrialists

Since the Enlightenment, technocracy has taken numerous forms in different countries. Because much of what follows in this book pertains to the U.S. experience, this chapter shifts to the history of American technocratic thought. Toward this end, we first turn our attention to the Progressive era.

The connection between the European origins of technocracy and the appearance of technocratic writings in the United States is easy to establish. During the last quarter of the nineteenth century, numerous American writers associated with various facets of the "Progressive" political movement began to take an interest in the ideas of the European technocrats, particularly those identified with the newly emerging social sciences.

It is impossible to adequately summarize the Progressive movement and its attraction to technocracy.[1] As a political movement that elected two presidents of the United States, Theodore Roosevelt and Woodrow Wilson, Progressivism was essentially a response to a number of long-term structural and ideological changes that accompanied rapid industrialization. Between 1870 and 1920, these changes gave rise to a veritable "organizational revolution" in the American political economy.[2] The term is used to identify the appearance of a distinctive national system

of large-scale organizations that was gradually to redefine the basic outlines of the new organizationalism and its relation to the reform agenda
advanced by the Progressive party.

The Progressives and the
"Organizational Revolution"

The most important feature of this new organizational system was the
large industrial corporation. By the 1920s, the corporation had emerged
as the dominant economic and social institution of American society. As
a new form of capitalist organization, it gave rise to a much more centralized and oligarchic mode of economic competition. Introducing high
ratios of fixed capital per worker and the use of expensive machine technologies, this new system necessitated that special attention be given to
the planning and regulation of the factors of production. In the process,
its emphasis on planning and technology brought about an unprecedented need for expertise. Indeed, in a relatively short period of time
managerial expertise replaced entrepreneurship as the central feature of
the new economic system. James Burnham was later to herald this process as the "managerial revolution."[3]

Beyond the corporation's internal uses of planning, the system also
gave rise to the need for external planning and regulation. This took the
form of increasingly centralized power and decision making in the political system. Specifically, this meant an emerging role for the federal government in such areas as monetary stabilization, economic regulation,
financial assistance for technological development, and the provision of
basic social assistance. As the federal role continued to expand during
those decades, it also spurred the consolidation of competing interest
groups—business associations, labor unions, farm groups, consumer
organizations, and the like—that took their constituencies' demands
directly to the state. By the end of the Great Depression, this transformation was to emerge as the modern "welfare state."

Contrary to the conventional rhetoric, then, the corporation—not the
state—gave rise to a process of bureaucratization that subsequently
advanced in both the economic and the political spheres. It was a process that provided the structural foundations for a new technocratic
ideology based on science and efficiency. The new ideology was largely
designed to legitimate this emergent system of corporate-state power,

often called "corporate liberalism."[4] Both the method and the world-view of this new ideology were based on an appeal to the rationality of science. Authority under corporate liberalism was to be lodged in the technically trained experts of the bureaucratic institutions. As a consequence, this new corporate-state system established and legitimated an attractive niche for growing numbers of middle-class professionals who increasingly found work in these institutions.

One of the main political vehicles for this broad social transformation was the Progressive movement. In large part, the movement was a response to the social turmoil that accompanied the transition to corporate industrialism. For the Progressives, industrialization, immigration, and urbanization had set America adrift. Often the chaos reflected blatant social contrasts that clashed sharply with traditional American values. At the same time that millionaire "Robber Barons" rapaciously gathered social wealth in the name of individual achievement and Social Darwinism, masses of impoverished immigrants became the pawns of egregious political machines that controlled city ghettos. While the immigrants lived in squalor, the machine bosses often used immigrant votes to line their pockets with public largess. No other group suffered greater losses of power and deference as a result of this urban-industrial malaise than the middle classes. Progressivism, in the main, emerged as a middle-class professional reform movement aimed at addressing these social ills.[5]

Historians still struggle to explain this unique political movement. For present purposes, it is sufficient to limit our focus to those aspects of the movement pertaining to the rise of American technocratic thought. Among the important contributors to such thought were some of the most influential journalists and social scientists of the day. Among them were Herbert Croly, Lester Ward, and Walter Lippmann.

Herbert Croly, founder of the *New Republic* magazine, was one of the most forceful and articulate of the Progressive writers.[6] Deeply influenced by August Comte, Croly advocated a mixture of strong political leadership and the use of social scientific techniques to identify and mobilize the national interest in the face of competing special interests. Working with public leaders, particularly those who supported the scientifically identified national interest, social scientists would be able not only to formulate the wisest public policies but also to organize them into master plans for societal change.

Lester Ward, a distinguished sociologist, attempted to rigorously formulate this new scientific vision of society. Ward accepted the basic structure of capitalism but recognized that it generates a number of destabilizing forces—the abuse of wealth, political deception, social ignorance, and extremist movements, among others. To fend off impending crisis, these forces had to be brought into line with human intelligence. The solution was to be found in a widespread application of the principles of sociology.[7] In an essay on the "use and abuses of wealth," Ward called upon the wealthy elites of society to join force with scientific sociologists and forge a system of governance based on the emerging laws of sociology. "If government could be in the hands of the social scientists, it might be elevated to the rank of an applied science, or the simple application of the scientific principles of social phenomena."[8] Education was the key to his strategy. Both citizens and politicians were to be instilled with the principles and values of Progressive sociology. Legislators, for example, would either themselves become social scientists or work closely with those who were. They "would then set for themselves the task of devising means to render harmless those forces" threatening the fabric of society.[9]

Similarly, Walter Lippmann envisioned the need to elevate professional experts to a central role in the political process.[10] Like many other leading progressive intellectuals, Lippmann was highly influenced by the writings of Frederick Taylor, the founder of "scientific management."[11] Although Taylor was primarily concerned with rationalizing work procedures in industrial organizations, Lippmann sought to bring his techniques to bear on the public sector. Scientific management was to provide theory and methods for disinterested professional experts who would formulate and carry out plans for social change.

Daniel Bell has suggested that Taylor bears the same relationship to Saint-Simon that Lenin does to Marx.[12] Where Saint-Simon was the grand theorist of technocracy, Taylor was its master technical strategist. Central to Taylor's influence was his emphasis on organizational efficiency. Scientific management, as the study of efficient organizational relationships, was to be embodied in the modern organization through the introduction of a planning staff and the development of managerial expertise. The new system was offered as the basis for increased industrial output and greater social harmony, largely defined as industrial peace. Indeed, for many contemporary writers, Taylorism is interpreted as a system designed to bring labor under strict managerial control as much as it is a technique for efficiency (see Chapter 12).

Corporate-business leaders were by and large sympathetic to Taylor's efforts to rationalize and control the labor process, but they were quite hesitant to share control of the enterprise with an independent group of "experts," science or no science.[13] Scientific management, for this reason, had difficulties taking hold in the private sector during this period. In the realm of public affairs, however, the story was quite different. The Progressives received scientific management with open arms. Under the influence of Progressive social scientists, for example, the discipline of public administration was literally to emerge as scientific management applied to public affairs.

Public administration was a core element of the Progressive reform strategy.[14] Essentially, it was designed to engineer the transition to a new and "more rational" form of governance (i.e., the liberal corporate-state system). It involved bringing the decision techniques and processes pioneered in the corporate realm to bear on the chronic disorders confronting the social system. Specifically, the strategy was an attempt to transfer the corporation's "rational" methods of administration and planning to the political sphere. By turning to social scientific methods of public planning and rational policy development, politicians could replace the "drift" of an apparently aimless change with predictability and accountability. In short, the movement sought to replace the ensuing political "irrationality" with scientifically designed decision processes.[15]

The scientific management strategy was organized around a proliferation of governmental reserach bureaus and commissions devoted to collecting "objective" data on the operations of municipal government. The approach was based on the belief that municipal corruption and inefficiency were largely based on the failure, both popular and official, to grasp the principles of efficient, orderly management. The solution was to be found in rigorous data collection and its scientific assessment.

Consider the case of scientific management applied to municipal reform in New York City.[16] In 1912, the New York Bureau of Municipal Research presented the outline of a city reform strategy aimed at ameliorating the corruption and mismanagement that plagued the city under the Tammany Hall political machine.[17] The solution was to be found in the introduction of orderly scientific procedures. Such procedures were based on an elaborate financial accounting system for codifying the duties and responsibilities of municipal officials, their actions in executing their duties and responsibilities, the costs of all personnel and equipment, and so on. Cities were to be scored on almost everything: the number of disorderly persons, the frequency of financial auditing, the protection of the milk supply, the incidence of prostitution, the management of city properties, and so on. As Judd reports, "In all, cities were

rated on 1,300 standardized questions." They were "advised to codify
all aspects of their operations so that 'inefficient' practices could be
identified and eliminated."[18] In 1913, the author of the proposal was appointed to serve as the mayor's policy adviser and he began to systematically implement the various phases of the strategy. Suffice it to say, the
strategy encountered many difficulties, both technical and political,
which led to its demise. But the very fact that the city attempted to
implement it is in itself a highly significant indication of the influence of
technocratic ideas during this period.

Scientific management also had another type of influence. In addition
to its techniques for engineering practical reforms, it served a powerful
legitimating function. For professionally oriented middle-class Progressives, the operational assumptions of scientific management meshed
smoothly with their basic values. As Haber points out, it integrated the
personal virtues of discipline and hard work, the energy input-output
ratio of the machine, the relation between profits and costs in a commer-
cial enterprise, and a concept of "social efficiency" defined as "leadership by the competent."[19]

Beyond the Progressives per se, the ideology of scientific management had general appeal to the growing numbers of Americans who
found themselves disheartened by the economic and political conditions of the country during this period. In a system corrupted by the
rampant play of vested interests, an emphasis on science and efficiency
addressed evident societal failures. Many were thus attracted to the possibility of replacing political corruption with scientific planning. Not
only could science serve as "the chief instrument for mastery and control over the physical and social environment, but also as the ultimate
legitimation for practical choices and everyday courses of action."[20]

One of the most important features of this ideology, according to
Progressive theorists, was its ability to eliminate political conflicts
between social classes. There were several dimensions to this argument.
One pertained to the level of state policy. Insofar as the proper management of science and technology could offer the possibility of an
unprecedented expansion of economic resources and industrial growth,
a large-scale corporate-state partnership could harness these forces to
mitigate—if not eliminate—the long-standing sources of class conflict,
namely, scarcity and unequal distribution of wealth.

Analogously, at the level of the industrial workplace, class conflict
could be attenuated if both workers and employers would submit to the
laws of scientific management. Supreme Court Justice Louis Brandeis, an

influential Progressive writer, expressed the scientific approach to industrial democracy in these words: "Those aspects of management to which the laws of science did not as yet apply were to be subject to collective bargaining. Where science did apply, a union representative might serve as a watchdog to make sure that it was the laws of science and not class interest which were obeyed."[21] In a time of intense labor strife, the possibility of such an arrangement was attractive to many. Indeed, it was to become a "core legitimation" of corporate capitalism.

The implications of this transition for managerial and technical experts were profound. Lodged in this appeal to science is the general cognitive and normative legitimation for the rise of a "new class" of trained and credentialed experts. Not only were experts assigned a central directive role in the corporate-state system, they were also seen as being emancipated from the political conflicts arising from traditional class allegiances and interests.

During this period, professional associations sprung up in occupation after occupation: engineering, economics, law, sociology, urban planning, and political science, among others. Each sought "to constitute and control a market for their own expertise"; each sought "to translate one order of scarce resources—special knowledge and skill—into another—social and economic rewards."[22] In Wiebe's words, this development was a central part of the emerging middle class's attempt "to fulfill its destiny by bureaucratic means."[23]

Public discussions about the uses of Progressive expertise were also mirrored in the theoretical discourse of the professions themselves. In the social sciences, it took the form of an epistemological controversy that centered on two competing approaches. One was the traditional view of social determinism that held sway over late nineteenth-century economic and political thought. For determinists, the main quest of the social sciences was the discovery of the general laws that move societies in predetermined, unalterable directions. The other position was an emerging "pragmatic" or "instrumental" conception of social science. It was largely advanced by Progressive social scientists who sought a more problem or policy-oriented conception of the disciplines. If social scientists were to assume the role opening up for them in the new corporate-state system, they needed more action-oriented theories and methods to guide policy interventions. The assault on the traditional view was led by men such as John Dewey, Thorstein Veblen, Lester Ward, and Charles Beard. Motivated by a new Progressive "instrumentalism," they sought in the face of turbulent societal change to bring the social sciences to bear

on the tasks of reform. In concrete terms, this meant an emphasis on the
analysis of social problems and the exploration of techniques for rational
(scientific) planning in public affairs. It also required a new organizational ethos for the social sciences. The political detachment associated
with determinism had to be replaced with a new professional image
oriented to a pragmatic involvement in the affairs of the day.[24]

Reform from Above: Engineers and the "Managerial Revolution"

Between World War I and World War II, America entered what was to
be called the "Age of the Machine." Although the intitial advances in
American technology took place in the nineteenth century, it was not
until after WWI that the rapid growth of machine technologies became
diffused throughout the society. During this period, the machine
emerged as the symbol of a new society based on order and efficiency,
power and progress. In the course of the transformation, the engineering
profession was often taken to embody the basic ideals of the new social
system.

One of the most important writers to stress the role of the engineer
during this period was Thorstein Veblen. Veblen's book, *The Engineers
and the Price System*, was to become a classic influence on technocratic
thinking.[25] Seeking a strategy for eliminating waste and encouraging
efficiency in the American economy, Veblen pinned his hopes, at least
initially, on the political possibilities posed by the newly emerging
professional class.

Veblen's program was by all standards quite radical. First and foremost, it called upon the "absentee owners" of corporate America to
transfer their power to reform-minded technocrats and workers. At the
same time, it advocated the eradication of free enterprise's "artificial"
price system. The allocation of goods and services could subsequently
be supervised by a national technical directorate. Such changes, Veblen
maintained, would dramatically increase the country's industrial
growth, perhaps by more than 1,000%.

How was such a system to be brought about? One possibility was a
national work stoppage on the part of technicians and workers. In an
argument not unlike the one put forward by Saint-Simon in his "parable
of the idlers," Veblen argued that, by withholding their indispensable

knowledge and skills, an alliance of these groups could easily paralyze industry and government. Such an alliance, he averred, might take the form of a "Soviet of Technicians."

One union, the International Workers of the World, accepted and advocated the idea of a worker-engineer alliance, but few others joined in. Even worse was the engineers' receptivity to the idea.[26] At the New School for Social Research, Veblen sponsored a program of lectures to interest engineers in the politics of his ideas, but the very limited success of the effort forced him to acknowledge the slim possibility of success of such a strategy. He attributed the failure of the engineers to embrace his "engineering radicalism" to their comfortable position in the capitalist system. As he put it, "By settled habit the technicians, the engineers and industrial experts, are a harmless and docile sort, well fed on the whole, and somewhat placidly content with the 'full dinner-pail' which the lieutenants of the Vested Interests habitually allow them."[27] The possibility of a radical reform movement led by the "new class" professionals was, in reality, more elusive than Veblen and the earlier Progressives had hoped.

Short of a radical engineer-worker alliance, however, Veblen's theory laid the ideological foundations for a more conservative—and curiously bizarre—"technocracy movement" in the 1920s and 1930s. The technocracy movement—which at various times called itself the Technical Alliance; Technocracy, Inc.; and the Continental Committee on Technocracy—consisted of a group of engineers who adopted Veblen's concern about energy production and the inefficiencies of waste.[28] Howard Scott, the movement's primary leader, argued indefatigably that scientific analysis of industrial production would show the path to lasting efficiency and unprecedented abundance. An early pamphlet put it this way:

> In Technocracy we see science banishing waste, unemployment, hunger, and insecurity of income forever . . . we see science replacing an economy of scarcity with an era of abundance. . . . [And] we see functional competence displacing grotesque and wasteful incompetence, facts displacing disorder, industrial planning displacing industrial chaos.[29]

Although the movement had a significant following for a period of time, including an academic base at Columbia University, it was ultimately short-lived. Its greatest moment was during the early years of the Great Depression, when it was virtually a sociocultural phenomenon.

Organized around a rigid hierarchical structure, the members of technocracy featured gray uniforms with special insignias, drove a fleet of
gray automobiles, and greeted one another with a special salute. The
resemblance of Technocracy, Inc. to the European fascist movements of
the day was not lost on many observers, including a number of dissident
groups among the organization's followers. In fact, this concern gave rise
to an internal factionalism between conservative members and the
leadership. Worried about the specter of authoritarianism, conservative
members split off into "safer" technocratic groups. Afterward, the movement died out rather quickly, although it formally persists even today.[30]

In some ways an assessment of Technocracy, Inc. is more elusive than
it first appears. Even though its direct impact on American society was
negligible, it was not entirely out of step with the new managerial ideologies that were becoming prominent during the New Deal administration. Some commentators have argued that the technocracy movement
failed more because of the *presentation* of its ideas than their substance
per se. James Burnham put it this way:

> Technocracy's failure to gain a wide response can be attributed in part to
> the too-plain and open way in which it expresses the perspective of
> managerial society. In spite of its failure to distinguish between engineers
> and managers (not all engineers are managers—many are hired hands—
> and not all managers are engineers) yet the society about which the Tech-
> nocrats write is quite obviously the managerial society, and within it their
> "Technocrats" are quite obviously the managerial ruling class. The theory
> is not dressed up enough for major ideological purposes. It fails also in
> refusing to devote sufficient attention to the problem of power, which so
> prominently occupies communism and fascism.[31]

In the early 1940s Burnham himself sought to supply the broader
managerial context for understanding technocracy. His famous book,
The Managerial Revolution, examined the "triumph" of the managers
in the modern corporate world.[32] Its thesis rested on the assumption
that *function* rather than *ownership* had become the crucial category of
power in a technical society. From this premise he constructed a theory
of historical succession in which both the proletariat and the bourgeoisie
would be replaced by the "managers." As the new ruling class, the managers would wield power on the basis of their *technical* superiority. This
would happen in both government and industry.

The principal element of control in the new corporate world was the expertise of management. (By *management*, Burnham referred to production managers, administrative engineers, and supervisory technicians.) Because it took managerial knowledge and expertise to keep the modern organization running, the new organizational form inevitably led to an elitist oligarchy. Burnham's theory, in this respect, converged with Michels's famous theory of the "Iron Law of Oligarchy."[33] Like Michels, Burnham argued that democracy would invariably conflict with the immutable needs of the organization. The result was always a "tyranny of expertise."

Because of management's indispensability, its new role had to be legitimated. This gave rise to what Burnham called the philosophy of "managerialism." Simply stated, in modern organizations power accrues to those who have expert knowledge in management; those who occupy the key managerial posts constitute a governing elite. Given their superior knowledge, this elite—at least in the ideal—would at once be technically efficient and morally good. Although often disguised with democratic euphemisms, even today this remains an accurate outline of the operant ideals of modern managerial theory and practice.

Burnham put his theory forward largely as a description of a future to come. For most writers today, Burnham is an anachronism. Although he correctly foresaw the rise of an America dominated by large-scale organizations, this theory of a governing managerial elite has failed to conform to subsequent events and is now largely discussed in footnotes. Nonetheless, while it is true that the managerial elite per se has yet to become *the* dominant elite, it is at present easy to discern a high percentage of top-level managers among the ruling elites of the country.[34] Surely this reality represents a significant step in the gradual but steady expansion of technocratic decision making.

The issues raised by the Progressives, then, proved in subsequent decades to be more subtle and complicated than they first seemed. For one thing, much to the chagrin of social reformers, the political proclivities of the technocrats could not be taken for granted. Many of them, in fact, seemed to lean more toward the status quo than Progressive politics. At worst, some exhibited fascistic tendencies. Second, the question of defining the relation of expertise to power began to raise complex questions that initially escaped the attention of the earlier enthusiasts of technocracy. Increasingly, it became clear that technocrats were being comfortably subordinated to the top managers of corporate capitalism. In short, they were easily being integrated—and co-opted—by the new power structure. But this is not to suggest that the question of technocrats assuming a more progressive reform orientation has disappeared. Today, as we shall see, the political allegiances of the experts have a priority on the agendas of both the political left and the right. In an era of high technology it is safe to assume that the issue will remain an important concern.

Toward "Scientific" Planning: Tugwell and the New Deal "Brain Trust"

The New Deal administration of Franklin D. Roosevelt represented a major expansion of the technocratic project. In face of the dire economic circumstances brought on by the Great Depression, many political and economic leaders were willing to turn to otherwise alien ideas, and public planning was one such idea. As a leading historian of the period put it, "Interest groups normally hostile to any suggestion of government direction of the national economy were close to desperation by the end of 1932, and allowed themselves to remember what they had gained during the short war (WWI) experience."[35] In short, public planning could lead to profits.

Talk about planning cropped up everywhere. During this early period, the question seemed to be less whether planning should be instituted and more what form it should take. The arguments ranged from a call for the expansion of the government's role in the collection of statistics to more radical proposals for economic and social planning. For many of those in the latter camp, these activities were seen as a direct evolution of ideas from the Progressive period. It was perceived as a return to the idea of planning, and many former Progressives were eager to take part in the social reconstruction.[36]

Roosevelt was by no measure a radical, but he was ready to undertake the steps necessary to save the country from complete economic collapse. One of his first initiatives was to assemble his famous "brain trust," constituted by Ramond Moley, Adolph Berle, and Rexford Tugwell. None of these men had known each other prior to their arrival in the Capitol, but they had one thing in common: all were talking about the need for economic planning. FDR, moreover, was ready to listen. Influenced by his advisers, he spoke in his early speeches of the need for "social experimentation," economic "collectivism," and "government planning." Roosevelt, in brief, had adopted the technocratic language of his top advisors.[37]

In the throes of economic crisis, the president took the advice of his advisers—especially Tugwell—and seized the moment. The result was an early and unprecedented spate of planning initiatives. Most important were three programs designed for comprehensive planning: the National Recovery Act, the Agricultural Adjustment Act, and the Tennessee Valley Authority. Social scientists and policy experts flocked to Washington to man the machinery that these efforts put into place.[38]

The National Recovery Act was truly the boldest planning experiment in American political history. It was designed to bring together the principal economic actors for the purpose of setting production priorities. From the outset, however, it was destined to fail; it scarcely lasted two years (1933–35). The reasons for its quick demise were numerous. One was the hostility toward the program that coalesced in the business community. Another was the enmity of the Supreme Court, which declared the program unconstitutional. But perhaps most important for our purposes was the discovery that the federal government had neither the know-how nor institutional capacity to plan. Looking back on the experience, economist Mordakai Ezekeil wrote that it would have taken ten years to develop and train the personnel and data bases needed to make the NRA effective.[39]

This absence of administrative infrastructure was not lost on Roosevelt. In the wake of defeat, he began to see administrative reorganization as the essential first step toward effective governmental planning. He thus shifted the discussion from planning to management. In an effort to build the government's administrative capacities, the president formed a study commission to examine the problem and make recommendations. With distinguished political scientists such as Charles Merriam and Luther Gulick among its members, the report of the President's Committee on Administrative Management was destined to become a landmark in the field of public administration.[40] It represented a major step in government toward the new "managerialism" that was taking hold more generally.

Most of the committee's recommendations focused on the need for the functional consolidation of government agencies and staff expertise. The need for expertise involved two components: the development of top-level administrators to help the president in the White House, and the formation of a planning board to provide the chief executive with advice and direction. The idea of a planning board was an attempt to institutionalize the already existing National Resources Planning Board, headed by Wesley Mitchell and Charles Merriam. As the central agency for policy coordination, it was to provide the president with economic advice, policy formulation, policy view, and research on social problems.

Through the Reorganization Act of 1939, the president obtained the rudiments of an administrative staff (described by one conservative congressman as consisting of "theoretical, intellectual, professional nincompoops").[41] But he lost the planning board. Already the National Planning Board had become a heated political issue. Its report, "Plan for Planning," set off an enormous controversy. Conservatives painted the board and its report as "socialism in disguise." They were having none of it, and removing it from the Reorganization Act was the price for the bill's passage. After this, the board drifted into a back-room research and brainstorming function. Although the board itself slowly withered away, the idea of a planning group continued to live on. After the war it re-emerged with the Full Employment Act of 1946 and the establishment of the Council of Economic Advisors, now largely viewed as the elite technocratic institution par excellence.[42]

Tugwell was the administration's most ardent advocate of planning. In every respect he represented the views of the earlier Progressive social scientists. At one point, he even foresaw the need to replace the capitalist "business system" with a planned economy. At another, he advocated that governmental policy decisions be turned over to an independent elite group of scientific planners.

Some of these ideas were most explicitly stated after Tugwell left the New Deal federal government and assumed the position of chairman of New York City's Planning Commission. For instance, in a 1939 address to planners, he spoke of the need to institutionalize planning experts in a separate branch of the national government. Drawing on the frustrations encountered as a New Deal "Braintruster," Tugwell argued that such experts should have equal status with the other branches of the federal system. He suggested that the new institution be called the "directive branch" and that, employing the latest techniques of scientific forecasting, it be mandated to establish major economic and social policies. Like the members of the judicial branch, these experts would be given long-term appointments to insulate them from political influence.[43]

Concerned with empirical facts rather than political, legal, or bureaucratic interests, the "directive branch's" dedication to the procedures of science would protect the public from those who might attempt to manipulate it for their own purposes.[44] Tugwell put it this way:

The margin of safety which the community possesses in entrusting power to the directive is widened by its persistent orientation to the future, a future discovered by charting the trends of the past through the present. And this projection is not subject to opinion or to change as a result of pressure from special interests. In this forecasting of the shape of things to come, it can succeed, aside from maintaining the most honorable relations with facts, only by possessing them and using the most modern techniques for discovering them. It thus has an interest in progress and in modernization which is quite different from the traditional interests of the other powers.[45]

Given its emphasis on "facts," he argued, social service is more important in the long run than law or political constituencies.

It may thus establish a genuinely social policy, as contrasted with private policies, dictated by contemporary resources, techniques and circumstances, rather than by political expediency; tuned to the universe, the continent, the region, and the times, rather than to an imaginary environment in some past utopia for speculators in private advantage.

Furthermore, social science planning is not designed to satisfy political or economic advantage.

It will be distilled with modern devices from the then controlling conditions for the success of society. It will take account of all there is to work with and allow itself to be guided only by the interests of all there are to work for.[46]

Tugwell, as Goodman writes, presented the "classic vision of the expert as free of politics, scientifically working in the interest of everyone."[47] Both his general thesis and his specific institutional solutions, namely, the directive branch, scarcely hid their earlier Progressive roots in social scientific planning. Perhaps the only difference was that, during the intervening 30 years, technocracy had, thanks in large part to the New Deal, begun in significant ways to manifest itself in the bureaucratic institutions of the federal government. What had earlier been little more than a theory was now beginning to take shape as a recognized practice.

Post-WWII: Big Science and the "End of Ideology"

It wasn't until World War II that the federal government succeeded in effectively pulling together its administrative machinery. In fact, it took the exigencies of a national war effort to catalyze the process that Roosevelt had begun earlier in the 1930s. World War II was truly a benchmark in the evolution of technocratic planning in the United States. During this period, the country was geared to a full-scale program of public planning. The major thrust of its efforts was administered by the Office of War Mobilization, the War Production Board, the Office of Price Administration (which developed elaborate economic input-output techniques to regulate supply and demand), the Office of Scientific Research and Development, and the Office of Strategic Services. The war thus brought a vast expansion of economic intervention, administrative machinery for the coordination of national military and production efforts, and elaborate institutions for data gathering and forecasting. All were important influences on a technocratic restructuring of American society that began to emerge after the war.[48]

The technological revolution initiated during the war, and later intensified by the "cold war" of the 1950s, was a primary impetus behind this technocratic restructuring. Scientific and technological innovation had always been a basic engine of industrialization, but after the war the relationship reached a new plateau, generally described as the rise of "Big Science." Evolving under the wing of the Pentagon and the corporate defense industry, Big Science gave birth in the postwar years to the "military-industrial complex."[49] Increasingly, as President Eisenhower explained, this military-industrial connection was becoming the foundation of the U.S. economy.

Both the complex organization and the financial capital needed to manage this technologically driven economy initiated a new emphasis on technology policy planning. It was in this context that governmental and corporate planners began to work out a new set of technocratic structures designed to guide the emerging technological system. In the name of economic growth, technological development was institutionalized in a new and carefully shielded relationship between governmental and top corporate executives. During the cold war, the government's role in this partnership at times took on the character of a national emergency. The Soviet launching of the "Sputnik" satellite precipitated the most dramatic of these national efforts. No expense was spared in the race for outer space. By and large, that is still true today.

One of the most significant aspects of this new governmental commitment to technology was the blurring of traditional institutional boundaries between the private and public sectors. As national policy unfolded, the government took major responsibility for financing military and nuclear technologies. So close was the relationship between the government and the defense industry that over time leading contractors became almost entirely dependent on multimillion-dollar contracts. Generally taking the form of quasi-governmental corporations, these public-private partnerships virtually negated any semblance of the traditional free market concepts purported to govern private industries. In the words of one writer, this new arrangement was "more like the administrative relationship between the industrial corporation and its subsidiary than the traditional relations of a buyer and seller in a free market."[50] It was necessitated, according to industry executives, by the uncertainties of the research and development process. For those who supported the arrangement, there was in the age of advanced technology no way to maintain the traditional public-private separation.[51]

These emerging relationships had a profound impact on the growth of technocracy. Big Science and the corporate-governmental partnership that evolved with it were, of course, primarily a boon to the physical and engineering sciences. In response to a new image and status conferred by these relationships, the ethos and organization of science underwent significant changes. Such changes were materially reflected in the form of new financial resources and institutional statuses. President Eisenhower, for example, instituted a new White House-level post of science adviser to the president. Indeed, it wasn't long before some began to speak of the scientific community as the "new priesthood."[52]

The postwar system was to hold out possibilities for the social science community as well. During the war, many social scientists had played important roles in government planning agencies. Their experiences in those agencies taught a number of lessons that were influential in shaping many new directions in the social sciences, particularly the emerging policy science movement. Perhaps the most significant was a realization that government could successfully intervene in the affairs of society. This, of course, was not the first time government had intervened in such affairs, but it was the first time the experience had actually bred confidence in the possibility of future interventions. Not only had government power been employed effectively in gearing the economy to the war effort, the war itself also illustrated that government could quite literally triumph over "evil forces." Government, in short, had demonstrated its potential as an instrument for social peace and progress.[53]

Intrigued by these developments, many social scientists began to play larger roles in policy issues, especially domestic issues. One of the leaders of this new impetus was Harold Lasswell.[54] Drawing heavily on his own wartime experiences, Lasswell called for the development of an empirically rigorous conception of the social sciences.[55] Particularly important in the evolution of this project was the outline of a multidisciplinary "policy science." Donning a new problem-solving orientation, policy science was designed to gear American policy-making to the "realities" of the modern technological era.[56]

For the political system, these realities were seen to dictate important structural reforms. In the context of big government and the complexities of technology, political decision making was increasingly limited to top-level organizational and technical elites. In the transition, the traditional concepts of democratic participation were rapidly losing their theoretical plausibility. Confronted with this problem, many social scientists began to rethink the forms of popular control. One of the most subtle but significant responses to emerge was the idea that the social sciences themselves could begin to bridge the gap between elite decision makers and the public. Through the development of "interventionist" theories and methods, ranging from survey research and polling studies to the creation of new political symbols of legitimacy, social scientists could begin to mediate between individual citizens and their political leaders. An interventionist social science could establish the appearance—if not the reality—of a new form of popular consultation. As we argue in Chapter 13, policy science, as conceived by Lasswell, can easily be interpreted as a contribution to this interventionist strategy.[57]

The idea of an interventionist social or policy science converged with another closely related postwar theme. During the 1950s, many social and political theorists—particularly Edward Shils, Raymond Aron, and Daniel Bell—began to speak of the "end of ideology."[58] After the war, the "American Model" of liberal democracy was taken in many quarters as an operational ideal. Writing in the context of the cold war, these theorists asserted the fundamental triumph of liberal corporate capitalism. For them America had achieved, or was at least well on its way to achieving, "the Good Society." In significant part, this situation was attributable to corporate capitalism's ability to harness the forces of technological progress and produce an unprecedented degree of material prosperity. Modern capitalism, in short, appeared to offer an answer to the old social antagonisms. In the face of this success, further debate about capitalism only seemed to impede the advance of prosperity. The remaining tasks were largely *technical* in nature. It was time for the ideologue to step aside and make way for the social engineer. Through technical expertise, such as that to be provided by policy science, the job ahead was largely a matter of fine-tuning the technological engines of corporate capitalism.

These ideas began to give rise to a new technocratic creed (ironically, the *new* ideology for the *end* of ideology). Rooted in the myths of technological progress, the creed stressed the belief that traditional political ideology could be replaced by the ascendant scientific, technological, and rational-instrumental modes of reason. Basic to this outlook was the idea that the guidance of complex economic and social processes could be anchored to the empirical propositions of the social and policy sciences. Drawing on the scientific modes of systems and cybernetics theory, the challenge was to employ technically "objective" information to smoothly regulate the process of social and political change.

Beyond the strengthening of the scientific bases of policy guidance, this new technocratic ideology also recognized the need to readjust the traditional political system to the requirements of "scientific politics." This meant an increase in the willingness of political institutions and actors to seek out scientific expertise as well as in the ability to transform this new knowledge into policy decisions. As Wagner and Wollmann explain, this necessitated major reform efforts aimed at reorganizing political and administrative processes. It meant the "quantitative approaches to political science, the sociology of organizations, and the administrative sciences became . . . of value for policy makers."[59]

No other institutional arrangement gave more currency to this technical orientation than the Council of Economic Advisors established during the postwar period. Increasingly swayed by the Keynesian approach to economic policy intervention, this presidential-level advisory group began to give concrete meaning to the technical conception of fine-tuning.[60] Under the Kennedy administration, which introduced the first official experiment with Keynesian policy techniques, the council's economists moved rather dramatically into the spheres of power. During this period it was not uncommon for journalists and other political writers also to celebrate this new breed of policy-oriented economists as "the new priesthood." Impressed by the new status of the economists, sociologists and political scientists began to emulate this new model of expertise. Indeed, in the latter half of the 1960s, the efforts of sociologists and political scientists gave rise to the call for a Council of Social Advisors (an idea that was submitted in Congress in the form of a legislative proposal).

The intellectual spirit of President Kennedy's administration was certainly a major motivating force behind this new resurgence of liberal expertise. Nowhere did he give greater impetus to this movement than in his famous address at Yale University in 1962:

> Most of us are conditioned for many years to have a political viewpoint, Republican or Democratic—liberal, conservative, moderate. The fact of the matter is that most of the problems . . . that we now face are technical problems, are administrative problems. They are very sophisticated judgments which do not lend themselves to the great sort of passionate movements which stirred this country so often in the past. Now they deal with questions which are beyond the comprehension of most men, most governmental administrators, over which experts may differ, and yet we operate through our traditional political system.[61]

Kennedy's statement was taken by many to indicate the impressive success of the technocratic thrust. Technocracy was seen to be supplanting the political system at the highest levels of power. In much the same way technocrats had served in the New Deal, they flourished in nearly every domain of the administration of Kennedy's successor, Lyndon Johnson.[62] Social scientists not only played a major role in two wars—the Vietnam war and the War on Poverty—they also advised and implemented throughout the federal government a comprehensive technocratic system of social planning and budgetary decision making—the Planning, Programming, and Budgetary System (PPBS). It was a high moment in the technocratic movement. In the words of one writer, it represented the "professionalization of reform."[63] Another leading observer of the period described it as "the Golden Age" of the "action intellectual."[64] For many, it represented nothing less than the appearance of a *new* system of power in American politics.

In Chapter 6 of the book we assess the technocratic politics of this period in some detail, particularly as it pertained to the War on Poverty. At this point, we turn to two of the most systematic and influential statements of technocratic power to appear during this period, the theories of John Kenneth Galbraith and Don Price.

The Technostructure and the Scientific Estate

In the late 1960s, John Kenneth Galbraith argued that, since World War II, large-scale technological development had imposed a new form of power and decision on the modern organization, both private and public, capitalist and socialist. Indeed, much like Veblen and Burnham, Galbraith proclaimed the arrival of a contemporary technocracy, now firmly lodged in the structures and practices of the "New Industrial State."[65]

Moving beyond Burnham's emphasis on a broadly conceived managerial elite, Galbraith located this new locus of power in the hands of those with technical expertise per se. The term "manager," he maintained, includes "only a small portion of those who as participants, contribute information to group decisions." "This latter group," in his words,

> is very large; it extends from the most senior officials of the corporation to where it meets, at the outer perimeter, the white and blue collar workers whose function is to conform more or less mechanically to instruction and routine. It embraces all who bring specialized knowledge, talent or experience to group decision-making.[66]

This larger decision group Galbraith called the "technostructure." The technostructure—not management—is the guiding intelligence of the organization, the brain of the enterprise.

In a discussion that reads like an update of Weber's analysis of bureaucracy and expertise, Galbraith described the technostructure as an organizational response to modern "technological imperatives." Such imperatives, he illustrated, have a profound impact on organizational management. They necessitate the accumulation of enormous amounts of capital; require the development of sophisticated organizational structures and managerial techniques; mandate a relatively inflexible deployment of financial and physical resources; and require the use of large numbers of technically trained workers. It is the task of the technostructure to shape and coordinate these requirements into an effective organization system.

Planning is the basic technique for achieving this technocratic mission. Galbraith argued that, both within the organization and in its relevant external environment, the technostructure acts to overcome the barriers—uncertainties, limitations, and interferences—that impede organizational success. In the case of the capitalist organization, this involves overcoming the hazardous vicissitudes of the free market. Strategic planning, in short, replaces the "invisible hand" of supply and demand. In the process, emphasis shifts from the pursuit of "maximum profit" to the criteria of an "acceptable profit" accompanied by institutional growth.[67]

The tasks of the technostructure give rise to a "technically trained collegia" dedicated to the effective use of planning and technology. According to Galbraith, few of the thoughts and deeds of this technocracy conjure up the image of a new ruling elite self-consciously striving for autonomous power. The technocrats' image of themselves is, in fact, one of service to society. One writer captured the point this way: Rather than a picture of tyrants or despots harboring ambitions to power, technocrats see themselves as "technical soul brothers acting in the best interest of the corporation and, since corporations are presumably a reflection of the society they serve, the social interests as well."[68]

But even a relatively selfless dedication to the criteria of the vast new technological system requires a strategic organization of power. To carry out its functions, the technostructure must garner power to ensure a measure of independence. This is particularly the case in those matters that extend beyond the boundaries of the corporation itself. To surmount this problem the technostructure has reached out to the state for assistance. In the interest of stabilizing the corporation's economic and social environment, the state (through its own technostructure) endeavors to plan and regulate the factors of production: consumer demand, the availability of new technologies, price levels, wages, the supply of labor, and so on. The result is an elaborate industrial-state network that Galbraith called the "planning system." In the planning system, government agencies and corporations often work so closely together that it becomes difficult to draw clear-cut lines between them. This is particularly the case in military-industrial relations, which have come to play a critical role in the planning system. Here planners learned that the easiest solution to the problems of maintaining a large supply of capital, ensuring security against market instabilities, and ensuring exemption from close political scrutiny is to do business with the Pentagon. Defense procurement is the best illustration. The significance of the relationship is reflected by a simple fact: through the military procurement process, the state today underwrites many of the advanced technologies used by modern industrial corporations.[69]

Galbraith's purpose was not to dismantle the New Industrial State and its reliance on the technostructure. In general, he accepted the technostructure as an *inevitable* outcome of a technological society. To the degree that he had concerns, they were largely reformist in nature. His main worry was that technocratic power, too closely geared to the needs of the corporate system, rests on an unnecessarily limited set of social and political values. Specifically, Galbraith was troubled that the planning system increasingly functions as a self-perpetuating process with little public accountability.

How was such accountability to be built into the planning system? Who was to speak for those interests that have not gained access to the technostructure? For Galbraith, the answer was the "scientific and educational estate." Essentially, it was only the intellectual community that could give voice to the wider spectrum of social interests and values. As Galbraith put it, "Unlike members of the technostructure, the educational scientific estate is not handicapped in political action by being accustomed to function only as part of an organization. It gains power in a socially complex society from its capacity for social intervention."[70] In a technological society, "scientists must assume responsibility for the consequences of science and technology." The very community engendered to serve the intellectual and scientific needs of the New Industrial State will hopefully "reject its monopoly of social purpose." Or, as Winner has translated the message, "the scientific and educational estate becomes the universal human class, carrying the banner of truth and virtue."[71]

Finally, it is important to note that Galbraith borrowed the idea of the scientific estate from Don K. Price, whose own work during this period deserves mention. In *The Scientific Estate*, Price outlined a profound dilemma facing the U.S. constitutional system.[72] The rise of science and technology, he argued, has uprooted many of the traditional principles upon which American government was founded. In particular, according to Price, the problem can be traced to a closer relationship between the private and public sectors and a new level of complexity that has necessitated the dramatic growth of bureaucratic government. Greatly exacerbated by the scientific revolution, both of these trends have posed serious challenges to our traditional understandings of the federal system of checks and balances. In Price's words, "our traditional reactions—our automatic political reflexes . . . [are] unreliable in dealing with our present problems."[73]

Price's purpose was to show that technological forces have begun to give rise to an "unwritten" set of political arrangements. This new system is largely a response to a dramatic increase in pluralistic ferment wrought by the growth of science and technology. To grapple with the complexity of the new issues that face governmental decision makers, a configuration of four "estates" has begun to emerge—the pure scientists, the professionals, the administrators, and the politicians. Each estate has its strengths and weaknesses; together they form a new functional system of checks and balances. Politicians and administrators, in this "informally" evolving system, learn to refrain from taking actions that defy the principles of scientific rationality, thus avoiding conflict with the professional and scientific estates. Likewise, scientists and professionals are only able to garner power by winning acceptance of their ideas through the political and bureaucratic systems. As Price explained, "The scientists and professionals in order to do their jobs, must be involved in the formulation of policy, and must be granted wide discretion in their own work." Conversely, politicians and administrators must control the key aspects of technological plans to make responsible decisions. As a consequence, "We have been establishing new kinds of checks and balances within the governmental system that depend on no legal provisions, but on a respect for scientific truth and professional expertise.[74]

Although Price portrayed these new arrangements in a benign light, they do not hold out a great deal of hope for our traditional conception of democratic participation. Winner has put it this way:

> In the end, the system of government Price describes is not one that encourages or expects citizen participation, not one that relies upon any effective representative process, not one that includes much of a role for traditional politics at all. His checks-and-balances argument, heralded as a way of salvaging representative democracy, is actually a way of showing why it is unnecessary to worry about such things. At the higher levels where the important policies are made and carried out, government takes place through interdependent, self-limiting collegia of expert knowledge holders.[75]

For Price the actors of the new technological system emerged as inherently responsible players. The "process of responsible policy making," as Price wrote, "is a process of interaction among the scientists, professional leaders, administrators and politicians; ultimately authority is with the politicians but the initiative is quite likely to rest with others, including scientists in or out of government."[76] Again, it is the wisdom of expertise that will save us.

By way of concluding this section, it is important to stress the degree to which Galbraith and Price take the realities of this new form of technocratic organization for granted. Often using technocratic language themselves, both basically accept the new system of technocratic decision making and devote their attention to reforms compatible with its own basic contours. In a nutshell, they call on technocrats to serve as agents of these reforms. As the saying goes, the fox is placed in charge of the chicken coop.

The Coming of Postindustrial Society

If Galbraith and Price signaled the arrival of technocratic decision making in America, in the 1970s its future evolution has been both theorized and hailed under the banner of "postindustrialism." Indeed, as Giddens puts it, contemporary technocratic theories are now theories of postindustrial society.

Daniel Bell was the first to describe the shape of the coming postindustrial society.[77] Bell's theory of postindustrial society can be conceived of as an attempt to theorize the broad social trends associated with the rise of the technostructure. It is, however, difficult to define postindustrialism in very specific terms. One reason is that Bell himself is not always clear about what it designates. In general, the term is used to refer to the outlines of an emerging transition from the traditional industrial system based on manufacturing to a new order founded on the production and exchange of goods and services. More specifically, it points to changes in the nature of work and work relationships, the increasing role of scientists and technicians in the social order, and the allegedly central role of theoretical knowledge in social change and the making of societal decisions. Large and relatively insulated private and public bureaucracies are the primary arenas for decision making; and, within the decision processes, emphasis is placed on the role of new information technologies—computers, telecommunication, and scientific techniques. The postindustrial decision maker, as in the New Industrial State, is characterized as a planner. Economic and social planning are the defining features of both production strategies and governmental policy.

The basic commodity of this new social system is information. Information is defined "as the bundle of activities that produce, process, and distribute *symbols* as opposed to *things*."[78] The "information society" is one in which most people are divorced from the material economy, including industrial, craft and agricultural production. The smokestack world, in which energy and matter are transformed from one state to another, is replaced with the symbolic manipulation of abstract patterns. Basic to this process are the "new information technologies."

Central to Bell's concept of postindustrialism is his claim that new intellectual technologies—particularly computers, systems theory, and cybernetics—are now transforming American society. Computers, in fact, are seen as both the Logos and the metaphor of the "cybernetic society." (To better capture the character of postindustrial production and organization, Alain Touraine calls the new system the "programmed society."[79]) The development of these information methodologies extends on a higher level of rationalization the transformational role that machine technologies played 100 years ago. As Bell puts it, the process of rationalization has been extended in much the way Weber predicted. Formalized in the workplace by Taylorism, it now emerges at the level of central policy guidance.[80]

Bell's purpose is to sketch out the "axial" principles that are shaping the new society. In this respect, postindustrialism is a theory about the interrelations of economic, social, and technological factors in an evolving society shaped by information and its technologies. The major factors that underlie its evolution can be summarized in these points:

(1) The "service industries," as opposed to basic production industries, are becoming increasingly important in the economic system. The service section (comprising finance, trade, real estate, insurance, professional business, personal and repair services, and general government) now accounts for much more than half of both total employment and the gross national product.

(2) A major shift takes place in the kinds of work people do. Increasingly, workers are more educated and the professional and technical workers constitute much higher percentages of the labor force. (It is estimated, for example, that industries engaged in the collection, storage, collation, and distribution of information by computers now generate one-half of the gross national product of the United States.) Accompanying this shift is an increasing substitution of "theoretical" knowledge for property as the foundation of the social system.

(3) There is an increasing reliance in the political system on technical expertise for the definition of, if not the actual resolution of, social and political problems. As a result, there will be more and more emphasis on the planning of political and social life.[81]

These trends are presented as forces behind an unprecedented societal formation. Although postindustrial theorists are vague about the precise nature of this system, they see these trends as adding up to a dramatic historical change. One of them concerns the rise of a technocratic system of governance. As in all technocratic theories, the rise of professional expertise is said to portend the emergence of a social order in which a technical elite assumes a critical role in the governance of society. The main features of this new role give rise to a theory of "technocratic guidance." Founded on the idea that contemporary organizational interdependencies, technological complexity, and rapid socioeconomic change demand new forms of knowledge, the theory emphasizes the role of professional experts in the production of the appropriate types of policy-relevant knowledge and the resultant dependence of politicians on professional experts.[82] The degree to which technical experts will erode the power of traditional politicians remains a source of disagreement. For some postindustrialists this technical elite evolves as a powerful group *sharing* governance with traditional economic and political elites. For others, the scientific/technical elite will eventually become the dominant partner in a system of elite governance. Brzezinski, for one, sees the new elite taking command of the essential flow of information and production. Increasingly, scientific knowledge will be used directly to plan almost every aspect of economic and social life. In the process, Brzezinski avers, class conflict will assume new forms and modes: Knowledge and culture will replace material needs in the struggle between the scientific/technical elite and the masses of people who will have to be integrated into and subordinated in the postindustrial system.[83]

A closely related theme underlying this change is a decline of ideology (reminiscent of the "end of ideology" thesis, of which Bell himself was a leading proponent). For instance, Brzezinski—who prefers the term "technetronic" to "postindustrial"—maintains that the contemporary information revolution must be grasped in terms very different than those used to describe earlier revolutions, such as the French or Bolshevik. These earlier revolutions, violent in nature, were largely fueled by competing ideologies: they represented struggles to replace the dominant ideas of one ruling elite with those of another. As such, their impacts were mainly registered as changes in the distribution of political power and the legitimating beliefs that justified it. By contrast, the contemporary technetronic revolution is essentially silent and nonideological. Driven by the development of new sciences and technologies, it portends a much more fundamental transformation that works across—and generally undercuts—existing ideologies. In Brzezinski's view, it is literally remolding the nature of society and human existence. The technological foundations of this new societal formation, of course, necessitate new social structures and forms of governance; these innovations are the job of the technologists and the social engineers.

Although postindustrialism has yet to emerge fully, its enthusiasts point to various manifestations of its progress. Many, for instance, single out high-technology areas such as Los Alamos, Route 128 around Boston, and "Silicon Valley" south of San Francisco. While the emergence of such computer technology centers (or "industrial parks") does not in itself constitute postindustrialism, it does present a powerful new image of a changing information-based economy—one symbolized by technicians in smocks rather than workers in overalls. Some, moreover, see utopian outlines in this embryonic postindustrial form. It is said to represent the beginnings of "science cities," or "technopolises," based on a systematic integration of science, economy, and society.[84]

Basic to this information society is a new set of social values. In the process of transformation, the capitalist values associated with property, wealth, and production steadily give way to values based on knowledge, wealth, and intellect. In place of the entrepreneur the primary social model emerges as the professional man. Indeed, professionalism assumes the role of a postindustrial ideology. As such, it fulfills two important functions. First, it emphasizes the essential component of technocracy: the translation of knowledge into applied practices. And, second, professionalism stresses social service and responsibility to both clients and society. This, in fact, is presented as a major principle supplying social legitimation to postindustrialism. Like Progressivism before it, postindustrialism is to be guided by those beholden to the canons of professional responsibility.[85]

One of the most explicit formulations of the role of the professions in the new society is put forward by Eulau. In the context of postindustrialism and the emergence of the "professional state," Eulau focuses on what he calls the "skill revolution" and the future appearance of a "Consultative Commonwealth." In this emerging political constellation the professional expert is elevated to a status equivalent to that of the political elites in the governmental decision processes. It is a vision of a governance system "in which human needs are discovered, human purposes formulated, and human problems handled by political processes better adapted to the requirements of a rapidly changing technological society than are participative, representational, or bureaucratic processes alone."[86] Participation, in sum, takes a backseat to technical expertise.

The professions, described as the "vanguards" of expert knowledge, are the cornerstones of the Consultative Commonwealth. Professional expertise, in Eulau's view, will serve as the "solvent" for the political and social divisions of the new order. Greater reliance on professionals will bring new "norms and modes of conduct" that will become "acknowledged components of individual and collective choice-making at the level of both policy and administration."

Eualu's conceptualization of the Consultative Commonwealth leaves many questions and contradictions unanswered. On the one hand, for instance, he recognizes that many social groups are distrustful of the professions and that such a project will encounter substantial resistance. On the other, he seems to treat these tensions as essentially non-problematic, at least in the long run. Rather than emphasizing the problems, Eulau prefers to stress the analytical and ideological advantages of a greater reliance on professionals. Not only are professional skills portrayed as key to effective governmental policy formation, their contribution to "disinterested" knowledge is seen to supply legitimacy to the process. Both points, of course, are technocratic touchstones.

According to Bell, a chief manifestation of this professionalism will be a "socializing" of the corporation. In the postindustrial society the corporation, as the dominant social institution, is seen to turn away from its traditional "economizing" mode of behavior (i.e., its narrow emphasis on the efficient production of material goods).[87] In its place will appear a new and broader professional emphasis on corporate social responsibility. America, in the process, will shift from a society based on a private market system to one in which the most important decisions will be made by top-level corporate and governmental managers. At this level, politically determined goals are consciously translated into planned priorities. The result is "a visible change from market to non-market political decision making."[88] Whereas the market disperses responsibility, the political center concentrates it. Not only are political decisions more visible, the question of who wins and who loses is more apparent. Government, as Bell puts it, becomes the "cockpit" of society.

At this point, Bell introduces a new and critically important wrinkle in the development of technocratic theory. Theorists from Saint-Simon forward have argued that, because experts would decide problems in a technocratic society, politics would disappear. Bell, on the other hand, does not see greater emphasis on expertise leading to the end of politics per se (an apparent departure from his earlier "end of ideology" thesis). Instead, he sees technology and expertise only leading to a *new* brand of politics. He puts it this way:

> The central point about the last third of the twentieth century . . . is that
> it will require more societal guidance, more expertise. To some extent, this

is an old technocratic dream. But an earlier technocratic visionary like Saint-Simon felt that in such a technocratic society politics would disappear since all problems would be decided by the expert. One would obey the competence of a superior just as one obeys the instructions of a doctor or an orchestra conductor or a ship's captain.[89]

But in the "knowledgeable society" of the postindustrial era the argument shifts. As Bell continues:

> It is more likely, however, that the post-industrial society will involve *more* politics than ever before, for the very reason that choice becomes conscious and the decision-makers more visible. The nature of a market society is to disperse responsibility and to have "production" decisions guided by the multiple demands of the scattered consumer. But a decision to allocate money to one scientific project rather than another is made by a political center as against a market decision. Since politics is a compound of interests and values, and these are often diverse, an increased degree of conflict and tension is probably unavoidable in the post-industrial society.[90]

The central role of knowledge and technology, then, only underscores the importance of political decision making. But it is a special kind of politics that is seen to emerge here. It is a politics said to be more responsible *to the criteria of knowledge*.[91] Politics, in short, becomes a *politics of expertise*.

What is the nature of this new politics? In the traditional political system, politics has its foundations in government and the public. In the postindustrial society politics is supposed to be much more rooted in empirical epistemologies and the logic of scientific inquiry. Such politics, according to Bell, will be extricated from traditional ideological contexts. Political leaders in the future will use knowledge to get beneath the conventional dogmas and ideologies that are seen to obscure the "objective realities" of society and thus impede the instrumental problem solving that new intellectual technologies make possible. Accordingly, the politics of expertise ultimately hinges on scientific opinion and the empirical validity of policy arguments.

The modern university, as the traditional home of science and expertise, is accorded a special status in this postindustrial formulation. It becomes a primary "productive agency" for the creation and dissemination of technical idea-systems. The organization of university research thus emerges as one of the critical issues of the new social order. In a passage that could have been written by Bacon, Bell argues that "in the post-industrial society the chief problem is the organization of science, and the primary institution the university or research institute where such work is carried out."[92] It is an organizational task geared to several objectives. One, of course, is the production of new knowledge. Another is the training and professional certification of experts who will take charge of the postindustrial apparatus. A third, largely mediated through professional training, involves bringing new knowledge to bear on the problems of "social guidance." Brzezinski captures this new role for the universities in these words:

> The university in an industrial society—in contrast to the situation in medieval times—is an aloof ivory tower, the repository of irrelevant, even if respected, wisdom, and for a brief time, the fountainhead for budding members of the established social elite. In the technetronic society the university becomes an intensely involved "think tank," the source of much sustained political planning and social innovation.[93]

In the face of this emphasis on think tanks and policy guidance, the university has increasingly become an institutional base for technocratic elites. Observing the movement of top-level policy advisers between Washington and the nation's campuses, some writers have portrayed leading universities as policy "command posts" for particular administrations, both liberal and conservative. Although an exaggeration of contemporary realities, this characterization does serve to underscore a very significant trend associated with policy guidance. The one important qualification that must be added to the argument is that the think tanks, largely because of the university's vulnerability to protest, are now primarily located outside of the universities.

These non-university-based think tanks, as Peschek points out in a recent study of "policy-planning organizations," play a central role in the technocratic strategy.[94] Both liberal and conservative, they have become key instruments for the organization of elite agendas. Bringing together top political and economic leaders from public and private sectors with influential policy intellectuals from academia, these institutions mobilize opinion and forge policy directives for the modern corporate-state system. It is in just such think tanks that the strategies for the postindustrial transformation and its "high-tech" agency are being formulated, planned, and legitimated.

Finally, it is essential to note the profound impact this emphasis on social innovation and guidance has had on the academic social sciences themselves. Whereas the social sciences traditionally justified their activities in the name of general enlightenment—that is, knowledge for its own sake—they now largely espouse an instrumental problem-solving orientation. As Schroyer explains, social research in the university as well as the think tank is increasingly dedicated to the production, directly and indirectly, of strategies for the planning of societal models that assist in the rationalization of complex systems. Through the development of "rules and priorities, analyzing available resources and costs, and projecting implications of alternative policies, the role of social theory becomes more and more essential for the management of organizations."[95] The social and political sciences thus—wittingly and unwittingly—become adjuncts to administrative and policy planning and, as such, are reduced to social technologies.

By way of concluding this section, it is important to concede that the postindustrial thesis is complex and its assessments must remain an open question. There is now a large and growing number of theorists struggling to identify and legitimate a future course for postindustrial development, both technocratic and participatory. Common to all of the scenarios—or what Frankel calls the "post-industrial utopias"—is a basic theme: the politics of expertise.[96] But here too not all postindustrial theorists conceptualize the politics of expertise in the same way. For the purpose of this work, the most interesting perspective is put forward by Alain Touraine.

Touraine agrees with those who argue that centralized technical guidance will intensify the politics of postindustrial decision making, although he sees the emerging political conflicts taking a very different form.[97] Like Bell, Touraine emphasizes the practical significance of theoretical knowledge, but he takes sharp exception to the argument that the planning strategies essential to a postindustrial system require a relatively autonomous cadre of experts involved in policy formulation. For Bell, the central problem is posed by the general populace's lack of the requisite economic and technical knowledge needed to understand the imperatives of central guidance. It is a concern heightened by his worry that mass demands are responsible for an overexpansion of economic and social entitlements (see Chapter 7). Lacking an understanding of the relationship of technical realities to economic processes, particularly the limits of growth, interest groups are seen to make demands that exceed system capabilities, thus threatening both future growth and political stability. In the context of this deep-seated concern, Bell has elevated his support of technical elites to the level of a major political polemic.

Alternatively, in his provocative essay, "What is Daniel Bell Afraid of?" Touraine concedes that basic political tension between the need for professional expertise and mass demands but draws a very different conclusion.[98] For him the contradition is an essential force underlying an expansion of antitechnocratic social forces that calls for the democratization of central decision processes. Specifically, he sees the growth of new social movements and their countercultural opposition to technological society as the most important democratic thrust to be found in Western societies today. The confrontation between the manipulatory policies of state-corporate technocrats and these countercultural movements is seen as a fundamental political tension shaping the future of contemporary political systems. Basic to the politics of expertise, it is a tension that underlies much of the analysis that follows. Moreover, it frames the specific topic of the final chapter.

Concluding Perspectives:
Toward a Politics of Expertise

Having completed our survey of technocratic writings, we can now offer a few general observations that help to focus the chapters that follow.

The most striking theme to emerge from this chronological outline is the continuity of the basic technocratic ideas. Largely a political response to industrialization and technological development, the essential ideas underlying the modern technocratic project were established by the time of Saint-Simon. In the United States these ideas were given currency by the Progressive movement and the rise of the liberal corporate state toward the end of the nineteenth century. From Croly to Bell, technocratic writings have emphasized the rise of scientific and technical elites, positivist methodologies, planning techniques, management and organization theory, the administrative state, and the new class. Underlying these concepts, as we saw, was a commitment to a single but often forceful thesis: the belief that scientific and technical decision making must increasingly take precedence over political decision making. Although the thesis remains controversial, the concepts that accompany it are now commonplace in the parlance of political science and sociology. Ferkiss captured this point when he wrote that a Progressive sociologist at the turn of the century would find little new in the basic concepts of postindustrialism.[99]

If the concepts have remained relatively constant, however, the realities associated with them have changed dramatically. Adjectives such as *technological, informational,* and *postindustrial* are now mainstream sociological concepts used to describe the central role of technical expertise in modern society. Indeed, scholars on both the political left and the right largely take these terms for granted. Often they dominate the intellectual struggle to discern the future of the American economy and its politics.

The key issue in this study, of course, is the degree to which this growth of technical expertise leads to technocratic modes of governance (i.e., the attempt to solve political problems with technical solutions). Already, as illustrated, technocracy has firmly established itself in the corporate-governmental system. In the space of about 50 years it has gone from a political vision to an identifiable set of attitudes and roles in the extant economic and political processes, or what Galbraith identifies as the "technostructure." While the system as a whole still falls far short of a full-fledged technocracy, the technostructure and its technocratic ethos is solidly entrenched in the administrative structures of American government, the corporate sector, and the major universities. From this vantage point, the technostructure—policy planners, economists, engineers, management specialists, computer analysts, social scientists, and technologists—process the critical information essential to the stable and efficient operation of our contemporary institutions. These knowledge specialists now play a central—and indispensable—role in the corporate-governmental planning systems and their influence is clearly on the increase. Such influence can be found in all of the major policy arenas, but it is most powerful in areas related to technology policy, where decision making is generally dominated by those from the physical and engineering sciences.

Along with this growth of technocracy, there have been subtle but important changes in the technocrats' political orientations. For one thing, their political pronouncements are much less grandiose than they used to be. Whereas earlier technocrats were given to sweeping statements about the political payoffs to result from technological progress and expert guidance, today's technocrats tend to speak a more subdued and pragmatic language addressed to organizational and technical "imperatives." Rather than presenting themselves as "new men" of power, they modestly step forward as the servants of the modern organizational systems.

Accompanying this new political style is a more fundamental change in the technocrats' theoretical approach to politics itself. Until the postwar years, technocratic theorists generally spoke of replacing politics with scientific and technical decision making. As technocrats have moved closer to power, however, this theme has undergone significant modifications. Today, it appears to be less a matter of replacing politics than an issue of changing its procedures and content. Instead of stressing an open exchange of public opinion—the essence of democratic politics—writers such as Bell, Lane, Eulau, and Price now emphasize the need for expert opinion. Political arguments in the postindustrial society, they assert, are increasingly based on the criteria of knowledge; the best decision is the one determined by the persuasive force of the valid scientific argument. Technical decision making does not formally replace interest-group politics, but expert opinion does take precedence over public opinion. Politics, in short, becomes a politics of expertise.

Contemporary technocrats typically seek to sidestep the political implications of this process by professing a "neutral" posture. Their role is said to be limited to the clarification of issues and options; they only bring intellectual order and rationality to the political decision-making processes. While expert advice can indeed be used to focus political issues and guide deliberation to productive directions, this obscures the fact that issues can be channeled very differently by competing experts. This reality, moreover, is often greatly exacerbated by the limits of expert knowledge. Experts generally have a better command of the facts than many decision makers, but their own knowledge—in part due to the state of the analytical arts—remains incomplete. The fact that expert advice is itself open to different interpretations only facilitates a politics of expertise.[100] Indeed, as we shall see in Part V, in expert circles this has raised basic epistemological questions concerned with what constitutes "usable knowledge" and how we get it. The resulting polemic has been described as a "politics of epistemology."

Another factor that helps to explain the technocrats' changing political orientation is the very success of their project. As technocrats increasingly share the policy-making processes with political elites, they find it necessary—and certainly advantageous—to accommodate their professional activities to the political processes. In a system that has long justified itself on democratic principles, it would be difficult to adopt publicly the traditional technocratic posture toward politics. Much less problematic is a new formulation of politics—a politics of expertise—based on the "technical realities" of postindustrialism.

One of the significant questions that will determine the future of such a politics is the relation of the technostructure to the traditional elites. Already there is suggestive evidence to indicate a receptivity on the part of elite decision makers to a greater emphasis on technocratic politics. Many among the political elites talk of a "governance crisis" resulting from an overload of interest-group politics and speak of depoliticizing policy issues through improved planning and management. Dickson identifies this as the replacement of the "democratic paradigm" with the "technocratic paradigm." [101] Understood in these terms, a close alliance between elites and technocrats holds out the potential for a mutually beneficial strategy. Not only are technocrats specialists in policy management and planning, their techniques are packaged in an ideology strategically suited to the elite conception of the political situation. Technocratic ideology, in short, holds out the possibility of a new—and often seductive—form of elite politics. Grounded in technical competence of professional expertise, such a system not only shrouds critical decisions in what would appear to be the logic of technical imperatives, it also erects stringent barriers to popular participation. Only those with knowledge (or credentials) can hope to participate in deciding the sophisticated issues confronting postindustrial society. Some, in fact, have averred that a politics of expertise will give rise to a new type of elite politician: the "politician-technician." Indeed, according to one writer, in European countries today one of the significant trends in elite composition is the politician with technical training. [102]

For political systems that call themselves "democratic," the implications of these technocratic trends are profound. Most of them have been recognized, but none of them has yet to receive the attention it deserves. In the chapters that follow, we will attempt to further open the manifestations of contemporary technocracy to critical scrutiny. In particular, we will focus on the ways in which power accrues to the technostructures of modern society, the implications and consequences of this technocratic thrust, and, last but not least, we suggest ways to think about the development of alternative, more democratic forms of expertise.

Notes

1. See Robert H. Wiebe, *The Search for Order, 1877–1920* (New York: Hill and Wang, 1967); and Richard Hofstadter, *The Age of Reform* (New York: Vintage, 1955).

2. Kenneth Boulding, *The Organizational Revolution* (Chicago: Quadrangle, 1968).

3. James Burnham, *The Managerial Revolution* (New York: John Day, 1941).

4. James Weinstein, *The Corporate Ideal in the Liberal State, 1900–1918* (Boston: Beacon, 1968).

5. Wiebe, *The Search for Order.*

6. See David Levy, *Herbert Croly of the New Republic: The Life and Thought of an American Progressive* (Princeton, NJ: Princeton University Press, 1985).

7. Dusky Lee Smith, "Scientific Liberalism: Ward, Galbraith, and the Welfare State," in *Politics in the Post-Welfare State,* ed. M. Donald Hancock and Gideon Sjoberg (New York: Columbia University Press, 1972), p. 72.

8. Lester Frank Ward, *Dynamic Sociology* (New York: D. Appelton, 1911), pp. 30 and 75.

9. Ibid.

10. Walter Lippmann, *Drift and Mastery* (Englewood Cliffs, NJ: Prentice-Hall, 1961).

11. Frederick Winslow Taylor, *Scientific Management* (New York: Harper, 1947). See also Judith A. Merkle, *Management and Ideology: The Legacy of the International Scientific Management Movement* (Berkeley: University of California Press, 1980).

12. Daniel Bell, *The Coming of Post-Industrial Society* (New York: Basic Books, 1973), p. 353.

13. Daniel Nelson, *Managers and Workers* (Madison: University of Wisconsin Press, 1975).

14. Samuel P. Hays, "The Politics of Reform in Municipal Government in the Progressive Era," *Pacific Northwest Quarterly* 55 (October 1964): 157–69.

15. Ibid.

16. See Jane S. Dahlberg, *The New York Bureau of Municipal Research: Pioneer in Government Administration* (New York: New York University Press, 1966).

17. Dennis R. Judd, *The Politics of American Cities* (Boston: Little, Brown, 1979), p. 100.

18. Ibid.

19. Samuel Haber, *Efficiency and Uplift* (Chicago: University of Chicago Press, 1964).

20. Magali Saratti Larson, *The Rise of Professionalism* (Berkeley: University of California Press, 1977), p. 141.

21. Haber, *Efficiency and Uplift,* p. 96.

22. Larson, *The Rise of Professionalism,* pp. xvi–xvii.

23. Wiebe, *The Search for Order,* pp. 111–32.

24. Mary O. Furner, *Advocacy and Objectivity: A Crisis in the Professionalization of American Social Science: 1865–1905* (Lexington: University of Kentucky Press, 1975).

25. Thorstein Veblen, *The Engineers and the Price System* (New York: Viking, 1933).

26. Donald Stabile, *Prophets of Order: The Rise of the New Class, Technocracy and Socialism in America* (Boston: South End Press, 1984), p. 220.

27. Veblen, *The Engineers*, p. 135.

28. William E. Akin, *Technocracy and the American Dream: The Technocratic Movement, 1900–1941* (Berkeley: University of California Press, 1960).

29. Quoted from Ralph Chaplin in Howard Scott, *Science Versus Chaos* (New York: Technocracy, Inc., 1933), foreword.

30. See, for example, Technocracy, Inc., *Technocracy: Technological Social Design* (Savannah, OH: Technocracy, Inc., 1978).

31. Burnham, *The Managerial Revolution*, p. 203.

32. Ibid.

33. Robert Michels, *Political Parties: A Sociological Study of the Oligarchical Tendencies of Modern Democracy* (New York: Dover, 1915).

34. William G. Scott and David K. Hart, *Organizational America* (Boston: Houghton Mifflin, 1979).

35. Richard Kirkendall, *Social Scientists and Farm Politics in the Age of Roosevelt* (Columbia: University of Missouri Press, 1966).

36. Ibid.

37. Otis L. Graham, Jr., *Toward a Planned Society: From Roosevelt to Nixon* (New York: Oxford University Press, 1976).

38. Ibid.

39. Ibid., p. 30.

40. Ibid., p. 52.

41. Ibid., p. 62.

42. Ibid., pp. 86–125.

43. Rexford Tugwell, *The Fourth Power* (Pamphlet published by the American Institute of Planners, 1939).

44. Ibid.

45. Ibid., p. 31.

46. Ibid.

47. Robert Goodman, *After the Planners* (New York: Simon & Schuster, 1971), p. 158.

48. Gene M. Lyons, *The Uneasy Partnership* (New York: Russell Sage, 1969).

49. Don K. Price, *The Scientific Estate* (Cambridge, MA: Harvard University Press, 1965), p. 37.

50. Ibid.

51. Ibid.

52. Ralph Lapp, *The New Priesthood* (New York: Harper & Row, 1965).

53. Henry J. Aaron, *Politics and the Professors* (Washington, DC: Brookings Institution, 1978), p. 148.

54. Harold Lasswell, "The Policy Orientation," in *The Policy Sciences*, ed. Daniel Lerner and Harold Lasswell (Stanford, CA: Stanford University Press), pp. 3–15.

55. See, for example, Harold D. Lasswell, *The Future of Political Science* (New York: Atherton, 1963).

56. Lerner and Lasswell, *The Policy Sciences*.

57. Richard M. Merelman, "On Interventionist Behavioralism: An Essay in the Sociology of Knowledge," *Politics and Society* 6, no. 1 (1976): pp. 57–78. Also, see Chapter 13 of this book.

58. Chaim I. Waxman, ed., *The End of Ideology Debate* (New York: Funk and Wagnalls, 1968).

59. Peter Wagner and Hellmut Wollmann, "Fluctuations in the Development of Evaluation Research: Do 'Regime Shifts' or 'Structure' Matter?" (Paper delivered at the XIIIth World Congress of the International Political Science Association, Paris, July 15–20, 1985).

60. Jeffrey D. Straussmann, *The Limits of Technocratic Politics* (New Brunswick, NJ: Transaction, 1978), pp. 41–64.

61. John F. Kennedy, "Commencement Address at Yale University," in *Public Papers of the President of the United States: John F. Kennedy, 1962* (Washington, DC: Government Printing Office, 1963), pp. 470–75.

62. Straussman, *The Limits of Technocratic Politics.*

63. Daniel P. Moynihan, "The Professionalization of Reform," *The Public Interest*, Fall 1965, pp. 6–16.

64. Theodore H. White, "The Action Intellectuals," *Life*, June 9, June 16, and June 23, 1967.

65. John Kenneth Galbraith, *The New Industrial State* (Boston: Houghton Mifflin, 1967).

66. Ibid., p. 82.

67. Ibid., pp. 176–88.

68. Langdon Winner, *Autonomous Technology*, (Cambridge: MIT Press, 1977), p. 165.

69. Galbraith, *The New Industrial State*, chap. 29.

70. Ibid, pp. 386–94.

71. Winner, *Autonomous Technology*, p. 168.

72. Price, *The Scientific Estate.*

73. Ibid., p. 17.

74. Ibid., p. 153.

75. Winner, *Autonomous Technology*, p. 159.

76. Price, *The Scientific Estate*, p. 68.

77. Bell, *The Coming of Post-Industrial Society.*

78. Marc Porat, *The Information Economy* (Stanford University Ph.D. diss., 1976, University Microfilms, Ann Arbor), pp. 2–3.

79. Alain Touraine, *The Post-Industrial Society* (New York: Random House, 1971).

80. Bell, *The Coming of Post-Industrial Society.*

81. Ibid. For an excellent discussion of these points, see Victor Ferkiss, "Daniel Bell's Concept of Post-Industrial Society: Theory, Myth and Ideology," *The Political Science Reviewer* IX (Fall 1979): pp. 61–102.

82. Straussman, *The Limits of Technocratic Politics*, pp. 41–64.

83. Zbigniew Brzezinski, *Between Two Ages: America's Role in the Technetronic Era* (New York: Viking, 1976).

84. For a discussion of the concept of "technopolis," see Raymond W. Smilor, George Kozmetsky, and David V. Gibson, *Creating the Technopolis* (Cambridge, MA: Ballinger, 1988).

THE TECHNOCRATIC PROJECT

85. Bell, *The Coming of Post-Industrial Society*; and George Frederick Goerl, "Cybernetics, Professionalization, and Knowledge Management: An Exercise in Assumptive Theory," *Public Administration Review*, November–December 1975, pp. 585–87.

86. Heinz Eulau, *Technology and Civility: The Skill Revolution in Politics* (Stanford, CA: Hoover Institution, 1977).

87. Bell, *The Coming of Post-Industrial Society*, pp. 267–98.

88. Ibid.

89. Ibid., p. 263.

90. Ibid.

91. Robert Lane, "The Decline of Politics and Ideology in a Knowledgeable Society," *American Sociological Review* 31 (October 1966): 549–662.

92. Bell, *The Coming of Post-Industrial Society*.

93. Brzezinski, *Between Two Ages*, p. 12.

94. Joseph G. Peschek, *Policy-Planning Organizations: Elite Agendas and America's Rightward Turn* (Philadelphia: Temple University Press, 1987).

95. Trent Schroyer, "The Coming of Post-Industrial Society" (Book Review), *Telos*, no. 19 (Spring 1974), p. 162.

96. Boris Frankel, *The Post-Industrial Utopians* (Madison: University of Wisconson Press, 1987).

97. Alain Touraine, "What Is Daniel Bell Afraid of?" *American Journal of Sociology* 83, no. 2 (1977): pp. 469–73.

98. Ibid.

99. Ferkiss, "Daniel Bell's Concept."

100. For a statement of this view, see Frank Press in Don I. Phillips, Gail J. Breslow, and Patricia S. Curlin, eds., *Federal R&D* (Colloquium Proceeding, A.A.A.S., June 19–20, 1979), pp. 21–22. As Press puts it, "Where the stakes are high, there is ample incentive for the parties involved to interpret the data in ways which suit their own purposes. We need to develop ways of fencing in these areas so that the debates can be confined to legitimate differences in value."

101. David Dickson, "Limiting Democracy: Technocrats and the Liberal State," *Democracy* 1 (January 1981): pp. 61–79.

102. Robert Putnam, "Elite Transformation in Advanced Industrial Societies: An Empirical Assessment of the Theory of Technocracy," *Comparative Political Studies*, 10(3), (October 1977): pp. 385–87.

PART III

THE POLITICAL USES OF EXPERTISE: ILLUSTRATIONS FROM ORGANIZATION AND POLICY

Specialists without spirit, sensualists without heart; this nullity imagines that it has attained a level of civilization never before achieved.

—MAX WEBER

Since the post-industrial society increases the importance of the technical component of knowledge, it forces the hierophants of the new society—the scientists, engineers and technocrats—to either compete with politicians or become their allies.

—DANIEL BELL

Part III is designed to provide two specific examples of technocratic expertise in practice. Chapter 5, "Managerial Expertise and Organizational Control: The Politics of Behavioral Science," focuses on the uses of psychology in the development of managerial theory and practices. The topic is approached through the evolution of the Human Relations School of management theory. The objective is to show that human relations theory, generally accepted to be a "scientific" advance over Taylor's scientific management, evolved in reality to serve a very specific task of political control in the workplace.

Examining the historical and ideological origins of the Human Relations School, the discussion explores the relationship of ideology to authority in the evolution of the capitalist workplace, the uses of bureaucratic authority to mitigate class conflict on the shop floor, and the role

117

of science as an ideology for legitimizing such authority. Toward this end, the analysis focuses on the development of "scientific personnel management," Ford's "welfare capitalism," and the rise of the "company union," all emerging around World War I. The discussion then takes up the Hawthorne experiments, the work of Mayo, and the formal emergence of the Human Relations School. After illustrating the ideological and social implications of human relations theory for labor conflict, the chapter points to ways in which these psychological techniques and their modern variants are employed in the workplace today.

Chapter 6 is titled "Technocracy and Policy Expertise: The Politics of the 'New Class.'" In the context of public policy analysis, the chapter explores the contemporary manifestations of an issue long associated with technocracy—namely, the "new class." Specifically, it examines the neoconservative contention that liberal policy experts have emerged as a new political force threatening the future of representative government. Liberal policy experts, according to neoconservatives, are to be seen as part of a new class striving for political power. Such power is said to be most vividly reflected in the leading roles policy experts now play in the formulation of public policy (the Great Society period of the 1960s typically serving as the classic example of the phenomenon). In sharp contrast to this contention, the chapter argues that the contemporary role of the policy analyst is less the product of a new and unprecedented elite conniving for power than a manifestation of the emerging ideological and technical realities of postindustrial politics. Furthermore, it is shown that the neoconservative response to the phenomenon itself serves to support the same technocratic ends that it is purported to challenge. Here the discussion points to the effort to counter liberal expertise with the development of a conservative "counterintelligentsia." Manifested in the growth of right-wing think tanks and an emphasis on policy techniques more compatible with conservative objectives, the result has been a significant politicization of policy expertise.

5

Managerial Expertise and Organizational Control: The Politics of Behavioral Science[†]

During the past two decades an increasing number of writers have turned their attention to the ideological role of the social sciences.[1] In general, this work has evolved from an epistemological critique of the social sciences' dominant methodological orientation, empiricism. Such critiques range from an assault on the traditional "value-neutral" conception of an empirical science, which rules out social and political evaluation, to an attempt to locate an interest in sociotechnical control within social science methodology itself.[2] Various writers have ascribed ideological consequences to such a methodology ranging from a bias toward social stability and the status quo to political domination and repression.

One of the areas of social science that has come under relatively sharp criticism is the field of organizational theory. The purpose of this discussion is to illustrate the ideological character of one major component of organization theory, organizational psychology and the human relations school.

†SOURCE: This chapter is a revised version of "Ideology and Organization Theory," in *Critical Studies in Organization and Bureaucracy,* edited by Frank Fischer and Carmen Sirianni (Philadelphia: Temple University Press); used by permission.

Ideology and Authority

To put the issue bluntly, organizational psychology emerged to facilitate the bureaucratic processes of twentieth-century corporate capitalism. As unabashed students of industrial efficiency and stable work relations, its first theorists laid the groundwork for a discipline designed to supplement and support the bureaucratic mode of authority and control. Since then the study of organizational behavior has never swung far from the narrowly defined objectives of corporate organization. Always closely affiliated with a school of business or an institute of labor relations, the discipline has emerged as one of the most well-financed but carefully insulated areas of social research.

The outcome, as Paul Goldman explains, is an organization theory that has "by its assumptions and procedures systematically narrowed its field of inquiry and, consequently, presented an incomplete and distorted picture of organizational reality."[3] Similarly, Alasdair MacIntyre maintains that the methodology of organization theory itself has become the ideology of bureaucratic authority. In his words, organizational science represents little more than an "ideological expression of that same organizational life which the theorists are attempting to describe."[4] For both Goldman and MacIntyre, the result of this narrowed field of interest is an elite-oriented ahistorical theory that is insulated from the critical concepts of social and political theory, particularly the concepts of power, authority, and class.

By distorting the picture of workplace realities, organization theory has taken on the standard functions of an ideology, in both the descriptive and the pejorative meanings of the term. As a workplace ideology, organization theory has conventionally represented a managerial "worldview." In this sense, it has programmatically embodied the interests, values, and objectives of the professional-managerial classes.

For example, Daniel Bell defines ideology in programmatic terms as "a way of translating ideas into action" and explains a "*total* ideology" as "an all inclusive system of comprehensive reality," which includes "a set of beliefs, infused with passion, that seeks to transform the way of life."[5] A total ideology, as such, is a program or plan of action based on an explicitly systematic model or theory of how society works, which is held with more confidence (passion) than the evidence for the theory or model warrants.

It is when we raise this issue of warrantability that an ideology loses its descriptive or nonjudgmental function and takes on a pejorative connotation. In the pejorative sense, the term is used when agents in the society are deluded about themselves, their position in society, or their interests. Jürgen Habermas, for instance, speaks of an ideology as a "world picture" that stabilizes or legitimizes authority and domination.[6] It is by virtue of the fact that it supports or justifies reprehensible social institutions, unjust social practices, relations of repressive authority, exploitation, or domination that a form of consciousness is an ideology.

Ideologies in organizations, in this regard, must be understood as efforts to justify the struggle for power and authority. Generated by conditions of conflict and contradiction, Reinhard Bendix has defined the function of organizational ideologies as "attempts by leaders of enterprises to justify the privilege of voluntary action and association for themselves, while imposing upon all subordinates the duty of obedience and of service to the best of their ability."[7]

The objective here is to offer an interpretation of the ideological functions of organizational psychology and the human relations movement. Bringing the perspective of the political and social theorist to bear on an "applied" behavioral science, the purpose is to show how the human relations movement, cloaked in the garb of scientific warrantability, has served to ideologically translate images of repressive authority into a widely accepted form of workplace consciousness.

Authority in Organization Theory

For Max Weber, the founder of modern organizational sociology, the problems of power and authority lay at the very heart of bureaucratic organization. Weber's principal objective was essentially to both describe and legitimate the replacement of "old world" forms of state authority based on traditional and charismatic leadership with a "rational-legalistic" mode of authority that facilitated industrial development.[8]

Based on emotion and mystique, rather than calculation and orderly change, the traditional and charismatic forms of monarchial and clerical authority thwarted the development of profit maximizing in the wider society. In place of these earlier forms, Weber sought to both describe and promote an alternative mode of authority based on fixed rules and routines, which he called "legal-rational" authority. As the foundation of managerial power in both state and industrial organizations, rational authority is linked to clearly defined, procedurally determined rules and regulations for coordinating relationships among administrative units.

For analytical purposes, Weber posited an ideal model of bureaucracy as the quintessential form of legal-rationalistic authority. This legal-rationalistic model represented the purest form of administrative control. As an analytical construct, it emerged as the basic conceptual foundation of organizational analysis. Contemporary theory, however, has underplayed Weber's emphasis on authority as a form of *power*, stressing instead the *efficient* aspects of legal-rationalistic authority. In a turn from Weber's social and political perspective on bureaucracy, the modern literature has adopted a narrower orientation: Bureaucratic administration is represented more as a model of technical efficiency than as a form of power and domination.

At this point, Weber's conception of bureaucracy as a model of efficiency converges with the emerging "value-neutral" science of management, designed to uncover the efficient rules governing the rational pursuit of goals. In the process, Weber's modern-day followers have underplayed his original concept of authority. Shunning his broad political perspective on entrepreneurial legitimation, they have restricted the concept of authority to an emphasis on its functional contribution to efficient organization practices, such as the uses of hierarchy, technical competence, and leadership.

Organizational Authority and Class Conflict

Bendix is one of the few theorists in the mainstream literature who has maintained Weber's early emphasis on power and authority. Based on a comparative examination of managements' justifications for workplace authority in major industrial countries, Bendix defines the function of a management ideology this way:

> Such ideologies interpret the facts of authority and obedience so as to neutralize or eliminate the conflict between the few and the many in the interest of a more effective exercise of authority. To do this, the exercise of authority is either denied altogether on the ground that the few merely order what the many want; or it is justified with the assertion that the few have qualities of excellence which enable them to realize the interest of the many.[9]

In the United States, the problem of legitimating management assumed special import. Managers in the United States faced a particular dilemma or contradiction. On the one hand, democratic ideologies stress liberty and equality for all. On the other, large masses of workers had to submit to the arbitrary authority of the enterprise's managers, backed up by local and national police forces and legal power, for 10 to 12 hours a day, six days a week. Moreover, in face of this fact, the workers' right to form unions of their own was severely limited or simply prohibited.

The problem, as Bendix put it, was this: How could a managerial elite legitimate its own privileges while imposing a harsh subservience upon its subordinates? The solution was sought at the level of symbols. Designed "as weapon(s) . . . in the struggle for industrialization," managerial ideologies emerged to confer advantage upon the privileged capitalist class.

Prior to industrialization, managers took little interest in the attitudes of their workers. Only when workers became antagonistic did early industrialists intervene in the work process. And then, to stem the tide of rebellion, they principally relied upon the prerogatives of ownership, backed by the physical force of the state. After the turn of the century, however, there was a dramatic turn to the promulgation of managerial ideologies to foster the compliance of labor. In this phase of the struggle, as DiTomaso points out, the loyalty of the worker, or at least the pretension of loyalty, becomes as important as doing a good job.[10] Rather than only specifying rules and regulations to govern various work situations, managerial ideologies function to promote an atmosphere or attitude of loyalty. As Bendix explains, they are aimed at the "spirit" rather than the letter of the rules.

The purpose of the remaining discussion is to illustrate the role of one managerial ideology—human relations theory—in class conflict at the level of the workplace.

Scientific Authority and Class Conflict

In the textbook conception of the human relations movement, its task has been to compensate for the empirical deficiencies of scientific management through the introduction of behavioral science methods and techniques.[11] Accepting the basic postulates of classical organization theory, the neoclassical human relations school sought to empirically build the *human* element into Frederick Taylor's "machine model" of management. In this regard, human relations psychologists attempted to scientifically modify Taylorism by introducing the role of individual behavior and the concept of the "informal group."

In addition to the general introduction of behavioral science methodology, the lasting theoretical contribution of neoclassical human relations theory clearly has been its conceptualization of informal group processes. In contrast to the focus upon formal hierarchical structures within scientific management, neoclassical theory emphasized informal work groups, defined as the natural social groups that emerge in the workplace. Unaccounted for by the formal "table of organization," such groupings appear, according to human relations theory, as a response to the worker's social need to associate with others. Generating an internal culture of norms for group conduct, the informal group can serve as an agency for worker identification, socialization, and control.

From the viewpoint of management, the informal group operates as a system of status and communication capable of thwarting managerial policy and control. In this respect, human relations theorists have often sought ways to coordinate the activities of the formal and informal organizations. William Scott puts it this way:

> Management should recognize that the informal organization exists, nothing can destroy it, and so the executive might just as well work with it. Working with the informal organization involves not threatening its existence unnecessarily, listening to opinions expressed for the group by the leaders, allowing group participation in decision-making situations, and controlling the grapevine by prompt release of accurate information. [12]

What none of this says is that in practice human relations psychology actually took hold as a response to the earlier successes of labor unions by the 1920s. Mainstream theorists are correct to see human relations as a response to the limitations of scientific management, but not for the reasons of science alone. Rather than a theoretical problem in experimental design, we must first look at human relations in the context of scientific management's experience with worker unrest.

By 1915, there was growing opposition to Taylorism and scientific management. One result was a major strike against scientific management practices at the government's Watertown Arsenal. The strike prompted extensive congressional hearings that elevated Taylorism to the level of national concern.

At the root of the problem was the issue of workplace control. As Harry Braverman and Dan Clawson have illustrated, to understand scientific management properly, it is essential to penetrate its scientific rhetoric and to recognize it as a response to labor's authority over actual work processes.[13] Above all else, scientific management emerged as a managerial strategy to gain greater control of the workplace during the labor struggles that accompanied rapid industrialization, especially from 1880 to 1920.

Fundamentally, Taylor recognized that capitalists could never win the struggle with labor under the divided authority that characterized nineteenth-century workplace organization. As long as capitalists continued to take for granted that the workers' craft organizations would retain control of the details of the labor process, they were forced to depend on the voluntary cooperation and active initiatives of these workers. Taylor recognized that capitalists had to conceive and implement an alternative organization of production. That clearly became the task of scientific management. The functions of scientific management experts were twofold. First, they were to enter the workplace to learn (through time and motion studies) what the *workers* already knew: how to plan and direct the details of the work process. Second, through managerial planning and analysis, Taylorites were to employ this newly gained knowledge to "efficiently" redesign the production process under *management* control. (See Chapter 12, pp. 303–308, this volume.)

Although Taylorism in the standard textbook is presented only as a stage in the scientific evolution of organization theory, its *real* contribution was less the development of scientific techniques for measuring work processes than the construction of a new mode of organizational control. In fact, according to Clawson, Taylor never conducted anything that approximated a scientific experiment. Thus, while Taylorism was able to show productivity increases, there is little basis for telling whether such increases resulted from *improved* work procedures or were merely obtained by speeding up the existing practices.

Scientific management's primary contribution to the work process was thus to wrest authority from the craft organizations of the nineteenth century and to place it in the hands of a newly emerging profession of management. As a set of *practical* procedures for the shop floor, however, it was less than a success. Labor found fault with it for political reasons, while management troubled over its technical failures. From management's point of view, Taylorites had properly identified the issue of workplace authority, but, as Richard Edwards put it, they "had not found quite the right mechanism."[14] The human relations movement can be understood as the culmination of a series of interrelated attempts to find the "right mechanism." Early interest in human relations by industrialists can, in fact, be interpreted as a response to the upsurge of organized labor, significantly facilitated by hostilities toward Taylorism itself.

Hugo Munsterberg's industrial psychology was the earliest forerunner of the human relations movement. As father of the newly emerging discipline, Munsterberg couched his 1913 book, *Psychology and Industrial Efficiency*, in language borrowed from Taylor's *Principles of Scientific Management*. Writing at the height of national interest in scientific management, Munsterberg's purpose was to elevate the study of human behavior to the same level of concern. The central focus of his book was to develop psychological techniques to identify the "best possible man" for the job.[15] Despite major opposition by many industrialists to psychological techniques, others began to recognize the need for the development of a "scientific personnel management" as a logical extension of Taylorism.

With the increasing pace of labor instability in the second decade of the century, particularly reflected in the problems of work stoppages, absenteeism, and turnover, this concern was expressed in the emergence of specialists to aid line managers in the selection and testing of workers as well as to perform other functions such as the administration of wages. The development of such specialists was one of the first steps in the widespread growth of the personnel department as a primary organizational function. Munsterberg's industrial psychology set the agenda, touching off study in vocational counseling and placement testing in both business and public administraton.

Industrial psychology and the "personnel movement" received big pushes during both World War I and its aftermath. Facilitated by discussion between Munsterberg and government officials—including President Wilson, as well as the secretaries of both Commerce and Labor—psychological techniques were widely put to use during the government's war efforts. Not only were soldiers tested and selected by psychological techniques, such methods were also extended to job analysis and problems of morale. After the war, facing the enormous task of making a transition to a peacetime economy, military and government psychologists were turned loose to work on the problems of industrial personnel. Psychological consulting firms developed into a thriving business.

During the same period, another approach gave credibility to the importance of the human dimension of organization, or what came to be known as the "labor problem." Dubbed "welfare capitalism," it involved bribing workers with selected nonjob benefits to undercut the militance created by the oppressive, alienating conditions of factory work, especially those associated with the newly emerging system of assembly-line production.[16]

Henry Ford, the founder of "welfare capitalism," startled the industrial world in 1914 with the announcement of a bold and unprecedented program.[17] To both win the loyalty of his workers and spur productivity, Ford agreed to more than double hourly production wages. Ford's "welfare" scheme was, however, largely designed to undercut a growing labor crisis wrought by assembly-line techniques, which were introduced to the industrial world by Ford himself. While the assembly line dramatically increased the rate of production, it had the simultaneous effect of increasing the ranks of the unions, particularly the ranks of the militant Industrial Workers of the World (IWW) at the Ford plant.

Ford's pay increase solved his basic labor problem. Because the new wage scale was so much higher than prevailing wages, it enlarged the pool of labor from which the company could choose. Moreover, because workers were now anxious to hang on to their jobs, it was easier for the plant to increase the pace of production. But this was only the beginning. To further ensure labor tranquility, Ford required participating workers to submit to the ministrations of his "Sociological Department." Basically, this meant that workers agreed to permit one or more of the department's 100 investigators—or "advisors"—to inspect their homes for cleanliness, to monitor their drinking habits, to investigate their sex lives, and generally to ensure that their leisure time was used "properly."

Heralded as a success by the business community, Ford's experiment proved a point. If management would devote time, effort, and a little money to the consideration of the human element of business, production and profits would rise. It was at least equivalent to the introduction of better machinery.

The lesson was not wasted on the larger community. Organizations of prominent industrialists (such as the National Civic Federation) incorporated "welfare capitalism" into their strategies for "harmonizing" the interests of labor and capital. Designed to combat a combination of tight labor markets and socialist union militance (both of which threatened military production in the coming world war), the capitalist welfare program "represented a sophisticated, well-financed, and widely implemented plan for controlling labor."[18] It continued well into the mid-1920s.

Closely related to the idea of welfare capitalism was the concept of the "company union." The chief stimuli for company unions were the labor settlements negotiated during the war. While army psychologists were busy developing techniques for selection and control, the government mandated companies to introduce "work councils" or "plans of representation" in the hope of stemming the dramatic rise of labor militance threatening to cripple military production. After the United States entered the war, President Wilson established the War Labor Board and a new labor policy mandating worker council participation in labor-management arbitration. In exchange for peace, specifically a moratorium on strikes, labor was guaranteed the right to organize and bargain collectively through the representation plan.[19]

However, the policy had a loophole. Because the law was vague on the type of labor organization permitted by the War Labor Board, big companies turned eagerly to a new experiment, the "company union." To meet the War Labor Board's requirement for a "work council" or "plan of representation," many large corporations quickly set up their own company-controlled unions before real unions could be established.

The idea of a company union was simple: establish a formal grievance procedure within the context of rigorously defined limits. Given a channel for expression of legitimate grievances, "loyal" workers would not be driven to join a labor union. As such, these channels represented a substantial roadblock to independent unions as well as extensive possibilities for company propaganda. The administration of the company plan became an important function of newly emerging personnel departments.

During the war, the government's War Industry Board set up special procedures to facilitate and promote the training of "employment managers," often essential for the administration of the company union. In all plants manufacturing munitions, war supplies, and ships, the government mandated the existence of a personnel department. Although "labor administration" had begun to slowly emerge before the war, the managerial requirements generated by the war were the primary catalyst behind the full-scale appearance of personnel departments. Their functions included recruiting, testing, selection, training, discipline, grievance procedures, research, company unions, and welfare provisions. One writer estimates that over 200 departments were added during this period.[20]

Although the company council and the personnel department were too transparent to stifle the intense workplace conflicts of the depression era, they were highly effective in delaying unionism during the postwar decade. Furthermore, they offered valuable lessons that advanced the human relations movement, the most important of which was the legacy of the grievance procedure. Corporate capitalists came to realize that formal grievance appeals procedures were actually quite useful. Rather than a threat to management prerogatives, they could be used to protect management's authority. Not only did they permit the company to redress individual grievances at little cost, such procedures also focused attention on individual cases rather than on company policy itself. Often this prevented grievances from festering into union militance.

From these activities—psychological testing, personnel administration, welfare capitalism, and company unions—emerged a growing recognition of the value of the human element, particularly in regard to the use of grievance procedures and the supervision of workers' needs. Yet these practical techniques were not provided with theoretical underpinnings until the final development that cinched the success of the human relations movement: the Hawthorne experiments and the writings of Elton Mayo.

The Hawthorne studies, usually posited as the starting point for the human relations tradition in conventional theory, were initiated and publicly financed by the congressionally chartered National Research Council of the National Academy of Sciences.[21] At the outset, the project began as an experiment in scientific management at the Western Electric Company near Chicago, a plant well known for its opposition to organized labor. The purpose of the Hawthorne experiments was to determine the effects of lighting on work performance.

To summarize a lengthy and complex set of investigations, the light experiments were conducted on two groups of women. One group was placed in a test room where the intensity of illumination was varied, and the other group worked in a control room with a supposedly constant environment. The investigation was to determine the specific conditions governing work efficiency.

The results were baffling to the researchers: Productivity increased in both rooms. The predicted correlations between lighting and output in the test room were thus undermined. In fact, to the astonishment of the investigators, the production of the women in the test room continually increased whether the lighting level was raised, was retained at the original level, or even was reduced so low that the workers could barely see. Obviously, some variables in the research were not being held constant under experimental controls. Something aside from the level of illumination was causing the change in productivity.

That something turned out to be the "human" variable. After additional experiments, Elton Mayo theorized that the variations were a function of the changing "mental attitude" of the group. The subjects in the test room of the experiment, as it turned out, had formed an "informal" social group that enjoyed the attention of the supervisors and developed a sense of participation in the project. Believing that they had been specially chosen to participate in an important experiment, the women in the test group informally banded together to provide the researchers with their best performance, even in the face of worsening physical conditions.

From all the theories about the Hawthorne studies, the most important finding for management has been recognition of the *supervisory* climate. Mayo hypothesized that the experimenters, having taken an interest in the workers, had assumed the role of de facto supervisors. This led to a second series of studies designed to examine the effects of supervision. Largely under the direction of a Harvard research team headed by Fritz Roethlisberger and William Dickson, these experiments initiated an "interviewing program" to further explore the connection between morale and supervision.

With the aim to improve supervisory techniques, the researchers sought to reeducate shop floor supervisors by teaching them to play the role accidently assumed by the experimenters in the original light studies. During this second phase, counselors were appointed to the various departments under investigation. No educational or professional experience was required, though the company gave them in-plant training. The principal requirement for counselors was that they be well liked by the people in the department. The counselor's function was to deal with the workers' *attitudes* toward their problems, but not the problems themselves. As Loren Baritz explained, "Regardless of all the technical gobbledygook that has been written about the function of the counselor, it all simmers down to a plain injunction that he was to listen to any problem of any employee, good worker or not; that he was not to give advice or argue; and that he should make no promises about remedial action."[22]

In short, the counselor, who was not to be guided by a problem- or efficiency-oriented approach, was just to listen to the employee. According to a Western Electric publication, the counselor "was to watch constantly for signs of unrest and to try to assuage the tension of the worker by discussion before the unrest became active." Counselors were to try to dilute or redirect dissatisfaction by helping the employees to think along "constructive lines." Through this process of adjusting people to situations, rather than situations to people, management hoped that absenteeism, low production, high turnover, grievances, and militant unionism could be reduced, if not avoided.

In addition, the company hoped to achieve a secondary benefit from the counseling program. One of the major themes throughout its interest in the role of counseling, as Baritz stated, "was that a well-trained counselor would be a likely candidate for promotion to a supervisory position, and it was thus hoped that counseling would . . . provide a recruitment pool for managerial positions."[23] In short, the counseling program could serve as a managerial screening device.

The Hawthorne studies probably remain the most widely analyzed and discussed experiments in the history of the social sciences. Many have criticized the findings for methodological errors; writers such as Alex Carey have argued that no valid generalizations emerged from the experiments, while others such as Paul Blumberg maintain that the Harvard researchers failed to see the real implications of their experiments.[24] As Donald Wren points out, however, most of the complaints have generally missed the overarching implications of the study: Regardless of their validity, the experiments opened up "new vistas" for supervision. Management could train supervisors to establish a harmonious work climate, free of idiosyncratic, personal authority.[25] This link between supervision, morale, and productivity became the foundation of academic human relations theory.

For Mayo, the Hawthorne studies offered nothing less than a foundation for a new *political* vision of industrial civilization. Basic to his philosophy was the view that twentieth-century industrial institutions were organized for conflict rather than cooperation. Class politics under capitalism, as he saw it, was nothing more than a "confused struggle of pressure groups [and] power blocs." In his own conception of the ideal community, small cooperative social groupings would replace the need for community.

Mayo maintained that the cooperation of individuals and groups is the supreme principle of the ideal community. Cooperation, he wrote, is a "balanced relation between various parts of the organization, so that the avowed purpose for which the whole exists [defined as the 'common interest'] may be conveniently and continuously fulfilled." Where there are different group interests, even certain inevitable conflicts, their elimination is merely a matter of "intelligent organization that takes careful account of all the group interests involved."[26]

Much of Mayo's political and social theorizing was based on a "psychopathological" analysis of industrial life. Essentially, he argued that workers tend to be motivated by emotions and generalized feelings, while management acts on the basis of logic and rationality. Unable to find satisfactory outlets for the expression of personal dissatisfactions in their work lives, workers became preoccupied with latent "pessimistic reveries," which are manifestly expressed as an apprehension of authority, restriction of output, and a variety of other forms of behavior that reduce morale and output. According to Mayo, industrial society, as presently organized, leads to the social maladjustment of workers and eventually to obsessively irrational behavior, including the formation of adversarial unions.

For Mayo, social class conflict is thus a "deviation" from the normal state of human actions and attitudes. For instance, he argued that "Marx detested 'the bourgeoisie' on grounds that will someday probably be shown to have been personal." Similarly, he described labor leaders as psychological deviates: "These men had no friends. . . . They had no capacity for conversation. . . . They regarded the world as a hostile place. . . . In every instance the personal history was one of social privation—a childhood devoid of normal and happy association in work and play with other children."[27]

Class conflict was, therefore, little more than a primitive expression of human imperfections. In Mayo's ideal community, there would be no need for political confrontations between labor and capital: "Where cooperation is maintained between the individual and his group, the group and the union, the union and management, the personal sense of security and absence of discontent in the individual run high."[28]

The remedy for class conflict is the proper application of psychological techniques. The objective is to eliminate class tensions through the development of "social skills" education. With the proper introduction of human-relations-oriented supervisors and psychological counselors, workers' desires for recognition, security, and the expression of grievances would be adequately fulfilled, obviating the need for union representation altogether.

For Mayo, as well as later Mayoists, the obligation for cooperation always remains in the hands of the management.[29] As the embodiment of logic and rationality, management always knows best. Its interests are thus presented as synonymous with the interests of the organization and society as a whole. For this reason, according to Baritz, Mayo only bothered to discuss the role of unions twice in all his writings.

Given the implications of his theory, Mayo was eager to justify human relations research to corporate management. From his academic post at the Harvard Graduate School of Business, he sought to convince top management that he knew their problems, understood their needs, and sympathized with their goals. Human relations techniques were presented as a means for discovering the true causes of management's problems, which could be revealed by nondirective psychological skills training. As Baritz stated, "Management was encouraged and instructed to enter not only the intellectual, social, and financial lives of the workers, but through counseling, to expose their most personal thoughts and aspirations."[30] In short, management's problems were caused more by management's failure to convert the worker to its point of view than by labor's failure to understand the principles of cooperation.

Given the managerial bias of his theory, it didn't take long for Mayo to find staunch supporters. By the 1940s, his work was widely viewed as the theoretical successor to scientific management. In industry generally, as Peter Drucker and others have pointed out, the human relations philosophy was widely adopted as the creed of the modern personnel department.[31] By the 1950s, groups such as the American Management Association asserted that human relations skills and supervisory training were the most important ingredients of good workplace management. Moreover, a quick look at the curriculum of any contemporary management program, not to mention industrial psychology departments, will attest to the enduring value of the conviction.

As the theoretical capstone of the human relations movement, Mayo's work succinctly expressed the culmination of a 30-year search for the "right mechanism," from the rise of industrial psychology and personnel administration to the development of company unions and welfare capitalism. From the foregoing discussion, it is clear that Mayo's contribution was much more than an empirical step in the evolution of modern organization theory. Regardless of the experimental orientation of the Hawthorne studies, Mayo's most profound contribution was to lift the findings to the level of a managerial *ideology*.

Not only does human relations philosphy offer a justification for the dominance of management over labor, it also provides psychological techniques for blurring the realities of workplace control. As a managerial worldview it posits the logical, "rational" authority of management over the "irrational," psychologically immature behavior of workers and their unions. Management is the agent of cooperation, while unions are the embodiment of social and political conflict.

In programmatic terms, human relations ideology masks a strategy to stabilize or legitimate managerial authority and domination. Through the manipulation of the organization's psychological climate, the purpose is to promote an atmosphere or attitude of loyalty to management. Although never stated formally, the specific objective is to blur the worker's consciousness of the general issues of power, authority, and class; particular unjust practices; and repression.[32] Depicting the union as an external interloper between the worker and management, workers are socialized to accept a paternalistic conception of "management-knows-best." In psychological terms, management portrays the all-knowing, benevolent father who offers guidance and protection to his children, the workers.

Finally, human relations theory, like ideologies in general, came to be accepted with more confidence than the evidence would warrant. This is attested to by the number of studies that have shown the Hawthorne experiments to be either unscientific or inconclusive at best. As Carey put it after his detailed study of the purported evidence, one wonders "how it is possible for studies so nearly devoid of scientific merit, and conclusions so little supported by the evidence, to gain so influential and respected a place within the scientific disciplines and to hold this place so long?"[33]

The answer is found in the theory's ideological appeal, especially to those who have generally funded organizational research. No one has more succinctly expressed this appeal than Michael Rose. Describing Mayoism as the "twentieth century's most seductive managerial ideology," Rose has captured its appeal in these words: "What, after all, could be more appealing than to be told that one's subordinates are nonlogical; that their uncooperativeness is a frustrated urge to collaborate; that their demands for cash mark a need for your approval; and that you have a historic destiny as a broker of social harmony?"[34]

In 1949, the United Auto Workers' (UAW) monthly education magazine expressed the union's hostility to human relations: "The prophet is Elton Mayo, a Harvard University professor who has been prying into the psychiatric bowels of factory workers since around about 1925 and who is the Old Man of the movement." Further satirizing management's devotion to Mayoism, they continued:

> The Bible is the book, the Human Problems of an Industrial Civilization.
> The Holy Place is the Hawthorne Plant of the Western Electric Company
> (the wholly owned subsidiary of one of the nation's largest monopolies,
> the AT and T). At Hawthorne, Ma Bell, when she wasn't organizing com-
> pany unions, allowed Professor Mayo to carry on experiments with a
> group of women workers for nine years.[35]

Criticizing Mayo's assertion that the women produced more because of
the expressed interest the supervisors and psychologists took in their
personal problems, they sarcastically concluded that his finding "is the
greatest discovery since J. P. Morgan learned that you can increase profits
by organizing a monopoly, suppressing competition, raising prices and
reducing production." While the union's view offers little to refine our
understanding of the human relations approach, it does help to convey
the labor-management tensions that it was designed to address.

Beyond the UAW, however, the human relations school was greeted
by labor with relative silence. Given the fact that human relations techniques were motivated by a desire to undercut the growth of unionism,
it is surprising that they never elicited the full outcry that was accorded
to Taylorism. In part, this was probably because psychological techniques are more subtle than the industrial engineer's stopwatch. The
human relations approach, therefore, appears as a less explicit threat and
in many quarters may have passed over the heads of union leaders.
Another reason may be the fact that by the 1940s the leaders of organized
labor had substantially moved toward a more conciliatory relationship
with management. Unions, as a result of Gomper's legacy, concentrated
on wage gains and left workplace authority to management.

Workplace Psychology Today

Before closing it is interesting to offer a brief update on the use of
human relations techniques in the contemporary workplace. As might be
anticipated, the movement is still very much alive today, although it is
now dressed in a more sophisticated theoretical language.

By 1960, human relations theory was said to be on the wane. As modern organizational theory began to shift its emphasis to top-level
managerial concerns, such as strategic planning and systems analysis, the
human relations tradition was seemingly relegated to a story in the his-

tory of organization theory. To the degree that its contribution lived on, it was subsumed under specialized areas of industrial and personnel psychology.

During the 1970s, however, when recessionary conditions began to put new pressures on corporate profit margins, management unleashed the most explicit offensive against trade unions since the 1930s. In the process, the concerns of human relations practitioners began to resurface on the managerial agenda. Sometimes called the "new industrial relations," the offensive has essentially taken two principal forms, one quite sophisticated and the other rather crude. Respectively, they have involved the development of Quality of Work Life programs and a new type of management consulting aimed explicitly at union-busting. Both are easily recognized as carrying forward the basic objectives that motivated the earlier human relations movement. Here in the closing section of this chapter, we point to a few of the basic aspects of these two developments.

First, we turn to Quality of Work Life programs (QWL), which have grown dramatically in the U. S. workplace in recent years. Most major corporate employers in the United States now have established some form of program that falls under the QWL rubric. They have also grown quite rapidly in the public sector. In 1983, for example, the secretary of the International Association of Quality Circles estimated that over 135,000 QWL circles operated at 8,000 locations in the United States, involving approximately 1 million workers.

There are a number of good things that can be said about QWL programs. Compared to earlier human relations approaches, they are based on a much broader understanding of the workers' relationship to organizations and jobs. QWL programs, in this respect, are built upon a number of important advances in organizational psychology, particularly those identified with "human resources psychology." The human resources approach, grounded in the theories of Douglas McGregor and Frederick Herzberg, among others, has focused primarily on the task of "job enrichment." Perhaps the most important aspect of this work has been the recognition that at times it may be the organization—not the individual—that needs to be changed.

Moreover, in recent years QWL programs have incorporated innovative techniques from other social and cultural contexts. Expecially significant has been the appropriation of "quality circle" concepts and techniques from the Japanese. Quality circle programs, often credited with boosting Japan's rate of industrial productivity, are basically a set of methods designed to turn workers into organizational problem solvers. In many places in the United States QWL programs have, in fact, become synonymous with quality circles.

It is essential, however, to see QWL programs in the political-economic context that gave rise to their wide-scale adoption. While much of the popular discussion of these programs emphasizes the role of modern psychological theories, the reason for the dramatic growth of QWL programs can be traced to the economic crisis of the late 1970s. Here, of course, it is impossible to discuss these economic difficulties in any detail. Suffice it to say that aggressive competition from foreign producers began to make clear the fact that the unilateral rule of the world economy by U. S. corporations was coming to an end. Indeed, the situation began to raise questions about the general health of the American economy. Much of the discussion has centered on industry's declining rate of productivity, especially when compared with Japan. In particular, this posed serious questions about U. S. labor-management practices. Many of the corporation's critics argued that productivity had fallen because of rigid managerial structures, often responsibile for worker apathy and alienation. Corporate leaders also focused on worker apathy but largely blamed the presence of unions in the workplace. Both groups, however, sought a solution through the "new industrial relations." For many concerned with worker apathy, it offered a new set of techniques for reviving worker motivation. For those who pointed to the unions, it was seen as a new opportunity for reasserting management's social control of the workplace.[36]

The result has been the dramatic growth of QWL programs and many of the experiences with these schemes have been remarkably similar to those associated with the earlier human relations programs. Corporations rapidly hired human resource specialists to hurriedly put these new programs in place at the same time that they launched a major attack on the unions. Typically, this took the form of demanding major contract concessions in the name of declining growth and productivity. In place of the cutbacks, corporate managers offered Quality of Work Life programs.

Many QWL programs were put into place so quickly that they caught many people—including union leaders—off guard. Structures, guidelines, and training were seldom worked out in advance. Lip service was initially paid to the idea that QWL programs were for job satisfaction, but, as Parker points out, this was largely to mollify worker and union objections.[37] Later, after programs were well established, many companies openly declared increasing productivity and economic competitiveness to be the goal of QWL programs. By the 1980s, little was heard about job enrichment per se. Today it is significant only insofar as it leads to well-defined productivity gains.

Union leaders, despite the fact that they are primary targets of QWL programs, have seldom been openly hostile to these programs. High levels of unemployment and dwindling union membership put union leaders and their staffs on the defensive. Under these conditions, unions have had very little influence over the shape of the programs. This, of course, was clearly an important component of the corporate strategy.

There is an unmistakable déjà vu associated with these QWL programs. For many corporate leaders, it is clearly a second opportunity to shape the human side of work for their own political advantages. The strategy is more sophisticated but the basic objective differs very little from human relations theory. Essentially, the tactic is to get workers involved in the production process. As one consultant put it: The goal is to get workers to think and act like managers without, at the same time, sharing managerial power. Basic to the approach is an attempt to blur the conflicts between labor and management. The hidden message, as another consultant puts it, is that "we're all in it together." Unions may have been necessary in an earlier period, but the times have changed. In short, leave the union and join the "corporate family."

Finally, we turn to the new breed of management consultants explicitly engaged in a much more obvious form of union-busting. Like human resource psychologists, these new consultants purport to specialize in the application of updated human relations techniques. But unlike human resource psychologists, who generally stand behind the guise of disinterested science, these "human relations consultants" are much more politically explicit in their efforts to assist management in tightening administrative control. In significant part, they have done this by wedding specific techniques of behavioral psychology to the classical political problems of industrial relations. The result has been the growth of a small industry devoted to the techniques of employee manipulation and union-busting. It is estimated by labor sources that they are presently assisting management to oppose about two-thirds of all union organizing drives, including efforts in both the private and the public sectors.

As in the Mayoist tradition, their approach is grounded in a basic ideological opposition to the labor movement. Emphasizing a new vision of "humanistic" workplace relations, introduced by an "enlightened" and "benevolent" management, conflict between workers and management is to be eliminated by good communications and improved supervision. Through a variety of techniques designed to socialize and "indoctrinate" workers to management's point of view, particularly during union-organizing drives, these specialists (like their predecessors) often establish the informal group as the central focus of their assault.

According to these consultants, up to 90% of all organizing drives are initiated by informal employee groups rather than by union organizers. Recognizing that unionization is the product of troubles that first find expression in the organization's informal groups, such modern-day consultants are quick to advise management on the merits of an internal grievance process to undercut such channels of communication. As with the earlier human relations movement, the purpose is to isolate and stifle dissatisfaction before it festers to the widespread dissent that fosters unionization.[38]

Only in recent years have unions begun to take steps to counter the union-busting firms. For instance, union charges that such consultants are abusing the nation's labor laws has prompted the House Education and Labor Committee's subcommittee on labor-management relations to conduct hearings that linked such consultants to unfair labor practices and union-busting.[39]

Concluding Perspectives

Max Horkheimer wrote that "the surface appearance or even the thesis of a doctrine rarely offers a clue to the role it plays in society."[40] The developments presented here clearly show that organization theory can be offered as evidence to substantiate his premise. In sharp contrast to an objective science of organizational behavior, what emerges from the history of organizational psychology is a picture of ideological corruption. Both wittingly and unwittingly, organizational psychology has evolved into a tool of manipulation and control in the ongoing struggle for command of the workplace.

The example of human relations theory thus demonstrates the need for a *political* theory of organizational science. While the articulation of such a theory is beyond the scope of the present chapter, from the foregoing analysis it is nonetheless possible to specify a number of factors that must be included in such a theory. Consider, for example, the relationship between organizational expertise and class politics.

An adequate theory of the role of organizational expertise must begin with the premise that knowledge has become a critical resource in the politics of class struggle, both inside and outside the workplace. In an age of bureaucratic organizations, characterized by hierarchy and functional compartmentalization, the very premises that determine political consciousness and class conflict are significantly shaped by the control of knowledge and information. Therefore, political scientists and sociologists must examine organizational psychology not only for its contribution to work processes but also for its critical force in shaping the political attitudes and actions of the working classes.

Second, in the elaboration of such a theory, one must recognize the complexity of the role of organizational expertise in the larger class struggle between capital and labor.[41] Men like Mayo were more than "tools" of capitalist power. While human relations psychology, like scientific management, has helped to mitigate the capitalists' conflicts with labor, it must be perceived as the commodity of a *new* class vying for position in the evolving world of bureaucratic capitalism.

Here we can benefit from Stark's analysis of scientific management.[42] Like scientific management, human relations theory must be understood as an emergent ideology of organizational psychologists bent upon earning a niche for themselves in the structures of modern industrial society. Positioned between capital and labor, they have sought the basis for a new professional recognition and autonomy by mediating class conflict. In this regard, Baritz, too, has shown that industrial and human relations psychologists required little prodding by the leaders of industry and government. Like the industrial engineers before them, they sought to legitimate themselves as members of a new professional-managerial strata. The justification for the role was to be provided by the experimental knowledge of human relations research developed by the industrial and organizational psychology community. Appeals to the "objective" laws of human behavior provided the basic ideological underpinnings for the psychologist's autonomy; psychological measurement offered the necessary data for display of their expertise; and the newly developed departments of personnel administration established an organizational base of operations.

Finally, a few comments should be made about the role of government. From the foregoing discussion, it is clear that the federal government has consistently sponsored the development of managerially biased organizational techniques. Thus the focus of labor relations policy should be extended beyond its primary emphasis on collective bargaining to include government's role in shaping specific workplace practices. Like the scientific management approach introduced at the government's Watertown Arsenal, the major strides in the development of industrial psychology, personnel management, and company unions were facilitated by the government's war efforts and later through public financing, as exemplified by the Hawthorne studies. Today, the research offices of the federal government, particularly those of the army and navy, remain among the most significant financial contributors to organizational research.

Consideration of these various elements leads to the following conclusion: If organization theory is to contribute to the construction of a socially just society, it must more directly confront the political motivations that shape its uses. In the realm of practice, social scientists must begin with the understanding that theory does not directly dictate practice. Unable to control the implications of their own work, they must recognize that even the most humanistic techniques can be employed to further unjust ends. Only with such caveats clearly in mind can organizational theorists realistically hope to address the need for legitimate practical reforms.

Notes

1. The distinction between the social and the behavioral sciences is largely a matter of professional convention. In large part, the term *behavioral science* was introduced to refer to those disciplines that strive for a rigorous, objectively detached, empirical orientation, in contrast to the "softer" more value-laden and less scientific disciplines. For instance, political science is typically designated as a social science while psychology is considered to be a behavioral science. It has been argued that the distinction was contrived in part to dissociate specific disciplines and approaches from the more contentious and controverisal concerns typically surrounding the social sciences, thus increasing their social respectability. On the ideological role of these sciences, see, for example, Robin Blackburn, ed., *Ideology in Social Science* (London: Fontana, 1972).

2. On the critique of "value-neutrality," see Frank Fischer, *Politics, Values, and Public Policy: The Problem of Methodology* (Boulder, CO: Westview, 1980). For an attempt to locate an interest in sociotechnical control in social science methodology, see Herbert Marcuse, *One-Dimensional Man* (Boston: Beacon, 1964).

3. Paul Goldman, "Sociologists and the Study of Bureaucracy: A Critique of Ideology and Practice," *The Insurgent Sociologist* 3 (Winter 1978), p. 21.

4. Alasdair MacIntyre,"Social Science Methodology as the Ideology of Bureaucratic Authority," in *Through the Looking-Glass*, ed. Maria J. Falco (Washington, DC: University Press of America, 1979), 42.

5. Daniel Bell, "The End of Ideology in the West," in *The End of Ideology Debate*, ed. Chaim I. Waxman (New York: Funk and Wagnalls, 1968), pp. 88, 96.

6. Jürgen Habermas, *Toward a Rational Society* (Boston: Beacon, 1970).

7. Reinhard Bendix, *Work and Authority in Industry* (New York: John Wiley, 1956), p. xxiii; Michael E. Urban, "Bureaucracy, Contradiction, and Ideology in Two Societies," *Administration and Society* 10, no. 1 (May 1978): 49–85.

8. Max Weber, *The Theory of Economic and Social Organization* (New York: Oxford University Press, 1947).

9. Bendix, *Work and Authority in Industry*, p. 13.

10. Nancy DiTomaso, "The Organization of Authority in the Capitalist State," *Journal of Political and Military Sociology* 6 (Fall 1978): 189–204.

11. William G. Scott, "Organization Theory: An Overview and Appraisal," *Organizations*, ed. Joseph A. Litterer (New York: John Wiley, 1969), pp. 15–29.

12. Ibid., p. 20.

13. Harry Braverman, *Labor and Monopoly Capital* (New York: Monthly Review Press, 1974); Dan Clawson, *Bureaucracy and the Labor Process* (New York: Monthly Review Press, 1980), p. 47.

14. Richard Edwards, *Contested Terrain* (New York: Basic Books, 1979), p. 104.

15. Donald A. Wren, *The Evolution of Management Thought* (New York: Ronald Press, 1972), pp. 195–208.

16. Stuart Brandeis, American *Welfare Capitalism, 1880–1940* (Chicago: University of Chicago Press, 1976).

17. Loren Baritz, *The Servants of Power: A History of the Use of Social Science in American Industry* (Middletown, CT: Wesleyan University Press, 1960), pp. 32–35; Braverman, *Labor and Monopoly Capital*, p. 149.

18. Edwards, *Contested Terrain*, p. 95.

19. Ibid., pp. 105–10.

20. Henry Eilburt, "The Development of Personnel Management in the United States," *Business History Review* 33 (Autumn 1959): 345–64.

21. Baritz, *Servants of Power*, pp. 76–116; Wren, *Evolution of Management Thought*, pp. 275–99.

22. Baritz, *Servants of Power*, p. 105.

23. Ibid.

24. Alex Carey, "The Hawthorne Studies: A Radical Criticism," *American Sociological Review* 32 (June 1974): 403–16; Paul Blumberg, *Industrial Democracy* (New York: Schocken, 1976), pp. 14–46; A. J. M. Sykes, "Economic Interest and the Hawthorne Researchers," *Human Relations* 18 (August 1965): 253–63.

25. Wren, *Evolution of Management Thought*, chaps. 13 and 14.

26. Elton Mayo, *The Social Problems of an Industrial Civilization* (London: Routledge, 1949), p. 128; Mayo, *The Political Problems of Industrial Civilization* (Cambridge, MA: Harvard University Printing Office, 1947).

27. Mayo, *The Social Problems of an Industrial Civilization*, p. 24; Baritz, *Servants of Power*.

28. Mayo, *The Social Problems of an Industrial Civilization*, p. 111.

29. For a good illustration of the anti-trade-union interpretation of the Hawthorne findings, see T. North Whitehead, *Leadership in a Free Society* (Cambridge, MA: Harvard University Press, 1936), p. 155.

30. Baritz, *Servants of Power*, p. 115.

31. Peter Drucker, *The Practice of Management* (New York: Harper & Row, 1954), pp. 273–88.

32. For a discussion of how the vocabulary of human relations experts blurs the facts of organizational power, see C. Wright Mills, "The Contributions of Sociology to Studies of Industrial Relations," *Proceedings of the First Annual Meeting of the Industrial Relations Association* (1948), pp. 212–13.

33. Carey, "Hawthorne Studies." p. 403.

34. Michael Rose, *Industrial Behaviour: Theoretical Development Since Taylor* (London: Allen Lane, 1975), p. 124.

35. Baritz, *Servants of Power*, pp. 11–15.

36. Guillermo J. Gremier, *Inhuman Relations: Quality Circles and Anti-Unionism in American Industry* (Philadelphia: Temple University Press, 1988).

37. Mike Parker, *Inside the Circle* (Boston: South End Press, 1985).

38. See, for example, Steve Lagerfeld, "The Pop Psychologist as Union Buster," *American Federationist*, November 1981; pp. 6–12; Damon Stetson, "New Kind of Law Firm Keeping Labor at Bay," *New York Times*, 25 October 1981, p. 53.

39. Committee on Education and Labor, House of Representatives Oversight Hearings Before the Subcommittee on Labor-Management Relations, 96th Congress, 1st session, *Pressures in Today's Workplace*, 4 vols. (Washington, DC: Government Printing Office, 1979).

40. Max Horkheimer, *The Eclipse of Reason* (New York: Oxford University Press, 1947), p. 85.

41. For an illustration of a Marxist attempt to explain organizational psychology in terms of the larger class struggle between capital and labor, see Walter R. Nord, "The Failure of Current Applied Behavioral Science—A Marxian Perspective," *Journal of Applied Behavioral Science* 10, no. 4 (October, November, December 1974): 557–78.

42. David Stark, "Class Struggle and the Transformation of the Labor Process: A Relational Approach," *Theory and Society* 9 (January 1980): 102.

6

Technocracy and Policy Expertise:
The Politics of the "New Class"

During the past 20 years policy experts have emerged as increasingly significant players in the game of politics. Most of the policy-oriented literature, however, has failed to grapple with the broad sociopolitical issues raised by this important development. One of the best examples is provided by the policy analysis literature. Largely a response to the need for policy expertise, public policy analysis has been one of the fastest-growing specializations in the social sciences. But most of the literature of "policy science" has assumed a rather narrow technical orientation. Much of it, in fact, has been devoted to methodological issues. Opting for an emphasis on procedure and technique, policy analysts have largely shunned the political questions that accompany their new presence.

In view of this new role, it is fair to say that the policy science movement and its literature naively cling to a number of outdated assumptions. One is the overly simplistic assumption that better policy knowledge will lead to improved policy decisions. Another is the idea that good policy science is "value-neutral." There is little in the contemporary experience that demonstrates the reliability of either assumption, although both remain firmly grounded in the discipline. Taken together, they perpetuate one of the discipline's most powerful myths: namely, that the concerns of policy science, if not all policy experts, transcend the play of politics.

One important exception to this trend in recent years has been the

policy-oriented writings of the neoconservative movement.[1] Neoconservative social scientists, in large part writing in reaction to the uses
of social science in the Great Society era, have singled out policy expertise as a political phenomenon that now threatens the future of representative government. The rise of these policy experts, increasingly taking
the form of a "new class" striving for political power, portends the
appearance of a technocratic system of government. The role these
experts now play in the formulation of public policy is, according to the
neoconservatives, the measure of their new power.

The neoconservative thesis is important for several reasons. It is put
forward by a group of intellectuals, many of them so-called policy
intellectuals, who have helped to shape the contemporary conservative
assault on big government, the primary consumer of policy expertise. It
also provides us with a usefully provocative literature that helps to cast
light on the neglected political issues that now surround the policy
expert's role. This chapter, as an effort to probe these issues, outlines the
neoconservative position and attempts to assess its new class thesis as it
pertains to both the expert role and the policy science movement. It proceeds in five parts. First, it examines the traditional patterns of policy
expertise, and, second, turns to a discussion of postindustrialism and the
new class thesis. Against this background, the third and fourth sections
trace the thesis through the Great Society experience and the conservative political response to it. Based on the themes developed in these sections, the closing discussion offers an alternative perspective on the
politics of policy expertise and draws out its implications for the policy
analysis profession.

Policy Expertise:
Basic Political Patterns

The relation of knowledge to power has long been a central theme in
social and political theory. Moreover, variants of the new class thesis are
as old as the social sciences themselves. In the American experience,
these issues have been most prominent in the Progressive era and the
New Deal.[2] In these periods, as well as the more recent Great Society in
the 1960s, both conservatives and radical theorists have typically portrayed top-level policy experts as members of a new class seeking to
install themselves as the political and moral arbiters of public policy.

In some cases there is truth in this view. Men as disparate as Harold Croly and Rexford Tugwell, for example, can be found in these earlier periods calling for the ascendency of the expert. But the experience in all of these periods has been one of dashed hopes. Such movements have invariably encountered powerful political opposition. Indeed, the degree of hostility with which such expertise has generally been greeted has at various times posed serious threats to the future of the larger policy science movement. In view of the precarious nature of such political activity, the rank and file of the professional discipline have traditionally opted for a politically cautious orientation.

In general outline, this historical experience has given rise to a narrow professional perspective purportedly grounded in the scientific principle of "ethical neutrality."[3] Eschewing ethical and political analysis, the policy science profession has been shaped around a methodological orientation that emphasizes technical advice concerning policy effectiveness and program efficiency. In this role, the policy scientist functions as a social engineer whose task focuses mainly on the calculation of costs and benefits of alternative means (for achieving goals hammered out by legitimate legislative processes). Some experts, swept into the enthusiasm of this orientation, have paradoxically gone so far as to view the value-laden political dimensions of the policy processes as irrational interruptions that impede the methodological requirements of efficient decision making.

Thus, as members of a professional movement, these applied social scientists have pursued the development of a functional relationship to those in power. This has generally taken the form of a close cooperative relationship with the "men of action" (those who, by virtue of their important political and economic responsibilities, are seen to possess superior practical knowledge). In this arrangement social scientists supply technical knowledge about the efficient achievement of goals deemed necessary by these practical men of affairs. Only these men are viewed to be in the position to judge which of the social scientists' recommendations can be used, when, and how.[4]

Under this functional or service model of policy advice, then, social scientists do not expect all of their advice to be accepted and used. But this is not to suggest that they exercise no policy influence or initiative in the processes. Within the context of this relationship, these "service intellectuals" have often promoted themselves and their ideas as the representatives of reason—largely defined as technical reason—in policy processes. In this respect the policy science movement, in the name of efficiency and cost-effectiveness, can be likened to an interest group vying for influence among competing interests in a pluralistic decision-making process.

Some have argued that this service model of expertise and its ideology nicely fit the pluralist theory of democracy and provide policy-oriented social scientists with a legitimate stance from which to ply their trade. Whether or not this is true, the practice of policy expertise has generally reflected something more than the impartiality that this theoretical justification would imply. Historian Barry Karl, for example, has shown that in practice this service model often takes the form of a political strategy, or what he calls a "methodology of social reform."

According to Karl, this reform methodology involves a number of basic steps. The first step concerns the assembly of a group of social science experts, usually by a reform-minded president. This group devotes its time to defining a social problem and spelling out the need for specific political reforms. A larger group of journalists, philanthropists, and business leaders is then gathered to discuss the problem. The objective in this phase is to develop a consensus and to broaden the reform coalition. Following this gathering a study is produced "containing all of the information and interpretation on which reasonable men, presumably in government, would base programs for reform."[5]

Such a reform methodology is clearly compatible with the service orientation but need not be limited by it. From the historical evidence it is far from clear that policy experts are necessarily constrained by an agenda preestablished by those they serve. Indeed, given the dynamics of this methodology, they can be deeply involved in determining the agenda. To be sure, such a role only confers an indirect form of power—namely, a power based on the ability to persuade political leaders that certain courses of action should be taken. But it is nonetheless very real power that can be used at propitious moments to shape the course of events.

Although both liberal and conservative politicians have used this methodology, it has been the liberal reform administrations that have provided most of the propitious moments. Because the liberal administrations of the Democratic party have typically shaped their political agendas around the call for social reform, it is not surprising that this methodology has largely served as a *liberal* reform strategy. The histories of the great liberal expansions—particularly in the Progressive era, the New Deal, and the Great Society—reveal a fairly regular and predictable pattern of political conflict generated by the use of this reform strategy. Given the fact that liberal reform agendas have generally borne the mark of liberal policy experts, the conservative attack on these agendas has typically included an attempt to discredit liberal social scientists and their ideas. Portraying them as impractical, power-seeking, and elitist, conservatives have generally sought their speedy return to the quiet life of academe.

Attacked in this manner, the social scientists have usually retreated under the banner of the service model. In short, they concede only to having served the programs of their elected political leaders (which, of course, is true but represents something less than the full picture). The fact that these leaders were generally of the Democratic party is thus portrayed as an issue for the political system, not the policy science profession.

Policy Expertise and the New Class

Having examined the basic patterns that formed the policy expert's traditional relationship to power, the discussion now turns to the neoconservative thesis: the argument that an elite group of policy experts has begun to play a leading political role in the formulation of public policy. Portraying these experts as members of a "new class," neoconservatives maintain that they have established a new and much more politically significant relationship to power.

The neoconservative thesis is grounded in an important reality that is not to be slighted. The preceding discussion has made clear the fact that the policy expert's role is not a new concern, but never has the issue been more salient than today. Not only has policy expertise become a pervasive phenomenon in contemporary society, many theorists now contend that its continuing evolution presages the rise of a new configuration of power. Indeed, some theorists write of a phase of societal development based on the production and administration of knowledge. Often called the "postindustrial society," this new social configuration is one in which capitalist values associated with property, wealth, and production are steadily giving way to values based on knowledge, education, and intellect.[6] Such a transformation is said to portend the coming of a new society in which a technical elite will take its place alongside traditional economic and political elites in the governance of society generally.

The emergence of expertise is thus not in doubt. Since the latter part of the 1800s a large degree of control over the day-to-day workings of complicated economic, political, and social processes has indeed been delegated to professional experts. Professional associations and policy experts generally now constitute the "hidden hierarchies" of all major policy arenas, prompting some to speak of the "Professional State."[7] One can debate the specific dimensions of this phenomenon, but it is abundantly clear from the available evidence that expertise has become deeply embedded in the bureaucratic structures of modern government.[8]

In recent years this concern has been reflected in the growing literature on the "new class." Disillusioned by the corporate-welfare state, in the 1970s theorists of both the political left and the right began to link many of the political problems of modern society to the rise of a new class. The challenge tended to come first from the radical critics. For example, Alvin Gouldner wrote of the "liberal technologues of the welfare-warfare state"; Noam Chomsky spoke of the "New Mandarins"; and Robert Goodman criticized the "planning mandarins" of the military-industrial complex.[9] Later in the decade, as well as into the 1980s, the same refrains could be heard, this time from the "neoconservatives," a group consisting of disheartened liberals from the Great Society period. Here we find theorists such as Irving Kristol, Edward Banfield, Jeanne Kirkpatrick, Nathan Glazer, and Samuel Beer, among others.[10] Although both radical and conservative writers have long been interested in the new class issue as an intellectual problem, in recent years neoconservatives have brought the topic into the mainstream of contemporary political discussion. Indeed, the neoconservative attack on the new class has figured prominently in the political assault on the welfare state, particularly the Reagan administration's emphasis on deregulation.

At base, the neoconservative's polemic against the new class is an attack on professional expertise and the modern role of the universities. The authority and legitimacy of this new elite are traced to their knowledge and professional credentials, the key commodities of the emerging postindustrial society. From this perspective the universities, as the purveyors of these commodities, constitute the institutional power bases of this new elite. Some argue that elite universities are increasingly being turned into policy "command posts." The "ivory tower" is described as becoming a sort of forward position from where the new elite can direct the government's weapons to policy targets, usually visible only to itself.[11]

Many concede that the grand outline of this "technocratic takeover" has in reality yet to fully materialize.[12] But as Banfield cautions, this must not overshadow the fact that the new class is emerging. Already it represents a significant challenge to our traditional democratic institutions, particularly the legislative system and political party structures. Banfield describes the unfolding threat in these terms:

> Policy science . . . appears as one in a long series of efforts by the Progressive Movement and its heirs to change the character of the American political system—to transfer power from the corrupt, the ignorant, and the self-serving to the virtuous, the educated and the public spirited. . . . These were the motives that inspired proposals to replace politicians with experts in the legislatures and to do away with political parties.[13]

Experts may not have replaced legislators yet, but neoconservatives are quick to point out that they are found everywhere *in* legislatures. Portrayed as part of the intellectual cadre of the liberal establishment, these policy experts are not only presented as ambitious, arrogant, and elitist, they are seen as the products of an adversary culture that is hostile to traditional American values, particularly the institutional practices of corporate capitalism. Defending democracy against these "unelected representatives" has become the defining agenda of the neoconservative movement.

How do we assess this neoconservative argument? Clearly these writers have identified an important political phenomenon, but coming to agreement on an interpretation of this development is another matter. Such an assessment is complicated by a number of factors. One longstanding problem has been the subtle and usually anonymous nature of the expert's power. Being neither publicly elected nor reviewed, the expert and his or her influence is generally difficult to measure. Indeed, for this reason the power of the expert has developed rather opaquely. To the degree that the phenomenon is upon us, it seems to have happened before we noticed it.

Another problem in assessing the new class thesis can be attributed to the fact that a good deal of the writing (on both the political left and the right) has been advanced to serve an ideological function. Often the intent has been to scapegoat the new class as an impediment to either market capitalism or democratic socialism. For this reason the new class literature tells us very little about the role of expertise in policy-making or about the struggles that have shaped its role.

To assess this thesis it is thus necessary to turn to other sources of data. Although such data have generally been hard to come by, over the past 10 or 15 years sufficient fragments have appeared to make such an assessment feasible. Much of the data pertain to the Great Society era and its aftermath, the touchstone of the neoconservative argument. Although this work has largely failed to capture the larger political dynamics of this phenomenon, it does provide an empirically oriented literature upon which to base an assessment.

Policy Expertise and the Great Society

The first step in the assessment is to set the neoconservative thesis in a substantive context. For this purpose the discussion turns here to the Great Society and the neoconservative interpretation of the liberal policy intellectual's role in the development of the War on Poverty.

A number of important political and intellectual events helped to set the stage for the Great Society. In particular it is essential to note that the period preceding this era was marked by a belief in the "end of ideology." Put forward by writers who could later be counted among the neoconservatives, the thesis asserted the fundamental triumph of liberal capitalism over bureaucratic socialism. According to this view, further debate about these ideologies would only impede progress toward the American ideal. The remaining task was seen to be largely technical in nature. It was time for the ideologue to step aside for the social engineer. Through technical expertise, such as that to be provided by the newly developing policy sciences, the task ahead was mainly a matter of fine-tuning the engines of liberal capitalism.[14]

Such ideas began to give rise to a new technocratic creed. Basic to this outlook was the idea that the guidance of complex economic and social processes could be based on the empirical propositions of the social and policy sciences. Drawing primarily on economics and systems analysis, the challenge was to technically employ "objective" scientific information to regulate smoothly the processes of social and political change.[15] These ideas reached their pinnacle in the Great Society of Lyndon Johnson. As a protégé of Roosevelt in the 1930s, Johnson was no stranger to the use of expertise in the formulation of government policy. Indeed, he was deeply committed to the kinds of liberal social reform developed by the policy advisers of the New Deal period. In his own words, in fact, the Great Society was to be the fulfillment of the New Deal legacy.

In much the same way that policy-oriented social scientists served the New Deal, they flourished in nearly every domain of the Johnson administration. Social scientists not only played a major role in two wars—the Vietnam war and the War on Poverty—they also devised and implemented throughout the federal government a comprehensive technocratic system of social planning and budgetary decision making, the Planning, Programming, Budgeting System (PPBS). In his statement introducing this new planning technique, Johnson hailed it as a revolution in policy decision making that would help to plan and coordinate his effort to end poverty in America. It was a high moment in the technocratic movement. To use Moynihan's phrase, it was clear evidence of the "professionalization of reform." [16]

Theodore White went so far as to describe this period as the "Golden Age of the action intellectual." For White it was nothing less than the appearance of a new system of power in American politics. These new intellectuals, acting in concert with political leaders in both the White House and Congress, were the "driving-wheels" of the Great Society. As a new generation of intellectuals with special problem-solving skills, they sought "to shape our defenses, guide our foreign policy, redesign our cities, eliminate poverty, reorganize our schools," and more. These policy professionals represented a "bridge across the gulf between government and the primary producers of really good ideas." The White House served as "a transmission belt, packaging and processing scholars' ideas to be sold to Congress as programs." [17]

Such enthusiasm was also reflected in the influential report issued by the National Academy of Sciences, *Government's Need for Knowledge and Information*. As a paradigm of the liberal methodology of reform in action the report was prepared by a blue-ribbon commission of social scientists and policy experts, and its message was widely disseminated to leading journalists, politicians, and philanthropic institutions. Reflecting on the fact that "the federal government confronts increasingly complex problems in foreign affairs, defense strategy and management, urban reconstruction, civil rights, economic growth and stability, public health, social welfare, and education and training," the report's message was this:

> The decision and actions taken by the President, the Congress, and the executive departments and agencies must be based on valid social and

economic information and involve a high degree of judgment about human behavior. The knowledge and methods of the behavioral sciences, devoted as they are to an understanding of human behavior and social institutions, should be applied as effectively as possible to the programs and policy processes of the federal government.[18]

In short, the social sciences had much to offer policymakers. Indeed, by implication the report can be read to argue that social scientists are better equipped for policy-making than the legislators and citizens who inform the traditional political processes. For this reason the report concluded that the social sciences needed increased financial support from the government to continue developing the theory and methods that were to contribute to better policy design.

The government did in fact contribute vast sums for applied social research. During this period it became customary to speak of policy expertise as a "growth industry." Spurred by the Great Society programs, the expenditures for applied or policy-related social research jumped dramatically. For example, federal agency spending climbed from about $235 million in 1965 to almost $1 billion in the ensuing decade.[19] Such funds brought into existence a number of major research institutions, both public and private, and greatly increased the amount of university-based policy-oriented social research. Accompanying this process was a sizable increase in the number of social scientists. During the decade of the 1960s this group increased by 163%, an increase larger than that registered by any other major occupational group.

No government programs were more closely associated with this policy research than the Great Society's antipoverty programs. It is not easy to generalize about complex governmental programs, but one thing that clearly stands out in the analyses of the antipoverty program is the central role of the "policy intellectual." Throughout the design and implementation of these programs the influence of such experts frequently played an important role in determining the course of events.

To be sure, the precise nature of the policy professional's role has been a sensitive and controversial issue in many circles, especially liberal circles. In part this can be attributed to the neoconservatives' polemical attack on the liberalism of the period. For neoconservatives, the antipoverty effort represented one of the most blatant exercises of new class power. The recognition and analysis of these events remain a basic touchstone upon which their movement was built.

To the neoconservative the critical question is this: Where did the antipoverty programs come from? Prior to the Great Society there was very little interest in poverty in America. As Glazer pointed out, there was nothing behind the War on Poverty "like the powerful political pressure and long-standing support that produced the great welfare measures of the New Deal—Social Security, Unemployment Insurance, Public Welfare, Public Housing."[20] The massive political and ideological support that produced these reforms of the 1930s simply did not exist in the early 1960s. Antecedent to initiation of the antipoverty programs, for example, there were no poverty protest movements per se. To be sure, poor black people were marching in the streets, but *formally* their demands were directed at achieving civil rights, not the elimination of poverty. Comparatively speaking, their numbers were usually small and their cause was far from popular in the nation as a whole. Moreover, there was little political discussion about poverty in the leading intellectual journals; and organized labor, to the degree that it was concerned, had little success in interesting its members in the plight of the poor.

About these facts the neoconservatives are largely correct. There was little political pressure on policymakers to focus on poverty. Indeed, one does not have to take the evidence here from the neoconservatives alone; radical social scientists such as Piven and Cloward make the same point.[21] What does remain controversial, however, is where such political initiatives did come from.

The answer is that they came from inside the White House. Essentially, the main pressure for this massive governmental assault on poverty was initiated *inside* the Kennedy and Johnson administrations. And it is here that the neoconservatives pick up their new class polemic. For them the poverty agenda was the work of a well-staffed cadre of intellectuals—in large part academics—assigned to the job of thinking about social reform. Some were old New Dealers, but many were drawn from the growing ranks of post-World War II social scientists. Together they constituted what one neoconservative called the "Great Society braintrusters."

The brain trust was indeed a significant political reality; about that there is no question. Enjoying easy access to President Johnson, these policy professionals discovered a chief executive who knew not only something about poverty but even a great deal more about politics. In a short period of time—perhaps six months from the time Johnson assumed the presidency in 1964—the array of programs and bills drafted by these policy experts was shaped into a major legislative program and delivered to Congress under the banner of the War on Poverty. The chief lobby for the program was the White House, which sent a parade of officials to speak in favor of the legislation. As Bibby and Davidson put it, "Congress was asked not to draft the war on poverty, but rather to ratify a fully prepared administration program, and invited though hardly encouraged, to propose marginal changes."[22]

Once a poverty bill was enacted, the White House and its policy advisers retained the initiative. For one thing, legislation for the Office of Economic Opportunity was written to assure that it could be managed from the top. This was accomplished by deliberately granting broad political discretion to professional administrators appointed by the White House. For another, the news media were inundated with facts and rhetoric emanating from the White House on the plight of the impoverished one-fifth of the nation, a group until then largely ignored. In conjunction with this effort, the president enlisted a host of private organizations—foundations, professional associations, and corporations—to proselytize the public to support the administration's war.[23] As Piven and Cloward put it, "very rapidly, poverty became a major newsbeat."[24] In a manner patterned on the techniques of the reform methodology, the Johnson administration and its policy elites had reinstated poverty as a major issue for the first time since the New Deal.

Beyond the issue of who initiated the poverty program, much has also been made of the specific influence of professional thinking on the content of poverty programs. Neoconservatives in particular are prone to underscore the Economic Opportunity Act requirement that community action programs be carried out with "maximum feasible participation" of the poor themselves. Many observers have argued that this was one of the most politically important aspects of the entire antipoverty program. Typical of the legislation in general, this provision was inserted into the law in the absence of any significant political demand from the poor. It was introduced, according to neoconservatives, largely because intellectuals of the social welfare profession believed the measure to be indispensable to effective social action. The literature of the field, as they point out, used such terms as the involvement of "indigenous nonprofessionals" to describe the community participation process.[25] Its effect, if not always its purpose, was to bring these nonprofessionals into a working coalition with poverty experts at the expense of elected local and state officials. Neoconservatives are not wrong when they argue that no other single program had less political consensus than this measure. Certainly none generated more political heat.

Conservative Policy Analysis: Politicizing the Political

The War on Poverty ran into many obstacles. For one thing, by the time the antipoverty programs were fully operational, the Vietnam conflict had unexpectedly claimed much of the fiscal dividend that was to be used for poverty programs. Whether or not it is fair to say that the War on Poverty was a failure remains a debated point. (In large part the answer depends on what criteria one uses to evaluate it.) On one point, however, there is little dispute: The program was a disappointment.

The public, in the face of disappointment, began to lose its fascination not only with a war on poverty but with the "action intellectuals" as well. This first began to surface over the conduct of the Vietnam war. As foreign policy experts became more deeply mired in a losing war, major divisions broke out among them. It wasn't long, given internal dissension, before the wisdom of the policy elites was being questioned by the larger public. And this concern soon spread to the antipoverty planners as well.

In the case of the antipoverty programs, the neoconservative movement played a primary role in articulating this dissatisfaction. In the years that followed, neoconservatives succeeded in elevating their critique of the "technocratic takeover" to a central issue in leading journals of political opinion. Indeed, thanks to these writers, it emerged as a major feature of the political dialogue of the 1970s reaching its acme in the election of Ronald Reagan. In this section I shall first examine the nature of their complaint, and then turn to a discussion of its influence on conservative politics and policy analysis.

It is not easy to ferret out the precise nature of the neoconservative complaint against technocracy and its policy science techniques. Invariably it is said that policy scientists, trained in the art of abstract model building, lack experience in practical politics. For another thing, it is frequently said that they are unable (or unwilling) to speak the language of either the policymaker or the ordinary citizen. Still another criticism stresses their failure to produce "usable knowledge." As one writer put it, "Study after study fails to turn up a direct link between data and decisions."[26]

If the analytical payoff of the policy sciences has been so divorced from the decision-making processes, why, then, all the concern about a new elite? Is it not just a matter of time before such a group withers away from ineptitude? The trouble seems to lie elsewhere. For writers such as Kristol and Banfield, it is in reality more a matter of the questions that are being raised than the solutions being proposed.[27] In their view policy scientists exhibit a special talent for finding fault with the American political system. One reason is rooted in the nature of their scientific methodologies; another is traced to the nature of politics in the emerging postindustrial society.

Committed to the ideals of scientific rationality, particularly the principles of technical efficiency, policy scientists are said to suffer from a distorted view of political realities. Against the ideals of technical rationality, nothing in the political world seems to work. Policy problems appear to abound in every area in a system that is described as slow and inefficient. But these are not *real* problems, according to neoconservatives. Political problems are not defined by scientific criteria external to the situation; they are determined by the political actors themselves. In the political world a problem exists only if political groups say that it exists. Perversely, then, the policy sciences busy themselves finding fault where none exists. For Banfield this constitutes a form of "metaphysical madness."[28]

Were it not for the cumulative effect of this phenomenon, the neoconservatives might be content to relegate such complaints to the intellectual realm of methodology. But in the emerging postindustrial society, where knowledge itself becomes a primary political commodity, these practices create pressure for policy change. By bringing to consciousness "problems" that would otherwise remain invisible to both politicians and the public, policy experts become an independent force for social change. The fact that experts tell people that a problem exists sets up a social disequilibrium that can be translated into a political demand for compensatory action.[29] Indeed, according to the neoconservatives, this dynamic has been a key component of the liberal strategy for social reform. The ability to translate such pressures into a political reform agenda has played a key part in the successes of liberal democratic reformers. The Great Society agenda is a primary example.

During eras in which policy intellectuals have managed to elevate themselves to significant positions of influence, conservative politicians and publicists have typically hounded them with harsh criticisms. One of the most common conservative strategies has been to portray them as the agents—witting or unwitting—of creeping socialism in America. Given the experts' precarious position in the political system, this tactic has almost always been sufficient to put them on the defensive, usually followed by a propitious retreat to the safe haven of the "ivory tower."

In the 1970s things started to change. The neoconservatives began to advocate a new strategy to sever the connection between liberal reform and policy expertise. In the face of the newly emerging "knowledge society," they counseled the more traditional conservatives to drop their typically one-sided animosity toward intellectuals in general and urged them to reach out to their own often forgotten conservative brethren in the academic realm. For neoconservatives the time had come to counter expertise on its own terms. A modern conservative movement, they argued, must itself get into the policy expertise business. Because of the inevitable coming of the "new class" phenomenon in a complex technological society, conservatives were exhorted no longer to view the phenomenon as an aberration in the patterns of American politics. According to the neoconservatives, expertise was now here to stay, and it was time for conservatives to train and hire their own experts, what William Simon called the creation of a "conservative counterintelligentsia."[30]

No one was more important in launching this movement than Irving Kristol. For Kristol, the new class had become the "permanent brain trust" of American politics. Having long sought their place in the sun, these new class members were now "in the process of seizing and consolidating" their political position. In view of their critical role in modern government and industry, conservatives must now launch a struggle to win their political allegiances. Kristol put it this way: "If one cannot count on these people to provide political, social, and moral stability—if they do not have a good opinion of our society—how long . . . can that stability and good opinion survive?"[31]

Traditional rhetoric aside, the new men, as Kristol cautioned his fellow conservatives, are not yet "doctrinaire socialists." Although it might prove impossible to convert them to the businessman's free market ideology, in Kristol's view they can nonetheless be educated in the realities of business and economics, particularly the need to maintain a sizable private sector. This requires the development of a new ideology to guide the politics of this emerging class. Steinfels, Berube, and Gittell, in fact, argue that the formation of this ideology has been the primary mission of Kristol and the neoconservative intellectuals generally.[32]

Such ideological work had to be buttressed by an active involvement on the part of the corporate leaders, a role heretofore largely shunned. Specifically, steps had to be taken to establish a working political relationship between business leaders and the conservative members of the new class. Most important, top executives were asked to invest in both conservative-oriented research and educational projects. And this they did. Throughout the 1970s corporate elites financed the development of a multimillion-dollar network of conservative think tanks, research centers, and educational programs.

One of the prime movers behind this effort was William Simon. In his conservative manifesto, *A Time for Truth,* he explained the agenda in these words: "Funds generated by business (by which I mean profits, funds in business foundations and contributions for individual businessmen) must rush by multimillions to the aid of . . . scholars, social scientists, writers and journalists who understand the relationship between political and economic liberty." In addition to supplying money "for books, books, and more books," he urged his fellow businessmen to "cease the mindless subsidizing of colleges and universities whose departments of economics, government, politics, and history are hostile to capitalism" and to redirect these grants to those with a more "pro-business" orientation.[33]

Much of this money has been channeled through a number of powerful conservative think tanks that have come to play a central role in shaping the conservative policy agenda. Most important are the American Enterprise Institute for Public Policy Research, the Hoover Institution, the Heritage Foundation, the Institute for Contemporary Studies, Freedom House, and the Institute of Educational Affairs, each of which produces a steady flow of books, pamphlets, and reports for the media, the public, and the universities.[34] Where for decades the prestigious Brookings Institution served Democratic administrations with both advisers and advice, these newer conservative institutes have become its counterparts for Republican administrations. It is, or course, difficult to measure the influence of these research institutes, but it is clear that they have been very influential in shaping the "Reagan Revolution." For example, it is estimated that more than two-thirds of the Heritage Foundation's policy recommendations were adopted by the Reagan administration in its first term.[35] In short, policy intellectuals were again shaping a presidential agenda. The difference was political: this time they were strictly conservative.

The result of these developments has been a significant politicization of policy expertise. Although policy analysis has always harbored political biases, in the past they have usually been fairly covert (thus providing the traditional claim of value neutrality with the appearance of plausibility). Today, however, many policy professionals openly operate in an adversarial style that makes their political biases quite explicit. Indeed, some policy analysts now readily concede their role as "hired guns." As recently as ten years ago, it would have been difficult to find a project director of a major research institution who would easily acknowledge the ideological character of his or her work. Today that has changed. Take, for instance, the remarks of Stuart Butler of the Heritage Foundation:

> It is naive, in the public policy area, to assume that people don't have an ideological predisposition toward things. Every economist subscribes to a school of economics. . . . Unlike other institutions that pretend ideological neutrality, we're conservative, no bones about it. We don't pretend to be anything different from what we are.[36]

Whereas the basic impetus for this adversarial style was the changing political climate, within the policy sciences themselves there were a number of technical considerations that helped to facilitate a conservative opposition to the traditionally dominant liberal bias. Particularly important was growing recognition of the complexity of the kinds of social problems that the Great Society had set out to resolve, as well as the limitations of the research techniques employed to measure their amelioration. To liberal policy analysts in the mid-1960s, solving social problems often seemed to be merely a matter of commitment and resources, but by the 1970s a more cautious breed of politicians and social scientists saw only complexity and unanticipated consequences. For instance, in the case of poverty research, Henry Aaron put it this way:

> Such puzzles as why earnings are distributed as they are and how policies of various kinds would affect the distribution, or what makes prices and wages increase and how to alter that rate of increase, are at least as complex as any addressed in the physical or biological sciences. Underlying these puzzles are all the variations in human personality and the mystery of its development . . . , the operations of labor markets involving the decisions of millions of businessmen and tens of millions of workers, and the myriad laws that guide and shape behavior, often indirectly and in surprising ways.[37]

In the face of this complexity "any particular set of facts will be consistent with a variety of theories and . . . it may be impossible or excessively costly to acquire the data that would permit analysts to reject false theories."[38] What starts in theory as an objective science of policy analysis thus turns out in practice to be a highly subjective and interpretive mode of inquiry. Given this reality, the political mood of the times, along with the persuasiveness or prestige of the policy advocate, will usually be the primary determinants of the acceptability of a particular policy proposal. In short, as the conservatives have demonstrated, the practice of policy analysis can become very political.

From Policy Innovation to Evaluation

The beginnings of this conservative approach to policy research first appeared during the Nixon administration. In his bid for the presidency, Nixon took advantage of the apparent policy failures associated with both the Vietnam war and the War on Poverty. Throughout his campaign he attacked both of these wars and the efforts of those who helped President Johnson direct them. After the election, the profile of policy intellectuals faded rapidly from center stage. Although Moynihan was recruited to bridge the political gulf between Nixon and the academic community, the political tone of the new administration was set by lawyers and businesspeople.

This is not to suggest that social science disappeared from the political scene. Indeed, retooled to address the conservative agenda, social science played an important role in the Nixon administration. One of the first steps in the ideological transition was a shift of federal spending toward conservative think tanks, particularly the American Enterprise Institute and the Hoover Institution. In fact, the Hoover Institution, traditionally involved in international studies, added a domestic policy analysis program to its activities in order to undertake the assignment.[39]

Under the aegis of this Republican administration and its conservative think tanks, this new orientation applied principally to the analysis of domestic social policy. Essentially the traditional reformist orientation of policy analysis—emphasizing social problem solving and the creative design of public programs—quickly vanished from the scene. In its place emerged an emphasis on a relatively new technique: evaluation research. Where policy analysis focuses largely on the implications of *prospective* public goals, evaluation research is *retrospectively* aimed at the measurement of program outcomes. Moynihan set the tone for this transition by arguing that the role of social science had been misunderstood. "The role of social science," as he put it, "lies not in the formulation of social policy, but in the measurement of its results."[40]

The role of evaluation research had already begun to emerge in the latter part of the Johnson years. It was largely a response to early signs of

disenchantment with a number of social programs. Increasingly prominent in these circles was the idea that many of the programs were
founded upon questionable social science assumptions and findings.
Antipoverty programs, it was pointed out, had been designed under the
constraints of both time and politics. For this reason much of the policy
advice behind their construction was based on the best *available* information. As Wilson put it, a good deal of what passed for "expert advice"
was necessarily based on educated guesses, personal opinion, or ideological assumptions.[41] Evaluation research was in part an attempt to
develop a more scientific basis for policy intervention. Emphasis in the
academy rapidly shifted from analysis to evaluation. Indeed, both on and
off the campus, evaluation research emerged as a growing industry.

Although politicans were seldom interested in the scientific foundations of policy research, they were nonetheless interested in finding out
"what works." Thus as early as 1967, Congress amended some of the
basic poverty legislation to include evaluation requirements. After 1969,
the Nixon administration significantly extended the practice by adding
newer and more stringent mandates for measurement of program outcomes. The primary reason given for the new practice was the sheer
increase in social spending, especially for human resources. Politicians
and the public were increasingly interested in what they were getting for
their money. Social scientists, as evaluation researchers, were to provide
answers.

For the Nixon administration, then, evaluation research was much
more than just another bureaucratic requirement. Essentially it was seen
as a core component of the administration's larger effort to bring management reform to the federal bureaucracy. Toward this end Nixon took
steps to upgrade evaluation and to institutionalize it as a managerial function. The most important step in this direction was the establishment of
the Office of Management and Budget (in place of the Bureau of the Budget). The reorganization was explicitly intended to strengthen the evaluation function by harnessing it to OMB's budgetary power.[42] In the
future programs would have to show results or lose their funding.

Through this institutionalization of evaluation in the budgetary process, OMB took a strong role in monitoring the progress of these evaluations. Ostensibly the agency's interest in these evaluations was largely
financial in nature; it sought to terminate those programs that did
not conform to the administration's conception of cost-effective results.
However, although the growth of social programs was reason enough
to justify a financial interest in program outcomes, the evidence

suggests political motives as well. In short, low-cost social experiments combined with rigid evaluation requirements were often used to subvert or eliminate expensive social programs beneficial to Democratic constituencies.[43]

A number of practices illustrate the administration's political use of evaluation research. One of the most important was the contrast between the evaluation criteria required for War on Poverty programs and those required for other programs aimed at assisting such interests as agribusiness, urban renewal, railroads, and the merchant marine. In the case of the former, every effort was made to demand rigorous results justifying continuation of the program, whereas none of the latter—described as "older, well-established and 'safe' domestic programs"—had such evaluation requirements attached to them. Particularly under scrutiny were those programs aimed at altering the established power structures, such as the community action program with its participation requirements. As Morehouse put it, "Program evaluation requirements were an important by-product of a general policy to bring controversial programs under control."[44]

The administration had chosen just the right methodology for this purpose. A close look at these techniques reveals an underlying bias that conveniently serves a conservative political orientation. The policy analyst (often in the role of planner or advocate) is generally biased toward social change; the evaluation researcher is biased in the opposite direction. Designed to review existing programs, evaluation research tends to be cloaked in skepticism. In part this skepticism is grounded in the nature of the sociopolitical role assigned to evaluators. Because they are asked to supply evidence to justify the continuation of public programs, evaluators are typically cast into a "show-me" attitude that puts the burden of proof on those who wish to continue a particular program.[45] It is essentially the attitude of the budget office. In short, the methodology nicely complements the role.

For the political decision maker, then, an emphasis on evaluation builds a conservative bias into the policy decision processes. But for the evaluation researcher the bias is usually less a function of his or her political orientation than the nature of the methodology itself. As an experimental mode of research, evaluation research—like science in general—is based on tough-minded doubt. Doubt and skepticism are inherent in the very theory upon which experimental science is based, particularly the principle of falsification (implemented through the concept of a "null hypothesis"). Based on falsification (or disproof) rather than proof per se, the experimentally oriented techniques of evaluation research require cautious skepticism. In a world of imperfect knowledge there is always one more variable that must be taken into account; there are experimental conditions that introduce uncontrolled variances; data that are invariably scarce; and so on. Given the fact that rigorous scientific verification remains the official standard for rendering valid policy judgments, the complexity of most policy problems can be marshaled to render an empirical assessment inconclusive, if not wrong.[46] Indeed, in these terms policy evaluations are beyond proof. As illustrated by the much-debated Head Start evaluations, they remain at best exercises in interpretation.[47]

Evaluation findings thus tend to be negative. In a situation in which it is difficult to prove anything, a mixed assessment is about the best one can hope for from evaluation research. Translated from the world of science to political decision making, a mixed assessment is usually enough for the conservative budget analyst to justify putting a program on the fiscal chopping block.

Nowhere was this process more clear than in the evaluation of poverty programs. Far from documenting the successes of these programs, the primary long-term effect of the massive accumulation of poverty-related findings generated by evaluation techniques was corrosion of the ideological faiths upon which these political programs were built.[48] In the mind of the general public, these findings left the impression that there was not a great deal to show for the money that had been spent on poverty programs. Evaluation research could not have provided better ammunition for the conservative opposition. In their eyes the War on Poverty had failed and they had the research to demonstrate their case.

The influence of this conservative orientation was soon to show up in the policy analysis profession more generally. By the mid-1970s the language of the discipline began to reflect this new emphasis. In place of the earlier bias toward liberal advocacy, much of the policy language began to emphasize the needs of public management. One sign of this was the focus of a prestigious new professional association, the Association of Public Policy and Management. The association's publication, *The Journal of Policy Analysis and Management*, is dedicated to bringing together the interests of policy analysts and public managers. In fact, this general concern gave rise to a new and expanding field of study called "knowledge utilization," largely designed to develop linkages between the creation of policy knowledge and its administrative uses.[49]

Cost-Benefit Analysis and Deregulation

Although the development of the conservative approach to policy research first appeared in the Nixon years, not until the Reagan era did it formally emerge as part of the new class challenge. Under Reagan this had been most vividly played out in the administration's efforts to dismantle the federal regulatory system.

Few presidents have been as anti-intellectual as Ronald Reagan. But even Reagan felt obliged to legitimate his policy agenda with an academic theory (in many ways an important political confirmation of the emerging "knowledge society"). Indeed, "Reagonomics" was put forward as the product of a new development in economic theory, "supply-side economics." Essentially, Reagonomics was a turn away from the evaluation of public programs to a more direct assault on their very existence. Beyond a determination of which programs work, the new emphasis was on limiting government programs altogether. The president enunciated his new policy emphasis in these words: "Government is not the solution to our problem . . . government is the problem."[50]

To effectuate this new political thrust, policy science was again called upon to play a special role. Following earlier but limited initiatives by the Carter administration, Reagan sought to employ cost-benefit analysis (CBA) as the major test for determining the future of public programs. Toward this end, cost-benefit analysis was institutionalized in the policy process through the Office of Management and Budget. Its job was to oversee and ensure that all programs pass this analytical test.

Cost-benefit analysis has, of course, long been a standard technique in the policy scientists' tool kit. Unlike evaluation research (designed to measure existing programs), cost-benefit analysis is generally a predecision technique used to compare alternative policy choices. In contrast to other prospective approaches in policy analysis, cost-benefit analysis stresses economy and efficiency over creativity and innovation. Thus, as in the case of evaluation research, conservative politicians have found cost-benefit analysis to be conveniently compatible with their own biases.

Largely a technique developed by economists, the basic logic of cost-benefit analysis is quite simple: It involves totaling up all of the costs and benefits of a policy or program to determine its net value. In practice, however, it is far from a simple operation. Although it has often been helpful in technical decision making (such as Defense Department decisions dealing with military procurement), its uses in the social and political realm have been the subject of a great deal of disagreement, both theoretical and practical. In social policy it has proven quite difficult to quantify policy inputs and outputs. Many have complained that the technique systematically underplays social objectives that cannot easily be measured in quantitative terms.[51]

In spite of these long-standing disputes, the Reagan administration elevated cost-benefit analysis to serve as the *primary* test for making policy decisions. With no shortage of support from conservative think tanks, administration officials persistently argued that such a test was the essence of rational decision making itself. And the message had an impact. In more and more quarters of the policy analysis profession cost-benefit analysis was largely the definition of good policy analysis.[52]

In particular, cost-benefit analysis had been directed at government regulation. Regulation was identified by the Reagan administration as one of the most malevolent aspects of the liberal welfare state. At the heart of the problem was the new class. The regulatory system, in this view, had been captured by new class reformers hostile to traditional capitalist values. As Weaver put it,

> The New Regulation . . . is the social policy of the new class—that rapidly growing and increasingly influential part of the upper-middle class that feels itself to be in a more or less adversary posture vis-à-vis American society and that tends to make its vocation in the public and not-for-profit sectors. Over the past decade it has come to be represented by a broad constellation of institutions—the "public interest" movement, the national press, various professions . . . , government bureaucracies, research institutes on and off campus, the "liberal" wing of the Democratic party, and the like. By means of its regulatory policy, the new class is . . . transferring power from the managerial class to [itself], and from [corporations] to more fully public ones—i.e., to the government.[53]

Essentially the effort to dismantle regulation was designed to undercut the political influence of these new class reformers. The first step, aimed at their purported hostility to capitalist values, was to subvert their use of noneconomic—social and political—criteria in the regulatory decision-making process. This was to be accomplished through the introduction of cost-benefit analysis. By mandating cost-benefit requirements for all regulatory and administrative agencies (a process called the "regulatory impact assessment," or RIA), the administration sought to impose an "economic grid" on all policy decision making.[54] Because of

CBA's basic market bias, its use would impose on the regulatory system a business-oriented decision-making framework that systematically deemphasizes social benefits. In the language of the RIA's architects—namely, conservative economists closely associated with the American Enterprise Institute and the Heritage Foundation—CBA would build the canons of economic rationality into the bureaucracy's incentive system. James Miller candidly described the nature of the system this way:

> The CBA executive order says to them: even if you get a nonconforming proposal past your agency heads, even if you've captured them or just plain fooled them, that proposal is likely to be caught at OMB—and there's not a chance in Hades of your capturing those people. So if you want to get ahead, you're going to have to write new rules and review existing rules in conformance with principles set forth by the President in the executive order. I believe that as internal agency procedures and the mechanisms for centralized review settle into place, agency personnel will voluntarily comply.[55]

Basically what these internal agency procedures were designed to do is impose a business language on policy discourse. Through a requirement that all decisions be explained and justified in terms of costs and benefits, a business bias is implicitly embedded in the deliberation process. Other modes of argumentation, particularly those grounded in the language of the "public interest," are rendered inadmissible—unless, of course, they should happen to pass the cost-benefit test.

Examination of those programs that did manage to demonstrate their cost-effectiveness sheds a revealing light on the politics underlying the administration's use of cost-benefit analysis. For programs or regulatory rules that pass the cost-benefit test, OMB has employed a number of backup tactics. One has been to tie up an undesirable regulatory rule in methodological analysis. As Zinke has argued, the purpose can be either to generate an alternative study with negative findings or merely to stall the implementation of an unacceptable regulation.[56] Because the determination of costs and benefits is frequently tied to a wide range of uncertain assumptions, it is almost always possible to challenge a particular analysis on methodological grounds. This point was underscored by Dr. Morton Corn, director of the Occupational Safety and Health Administration (OSHA) in 1976:

> After arriving at OSHA, I engaged in an indepth consideration of cost-benefit analysis, applying the methodology to the coke oven standard. . . .

With the dose response data at our disposal, various assumptions were used to ring in changes on different methodologies for estimating benefits. The range in values was so wide as to be virtually useless. The conclusion I reached after this exercise was that the methodology of cost-benefit analysis for disease and death effects is very preliminary, and one can almost derive any desired answer.[57]

The point that CBA can be used to justify almost any conclusion is perhaps best illustrated by Russell Settle.[58] Independent of OSHA, Settle studied the agency's 1972 asbestos standard. His conclusion shows that CBA results are in large part determined by policymakers' assumptions, particularly those pertaining to the identification, monetarization, and discounting of future benefits. Employing a wide range of reasonable alternative assumptions, Settle calculated as many as 72 different estimates of the net benefits of OSHA's asbestos standard, from high to low.

In numerous cases OMB was reported to have attempted to assist an agency's ability to generate desirable analytical results by funding efforts to improve available data. For example, in the case of Federal Trade Commission regulations, OMB poured a substantial amount of money into research that assists staff analysts in identifying the *costs* of trade regulations while, at the same time, helping the Environmental Protection Agency to eliminate research that makes it easier to quantify *benefits*.[59]

In other cases where there is fairly clear evidence from the outset that CBA calculations were unlikely to support the administration's preferences, OMB resorted to more direct political tactics. Ample evidence had been assembled to show that OMB, where deemed necessary, tabled its own request for a CBA review. Zinke, for example, points to cases in which the central budget staff squelched various analyses of housing industry subsidies at the Department of Housing and Urban Development (HUD). He quotes one official as saying that in some cases if HUD wanted to carry out a cost-benefit analysis of a particular housing rule, the agency would literally have to fight for the permission to do it.[60]

Cost-benefit analysis, then, had emerged as a major *political* methodology of the Reagan administration. This is not to say that information on the costs and benefits of a public program are not an important—and at times an essential—ingredient for policy decision making. Rather, it is to point out that the cost-benefit technique, like evaluation research or any other methodology, can be only one component of an adequate policy science. Given the full array of normative and empirical data that potentially bear on a policy judgment, to misrepresent one type of data as sufficient is to build bias and distortion into the decision-making process. Perhaps in one sense data can be neutral (and thus speak for themselves), but as soon as they are introduced into a political process, all such claims must be abandoned. Thus, in order to judge a policy methodology and its data, it is essential to know something about the political purposes of those who employ it.

An Alternative Perspective

At this point, the question of new class power, at least as it pertains to the policy scientists, readily yields to a more sophisticated explanation than the sort typically rendered by neoconservatives. Although the purpose here has not been to engage in a formal class analysis, it is important first to put to rest any formal pretentions to which the neoconservatives' new class theory might aspire.

Without belaboring the issue, it is fairly easy to show that the new class thesis at present fails the most critical test of a rigorous class analysis. It is clear, to be sure, that modern policy professionals occupy an important stratum in the advanced capitalist state, and that from this position they perform distinct functions that accord them a unique place in the social class structure. It is, moreover, possible to identify a number of specific characteristics that give policy experts a common class orientation, particularly their generally shared career goals, cultural interests, and common mode of discourse. One should also not overlook the role of their professional organizations in promoting these interests. But these concerns provide insufficient basis for classifying a new class in the *formal* sense of the term. Missing is an essential political orientation.[61] In short, professional policy scientists—and technocrats generally—have yet to set out an independent political position. Thus far, they continue to align themselves with the existing classes, especially the dominant economic and political elites. Indeed, the analysis provided here shows the ways in which the policy professionals' political allegiances are now divided between the liberal and conservative elites of the two major parties. For this reason, it is wrong at present to describe these technocrats as a class per se. Neoconservatives, it is fair to say, have merely appropriated the language of class for their own ideological purposes.

Beyond the class issue, however, neoconservatives have identified an important phenomenon in American politics that must not be overlooked: namely, that modern-day policy professionals play an increasingly important role in the policy-making processes. Indeed, in some cases, they may at certain moments be the prime movers behind a policy agenda, as the War on Poverty experience illustrated. Although policy professionals fell far short of becoming a "new priesthood," it is not inaccurate to speak of the professionalization of reform.

But the neoconservatives go a step too far. It is wrong to characterize this phenomenon as a "technocratic takeover." The discussion in this chapter makes clear the fact that technocrats have not become a dominant elite per se. While technocrats have hardly shunned their new political influence, the neoconservative emphasis on the political machinations of ambitious policy professionals is simplistic and insufficient. As the evidence presented here suggests, a more systematic explanation is required. Such an explanation must be grounded in the politics of a postindustrial society. From this perspective, the rise of the policy professionals would seem to be less a matter of a new and unrepresentative elite conniving for power than a matter of modern ideological and technical realities ushering experts to the fore.

These policy experts, however, continue to play their traditional role: that of serving as functionaries to the power elite. Little, if anything, in the foregoing account would suggest a transformation in the basic political relationship. The principal actors here are still the economic and political leaders of the two ruling parties. With the exception that the conservatives themselves have now strategically entered the technocratic game, the emergent pattern must be seen as a contemporary variant of the long-established patterns of policy expertise.

In cases such as the Great Society, where policy professionals would appear to have stepped beyond their role as functionaries, such expert behavior must be interpreted as something less than political autonomy. What neoconservatives fail to acknowledge is that such behavior only occurs at the discretion of political elites. Policy experts were busy pushing forward antipoverty legislation because Democratic party leaders, particularly President Johnson, sanctioned their role. Without this sanction, these activities would not have taken place.

This is not to deny that the process has conferred a new status on policy experts. Rather, it is to argue that this new role does not represent a *basic* change in the underlying political structure of society. What has begun to change, however, is the *terrain* of politics. In the "knowledge society," expertise has become a key commodity essential for political control.

What does it mean to say that knowledge is becoming the terrain of politics? It is clear, regardless of one's assessment of the postindustrial thesis, that knowledge and expertise now play important roles in mediating policy decisions. Experts may not make the final decisions about policy, but they increasingly serve as intermediaries between elite decision makers and the groups toward which specific policies are aimed. This confers an indirect but significant form of power upon experts. It usually means that, in the name of expert knowledge, policy advisers gain significant influence in shaping the discussion of policy alternatives, if not the specific outcomes. It also means that in some instances experts *broker* political options between elite decision makers and particular interest groups. In those cases in which the experts innovate an option acceptable to elite leaders, they will sometimes even appear to have initiated the policy itself. The antipoverty program is an important example of one such illusion.

The importance of this new terrain is underscored by the neoconservatives' efforts to cultivate their own policy experts. What is more, such efforts tell us a good deal about their understanding of the expert's relation to power. The neoconservatives' strategy, contrary to their rhetoric, is clearly compatible with the conviction that those who have expertise are not necessarily those who control it. Indeed, this chapter has shown that neoconservatives have turned the expert's commodity into an object of political struggle for control of the liberal capitalist state.

The terms of this struggle also reveal a significant ideological flaw in the neoconservative position. Neoconservatives regularly argue that knowledge elites are a threat to democracy. But if this is their primary concern, their solution is scarcely designed to remedy the problem. Indeed, by challenging the Democratic party's use of policy expertise with a counterintelligentsia, they implicitly accept—and approve of— the evolving technocratic terrain. Developing a conservative cadre of policy analysts cannot be interpreted as a measure designed to return power to the people.

Neoconservatives doubtless maintain that *their* policy advisers speak for different political values: Rather than the welfare state and bureaucratic paternalism, conservative experts advocate democracy and free market individualism. Such an argument, however, fails to address the critical issue. As a system of decision making geared toward expert knowledge, technocracy—liberal or conservative—necessarily blocks meaningful participation for the average citizen. Ultimately only those who can interpret the complex technical languages that increasingly frame economic and social issues have access to the play of power. Democratic rhetoric aside, those who nurture a conservative intelligentsia in reality only help to extend an elite system of policy-making.

As we saw earlier, this issue cuts to the core of the technocracy problem.[62] Laird argues that disempowerment of citizens, rather than the political ascendancy of experts, is the defining characteristic of the contemporary technocracy. In his view, the impact of technocracy has too often been judged in terms of the technocrat's rise vis-à-vis elite power-holders. The consequent failure to find technocrats emerging as a cohesive ruling elite has thus led many to underplay the importance of expertise. This, Laird argues, misses the crucial point. For him, the question is not so much who gains power but who loses it. In these terms, technocracy leads to a clear and unmistakable consequence: the shift of power away from citizens.

This conclusion, however, should not permit us to neglect altogether the technocrats' relationship to the power elites. The fact that technocrats have not become a cohesive ruling elite must not allow us to overlook the influence that accrues to them in an evolving information society. While such power is more subtle than the traditional forms of political power, and thus more difficult to measure, a convergence of contemporary technocratic roles and ideologies surely portends a continuing increase in the experts' political status. Indeed, neoconservativism appears to have itself become one such ideology. As Steinfels, Berube, and Gittell argue, neoconservativism is at base an elitist ideology aimed at promoting a new group of conservative technocrats. The result, as we saw, has been the rise of right-wing think tanks and the use of policy techniques more compatible with conservative biases. In the face of such realities, it would be a mistake to write off the technocrats' position in the political hierarchy. They may not become dominant counterelites in the near future, but expert politics will doubtless play an increasing role in the elite decision processes.

Finally, what are the implications of this analysis for the policy analysis profession and its principal standard of conduct, value neutrality? Policy experts are not entirely naive when it comes to the subject of political influence. The policy literature is filled with references concerning the influence of partisan politics on analysis. The implications of the discussion here, however, suggest that the standard professional perspective on the problem is basically one-sided.

Typically, the professional literature focuses on the politician's misuse or abuse of the policy expert's data. The analyst, by and large, is portrayed as a relatively impartial evaluator struggling against the pressure of partisan politics. Underplayed, if not altogether missing, is a sense of the degree to which the policy expert can (and often does) complicitly join the political fray. Rarely does the literature concede the kind of involvement portrayed in the analysis of the Great Society experience and its aftermath. Not only do we see the ways in which policy professionals—both liberal and conservative—commit themselves to particular politicians and ideologies, we also become aware of the ways in which both the techniques and the methodological assumptions of the discipline periodically shift to accommodate changing political winds. Although the profession continues to sell policy analysis as an applied science dedicated to an impartial pursuit of practical knowledge, in reality it is clear that the discipline's public image and methodological approaches are significantly shaped by external political influences. Indeed, we have seen here that the practice of policy analysis, if not the discipline, is increasingly adopting an adversarial orientation.[63] In this light it is not surprising to learn that some writers have begun to identify a new type of expert role on the political landscape: the "policy entrepreneur." The policy entrepreneur, as Polsby explains, is an expert who not only develops a policy idea but also actively works with interest groups and politicians to promote its adoption.[64] With the rapid growth of competing think tanks, such policy entrepreneurship is becoming increasingly prominent.[65]

Clearly, this advocacy role requires more attention than it is getting in the professional literature. Not only does it have profoundly significant implications for our understanding of the policy expert's role, it also raises very important questions about the nature of policy analysis training. Until these issues are addressed in the context of actual policy analysis practices, the discipline's self-proclaimed impartiality can only serve as a professional ideology that obscures the expanding power of the policy expert.

Coming to grips with these issues requires that we recognize the policy science movement to be, like any other scientific or professional movement, an organizational enterprise with interests beyond the production and dissemination of knowledge. Like other professional organizations, it is subject to the political pressures of its times, including the view of itself that it both creates and propounds. If we are to learn anything from the experiences reported here, it is this: An adequate understanding of the policy professions must not be limited to the methodological discussions that too often serve to define the subject.

Only when these methodological issues are couched in the larger political context that surrounds them can we begin to grasp the role of policy expertise.

Notes

1. Peter Steinfels, *The Neoconservatives* (New York: Simon & Schuster, 1979); and Lewis A. Coser and Irving Howe, eds., *The New Conservatives* (New York: Quadrangle, 1973).

2. Mary O. Furner, *Advocacy and Objectivity: A Crisis in the Professionalization of American Social Science: 1865–1905* (Lexington: University of Kentucky Press, 1975); and Richard Kirkendall, *Social Scientists and Farm Politics in the Age of Roosevelt* (Columbia: University of Missouri Press, 1966).

3. Frank Fischer, *Politics, Values, and Public Policy: The Problem of Methodology* (Boulder: Westview, 1980).

4. One of the early, influential statements of this position was advanced by John R. Commons. See Kirkendall, *Social Science and Farm Politics*, pp. 3–5.

5. Barry Karl, "Presidential Planning and Social Science Research: Mr. Hoover's Experts," in *Perspectives in American History,* vol. 111 (Cambridge, MA: Charles Warren Center for Studies in American History), pp. 347–409.

6. See, for example, Daniel Bell, *The Coming of Post-Industrial Society* (New York: Basic Books, 1973).

7. Corrine L. Gilb, *Hidden Hierarchies* (New York: Harper & Row, 1966); and on the "professional state," see Frederick C. Mosher, *Democracy and the Public Service* (New York: Oxford University Press, 1968).

8. Gene M. Lyons, *The Uneasy Partnership* (New York: Russell Sage, 1969).

9. Alvin W. Gouldner, *The Coming Crisis of Western Sociology* (New York: Avon, 1970), p. 500. As Gouldner puts it, "In the context of the burgeoning Welfare-Warfare State . . . liberal ideologues serve . . . to increase the centralized control of an ever-growing Federal Administrative Class and of the master institutions on behalf of which it operates. Liberal sociologists have thus become the technical cadres of national governance . . . [T]he liberal technologue . . . produces information and theories that serve to bind the poor and the working classes both to the state apparatus and to the political machinery of the Democratic party . . . "; Noam Chomsky, *American Power and the New Mandarin* (New York: Vintage, 1969); and Robert Goodman, *After the Planners* (New York: Simon & Schuster, 1971).

10. See Steinfels, *Neoconservatives.*

11. Ibid., especially chap. 10.

12. The term *technocratic takeover* is used by Samuel H. Beer, "In Search of a New Public Philosophy," in Anthony King, ed., *The New American Political System* (Washington, DC: American Enterprise Institute for Public Policy Research, 1978), pp. 44–55.

13. Edward C. Banfield, "Policy Science as Metaphysical Madness," in Robert A. Goldwin, ed., *Bureaucrats, Policy Analysts, Statesmen: Who Leads?* (Washington, DC: American Enterprise Institute for Public Policy Research, 1980), p. 5.

14. See Chaim I. Waxman, ed., *The End of Ideology Debate* (New York: Funk and Wagnalls, 1968).

15. Jürgen Habermas, *Legitimation Crisis* (Boston: Beacon, 1975).

16. Daniel P. Moynihan, "The Professionalization of Reform," *The Public Interest,* Fall 1965, pp. 6–16.

17. Theodore H. White, "The Action Intellectuals," *Life,* June 9, June 16, June 23, 1967.

18. National Academy of Sciences, *Government's Need for Knowledge and Information* (Washington, DC: Government Printing Office, 1968).

19. See Clark C. Abt, *Toward the Benefit/Cost Evaluation of U.S. Government Social Research* (Cambridge, MA: Abt Associates, 1976).

20. Cited by Moynihan, "Professionalization of Reform," p. 7.

21. Frances Fox Piven and Richard A. Cloward, *Regulating the Poor* (New York: Pantheon, 1971).

22. John Bibby and Roger Davidson, *On Capitol Hill* (New York: Holt, Rinehart & Winston, 1967), p. 236.

23. Elinor Graham, "Poverty and the Legislative Process," in *Poverty as a Public Issue,* ed. Ben B. Seligman (New York: Free Press, 1965), pp. 243–44.

24. Piven and Cloward, *Regulating the Poor,* p. 258; and Sar Levitan, *The Great Society's Poor Law* (Baltimore: Johns Hopkins University Press, 1969), p. 94.

25. Daniel P. Moynihan, *Maximum Feasible Misunderstanding: Community Action in the War on Poverty* (New York: Free Press, 1969); and Nelson W. Polsby, *Political Innovation in America* (New Haven, CT: Yale University Press, 1984), pp. 128–45.

26. Banfield, "Policy Science as Metaphysical Madness," pp. 6–7.

27. Ibid., p. 18; and Irving Kristol, "Where Have All the Answers Gone?" *National Forum* LXIX, no. 1 (1979): 12–14.

28. Banfield, "Policy Science as Metaphysical Madness," p. 1.

29. Robert E. Lane, "The Decline of Politics and Ideology in a Knowledgeable Society," *American Sociological Review* 31 (October 1966): 662.

30. William Simon, *A Time for Truth* (New York: Reader's Digest Books, 1979).

31. Irving Kristol, *Two Cheers for Capitalism* (New York: Basic Books, 1978), pp. 141–45.

32. Maurice R. Berube and Marilyn Gittell, "In Whose Interest Is the 'The Public Interest'?" *Social Policy* (May–June 1970), pp. 5–6; and Steinfels, *Neoconservatives,* p. 279.

33. Simon, *A Time for Truth.*

34. John S. Saloma, *Ominous Politics: The New Conservative Labyrinth* (New York: Hill & Wang, 1984), especially chap. 2.

35. See "Bad Advice from Heritage," *Public Administration Times,* January 1, 1985, p. 2; and Charles L. Heatherly, ed., *Mandate for Leadership: Policy Management in a Conservative Administration* (Washington, DC: Heritage Foundation, 1981).

36. Quoted in Martin Tolchin, "Working Profile: Stuart M. Butler," *New York Times,* July 22, 1985, p. 10.

37. Henry J. Aaron, *Politics and the Professors: The Great Society in Perspective* (Washington, DC: Brookings Institution, 1978), p. 57.

176 THE POLITICAL USES OF EXPERTISE

39. James Everett Katz, *Presidential Politics and Science Policy* (New York: Prae-ger, 1978), p. 204.

40. Moynihan, *Maximum Feasible Misunderstanding*, p. 193.

41. James Q. Wilson, "Social Science and Public Policy: A Personal Note," in Lawrence E. Lynn, Jr., ed., *Knowledge and Policy: The Uncertain Connection* (Washington, DC: National Academy of Sciences, 1978), pp. 82–92.

42. Larry Berman, *The Office of Management and Budget and the Presidency, 1921–1979* (Princeton, NJ: Princeton University Press, 1979), pp. 105–30.

43. Katz, *Presidential Politics,* pp. 200–205.

44. Thomas A. Morehouse, "Program Evaluation: Social Research Versus Public Policy," *Public Administration Review,* November/December 1972, p. 873.

45. Allen Schick, "From Analysis to Evaluation," *American Academy of Political and Social Science Annals,* 394 (1971): 57–71.

46. Mark H. Moore, "Statesmanship in a World of Particular Substantive Choices," in Goldwin, *Bureaucrats, Policy Analysts, Statesmen*, p. 33.

47. Frank Fischer, "Critical Evaluation of Public Policy: A Methodological Case Study," in *Critical Theory and Public Life*, ed. John Forester (Cambridge: MIT Press, 1986), pp. 231–57.

48. Aaron, *Politics and the Professors*, p. 159.

49. On "knowledge utilization," see the journal *Knowledge: Creation, Diffusion, Utilization*, published by Sage Publications.

50. John Schwarz, *America's Hidden Success* (New York: Norton, 1983), p. 22.

51. See, for example, Steven Kelman, *Cost-Benefit Analysis and Environmental Regulation: Politics, Ethics, and Methods* (New York: Conservation Foundation, 1982).

52. For a spirited defense of this position, see John McAdams, "The Anti-Policy Analysts," *Policy Studies Journal* 13, no. 1 (1984): 91–102.

53. Paul H. Weaver, "Regulation, Social Policy and Class Conflict," *The Public Interest* 50 (Winter 1978), p. 59.

54. Susan J. Tolchin, "Cost-Benefit Analysis and the Rush to Deregulate: The Use and Misuse of Theory to Effect Policy Change," *Policy Studies Review* 4, no. 2 (November 1984): 213.

55. "Deregulation HQ: An Interview on the New Executive Order with Murray L. Weidenbaum and James C. Miller, III," *Regulation*, March/April 1981, p. 16.

56. Robert Clifford Zinke, "Cost-Benefit Analysis and Administrative Decision-Making: A Methodological Case-Study of the Relation of Social Science to Public Policy" (Ph.D. diss., New York University, Department of Public Administration, 1984).

57. Cited in Office of Technology Assessment, *Preventing Illness and Injury in the Workplace* (Washington, DC: Government Printing Office, 1985), p. 283.

58. Russell Franklin Settle, "The Welfare Economics of Occupational Safety and Health Standards" (Ph.D. diss., University of Wisconsin, Department of Economics, 1974).

59. Nancy DiTomaso, "The Managed State: Governmental Reorganization in the First Years of the Reagan Administration," in *Research in Political Sociology*, ed. Richard G. Braungart and Margaret M. Braungart (Greenwich, CT: JAI Press, 1985), pp. 141–66.

60. Zinke, "Cost-Benefit Analysis," p. 257.

61. This argument draws on Stanley Aronowitz, "The Professional-Managerial Class or Middle Stata," in *Between Labor and Capital*, ed. Pat Walker (Boston: South End Press, 1979), pp. 213–42.

62. Frank Laird, "Technocracy Revisited: Knowledge, Power and the Crisis in Energy Decisions," *Industrial Crisis Quarterly* 3, no. 1 (1990).

63. On some implications of this adversarial style, see Jeanne Guillemin and Irving Louis Horowitz, "Social Research and Political Advocacy: New Stages and Old Problems in Integrating Science and Values," in *Ethics, The Social Sciences, and Policy Analysis,* ed. Daniel Callahan and Bruce Jennings (New York: Plenum, 1983), pp. 187–211.

64. Polsby, *Political Innovation in America,* pp. 167–74.

65. On think tanks and policy entrepreneurship, see Philip Boffey, "Heritage Foundation: Success in Obscurity," *New York Times*, November 17, 1985, p. 62. Also, see Edwin J. Feulner, "Ideas, Think-Tanks and Governments," *The Heritage Lectures*, no. 51 (Washington, DC: Heritage Foundation, 1986).

PART IV

TECHNOCORPORATISM: THEORY AND METHODS

From the political, social, and human points of view, this conjunction of state and technique is by far the most important phenomenon of history. It is astonishing to note that no one, to the best of my knowledge, has emphasized this fact. It is likewise astonishing that we still apply ourselves to the study of political theories or parties which no longer possess anything but episodic importance, yet we bypass the technical fact which explains the totality of modern political events.

—JACQUES ELLUL

Systems theory has emancipated itself from both reason and domination. . . . I do not see how the living conditions of mankind could be essentially changed or how human beings could educate themselves by discussing the truth of arguments which give validity to domination . . . and by trying to find a reasonable concensus on this matter. . . . This question [is] . . . "out of step" with reality.

—NIKLAS LUHMANN

This part of the book, "Technocorporatism: Theory and Methods," explores the technocratic theory and methodologies associated with a powerful political ideology in the postindustrial United States, or "technocorporatism" as it is called here. The discussion in Chapter 7 first describes this new paradigm as a response to specific economic and political circumstances thwarting the state-corporate system, such as economic decline and the need for technological innovation, the expansion of interest-group demands and the failures of the welfare state, energy shortages, and the environmental crisis. It then turns to the political structures and technocratic strategies inherent to the development of the "technocorporate state." They are examined in the context of "reindustrialization" in the United States and the political movement to institute an industrial (or postindustrial) policy, largely a euphemism for economic planning. The chapter concludes with an illustration that underscores the contemporary political significance of technocorporatism.

Chapter 8 focuses on the uses of techocratic methodologies in the central guidance of technocorporate systems. In particular, it outlines the ways in which the consummate technocratic methodology, the systems approach, analytically models the managerial and planning requirements of the technocorporate state. Systems theorists and planners are shown to provide two essential contributions to the project: (1) an apolitical "scientific" legitimation for the political transformation said to be essential for economic revitalization; and (2) specific information technologies designed for centralized postindustrial planning.

Taken together, these interconnected political and technocratic movements give rise to an elitist conception of "planning politics" that offers little room for democratic participation. Very clearly this new push for societal transformation elevates the following question to the top of the contemporary agenda in political theory: What is the relation of democratic participation to expertise? Unfortunately, it has yet to receive the attention it requires. These two chapters are designed to help widen the discussion in this direction.

7

Apolitical Politics:
The Theory of the Technocorporate State

Technocracy, as the preceding chapters make clear, has a long established place in social and political theory. But never before has it had the kind of significance that the contemporary "postindustrial" or "information" society now confers upon it. The purpose of this chapter is to explore the technocratic theory and practices evolving with this new societal formation, or what has been called "technocorporatism." Focusing specifically on the concept of the technocorporate state, the discussion examines the thought systems and techniques that both guide and legitimate the practices of the technocratic decision makers, or technostructure, of this emerging state formation.

Limited to the United States, the specific objective is to offer a general outline of the political and technocratic functions of the technocorporate state. Emphasis is placed on the economic and political circumstances that shape the evolution of the technocorporate state and its practices, the particular structures inherent in its development, and the strategies designed for its central guidance.

Technocratic Theory and the Technostructure

We begin with a discussion of the core theoretical component of contemporary technocratic theory, the "technostructure."[1] Essentially a product of the managerial function and its worldview, the technostructure constitutes the basic decision-making apparatus of the modern organization.[2] It consists of the policy planners, managerial specialists, computer analysts, social scientists, and technologists responsible for processing the information essential to the stable and efficient operation of modern large-scale organizations, in both the private and the public sectors. As the "guiding intelligence" of such organizations, the technostructure is a managerial response to modern "technological imperatives" and the organizational exigencies to which they give rise.[3] Employing the techniques of management and planning, the technostructure strives to overcome the barriers—uncertainties, limitations, and interferences—that impede organizational success (measured in terms of both profits and institutional growth).

In a society dominated by large, technologically based institutions, the technostructure thus commands a substantial degree of influence and discretion in the managerial processes. Although the degree of this influence remains the subject of debate, there can be no question that it is growing. Indeed, the ideas of the technostructure now have a powerful force of their own. It is fair to describe its assumptions and worldview—largely taken here to be synonymous with technocratic theory—as one of the most prominent ideologies of our time.[4]

Fundamental to the ideology of this technocratic group is a deep-seated aversion to political decision making and the proliferation of interest groups that seek to influence the outcomes of the contemporary decision processes. As we have already seen, one of the most imposing challenges to the management and planning of large-scale economic and technological development is the proliferation of political groups with an interest in the process. While some planners hold out the possibility of developing a participatory approach to planning (a topic we turn to in Chapter 14), technocrats are not to be found among them. For them, opening the planning process to politics is equivalent to courting Pandora's tragedy. Interest groups, from their perspective, are the virtual enemy of a systematic (or "scientific") approach to planning and management. Technocratic strategies, as we shall see, are in fact promoted to short-circuit this troublesome political tension. In essence, such strategies are designed to supplant political bargaining and compromise with technically rational decision-making procedures, or what has been called "methodological decision making." The task, in the ideal, is to translate—or redefine—political problems into administrative issues amenable to technical solutions. Political decisions are thus to be made on the basis of technical calculation rather than "untutored" value preferences. Oxymoronically, the approach has aptly been described as an "apolitical" form of politics—or, more succinctly, "apolitical politics."[5]

Although the contemporary state has yet to assume a technocratic form per se, the outlines of an emergent technocratic infrastructure are clearly visible. Much of this infrastructure is still confined to the administrative bureaucracies of the state; it is here that technocratic ideology has its greatest influence and support (no small consideration given the continuing expansion of the administrative state vis-à-vis the other branches of government). But the technocratic thrust is by no means limited to the administrative sector. With the assistance of powerful elites—particularly those closely associated with the top management of the dominant corporations—technocratic organizational ideologies are being elevated to serve as a theory of society itself, albeit an "organizational" or "managed" society.[6]

At the level of society, technocratic theory and strategy are becoming an essential component of the present-day state-corporate system. They are being used to shape a new political formation, which, for lack of a more felicitious term, can be described as the "technocorporate state." Even though this new formation is still very much in its developmental stages, and is thus difficult to specify with a high degree of precision, its primary technocratic features are clear: a stronger measure of central planning and the depoliticization of decision making, both of which are carried out through limitations on interest-group processes and a greater reliance on policy experts. Indeed, the technocorporate state may well portend a new plateau in the evolution of technocratic governance. For this reason, it is essential to come to grips with the basic ideas and methods that guide its development.

Technocorporate Theory: Complexity and Depoliticization

Focusing on the United States, we present in this section an outline of contemporary technocorporate theory. Because there is no single source of such theory, the sketch is loosely drawn from various technocratic perspectives. As a synthesis, its purpose is essentially illustrative. The place to begin is with the technostructure's relationship to modern American capitalism.

At the risk of oversimplification, three basic characteristics of advanced capitalism can be singled out as fundamental to the development of contemporary technocorporate theory: capitalism's high degree of technological complexity, the growth of organizational interdependence, and the rapid rate of economic and technological change.[7] In sharp contrast to early capitalism, characterized by a sphere of freely competing entrepreneurs, twentieth-century corporate capitalism gives rise to a system of large-scale and interlocking organizations that substantially restrict the movement of economic and political actors. Indeed, in the language of the economist, the system takes the form of a "sunk cost." Once in place, it generates its own risks and uncertainties, problems and commitments. The result is a simple but inescapable reality: Any attempt to "tinker with the system"—not to mention radically change it—is fraught with dangerous destabilizing consequences. In the face of these circumstances, the task of governance is more and more reduced to "keeping the machine running." The organizational system, in short, substantially narrows the realm open to political and administrative choice and begins to supplant consensually derived goals with its own "technical imperatives."[8] Economic guidance, in the process, becomes less an issue for political deliberation than one of improved management and planning. Herein lie the implications for political-economic governance; technocorporate theory steps forward to address them.

Technocorporate theory and the technostructure, then, supply modern technological capitalism with a system of governance more suited to the realities that it confronts. The theory is first an attempt to explain the need for this new system, and, second, an effort to provide the information technologies required for its central management and planning. Before turning to the theory itself, however, it is important to clarify the most important defining characteristic of the technocratic project. It is not the call for central management and planning per se that defines contemporary technocratic theory. Indeed, in an age of complex technologies a wide range of groups have come to accept the need for some form of central management and planning. What separates the technocrats from other groups is their fundamentally apolitical approach to these processes.[9]

The need for more rigorous management and planning is recognized to pose a fundamental challenge to American politics. The principal barrier to effective planning is seen to be nothing less than the cornerstone of American democracy, the pluralist system of interest-group politics. For technocrats, the development of a rationally coherent plan is either hin-

dered or blocked by the aggressive competition of self-interested groups
vying for society's scarce resources, or what Huntington has called the
contemporary "democratic distemper."[10] The solution has to be radical;
it must bring about a dramatic curtailment of interest-group politics.

In the United States, talk of the need for such a political restructuring
was especially prominent in the 1970s. Typically, such discussions were
grounded in the doomsday language that political and economic elites
evoked to describe the precarious conditions threatening the country's
future. Among the standard topics, in both the liberal and the conservative presses, were the decline of growth, high levels of unemployment,
accelerating inflation rates, the crisis of the welfare state, the stagnation
of the world economy, the dangers of nuclear war, terrorism, and the
demise of legitimate authority. Given the "crisis-prone" character of the
modern state, statecraft itself is seen to be largely an exercise in "crisis
management."[11]

It is in response to the incoherence and instabilities of this system that
contemporary political writers increasingly speak of the "ungovernabil-
ity" of American government.[12] The system, they argue, is overloaded
with interest-group demands, often attributed to an uncontrolled rise in
welfare state "entitlements."[13] Moreover, this "systems overload" has
occurred at a time when the economy was beginning to slow down significantly. Some began to describe the American system as a "zero-sum"
society (i.e., a system in which nobody can gain without doing it at the
expense of someone else).[14]

Little needs to be said to underscore the political import of this thesis:
Interest-group politics has long been accepted as the basic mode of policy formation in Western democratic regimes. Conventionally described
as a pluralistic process of "disjointed" and "incremental" decision making, interest-group bargaining has in fact been celebrated as the essence
of wisdom in the realm of political practice.[15] Indeed, for many of
pluralism's theorists anything more than an incremental system of
"piecemeal" change is seen to fall beyond the capabilities of human intelligence.[16] Political decision making under pluralism, in short, is a form
of "bounded rationality" limited by the processes of interest-group bargaining. Such bargaining establishes fairly strict boundaries within
which economic and social planning must confine itself. Under these
circumstances, planning can at best be partial in nature. As one writer
explains, "Planning can only be a piecemeal affair of making relatively
small adjustments."[17]

Even though incrementalism has been much celebrated by American theorists, it has suffered considerable criticism from many quarters during the past two decades. In an economy dominated by large-scale technological developments, incrementalism often appears to be an inadequate mode of decision making.[18] With the troubling return of economic decline, along with the threat of social malaise accompanying it, the need to replace this "outmoded" decision process strikes many as all the more urgent. The result has been a growing interest in "restructuring" the political system. Usually this takes the form of a call for the depoliticization of basic decision-making processes and the introduction of more comprehensive forms of planning.[19]

The policy issue that has most forcefully raised this concern in recent years has been that of "reindustrializing" the American economy.[20] In reaction to economic decline and the crises associated with it, political reformers across the spectrum have begun to propose the outlines of a new structural framework for postindustrial renewal. For the most part, it has been put forward in the name of "industrial policy," virtually a code word for national economic planning.

To be sure, such writers do not seek the elimination of interest-group processes altogether. Rather, they question the wisdom of the liberal pluralist philosophy that justifies their privileged position in American politics and propose a wholesale restructuring of the interest-group process itself. The remedy is to be found in the relative subordination of interest-group demands to a centralized system of decision making. In political terms, the general contours of this new system are largely "corporatist" in nature.[21] Corporatism, or, more precisely, "neocorporatism" in contemporary terminology, is seen as the essential condition for the introduction of a more comprehensive form of planning. One can see this combining of corporate political structures with a more comprehensive form of planning as an evolving theory of a "technocorporate state."[22] Writing in a somewhat different context, Heydebrand has referred to the convergence of these ideas as "technocratic corporatism."[23] Marin, analyzing the Austrian power structure, has similarly developed a concept of "technocorporatism."[24] We turn in the next section to a brief examination of the basic structural framework of this theoretical formulation.

Technocorporate Structures

Corporatism, or more typically "neocorporatism," is today a prominent feature of a number of European countries, especially West Germany, Sweden, Austria, and the Netherlands. As a mode of governance, it is concerned primarily with the "macro-structuring" of the primary economic and political interest-group processes in society.[25] In both Europe and the United States the approach, or some form of it, is increasingly advocated in elite political and intellectual circles as the appropriate political structure for the postliberal state-corporate complex. As a political theory, it is explicitly designed to confront the problem of aggressive interest-group competition. Essentially, it involves a strategy of integrating proliferating interest groups into larger political associations, which, in turn, do their bidding for them at the state level. Schmitter describes corporatism in these terms:

> [It is] a system of interest group representation in which the constituent units are organized into a limited number of singular, compulsory, non-competitive, hierarchially ordered and functionally differentiated categories, recognized or licensed (if not created) by the state and granted a deliberate representational monopoly within their respective categories in exchange for observing certain controls on their selection of leaders and articulation of demands and supports.[26]

At the top level of the corporatist structure is a small group of horizontally integrated elites. They constitute the dominant interest associations in society (corporate business, the military, the scientific establishment, professional groups, and major labor unions, to name the most significant). Rather than relying on traditional interest-group strategies, particularly lobbying and pressure tactics, these groups derive power from the institutionalization of privileged relationships in the state policymaking processes.[27]

Traditional interest groups, by contrast, are relegated to a secondary level of the political structure, where their link to the policy-making arenas is mediated through the vertical structures of the political matrix. Confined to these carefully organized vertical structures of the hierarchy, the upward flow of interest-group demands is much more indirect and limited. Interest-group politics, in the process, loses its traditional policy-making function. Instead of forging policy per se, traditional interest groups serve a secondary "feedback" function for top-level decision makers in the privileged center.[28]

Basic to the corporatist formulation is also the systematic integration of government and the economy. Manifestations of such interdependencies are already clearly evident in Western state-corporate systems. For example, in numerous areas of government regulation, planning, and tax policy, it is now difficult to discern practical distinctions between "public" and "private" interests. Moreover, it becomes increasingly difficult to find administrative organizations that fall squarely into one or the other of the two sectors. Corporate military defense contracting is the most commonly cited example.[29]

This linking of the two sectors gives rise to an elaborate network of organizations cutting across all levels of government and the economy (regional, national, and international). The political economy, in short, consists of a network of controlling and subordinate organizations, each commanded by elites who attempt to extend their domains of control. Insofar as these "interorganizational" arrangements have vertical as well as horizontal dimensions, they give the technocorporate complex a matrixlike structure.[30]

These corporatist systems, then, tend to be inherently bureaucratic.[31] In this respect, one of their primary manifestations is what Scott and Hart call the "national managerial system."[32] Fundamentally elitist in structure, it constitutes a vast set of interlocking management systems designed to coordinate and plan the technocorporate apparatus. Top-level managers in this network frequently move freely from organization to organization in both public and private sectors. Their common identity is based on the similarity of their positions, power, shared values, and skills. In short, they operate at the top levels of the organizational structures, speak the same managerial language, and pursue the same types of strategies (increasingly technocratic in nature).

This network of managerial elites is the core component of what can be called the "central guidance cluster" or "societal guidance system" of the state-corporate complex.[33] It is at this level that we find technocratic planners and other experts working in close cooperation with elite political leaders. The planners' task is twofold: first, to organize data about resources and needs, and, second, to assist political leaders in coordinating such data with information and demands that come up the political hierarchies. It is this act of coordination that constitutes the essence of corporatism generally; it is the reliance on technical data and analyses— both real and ideological—that constitutes the essence of technocorporatism specifically.

The result is a uniquely insulated and highly depoliticized "consultative mechanism" for governmental policy-making. Rather than permitting interest groups to negotiate their own differences (with public policy emerging as the outcome of these forces), the central guidance cluster organizes their political interests and demands according to the established priorities of the state-corporate complex. Who sets these priorities? It is the dominant political leaders with the assistance of the expert advisers.

Such elites frequently meet in a variety of contexts, but one site in particular has become of critical importance, namely, the policy-planning organizations that now serve both the liberal and the conservative camps.[34] Concerned with the "troubling trajectory of crises" that have plagued America in the 1970s and 1980s, these research organizations are engaged in the working out of ideological and policy positions designed to facilitate political-economic transformation. In Peschek's words, they are not only "objective producers of research and recommendations, but also active agents linked to power blocks and policy currents, reflecting and in turn shaping ideological shifts and political regroupings in a time of momentus transformations."[35] They serve, in short, as key policy instruments for the central guidance cluster of the modern state-corporate system. Although they vary in their ideological orientations, there is a remarkable convergence in their turn to technocratic and corporatist strategies. Indeed, it is in such planning organizations as the Trilaterial Commission, the Brookings Institution, and the American Enterprise Institute that the basic precepts of technocorporate strategy are being worked out.

Technocorporate Strategy:
A Contemporary Example

While the foregoing discussion focuses on the elements of a theory, in the United States today this technocorporate model is much more than just a theory. Not only is it advanced as the foundation for economic reform by influential spokespersons in current policy debates, it has in fact provided a rationale for the response to a major government crisis. It is to this example that we briefly turn in this final section of the chapter.

Specifically, the example concerns the issue of national economic "reindustrialization." In reaction to economic decline since the mid-1970s, political writers across the spectrum have begun to propose variants of technocorporatism as the structural model for postindustrial renewal. For the most part these proposals proliferated during the Carter administration as part of the search for an "industrial policy."

Although the Reagan administration quickly took the idea of industrial policy off the White House agenda, the ideas and concepts are still very much alive. They have remained a key element in liberal economic circles, even if the rhetoric has been somewhat muted to suit the political tenor of the times. (In fact, industrial policy emerged as a centerpiece of Governor Dukakis's bid for the Democratic party's presidential nomination.[36]) Moreover, it reemerged in conservative circles as a strategy for "industrial competitiveness," a term designed to avoid the specific planning connotations conveyed by "industrial policy."[37] Even more interesting, however, is the contention that the Reagan administration quietly pursued its own industrial policy. By the end of the president's second term, writers such as Reich could point to a well-developed governmental economic policy designed to actively encourage specific industries and technologies.[38]

The participants in the industrial policy debate, on both the left and the right, accept the need for planning as a given in the modern high-tech economy. Their differences revolve around the *form* such planning should take. The most influential of the proposals comes from a group of investment bankers and business leaders. Urgently advocating what *Business Week* calls "centralized government economic planning," the proposals of this group are firmly grounded in technocratic thinking.[39] The best known of these writers is Felix Rohatyn, a millionaire investment banker who has become a primary spokesman for the group. A frequent adviser to Democratic party politicians, no one better exemplifies the contemporary technocorporate push than Rohatyn.[40]

For Rohatyn, like technocratic theorists in general, the American economy is "out of control."[41] The current "crisis" rests on a variety of problems: the decline of the manufacturing sector, the collapsing economic infrastructure of the cities, budgeting deficits, and the need for increased high-technology investments, among others. Neither a revitalization of Democratic party liberalism nor laissez-faire Reagonomics, in Rohatyn's view, is equipped to confront the deep-seated nature of the crisis. The solution is to be found in basic structural changes, which, for Rohatyn, involve the introduction of a new form of corporatism accompanied by state planning of the economy. Given the complexity of the modern technological economy, he argues, only the federal government can orchestrate the needed structural changes. The specific mechanism for engineering the transition would be a new state agency with major responsibility for planning national economic investments.

Of most interest here, of course, is the technocratic character of this scheme. Basic to Rohatyn's proposal is an approach reminiscent of the earlier Progressive reform strategy. Essentially, it involves a key role for economic and financial experts backed by strong political leadership. To carry out the planning function, policy experts are to be "insulated from political pressures." The agency decision processes must be relatively inaccessible to elected officials and altogether sheltered from interest-group demands. In Rohatyn's words, planning is to be "publicly account-able but . . . run outside of politics."

This insulation of planning from the public is offered as a direct challenge to those who call for greater economic democracy. Economic "austerity and democracy," according to Rohatyn, "do not walk hand in hand in the United States." In reply to those who insist on the democrati-zation of the planning process as an end in itself, Rohatyn argues that greater political participation is a prescription for disaster. Debate over the goals of planning, he contends, does little but fuel an overheated interest-group struggle for government's scarce resources. Not only would such competition wreak havoc with the budgetary process, it would ruin the American economy's chances for revitalization. The solu-tion, according to Rohatyn, is to be found in a disciplined "allocation of pain," a task for which democracy is wholly unsuited. Only a central planning agency insulated from the public and backed by powerful elite support can implement this painful but necessary restructuring of the American political system.

The new planning agency, as envisioned by Rohatyn, should be pat-terned after the Reconstruction Finance Corporation of the 1930s. The agency would be an enormous investment banking operation with the powers needed to plan industrial growth. (It would be, in his words, a "vibrant instrument" equipped to establish a "comprehensive recovery program.") While the details of the program remain vague, three general elements are clear: massive public investments for the corporate sector, greater labor discipline combined with union wage cuts, and general social austerity. Taken together, they represent a fundamental economic transformation.

The basic tools for engineering this transformation are the carrot and the stick. To stimulate carefully selected investments, central planners would funnel federally guaranteed loans to specific companies or indus-tries. In particular, aid would be targeted to vitally important but "finan-cially distressed" companies. (If necessary, the agency could directly purchase company equity.) Before committing the money, however, planners would secure the major concessions essential for fundamental economic change. Businesses would be asked to limit their profits to predetermined levels, labor unions would have to agree to work rules, consumers must accept price increases, and so on. For many, the new state agency is viewed as the American counterpart to Japan's Ministry for International Trade and Investment, long credited with guiding Japan's "economic miracle." Only with such an agency, according to Rohatyn and his followers, can the United States hope in the long run to compete with its principal economic rival, Japan.

Rohatyn's ideas are anything but armchair theorizing. In the mid-1970s the fiscal crisis of New York City government afforded Rohatyn and a group of New York bankers a unique and unprecedented opportunity to restructure the governance of the city. In what was essentially an exercise in "crisis management," the banking community and key top-level politicians imposed on the city a new set of governance institutions that virtually constituted a "central guidance cluster." Three planning agencies were established to guide the transformation: the Municipal Assistance Corporation (which Rohatyn headed himself), the Emergency Financial Control Board, and the State Office of the Special Deputy Comptroller.[42] These agencies were directed by financial experts, urban policy planners, key members of the banking community, and a few carefully selected political leaders. In the name of fiscal planning, their job was first to save the city from impending bankruptcy (a reality that threatened to shake the entire financial community of the country), and, second, to chart the fiscal future of the city for the decades to come.

The objective of this central guidance was thus to balance the city's budget through a long-term financial plan. In the process, the city was to become a responsible debtor, thus offering much needed reassurances to an anxious investment community. At this level, such reforms seemed straightforward and were fairly widely accepted, given the dire implications of the city's fiscal situation. Much less obvious and far more controversial, however, were the deeper political goals that accompanied the introduction of these central agencies. Recognizing that the restructuring of the city's fiscal structure had implications for the entire governmental process, Rohatyn and his associates used this centralized financial control to forge a new political power structure in the city. The result, as Robert Bailey shows in his study of the "crisis regime," was the rise of a new "post-interest-group" system of governance.[43]

Post-interest-group politics is essentially neocorporatist in nature. Designed to limit interest-group participation, it is based on a dramatic reduction of the city's primary policy arenas—education, welfare, housing, and so on. Its overarching feature is an increasingly "centralized planning model" for political decision making. Orchestrated through a centralized aggregation of policy issues, the city's governance structure is more and more constituted by a small number of central decision processes governed by a few powerful elite groups (bankers, union leaders, top-level politicians, and the like). Politics, in the process, shifts away from groups per se to the relationships between them, that is, the larger political context that structures competition itself. It is this shift to *context* that makes possible the neocorporatist objective: central coordination of policy priorities. By imposing general policy criteria that apply to the entire range of city interest groups, group politics can be structured and channeled to correspond to central priorities. The result is a new style of politics planned from the top. By all standards, this "planning politics" represents an unprecedented departure from the traditional pluralist processes that long governed city policy-making.

Basic to this emergent political process is a blurring of the distinction between the public and private sectors, an essential feature of neocorporatism. For instance, a number of the members appointed to these fiscal planning agencies were publicly acknowledged to represent the business and financial communities per se. Bailey explains the political significance of these appointments in these words:

> Private groups have always been at the center of the policymaking process, but they were never among the formal authorities that legislated decisions. Now they are at the very center. Power over the cities was transferred to a powerful private elite.[44]

No one better describes the political consequences of this private elite's role than William Tabb.[45] Private bankers and their financial experts, he writes, laid out a very stringent program for the city and largely got what they requested: "fiscal cutbacks, the stripping of the mayor's powers, and the creation of an advisory group to run the city their way." Questions—such as "who was to go to the city's colleges, how often garbage was to be collected, which hospitals were to be closed—were decided not by officials but by the new 'government.'" In the process, large numbers of New Yorkers are disenfranchised by these "new men of power." The traditional political process, as Tabb puts it, becomes "an empty ritual."

Finally, it is important to note that Rohatyn has explicitly recommended his New York City strategy as the model for restructuring the federal governmental process. Maintaining that "the situation in America today is not so different from that of New York City in 1975," he likens the institutionalization of the Reconstruction Finance Corporation to the Municipal Assistance Corporation put into place in the city.[46] Such an arrangement will work only if political confrontation can give way to an era of business-labor cooperation. The incentive for this new era of cooperation is the threat hanging over the heads of the country's working and middle classes—an economic decline that brings a lower standard of living. The Reconstruction Finance Corporation is fashioned as the institutional mechanism for obtaining lower wage costs, union compliance, and the capital accumulation required for high-technology industries in the United States. The outcome is described as a more aggressive corporate state, both at home and in world markets.

Having now outlined the political structures and practices of technocorporatism, we turn in the next chapter to the role of planning in this evolving formulation. If neocorporatism is the political structure of the technocorporate state, technocracy is its ideal form of administration and control. Where neocorporatism supplies the system of political representation, technocracy provides the ideology and planning techniques of the top-level decision makers. In the next section, we examine the dominant methodology for the organization and planning of technocracy's central guidance function, namely, the methodologies of the systems approach.

Notes

1. John Kenneth Galbraith, *The New Industrial State* (Boston: Houghton Mifflin, 1967).

2. Alain Touraine, *The Post-Industrial Society* (New York: Random House, 1971), pp. 49–56. On technocratic planning and the managerial worldview, see Robert R. Alford and Roger Friedland, *Powers of Theory: Capitalism, the State, and Democracy* (Cambridge: Cambridge University Press, 1985), especially chaps. 7 and 10.

3. Galbraith, *The New Industrial State.*

4. See Jürgen Habermas, *Toward a Rational Society* (Boston: Beacon, 1968); and Alvin Gouldner, *The Dialectic of Ideology and Technology* (New York: Seabury, 1976), especially chaps. 11 and 12.

5. Guy Benveniste, *The Politics of Expertise* (San Francisco: Boyd and Fraser, 1972), p. 63.

6. See Bertram M. Gross, "Friendly Fascism: A Model for America," *Social Policy*, September/October, 1974, p. 47; and William G. Scott and David K. Hart, *Organizational America* (Boston: Houghton Mifflin, 1979).

7. Galbraith, *The New Industrial State;* and Robert L. Heilbroner, *The Limits of American Capitalism* (New York: Harper & Row, 1966).

8. Galbraith, *The New Industrial State.*

9. Jeffrey D. Straussman, *The Limits of Technocratic Politics* (New Brunswick, NJ: Transaction, 1978).

10. Samuel P. Huntington, "The Democratic Distemper," *The Public Interest*, no. 41 (Fall 1975): 36–37.

11. For a discussion of the political ramifications of these crises and the role of crisis management, see Claus Offe, *Contradictions of the Welfare State*, ed. John Keane (Cambridge: MIT Press, 1984), especially chaps. 1 and 2.

12. See, for example, Michael Crozier et al., eds., *The Crisis of Democracy* (New York: New York University, 1975).

13. Michael Crozier, in *The Governability of Democracies*, ed. the Trilateral Task Force on the Governability of Democracies (New York: Trilateral Commission, 1975), chap. 2, p. 3; Anthony King, "Overload: The Problem of Governing in the 1970s," *Political Studies* 23, (1975): 284–96; and Daniel Bell, "The Revolution of Rising Entitlements," *Fortune*, April 1975, pp. 98–103.

14. Lester Thurow, *The Zero-Sum Society* (New York: Basic Books, 1980).

15. See Charles Lindblom and David Braybrook, *Strategy of Decision* (New York: Free Press, 1963).

16. The classic statement on piecemeal change is Karl Popper, *The Open Society and Its Enemies*, vol. 1 (Princeton, NJ: Princeton University Press, 1963).

17. Benjamin Kleinberg, *American Society in the Postindustrial Age: Technocracy, Power, and the End of Ideology* (Columbus, OH: Charles E. Merrill, 1973).

18. See, for example, Amitai Etzioni, *The Active Society* (New York: Free Press, 1968), chaps. 11 and 12.

19. Trilateral Commission Task Force, *The Governability of Democracies.*

20. Amitai Etzioni, *An Immodest Agenda: Rebuilding America Before the Twenty-First Century* (New York: McGraw-Hill, 1983), p. 313.

21. On corporatism generally, see P. Schmitter and G. Lehmbruch, eds., *Patterns of Corporatist Intermediation* (Beverly Hills, CA: Sage, 1982). For a discussion of the corporatist foundations of reindustrialization policy, see Robert C. Grady, "Reindustrialization, Liberal Democracy, and Corporatist Representation," *Political Science Quarterly* 101, no. 3 (1986): 415–32; and Charles E. Lindblom, *Politics and Markets* (New York: Basic Books, 1977).

22. The term *techno-corporate state* is mentioned by Hoos, although she does not develop the concept. See Ida R. Hoos, *Systems Analysis in Public Policy: A Critique* (Berkeley: University of California Press, 1972), p. 13.

23. Wolf V. Heydebrand, "Technocratic Corporatism: Toward a Theory of Occupational and Organizational Transformation," in *Organizational Theory and Public Policy*, ed. Richard H. Hall and Robert E. Quinn (Beverly Hills, CA: Sage, 1983), pp. 93–114.

24. Bernd Marin, *Die Paritaetische Kommission: Aufgekleter Technokorporatismus in Oesterreich* (Vienna: Institute for Conflict Research, 1982); and Hajo Weber, "Technokorporatismus," in *Politik und die Macht der Technik*, ed. Hans-Hermann Hartwich (Opladen: Westdeutscher Verlag, 1986), pp. 278–97.

25. Claus Offe, "Corporatism as Macro-Structuring," *Telos*, Fall 1985, pp. 97–111.

26. Phillipe Schmitter, "Still the Century of Corporatism," in *Trends Toward Corporatist Intermediation*, ed. P. Schmitter and G. Lehmbruch (Beverly Hills, CA: Sage, 1979), p. 13.

27. Ibid.

28. See, for example, Etzioni, *The Active Society*; and Etzioni, "A Theory of Societal Guidance," in *Societal Guidance: A New Approach to Social Problems*, ed. Sarajane Heidt and Amitai Etzioni, (New York: Thomas Y. Crowell, 1969).

29. Galbraith, *The New Industrial State*.

30. Heydebrand, *Technocratic Corporatism*, p. 103.

31. Alfred Diamant, "Bureaucracy and Public Policy in Neo-Corporatist Settings," *Comparative Politics* 14 (1981): 101–24; Leo Panitch, "Recent Theorizations of Corporatism," *British Journal of Sociology* 31 (1980): 159–87; and Roger Marris, "Is the Corporatist Economy a Corporate State?" *American Economic Review, Papers and Proceedings* 62 (1972): 103–15.

32. Scott and Hart, *Organizational America*, pp. 88–89.

33. Bertram M. Gross, "The State of the Nation: Social Systems Accounting," in *Social Indicators*, ed. Raymond A. Bauer (Cambridge: MIT Press, 1966), p. 209. For a more recent statement on the need for central guidance, see Yeheskel Dror, "Retrofitting Central Minds of Government," in *Research in Public Policy Analysis and Management*, vol. 4, ed. Stuart S. Nagel (Greenwich, CT: JAI Press, 1987), pp. 79–107; and Amitai Etzioni, "U.S. Technological, Economic, and Social Development for the 21st Century," ibid., pp. 241–70.

34. See Joseph G. Peschek, *Policy-Planning Organizations: Elite Agendas and America's Rightward Turn* (Philadelphia: Temple University Press, 1987); Thomas R. Dye, "Oligarchic Tendencies in National Policy-Making: The Role of Private Policy-Planning Organizations," *Journal of Politics* 40 (May 1978), p. 309; John S. Saloma, *Ominous Politics: The New Conservative Labyrinth* (New York: Hill and Wang, 1984); and William Domhoff, *The Powers That Be: Processes of Ruling-Class Domination in America* (New York: Random House, 1978), p. 155.

35. Peschek, *Policy-Planning Organizations*.

36. "An Industrial Policy by Any Other Name," *Business Week*, May 2, 1988, p. 33.

37. Kevin P. Philips, *Staying on Top* (New York: Random House, 1986).

38. Robert B. Reich, "Behold! We have an Industrial Policy," *New York Times*, May 2, 1988, p. 33; also, see Andrew Pollack, "America's Answer to Japan's MITI," *New York Times*, March 5, 1989, sec. 3, p. 1.

39. Cited by Maurice Zeitlin, "The American Crisis: An Analysis and Modest Proposal," in *The Future of American Democracy*, ed. Mark E. Kann (Philadelphia: Temple University Press, 1983), p. 121.

40. Rohatyn's views are supported by a number of very significant business leaders, such as William McChesney Martin, ex-head of the Federal Reserve Board; George Ball of Lehman Bros.; Robert Roosa of Brown Bros., Harriman; Henry Ford II; Gustave Ley of Goldman, Sachs; Thomas C. Bradshaw, president of Atlantic Richfield; Alfred Hayes, ex-head of the Federal Reserve Board in New York; Ray Garrett, former chairman of the Securities Exchange Commission; and Henry Kaufman of Salamon Bros. See Zeitlin, ibid., p. 133.

41. Rohatyn's comments in this section of the chapter are taken from the following works: Rohatyn, "Re-Constructing America," *New York Review of Books*,

March 5, 1981, pp. 16, 18–20; "The Coming Emergency and What Can Be Done About It," *New York Review of Books*, December 4, 1980, pp. 20–24, 26; "Public-Private Partnerships to Stave Off Disaster," *Harvard Business Review*, November–December 1979; "America in the 1980s," *The Economist*, September 19, 1981, pp. 31–38; "Democracy's No Free Gift," *New York Times*, December 7, 1978, p. A23; and *The Twenty-Year Century: Essays on Economics and Public Finance* (New York: Random House, 1983).

42. Eric Lichten, *Class, Power and Austerity: The New York City Crisis* (South Hadley, MA: Bergin and Garvey, 1986).

43. Robert W. Bailey, *The Crisis Regime: The MAC, the EFCB, and the Political Impact of the New York City Financial Crisis* (Albany: State University of New York Press, 1986).

44. Ibid.

45. William K. Tabb, *The Long Default: New York City and the Urban Fiscal Crisis* (New York: Monthly Review Press, 1981).

46. Quoted in Lichten, *Class, Power and Austerity*, p. 197.

8

Technocratic Methodology: Central Guidance as Systems Planning

In this chapter the focus turns to a primary methodological orientation of technocratic management and planning, the "systems approach." The systems orientation is characterized as an intrinsic meta-logic of technocratic thought; it supplies fundamental codes that underlie technocratic decision making—its language, its schemas of perception, its values, its techniques, and its practices. The purpose is to outline the ways in which the "scientific" theory and logic of the systems approach have evolved to virtually model the governance of the technocorporate state as well as to provide the specific methodological techniques for its coordination and planning.

The planning literature makes clear the essential elements of the postindustrial task.[1] In analytical terms, it involves two interrelated activities. One is the intellectual calculation of scarce resources and their strategic implications for societal needs and goals. The other is the strategic planning of resource allocations to meet systemwide priorities and needs. These tasks involve the joining of intellectual technologies with the central administration of policy formulation and implementation.[2] Assignments for which the systems approach is uniquely tailored, its methodologies constitute the quintessential products of contemporary technocratic social science.[3]

Many of the techniques of systems planning have been elaborated—if not invented—by corporate planners. In the main, the advocates of public planning argue that private sector techniques must be extended to the public sphere. Most important, in this respect, is the introduction of corporate-style "strategic planning."[4] A systems-based methodology, strategic planning is presented as one of the most important components of the larger postindustrial effort to restructure American government.

Although systems theory has a history independent of neocorporatist and postindustrial theories of the state, it has nonetheless evolved in managerial and policy circles as the methodology best suited to deal with the kinds of guidance problems postindustrialists seek to solve. Indeed, it is essentially a theory concerned with the coordination of complex systems, both technical and social. Its development in the managerial and policy sciences, in fact, has been shaped by the study of complex organizations and their top-level managerial problems (generally at the behest of top-level managers). For this reason, no discussion of technocracy can be complete without a discussion of systems theory and its planning techniques.

To illustrate the technocratic functions of systems theory and methods, the discussion first illuminates the ways in which they analytically conceptualize the central guidance problems of the technocorporate state. Second, it shows how the intellectual technologies of the systems approach serve to facilitate the depoliticization of top-level political decision making.

Origins and Promises

The idea that systems theory is a primary intellectual foundation of technocratic governance is anything but new. From the very beginning, systems theory advocates have seen its implications for technocracy. Ludwig von Bertalanffy, founder of the "general systems theory movement," put it this way: "Systems design, systems analysis [and] systems engineering . . . are the very nucleus of a new technology and technocracy."[5]

By all standards, systems theory is a major intellectual project. Most fundamentally, it is the product of a series of converging theoretical developments. Work in various disciplines—theoretical biology, computer sciences, information theory, linguistics, economic game theory, political science, communication theory, cybernetics, operations research, and more—converged to shape a "general systems theory movement."[6] Giving rise to a very large literature in a short period of time, the purpose of this interdisciplinary movement has been profoundly ambitious: the search for overarching concepts and "general laws" that govern all systems—living organisms, societies, economics, languages, and so on.

In the managerial and policy sciences, the systems perspective emerged as the product of a number of developments that first took shape during World War II. Working on tactical and logistical problems concerned with the war effort, British and American scientists developed a technique called "operations research." After the war some of these groups were held together; one of them became the well-known Rand Corporation.[7] Early Rand research, like wartime operations research, dealt with the mathematical and statistical treatment (largely through linear programming techniques) of well-defined, low-level tactical decision problems. By the early 1950s, Rand had begun to emphasize what is now called "systems analysis."

A derivative of operations research, systems analysis was designed to deal with problems that have less clearly defined objectives, including a variety of economic and social problems. Systems analysis, for this reason, tended to rely less on the most rigorous quantitative techniques, reserving their use for selected aspects of particular problems. Its practitioners sometimes describe it as an attempt to supply systematic reasoning to the "structuring" of complex problems. As such, systems analysis is a way of thinking, one that emphasizes the technical side of problems over their social and political dimensions. Evolving at about the same time that "general systems theory" made its appearance, systems analysis was adopted as one of the subdisciplines of the general systems theory movement.

The "systems approach," as this convergence of methodologies came to be called in the managerial and policy sciences, is constituted by a set of techniques for the diagnosis, design, evaluation, and control of complex configurations of people, technologies, and organizations. Because of its use in the planning and evaluation of complex tasks associated with NASA's space program, the systems approach has been called the "Space-Age technology" for problem solving.[8] Often described as the most valuable spin-off of the aerospace program, it is portrayed as "revolutionizing management and planning in government, business . . . and human problems."[9] Having succeeded in putting a man on the moon, we are told, systems planning can also be used to redesign cities, eliminate poverty, improve education, and more.[10] No one has expressed greater enthusiasm for the systems approach than C. West Churchman, one of its leading interpreters. He puts it this way:

> In principle, we have the technological capacity of adequately feeding, sheltering, and clothing every inhabitant of the world. In principle, we have the technological capability of providing adequate medical care for every inhabitant of the world. In principle, we have the technological capability of providing sufficient education for every inhabitant of the world for him to enjoy a mature intellectual life. . . . Then why don't we do so? The answer is that we are not organized to do so.[11]

For Churchman there is nothing mysterious about our failure here. It is attributable to the fact that we have yet to avail ourselves of the special talents of modern systems engineers and their principles of organizational design. The modern systems engineer, as military-industrialist Simon Ramo elaborates, is a "multiheaded engineer," a "techno-political-econo-socio" expert. Such experts, he tells us, include in their heads "the total intelligence, background, experience, wisdom, and creative ability in all aspects of the problem of applying science." The integration of this intelligence is mobilized to generate "real-life solutions to real-life problems."[12]

Basic, then, to systems organization is the organization of expertise itself. Because the task of social problem solving combines knowledge from many disciplines—mathematics, computer sciences, physics, chemistry, psychology, sociology, business finance, political science, and so on—experts must be organized into "systems-engineering teams."[13] Such teams are the nucleus of a systems-based technology. Their purpose is to revolutionize managerial and policy decision making in ways that will open up new solutions to many of the most entrenched economic and social problems of our time. Boguslaw calls them "the new utopians"; Kuhns refers to them as "the post-industrial prophets."[14]

Systems Theory as Political Theory

Influenced by these extravagant claims for systems theory generally, many social scientists in the late 1960s and early 1970s took the theory to be "an analytical model for the planned reconstruction of society."[15] Among the most important efforts in this direction were those that drew on cybernetically based systems models. Particularly significant were the writings of Etzioni, Breed, and Luhmann in sociology, Deutsch in political science, and Schick in public administration.[16] For these theorists, the crises thwarting modern society were essentially the result of unresolved "steering problems." The solution was to be found in the development of new forms of central guidance patterned after cybernetically designed "self-regulating" steering systems.[17] (Habermas, quite appropriately, has described this approach as the highest expression of "technocratic consciousness.")

Briefly consider Schick's enthusiastic description of the "cybernetic state." In a "post-industrial cybernetic state," as he puts it, "government functions as a servomechanism conjoining the polity and the economy to achieve the public objectives."[18] The electoral process would still exist in this new system of government but "would not have its old importance." The lines between the public and private sectors would blur into one another, with governmental administrators largely superseded by systems engineers and planners. The result would be the narrowing of the scope of politics and thus a substantial reduction in the number of political conflicts plaguing society. The specific dynamics of the new political process are well illustrated in Schick's discussion of cybernetic decision making.

In the cybernetic state, decision making depends less on political deliberation than on economic and social indicators. Such indicators are designed to scientifically monitor the existing state of desirable social conditions and goals. (When a discrepancy emerges between existing conditions and goals, a set of defined action alternatives would be automatically implemented to bring the system back to the desired state of equilibrium.) The determination of systems goals and the prescription of alternative courses of action would still necessitate political discussion, but such discourse should be significantly circumscribed by the technical relationships undergirding a highly interdependent system. For this reason, both the nature and the locus of political dialogue would undergo significant transformation. Increasingly, it would take the form of a politics of expertise. No longer would government require the intermediation of interest groups for the communication of its policy goals, the discovery of interest preferences from the public, or the control of representative and bureaucratic institutions. When such communication is necessary, Schick explains, the chief executive will merely use mass communication to reach the public more effectively than through traditional party and interest-group processes. (If nothing else, this latter point would appear to have anticipated the coming of the Reagan presidency. In his battle against "special interest" groups, Reagan elevated the use of the media to an art form.)

Methodology for Central Guidance

Nearly 20 years have passed since such exaggerated claims have been advanced in the name of systems theory. It is now difficult to find a social scientist talking in such terms, thanks in no small part to the Reagan administration's hostility to government and planning. But this is not to say that systems theory and its technocratic politics have faded from the discourse of the social and managerial sciences. On the contrary, they have only receded to the less obvious but very influential level of methodology.[19] The contemporary fascination with the computer provides the best example. If the language of systems theory was the vogue of the 1960s and early 1970s, in more recent years it has been the language of the computer. The fact that the computer is itself a systems-based technology is merely taken for granted.

Operating at the epistemic level, systems theory now serves as a basic mode of organizing inquiry in the managerial and policy sciences. In fact, it is fair to say that, if scientific decision making is the commitment that links technocrats together as an identifiable group, systems theory is one of its primary theoretical manifestations.[20] It has been described as the meta-theoretical foundation of technocratic decision making. Borrowing from Foucault, it can be thought of as a basic "episteme" of the modern technocratic project.[21] As such, it provides the fundamental codes that govern technocratic decision methodologies—their schemas of perception, their conceptual languages, their values, their specific techniques, and their hierarchy of practices.

But what does it mean to say that systems theory is the meta-theoretical foundation of technocratic decision making? To be more concrete, it is necessary to examine systems theory itself. Toward this end, the remainder of the chapter is devoted to outlining the conceptual correspondence between systems theory and the concrete tasks of technocratic decision making. The specific purpose is to show the ways in which a purportedly "scientific" methodology in fact serves to organize the primary technocratic assignment, the analytic conceptualization of the central guidance problems of a postindustrial system. Essentially systems theory is shown to be a framework geared to the coordination of complex systems. In short, it supplies an apolitical model for the coordination and implementation of technocorporate planning.

In textbook terms, a system is typically defined as an "entity in which everything relates to everything else." Or, to put it another way, systems are said to comprise "components that work together for the objectives of the whole, and the systems approach is merely a way of thinking about components and their relationships."[22] Beyond such basic definitions, however, systems theory is generally couched in sophisticated scientific and mathematical terminologies. It is presented as an empirical-analytical explanatory model of the structures and processes that constitute and govern complex organizations, or what some call "organized complexity."[23] Toward this end, it focuses on the nature of complex interdependencies, examining the specific processes by which such relationships develop and unfold.

One of systems theory's most basic propositions is the idea that, as a system evolves, one of its parts invariably emerges as a central and controlling agent for the system as a whole. The unit's function, in brief, is that of central guidance of the system's development. Empirical evidence for the ubiquity of this phenomenon is said to be found everywhere, from embryonic development to telephone networks and national defense systems.[24]

Closely related to this emphasis on central guidance is the concept of hierarchy, also said to be a "natural property" of all systems development. The hierarchical structuring of systems is similarly held to be found in all realms: inorganic nature, organic nature, social life, and even the cosmos. Wherever systems development and growth occur, it takes a hierarchical form. Well-structured hierarchical systems, in fact, are believed to grow more rapidly than poorly structured systems, a proposition said to rest on mathematical evidence.[25]

Systems Management and Planning

In the managerial and policy sciences, the turn to the systems approach and its various techniques—strategic planning, computer simulations, cost-benefit and decision analysis, among others—is generally conceptualized as a "natural phase" in the evolution of managerial practices in complex organizational systems. Although various approaches differ somewhat, in all cases the ultimate objectives of systems planning are those of coordination and control (more often referred to as the "rationalization" of system processes). Typically, the exercise is defined as the functional coordination of subsystems processes for the purpose of efficient goal achievement.[26] The implementation of a systems plan is managed through the manipulation of hierarchical structures. The flow of information and instructions to subsystems is coordinated through the use of centralized data processing and managerial information systems.[27]

Much of systems planning's emphasis on information flows and management information systems comes from "cybernetics" systems theory.[28] In large part the outgrowth of computer science and the study of artificial intelligence, cybernetics is the study of the flow of information in complex systems. In these terms, systems are analyzed as centralized information networks. They are described with reference to their capacity to store, retrieve, and process information moving to and from the various parts of the system. Central systems guidance, or "steering" in the language of cybernetics, is thus geared to the quality and quantity of information available to top-level decision makers and their ability to process it effectively. This capacity depends in significant part on techniques—both administrative and analytical—designed to both collect and route information through systems channels. In all cases, the computer is fundamental to these techniques. Indeed, its processes become the model for organizational design itself.

Fundamental to the systems planning process is the central "management of information." Good planning and management are held to depend on the development of vast resources of information. The primary task of the centralized experts is to fill in the "information gaps." The basic tool for coordinating this activity is the "management information systems," often described as the "brain of the organization."[29] It is designed, at least in theory, to comprehensively and continuously code, store, and retrieve information about the organization's operations. As a result of advances in computer programming, these systems are now being upgraded to "expert systems."[30] Whereas the management information system helps decision makers retrieve the information needed to solve specific problems, the expert system is itself designed to provide answers. Decision makers merely punch in their problems and the expert computer (programmed with the latest principles in organization theory as well as "rules of thumb" designed by practitioners) simply prints out the solution. Expert systems are thus a significant step toward the ultimate technocratic solution—the replacement of human beings with computers.

The expansion of intelligence gathering and the continuing improvement of rapid data processing techniques are necessarily preconditions for such planning. Basic to this requirement is a high degree of quantification and measurement of economic and social life, an activity that has long been under way. (Macro-economic measurements undergo constant elaboration; the census continually expands its standardized social classifications—ethnicity, marital status, income levels, conditions of health, and so on—educational and personnel testing is steadily improved; quantitatively based institutional meetings are ascribed to social problems; and so on.) It is not surprising then that the collection and computerized processing of such data now constitute a major industry that only continues to grow. Information, in short, is the currency of planned societal guidance.

Based on the management and coordination of information, systems management gives shape to a specialized managerial language that stresses the quantitative expression of functions and goals, inputs and outputs, hierarchies and subsystems, equilibriums and control. Typically, systems structures and processes are represented in abstract diagrammatic models, matrices, flow charts, or computer printouts. Whenever possible, these structures and processes are translated into a quantifiable set of logically related variables (units, objectives, costs, and the like). Where data permit, variables are linked together through series of interrelated equations. The result is an analysis that is highly abstract, technical, and quantitative.

The specific purpose of systems coordination is described as the "reduction of complexity," particularly the reduction of the risk and uncertainty that it imposes on decision making. This is accomplished through the use of administrative mechanisms and indicators designed to monitor and manipulate the uncontrollable variables in an organization's internal and external environments. Sometimes the strategy is described as the managing of "planned change."[31] Ackoff refers to it as "redesigning the future."[32]

The planning of change takes place on two levels. Traditionally, it has evolved from efforts to rationalize the internal operations of a particular organization. In the modern state-corporate complex—or "organizational society"—it has also been extended to the relations *between* organizations themselves. In management theory, this has given rise to a new specialization called "interorganizational analysis." As a field of research, it is designed to supply theoretical and technical knowledge needed for the coordination, integration, cooperation, and management of institutions at the level of society.[33]

The specific policy criterion employed by planners to orchestrate systems coordination and coherence is that of optimality.[34] Instrumentally defined in terms of input and output ratios, optimality focuses on the efficient allocation of resources. Wherever possible, systems planners conceptualize the subsystems of both production and service organizations as "investment centers" governed by the optimal flow of material and financial resources. Depending on economic and social circumstances, the proper flow of resources will necessarily vary from organization to organization.

A number of analytical techniques, such as linear programming and decision and cost-benefit analysis, have been developed to define optimality under different organizational conditions.[35] Each focuses attention on goal realization. Internal organizational processes, largely based on established positions and interests, are only important insofar as they lead to specific optimal outcomes.[36] Short of that, they are to be reorganized until they do so.

Cost-benefit analysis, formally embodied in the concept of investment centers, is frequently enlisted as a tool for directing attention from processes to outcomes.[37] Focusing on what is obtained for a given amount of input, cost-benefit calculations are described as a workable alternative to political or process-oriented approaches in the management of governance conflicts. Not only is it said to permit the orderly resolution of amorphous issues confronting central guidance, it is believed to allow planners in many cases to discover the "rationally superior solution."[38] The validity of this contention, to be sure, is the subject of much dispute. Nonetheless, the claim itself is a consummate example of technocratic thought.

From this brief outline, it is easy to identify the correspondence between the systems model and the basic structural features of the technocorporate state. At the most general level, complexity, risk, and interdependence define the focus of both theories. More specifically, systems theory is constructed around the three structural variables most important to the technocratic state: central guidance, hierarchy, and the flow of information. Information, the commodity of expertise, is posited as the primary resource of complex systems; it is the currency of central guidance.

With regard to basic systems processes, the correspondence between systems planning and central guidance is also easily discernible. The techniques of systems planning are essentially the foundation of the new "information technologies" that Bell and others laud as the tools for central guidance. Systems planning's orientation to societal guidance becomes even clearer in the context of its more recent emphasis on "interorganizational analysis." The interorganizational perspective lifts the systems approach to the level of societal coordination. Translated into substantive economic and political issues, the explicit focus at this level is on the integration and rationalization of the vertical and horizontal networks—or "matrices"—of the neocorporate-state complex, or what we have called the technocorporate system. In short, interorganizational systems perspective is essentially that of technocorporate strategists.

Nowhere is the link between the political literature of technocratic corporatism and systems planning theory more interesting than in the discussion of "crisis management," largely accepted as a defining characteristic of modern economic and political governance. As a technique for reducing risk and uncertainty, systems planning is specifically advanced as an approach to crisis management. Essentially it can be used to engineer a long-term restructuring of the corporate-state system. Because systematic crisis management itself necessitates an increasing centralization of decision making, planners can exploit it to facilitate the introduction of technocratic corporatism's key structural element, namely, the administrative centralization of long-term planning (which, in turn, makes possible the depoliticization of policy decision making). As Scott and Hart explain, once centralized crisis management is in place, planners can literally attempt to orchestrate crises to advance system-defined ends.[39] The primary task is to merge short- and long-term goals in such a way that key elements of short-term crises can strategically be integrated into the framework of a long-term plan. Thus, according to Heydebrand, "the crises themselves are to be anticipated and incorporated into the system." The very problems that threaten the system are "internalized" into the system itself.[40]

Apolitical Theory

Systems theory thus supplies an apolitical language for talking about inherently political processes. Whereas technocorporate theory offers a political argument for the restructuring of the American political system, systems theory purports to supply scientific evidence for the inevitability of such arrangements in complex systems development. One theory seeks to mobilize political support for the reorganization of American governance processes; the other serves to supply the project with scientific legitimation. In this respect, systems theory performs the essential technocratic task: It translates the political agenda into a technical language of science. Invariably laden with abstract symbols and mathematical equations, it is a language cast in a specialized idiom accessible only to those trained in the intricacies of systems-based methodologies.

Virtually absent from this language is an understanding of society as a system of interactions among people consciously organizing their practices through politics.[41] In place of politics, systems theory substitutes a technical approach to basic decision problems. As a scientific conceptualization of central guidance, it provides a neutral (or "value-free") language divorced from the political context to which it is applied: Political decision processes become information channels, interest groups become subunits, participation becomes feedback, and so on. In fact, the very definition of the contemporary political "crisis" is defined as a "systems overload."

Whereas in politics the organization of society is the most basic concern, the systems perspective largely takes the social system for granted. Indeed, it appears as a relatively fixed "natural" phenomenon with an ontological status of its own. Social and political change does occur in this natural system, but it is largely understood to be the function of the internal adjustments of system parts. In this respect, component subsystems (vis-à-vis the system itself) are the primary focus of analysis. As such, emphasis is on means and functions rather than on ends per se. Systems ends, traditionally the stuff of politics, are derived from technical/organizational requirements. If they are not apparent—or given—they are identified by systems experts.

Systems theory thus attempts to short-curcuit the basic *political* task of securing consensus and legitimation. It does this by supplying the political agenda with what would appear to be a higher form of legitimation, the scientific legitimation accorded to a "natural process." Insofar as natural processes possess a dimension of inevitability, the effective course of action becomes the one that facilitates the centralized restructuring of subunits or parts. As the West German systems theorist Luhmann puts it, to resist the inevitable is only to court folly.[42]

While most systems theorists are remarkably silent about the methodology's apolitical implications, it would be wrong to altogether overlook those who find them troublesome. Concerned with the approach's overemphasis on efficiency and functional integration, theorists such as von Bertalanffy, Buckley, and Gawthrop have sought to counter this problem by building into the model countervailing values such as human choice and individual dignity.[43] Moreover, others like Ackoff have labored to recast systems planning as an "interactive" methodology for broad-based participation.[44] As Harmon and Mayer correctly point out, however, none of these approaches has succeeded in offsetting "the primacy and 'given-ness' of *system needs*," the very source of the problem.[45]

These writers, moreover, are the exceptions. Any influence they have had within the systems movement has been more than countered by those who choose to fully extend the instrumental implications of systems premises. One need only consider a few of the most prominent examples to grasp the nature fo the challenge. Ramo, for instance, uses systems precepts to argue that politics and democracy must be relegated to an instrumental role in modern societal guidance.[46] For Beer, the solution to politics is to be found in a cybernetic "redesign of freedom."[47] B. F. Skinner, the quintessential social engineer of our time, boldly argues in *Beyond Freedom and Dignity* that traditional political values are modern-day anachronisms that have no place in a scientifically designed social system.[48] Indeed, in his view, such values are little more than conventional myths that impede the scientific vision of a new society. Similarly, Luhmann forcefully argues that the contemporary discussion of democracy as "out of step" with the realities of systems complexity. The enormous pressures that technological and social complexity place on highly developed societies, he maintains, require instead of democracy a high degree of automony for central administrative systems. He provocatively challenges democratic theorists with these words: "To demand an intensive, engaged participation of all [those affected by decisions] would be to make a principle of frustration. Anyone who understands democracy in this way has, in fact, to come to the conclusion that it is incompatible with rationality."[49]

Summing Up

Technocratic theory and its methodologies, as we have seen, give shape to a very influential political strategy in the United States, namely, "technocratic corporatism." For most postindustrialists, some form of the technocorporate scenario is virtually inevitable. A variety of forces are said to be driving society in this direction (particularly the risks and uncertainties associated with the technological and organizational complexity of the postindustrial economy). Such forces give rise to the "trajectory of crises" confronting the American political economy—

environmental, economic, technological, and so on. The theory of technocratic corporatism, in this respect, is an intellectual reflection of these powerful economic and political realities. Its strategies and approaches to planning and crisis management are today seen to be far more in step with contemporary circumstances than much of the conventional economic and political wisdom, especially that of the free market variety. Many postindustrialists thus believe it to be only a matter of time before some version of the strategy becomes the explicit operating ideology of an American presidential administration.

At the methodological level, technocorporate theory was essentially seen to be an attempt to extend the organizational planning techniques of the technostructure to the political economy as a whole. It is in large part an effort to rationalize the interorganizational network that constitutes the corporate-state system. Basic to this rationalization process is the introduction of a depoliticized form of systems planning, the specific focus of this chapter. As the consummate technocratic methodology, the systems approach is designed to analytically model the central guidance problems of the postindustrial technocorporate-state. Indeed, as a technique for problem solving, it has been shaped by studies of complex organizational systems and their top-level managerial problems.

In political terms, systems planning has involved a deep-seated challenge to the interest-group processes that have long defined American democratic theory (if not always actual political practices). Although the calls for restructuring take various forms, the basic objective in all cases is to bring about a "better managed society." It is a society in which politics takes a backseat to administration.

The systems movement has thus been a major force in designing the theoretical framework that purportedly supplies technocorporate strategy with a scientific foundation. Insofar as the strategy is the program of a political movement, systems theory becomes as much an ideology as a scientific theory. For this reason, a key task for those interested in redirecting the managerial and policy sciences toward democratic ends must begin with the intellectual reconstruction of their methodologies. It is to this task that we turn in the second half of the book.

Notes

1. For a guide to the planning literature, see John Friedmann, *Planning in the Public Domain* (Princeton, NJ: Princeton University Press, 1987).

2. Daniel Bell, *The Coming of Post-Industrial Society* (New York: Basic Books, 1973); and Herbert I. Schiller, *Information and the Crisis Economy* (New York: Oxford University Press, 1986).

3. Jürgen Habermas, *Toward a Rational Society* (Boston: Beacon, 1970), pp. 81–122.

4. See, for example, John M. Bryson and William D. Roering, "Applying Private-Sector Strategic Planning in the Public Sector," *Journal of the American Planning Association* 53, no. 1 (Winter, 1987): 9–22. Also, see Susan Walter and Pat Choate, *Thinking Strategically: A Primer for Public Leaders* (Washington, DC: Council of State Planning Agencies, 1984); and John Olsen and Douglas Eadie, *The Game Plan: Governance with Insight* (Washington, DC: Council of State Planning Agencies, 1982).

5. Ludwig von Bertalanffy, *General Systems Theory* (New York: George Brazillier, 1968), p. 3; and John W. Sutherland, *A General Systems Philosophy for the Social and Behavioral Sciences* (New York: Brazillier, 1973).

6. See Robert Lilienfeld, *The Rise of Systems Theory* (New York: John Wiley, 1978).

7. Bruce L. R. Smith, *The Rand Corporation* (Cambridge, MA: Harvard University Press, 1966).

8. Cited in Ida R. Hoos, *Systems Analysis in Public Policy* (Berkeley: University of California Press, 1972), p. 1.

9. C. West Churchman, *The Systems Approach* (New York: Dell, 1968). See the cover of the paperback edition.

10. Richard R. Nelson, *The Moon and the Ghetto: Essays on Public Policy Analysis* (New York: Norton, 1977), p. 13.

11. Churchman, *The Systems Approach*, pp. 3–4.

12. Simon Ramo, *Cure for Chaos: Fresh Solutions to Social Problems Through the Systems Approach* (New York: David McKay, 1969), p. 15.

13. Ibid.

14. Robert Boguslaw, *The New Utopians: A Study of System Design and Social Change* (Englewood Cliffs, NJ: Prentice-Hall, 1965); and William Kuhns, *The Post-Industrial Prophets* (New York: Weybright and Talley, 1971).

15. Habermas, *Toward a Rational Society*, p. 106.

16. Amitai Etzioni, *The Active Society* (New York: Free Press, 1968); Karl Deutsch, *The Nerves of Government* (New York: Free Press, 1966); Nicholas Luhmann, *Trust and Power* (New York: John Wiley, 1979); Warren Breed, *The Self-Guiding Society* (New York: Free Press, 1971); and Allen Schick, "Toward the Cybernetic State," in *Public Administration in a Time of Turbulence*, ed. Dwight Waldo (Scranton, PA: Chandler, 1971), pp. 214–33.

17. Habermas, *Toward a Rational Society*.

18. Schick, *Toward the Cybernetic State*, p. 222.

19. Robert W. Backoff and Barry M. Mitnick, "Reappraising the Promise of General Systems Theory for the Policy Sciences," in *Policy Analysis: Perspective, Concepts, and Methods*, ed. William Dunn (Greenwich, CT: JAI Press, 1986), pp. 23–40.

20. Robert Lilienfeld, "Systems Theory as an Ideology," *Social Research* 42 (Winter 1975), p. 659; Habermas, *Toward a Rational Society*, p. 106.

21. Michel Foucault, *The Order of Things: An Archaeology of the Human Sciences* (New York: Vintage, 1973), p. xx.

22. Nicholas L. Henry, "The Systems Approach and Management Science," *Public Administration and Public Affairs* (Englewood Cliffs, NJ: Prentice-Hall, 1986), p. 110.

23. Ronald D. Brunner and Gary D. Brewer, *Organized Complexity* (New York: Free Press, 1971); and Todd R. LaPorte, ed., *Organized Social Complexity: Challenge to Politics and Policy* (Princeton, NJ: Princeton University Press, 1975).

24. Arthur D. Hall, "Some Fundamental Concepts of Systems Engineering," in *Systems Analysis*, ed. Stanford L. Optner (Harmondsworth: Penguin, 1973), pp. 111–12.

25. Ervin Laszlo, *The Systems View of the World* (New York: Brazillier, 1972), pp. 67–68.

26. See Churchman, *The Systems Approach*; and Henry, "The Systems Approach."

27. For a case study, see James N. Danziger et al., *Computers and Politics: High Technology in American Local Governments* (New York: Columbia University Press, 1982).

28. See W. Ross Ashby, *Introduction to Cybernetics* (London: Chapman and Hall, 1961); John D. Steinbruner, *The Cybernetic Theory of Decision* (Princeton, NJ: Princeton University Press, 1974), especially part I; and Stafford Beer, *Cybernetics and Management* (New York: John Wiley, 1964).

29. On management information systems, see Jerome Kanter, "Integrated Management Information and Control Systems," in Optner, *Systems Analysis*, pp. 198–219.

30. For a discussion of expert systems, see Dwight B. Davis, "Artificial Intelligence Goes to Work," *High Technology*, April 1987, pp. 16–27; and Paul Harmon and David King, *Expert Systems: Artificial Intelligence in Business* (New York: John Wiley, 1985).

31. Warren G. Bennis, Kenneth D. Benne, and Robert Chin, *The Planning of Change* (New York: Holt, Rinehart, & Winston, 1969).

32. Russell Ackoff, *Redesigning the Future: A Systems Approach to Societal Problems* (New York: John Wiley, 1974).

33. William M. Evan, "The Organization-Set: Toward a Theory of Interorganizational Relations," in *Approaches to Organizational Design*, ed. J. D. Thompson (Pittsburgh: University of Pittsburgh Press, 1966), pp. 175–91; and K. S. Cook, "Exchange and Power in Networks of Interorganizational Relations," *Sociological Quarterly* 18 (Winter 1977): 62–82.

34. Guy Benveniste, "Political Aspects of the Systems Approach," *The Politics of Expertise* (San Francisco: Boyd and Fraser, 1972), pp. 71–74.

35. On optimality, see E. S. Quade, *Analysis for Public Decisions* (Amsterdam: Elsevier, 1982).

36. Allen Schick, "Systems Politics and Systems Budgeting," *Public Administration Review* 29 (March/April 1969): 137–52.

37. Laurence H. Tribe, "Policy Science: Analysis or Ideology?" *Philosophy and Public Affairs* 2 (Fall 1972): 66–108; and Alasdair MacIntyre, "Utilitarianism and the Presuppositions of Cost-Benefit Analysis: An Essay on the Relevance of Moral Philosophy to the Theory of Bureaucracy," in *Ethics in Planning*, ed. Martin Wachs (New Brunswick, NJ: Center for Urban Policy Research, 1985), pp. 259–87. On cost-benefit analysis in systems analysis, see William S. Davis, *Tools and Techniques for Structured Systems Analysis and Design* (Reading, MA: Addison-Wesley, 1983), pp. 57–68; and J. Daniel Couger and Robert W. Knapp, eds., *Systems Analysis Techniques* (New York: John Wiley, 1974), part 3.

38. E. J. Mishan, *Cost-Benefit Analysis* (New York: Praeger, 1976).

39. William G. Scott and David K. Hart, *Organizational America* (Boston: Houghton Mifflin, 1979), pp. 118–21.

40. Wolf V. Heydebrand, "Technocratic Corporatism," in *Organization Theory and Public Policy*, ed. Richard Hall and Robert Quinn (Beverly Hills, CA: Sage, 1983), p. 101.

41. Manfred Stanley, *The Technological Conscience: Survival and Dignity in an Age of Expertise* (Chicago: University of Chicago Press, 1978).

42. Nicholas Luhmann, "Komplexität und Democratie," *Politische Vierteljahreschrift*, 1968, p. 319.

43. von Bertalanffy, *General Systems Theory*; Walter Buckley, "Society as a Complex, Adaptive System," in *Tomorrow's Organizations*, ed. Jong S. Jun and William B. Storm (Glenview, IL: Scott, Foresman, 1973), pp. 198–213; and Louis Gawthrop, *Public Sector Management, Systems, and Ethics* (Bloomington: Indiana University Press, 1984).

44. Ackoff, *Redesigning the Future.*

45. Michael M. Harmon and Richard T. Mayer, *Organization Theory for Public Administration* (Boston: Little, Brown, 1986), p. 187.

46. Simon Ramo, *America's Technology Slip* (New York: John Wiley, 1980), pp. 4, 7, 90–91.

47. Stafford Beer, *Designing Freedom* (New York: John Wiley, 1974).

48. B. F. Skinner, *Beyond Freedom and Dignity* (New York: Knopf, 1971); and Peter G. Stillman, "The Limits of Behavioralism: A Review Essay on B. F. Skinner's Social and Political Thought," *American Political Science Review* 69 (March 1975): 202–13.

49. Quoted in Jürgen Habermas, *Legitimation Crisis* (Boston: Beacon, 1973), p. 133.

PART V

POLICY SCIENCE AND THE POSTPOSITIVIST CHALLENGE: THE POLITICS OF DISCOURSE

The culture of critical discourse . . . is the deep structure of the common ideology shared by the New Class. The ideology of the intellectuals . . . is thus an ideology about discourse. Apart from and underlying the various technical languages . . . spoken by specialized professions, intellectuals and intelligentsia are commonly committed to a culture of critical discourse. [It] is the latent but mobilizable infrastructure of modern "technical" languages.

—ALVIN W. GOULDNER

[One must] make allowance for the complex and unstable process whereby discourse can be both an instrument and an effect of power, but also a hindrance, a stumbling block, a point of resistance and a starting point for an opposing strategy. Discourse transmits and produces power; it reinforces it, but also undermines and exposes it, renders it fragile and makes it possible to thwart it.

—MICHEL FOUCAULT

The political status of technocracy as a knowledge elite is based on its claim to superior knowledge—an empirically established knowledge—and the technical forms of discourse appropriate to it. Insofar as the argument is based on a neopositivist conception of scientific knowledge, technocracy is vulnerable to an epistemological critique of the neopositivistic conception of science and rationality. The validity of technocratic claims can thus be assessed by an analysis of neopositivist methods and procedures through which they are derived. Methodologi-

215

cal critique, for this reason, can take the form of politics at the level of theory. It is to this task that we turn in the two chapters of this section.

In policy science the methodological problem, stated more concretely, focuses on the technostructure's instrumental orientation: its emphasis on empirical analysis of *means* to given ends. The postpositivist challenge is an effort to move beyond the calculation of efficient means to include an assessment of the substantive ends of policy, that is, the rationality of goals, values, and attitudes toward various ways of life. At root, postpositivism confronts positivism's most fundamental principle, namely, the strict separation of facts and values. It is an effort to surmount a narrowly gauged commitment to the analysis of means by integrating empirical and normative decision criteria in a more comprehensive concept of rationality.

Chapter 9, "Beyond Technical Discourse: A Theory of Comprehensive Rationality," takes up this challenge directly. The chapter begins with an examination of the social and political turmoil of the late 1960s and 1970s. The intellectual strife surrounding the political crises of the period took the form of an explicit challenge to the dominant technocratic methodologies and opened the social sciences to the search for alternative methodological orientations. One of the most influential contributions to this effort has been that of Jürgen Habermas. Taken here to be the most promising foundation for the methodological reconstruction of the organizational and policy sciences, the remainder of the chapter is devoted to an explication of Habermas's postpositivist epistemology. Drawing in particular on his theory of comprehensive rationality, the discussion focuses on the way in which technical rationality can be methodologically situated within a wider framework of social values and interests.

Chapter 10, "Critical Discourse and Policy Expertise: A Methodological Case Study," presents a policy-oriented methodology based on the concept of comprehensive rationality and illustrates its uses in the context of a case study. Specifically, the chapter examines a compensatory educational program from a postpositivist multimethodological perspective. Insofar as the search for a postpositivist methodology is one of the most challenging problems confronting modern social science, the approach outlined here is modestly put forward as a suggestive beginning upon which a more systematic reconstruction might be founded.

9

Beyond Technical Discourse:
A Theory of Comprehensive Rationality

A discussion that seeks to transcend the limitations of the technocratic approach must directly confront the question of epistemology. Toward this end, we examine here the neopositivistic epistemological foundations of technocracy, particularly its conception of technical rationality, and advance a "postpositivist" (or "postempiricist") alternative.[1] In this respect, the analysis draws primarily on the postpositivist perspective of Jürgen Habermas.

The purpose of a postpositivist epistemology is to provide a methodological framework capable of transcending the limits of the technical conception of rationality that underlies much of empirical social science.[2] The task of such a project is the development of a methodological framework that incorporates both the rigor of empirical science and the classical traditions of normative theory.[3] In the language of epistemology, the objective is to situate the dominant neopositivistic conception of social science methodology within the structure of a more comprehensive theory of rationality.[4] More specifically, the task is to outline a methodological framework that not only includes but logically transcends empirical analysis by interpreting the meaning of its data in both the context of action and a larger critique of society.[5] Such a methodology is systematically structured to move inquiry from the most concrete level of empirical investigation up through the higher levels of abstract exploration of norms and values.

The search for a more comprehensive theory of rationality thus focuses on the question of how to methodologically relate the levels of social and political evaluation. In numerous ways, the pursuit is impeded by the long-standing antipathy that exists between empirical social scientists and philosophically oriented normative theoreticians. Empirical social scientists have tended either to dismiss abstract normative theory as speculative and irrational or to criticize the philosopher's contribution as hopelessly general at the level of concrete research; philosophers in turn have generally remained content to disdain the practical problems of empirical research. "In the abstract," as Forester writes, "each needs the other; in the concrete, each has little patience with the other's style."[6]

Although empirical and normative theorists both tend to devalue the necessity of each other, it has become increasingly clear to many that the strengths of one are in fact the weaknesses of the other, and vice versa. As yet, there has been little methodological investigation on the part of either that speaks to this problem. If the task of a comprehensive theory of rationality is to bring them together, the critical question is this: What is the logic of the methodological structure capable of systematically linking one level of evaluation to the other?

Addressed to the gap between these two levels of inquiry, the task in this section of the book is to provide a comprehensive methodological structure based on a synthesis of epistemological elements borrowed from the works of Habermas, Toulmin, and Taylor.[7] Given the intellectual distance and tensions between normative and empirical camps, there can be no hope of resolving their critical differences in these two chapters. The intended purpose is only to offer a suggestive beginning capable of facilitating the much needed dialogue between them.

The problems that arise at the empirical end of the dichotomy are taken as the point of entry for this discussion. As such, the angle of vision tends to be that of the social scientist rather than the philosopher or epistemologist. For this reason, the framework presented here is primarily a contribution to social science methodology. While no discussion of social science methodology can altogether ignore its epistemological implications, at the level of methodology it is necessary at times to temporarily "bracket out" the more philosophical questions of methodology. In social research, as in social life generally, inquiry is in reality forced to proceed in the absence of philosophical certainty.

Insofar as a distinction is employed here between *epistemology* and *methodology*, it is important at the outset to offer working definitions for these terms. Such a task, it should be noted, is somewhat complicated by the fact that these terms are employed differently by European and American writers (and frequently used interchangeably by others). For purposes here, *epistemology* and *methodology* are distinguished as two different levels of analysis with their own separate purposes and concerns. *Epistemology* is concerned with fundamental questions that arise in the pursuit of knowledge; it involves the search for ultimate principles. As matters of philosophical analysis, epistemological issues remain far removed from the concrete problems of technique (e.g., experimentation and data collection) that emerge in the process of research and analysis. By contrast, *methodology*, as it is understood here, focuses on the intermediate or middle-range problems that arise between philosophical principles and research techniques. Emerging from research rather than philosophy, methodology is an attempt to reconstruct the working logic of the investigatory process. Its objective is the development of a rational model of the inferential assessment process employed in social and political research.[8]

In the context of methodology, the assignment is to propose an alternative to the neopositivistic understanding of inquiry that dominates methodological thinking in the social sciences. Toward this end, the methodology is developed through a series of interrelated discussions. This chapter provides an introduction to the normative issues in political science and sociology that generate the methodological problem of the levels of evaluation; it then presents Habermas's concept of comprehensive rationality as an alternative approach designed to integrate these levels. In the subsequent chapter, Toulmin's model of substantial arguments and Taylor's logic of evaluation are employed to translate Habermas's epistemological framework into a methodology for evaluating public policy arguments. The methodology is illustrated with a specific case study.

The Problem of Methodology

The objective in this section is to illustrate how the methodological debate that emerged in the social sciences in the late 1960s and 1970s prefigured the need for a more comprehensive methodological framework capable of integrating normative and empirical theory. In large part the result of the urban crisis and the Vietnam War, the middle to late 1960s was a period of great social and political turmoil. In the social sciences this strife took the form of a search for "social relevance" in theory and research. Much of it was precipitated by the increasing use of social and political research to plan and legitimate the policies of this period. The fact that the use of such research was accompanied by one of the most fundamental challenges to political authority emerged as a source of considerable consternation and embarrassment to many social scientists. Why, for example, did Great Society policies, often influenced by (and in some cases designed by) leading social scientists, contribute to urban violence? Why was it that the contemporary social sciences, armed with sophisticated research methodologies, were unable to predict or foresee the implications of their own programs?[9]

During such periods of normative malaise, the academic community is often compelled to confront the epistemologies that underlie competing political perspectives.[10] In this respect, the polemic about "social relevance" can be traced, both directly and indirectly, to the political turmoil of the second half of the decade. In sharp contrast to the self-confidence exhibited in the early part of the decade by empirically oriented social scientists, the latter half of the decade brought polemical discussion and speculation about the relevance of their research to actual political problems. Complaints emanated from across the political spectrum. Those oriented toward the priorities of the established power structure increasingly lamented the failure of the social sciences to provide usable knowledge for social guidance and control; those committed to the causes of the poor and the minorities accused the social sciences of ideological manipulation.

Such debates invariably raised questions about the relation of knowledge to power. Who controlled the production of knowledge? And for what purpose was it employed? One result of this debate was an increasing recognition of the emergence of technocratic decision making and the forms of social and political control associated with it.

Technocratic decision strategies, as we have seen, are based on a positivistically oriented empirical conception of knowledge (reflected in a growing inventory of operational techniques such as cost-benefit analyses, operations research, systems analysis, strategic planning, and computer simulations).[11] Emphasizing the tenets of value-neutral objectivity, empirical operationalism, and professional expertise, modern technocracy stands or falls with the ideology of scientism. Thus, as Habermas explains, knowledge under technocracy "is defined by what the sciences do and can . . . be adequately explicated through the methodological analysis of scientific procedures."[12] For this reason, methodological research can take the form of politics at the level of theory.

In political science and sociology these methodological concerns emerged as a search for a postpositivist or postempiricist paradigm.[13] Influenced by Thomas Kuhn's theory of scientific progress, this search for an alternative paradigm began with an intense scrutiny of the basic methodological principles of "normal" social science, particularly the relationship of empirical evidence to theoretical models and their normative assumptions. These issues reopened questions about the viability of maintaining the "fact-value" dichotomy and the principle of "ethical neutrality" in the social sciences. In clear contrast to the view that values are emotive responses (matters of personal conviction, taste or faith) that lie beyond the reach of rational assessment, postpositivists argued that even the constitution of a fact, let alone a theory, is inherently tied to value assumptions lodged (explicitly or implicitly) in the foundations of the researcher's theoretical and ideological orientation. Beyond the narrow emphasis on empirical research, an adequate postpositivist methodology would have to place primary emphasis on the study of the theoretical and normative structures that guide data collection and assessments.[14]

The search for an alternative methodology initially followed several separate avenues. First, there was a phenomenological orientation drawn largely from sociology, expecially the work of Alfred Schutz.[15] For researchers who followed this path, a relevant social science must place primary emphasis on the social actor's normative point of view. They argued that the investigator must get inside the social situation to grasp the actor's own interpretations of events. Some concentrated on the elaboration of sophisticated methodological procedures for "unobtrusive" observation, while others offered detailed accounts of the effects of specific social events in everyday life. Both groups agreed that researchers must explain social action in terms of the impressions and outlooks of the actors themselves rather than in terms of empirical descriptions alone.

At the same time there was a resurgence of social and political philosophy. While political philosophers agreed about the need to begin with the actor's subjective viewpoint, writers as disparate as Leo Strauss and Sheldon Wolin insisted on pushing the level of analysis beyond the relativity inherent in the social actor's own common sense interpretations of everyday experience.[16] The task must also include the explication of fundamental value principles on which this experience was organized.

In this respect, the critical theory of the Frankfurt School began to attract special attention. As a thoroughgoing attempt to link philosophy and science, fact and value, the work of Max Horkheimer, Theodor Adorno, and Herbert Marcuse, followed by that of Habermas, represented a major effort to construct a theory capable of relating philosophical critique and political interpretation to everyday self-awareness.[17] The objective is defined as a critical theory and method intended to promote political consciousness and self-actualization.[18] Habermas's work, which began to appear in English in the early 1970s, is a comprehensive attempt to ground epistemologically the categorical framework of this project.

These phenomenological and philosophical critiques of mainstream social science methodologies raised profound epistemological issues about the empiricist treatment of the normative character of the social world. As Richard Bernstein has succinctly summarized it: They posed questions about fundamental categorical distinctions "between theory and 'practice,' where 'practice' is understood as the technical application of theoretical knowledge; the distinction between empirical and normative theory, where the former is directed toward description and explication of what *is*, while the latter deals with the clarification and justification of what *ought to be*; the distinction between descriptive and prescriptive discourse; and the distinction between fact and value."[19] Translated into research-oriented methodological terms, these categorical distinctions generate critical questions about the purposes of social and political evaluation, and the relationship of the various levels of evaluation to each other, including the relation of holistically oriented qualitative research methods (such as participatory observation and *verstehen*, aimed at social understanding and interpretation) to analytical empirical techniques (based on experimental design and statistical inference, employed in causal analysis and prediction).

Many mainstream social scientists were willing to accept the normative theoretical character of the problem but not the phenomenological or philosophical solutions. Disturbed by the antiempiricism of the interpretively oriented approaches, they advanced a third orientation closely aligned to the methodological tenets of scientific naturalism, a long-standing and respected tradition in normative theory. As an advocate of this position, David Easton stated that the critics were correct about the failure of social science to deal with value orientations but wrong in their responses.[20] Phenomenology and philosophy, in this view, were methodologically bankrupt, as they offered no procedure for inference between competing hypotheses. Wolin's emphasis on "tacit knowledge," Strauss's return to the classical traditions of Plato and Aristotle, as well as Schutz's *verstehen*, were held to represent a turn back to intuition and speculation. Some complained that they offered little more than a plea for a return to a liberal arts program. Rather than the methods of *verstehen* and critique, the proper response was to increase the empirical rigor of social science and apply its focus to the value-laden issues of public policy.[21]

The most significant effort undertaken by policy-oriented empiricists to promote a wider focus on values was the adoption of a systems framework. As a rigorous teleological methodology, systems analysis shifted the empirical focus from a narrow efficiency orientation to a broader framework emphasizing the multiple evaluation criteria of complex phenomena. A systems-based policy analysis, as Graham put it, represented a transition from the micro to macro level of evaluation.[22]

Supported by a rigorous statement of systems theory and its empirical methodology, the technocratic conception of social science managed to maintain its hold on the disciplines. However, the fact that the phenomenological and philosophical approaches succeeded in staking out valid contributions suggested that something more was involved than was readily apparent. The strident tone of the debate subsided but the problem continued to linger. Many, in fact, began to see the issue in a new light. Perhaps the question was not "which methodology is right?" but rather "what is the relationship between them?" In short, could they all be components of a larger methodological framework?[23]

The by-product of this recognition was a less strident and more rigorous turn to the study of the philosophy of science and its implications for social science methodology. A growing number of methodologists began to devote their energies to the development of "new directions."[24] A number of writers were willing to directly address the normative dimension of the problem on its own epistemological terms. Martin Rein, for instance, argued that the problem of methodological integration basically involves finding a way to translate the two distinct languages of facts and values into a common methodological framework. Values, as he puts it, are not inferior to facts; they are merely different.[25]

Recognition of the epistemological barriers that separate empirical and normative judgments opens the possibility of an alternative avenue of investigation. As Grauhan and Strubelt point out, to speak of a methodology capable of integrating empirical and normative judgments is to talk about the development of a more comprehensive concept of rationality.[26] It raises questions about the possibility of extending rational assessment beyond the concrete levels of empirical outcomes to the more abstract normative questions concerned with the assessment of social norms and political value judgments. In short, is it possible to find logical connections that systematically link the empirical and normative levels of evaluation?

It is in this context that neopositivistic social scientists have their strongest grip on the methodology issue. Despite the many diverse attacks on positivism's own self-understanding, the positivists' emphasis on rational procedures has proved to be a powerful foil. Bernstein formulates their position this way:

> Whatever disagreements there may be about the characteristics of the natural sciences, mathematics and logic, there can be no doubt that these disciplines are the exemplars of warranted knowledge. One of the depth motivations for restricting the domain of legitimate knowledge to these disciplines or those which have been molded upon them, was the revulsion against the belief that there are other forms of knowledge and other means of gaining knowledge. Positivists claimed that when we examine these other pretenders to knowledge, we discover that they lack what is characteristic of scientific knowledge: rational procedures for testing, validating and rejecting hypotheses.[27]

The demand for rigorous explication and precise formulation has been one of the most important contributions of positivism. To its adversaries it says: "If you assert that there are other forms of knowledge and other means for testing knowledge claims, you must clearly and rigorously state what these are."[28] The fact that this virtue has contributed to positivism's own epistemological troubles (namely, its failures to meet its own standards) does not offset the value of the thesis. It still leaves the critics with this question: "If positivism is fundamentally mistaken, then what is a proper account of science and knowledge?"[29] This has proven to be a difficult question to answer. The inability of phenomenology and philosophy to answer it certainly has been a prime reason that neopositivistic methodology has successfully maintained its grasp in the social sciences long after many of its tenets have been invalidated.

It is here that we are drawn to Jürgen Habermas's work on the relation of knowledge to human interests.[30] Fundamentally concerned with linking normative theory to practical action, Habermas has labored to develop a theory of comprehensive rationality that incorporates the methodological concerns of both science and philosophy, empirical and practical reason.[31] Central to this extraordinary effort has been his attempt to integrate the principal competing methodologies in the social sciences. As such, this work offers powerful insights into the nature of the task of methodological reconstruction in the contemporary social sciences.

The advantages of borrowing from Habermas's work are not without difficulties. One problem concerns the complexity of the epistemological project. McCarthy captured its complexity in these words:

> It is empirical without being reducible to empirical-analytic science; it is philosophical but in the sense of critique and not of first philosophy; it is historical without being historicist; and it is practical, not in the sense of possessing a technological potential but in the sense of being oriented to enlightenment and emancipation.[32]

Because of its scope and sophistication, which presupposes a good grasp of analytical philosophy linguistics as well as the social sciences, Habermas's work is often intellectually intimidating. As George Lichtheim put it, "the baffling thing about Habermas is that, at an age when most of his colleagues have painfully established control over one corner of the field, he has made himself master of the whole, in depth and breadth alike."[33]

A second difficulty arises from its provocative character. As an attempt to integrate methodological traditions that have long been hostile toward each other, such as historical materialism, phenomenology, linguistic philosophy, behavioral science, and functional systems theory, identification with Habermas's project draws opposition as well as enthusiasm. The present study attempts to "bracket out" these epistemological controversies by focusing on the more practical requirements of methodology. In this regard, elements of Habermas's work are borrowed only where they suit present purposes.

Furthermore, where we do borrow from Habermas, the value of the contribution rests not so much upon what has been proven but upon the fact that it offers (in the context of contemporary philosophical and scientific research) essential clues as to how these enduring methodological questions might be reformulated. To recognize the potential of this work as a program for further research does not imply the full validity of the project. Habermas offers such a caveat himself.

At this point, the discussion can turn to the pertinent elements of Habermas's theory of comprehensive rationality, particularly his theory of cognitive interests and its implications for a multilevel theory of social and political evaluation.

Comprehensive Rationality

The contemporary social sciences, Habermas argues, have been turned into a variety of social management theories.[34] Increasingly oriented toward providing information for social guidance and control, they have largely been relegated to the role of policy sciences (in the narrow technical sense of the term). The principal intellectual support behind this development has been the positivists' technocratic understanding of the relationship between theory and practice. Habermas thus takes the critique of this understanding as his point of departure. His objective is to place this relationship in a broader concept of rationality that extends from the level of empirical analysis to practical discourse and critical reflection.

The groundwork for the development of such a concept of rationality involves a wide-ranging examination of leading contemporary methodologies. Habermas's purpose is to criticize their claims to self-sufficiency while appropriating their essential contributions.[35] Starting with a critique of the neopositivistic "scientization of politics," he develops an approach very different from the one commonly adopted by critics of technocracy. Where others argue against science altogether, or claim that science itself will be radically transformed in a new society, Habermas attempts to preserve science by relegating it to a more limited realm of methodological activity. His objective is to criticize the scientific understanding of society without rejecting altogether the logical structure and purpose of science.[36]

The fundamental problem is found in positivism's restricted concept of rationality, largely instrumental and technical in nature. At the expense of a more substantive concept of reason or rationality, instrumental or "formal" rationality has become the evaluative standard against which social action in general is assessed. Positivistic social scientists argue that technical efficiency is the basic principle of all rational action, not just the special feature of a certain type of rational action.[37]

For Habermas, the solution lies in locating technical reason—and the policy-oriented social sciences that embody it—within a comprehensive theory of rationality that extends beyond efficiency. His theory is built around a number of interrelated components: the development of a theory of cognitive interest, a consensus theory of truth, a linguistically oriented theory of communicative competence, and the concept of an "ideal speech community." For present purposes, we can limit our attention to the theory of cognitive interests.

The Theory of Cognitive Interests

The theory of cognitive interests is an attempt to radicalize epistemology by unearthing the roots of knowledge in human life. Habermas's central thesis is that there are three generic areas in which human interests generate knowledge for the maintenance and survival of society. As "specific viewpoints" from which we apprehend aspects of social reality, each area of interest has its basis in the natural history of the species. Tied to the "imperatives of the sociocultural form of life," knowledge generated by these interests unfolds through the specific media of social organization. They are the media of work, linguistic interaction, and power. In this respect, an adequate theory of the epistemological foundations of a comprehensive approach to society must itself be anchored to a theory of society.[38]

Habermas identifies these human interests as "quasi-transcendental" spheres that determine the categories relevant to what we call knowledge in the three media. As such, they provide the basis for specific cognitive strategies that systematically guide inquiry within them—that is, they determine the modes of discovering knowledge relevant to each sphere and for establishing the warrantability of particular knowledge claims. These distinct but interrelated knowledge domains are specified as the three primary "cognitive interests." Identified as the technical, practical, and emancipatory interests, they are pursued through the methodologies of the empirical-analytic sciences, the (phenomenologically based) historical-hemeneutic disciplines, and critically oriented philosophical speculation and self reflection.

Presented by Habermas as the epistemological foundations of a comprehensively rational theory of society, it is relatively easy to recognize the implications of these interests for the mainstream debate in the social sciences (where, as we saw, the relationship between empirical research, social phenomenology, and political philosophy has become increasingly problematic). The character of these relationships becomes apparent as the specific logic of each cognitive interest is unraveled.

First, consider the technical cognitive interest. The technical interest, which governs the medium of work, is pursued through the application of the empirical-analytic sciences (including the natural and social sciences insofar as they aim at producing nomological knowledge). Identified by Habermas as the medium of "purposive-rational" social action, it is concerned with "expectations as to the behavior of external objects and of other men, and making use of these expectations as 'conditions' or 'means' for the rational, success-oriented pursuit of the agent's own rationally considered ends."[39] Within this sphere, Habermas locates the means-ends orientation of action and decision criteria upon which it is based—primarily the principles of economy and efficiency. As an epistemological orientation from which reality is apprehended, it originates in the cognitive interest of the species rooted in the activities of physical labor and work organization (defined as a primary level of action). It is designed to generate knowledge about how to secure the existence of the human species in systems of labor and self-assertion through physical effort, including force. As a practical technique, it is easily recognized as the type of knowledge pursued by the contemporary social or policy sciences—for instance, a comparison of the efficiency of alternative tax policies in promoting urban development or in the evaluation of an employment training program to determine its actual degree of success after implementation.

The type of knowledge characterized by the second cognitive interest—practical knowledge—is the object of the phenomenologically oriented historical hermeneutic disciplines.[40] It is concerned with uncovering the practical interest pursued through the medium of communicative social interaction. As a mode of inquiry, it includes the humanities, history, and the social sciences insofar as they aim at an interpretive understanding of the meaning of action. The practical interest that orients these disciplines must be sharply distinguished from the primary level of human action characterized as work or purposive-rational action. In contrast to causal laws, practical knowledge is governed by mutually shared or recognized consensual norms, which define reciprocal expectations about behavior. Such norms, enforced by binding sanctions, are objectified through ordinary language communication. Thus, while the validity of technical rules depends on the empirical truth or analytical correctness of propositions, the validity of social norms is grounded in the intersubjectivity of the mutual understanding of intentions and secured through normative discourse aimed at the identification of general social duties and obligations.

The essential epistemological point here is that communicative social interaction is a nonreducible type of action requiring a distinctive set of categories for its description, explanation, and understanding.[41] Individuals shape and determine themselves not only through their physical activities, such as work, but also through communicative action and language. If we are to understand the ways in which the human species has formed itself in the course of historical development, it is just as important to understand the historical forms of communicative social interaction as it is to understand the forms of purposive-rational action. Fundamentally, the task is to recognize the complex ways in which the two levels of action are interrelated.

Habermas draws upon a wide variety of literatures—including phenomenology and hermeneutics, interpretive sociology, and Wittgenstein's analysis of language games—to clarify what he means by "interaction" and to justify his claim that it is a nonreducible level of action. What he takes to be vital and correct in these seemingly disparate approaches is a primary emphasis on a level of communication and intersubjectivity that is basic for understanding social and political life.

To establish the autonomy and nonreducibility of communicative interaction, Habermas shows that we cannot comprehend empirical-analytical science itself without reference to historical, hermeneutic knowledge. Essentially, he argues that an attempt to give a rational account of empirical-analytic science by reference only to the concepts shaped by the technical interest is self-defeating.[42] If the scientific community can in principle provide us with a true and complete empirical account of knowledge and reality, then it should be possible within its own scientific framework to explain the very possibility of empirical-analytic knowledge. But, following Peirce's analysis of a scientific community of inquirers, we discover that the intelligibility of such a community (with its distinctive forms of intersubjective communication) presupposes a level of action—symbolic interaction—and a set of categories needed to account for that action, which are richer and more inclusive than those explicitly countenanced by the technical-cognitive interest. Thus Habermas maintains that the scientific disciplines are themselves grounded in a historical-hermeneutic process. As such, historical-hermeneutic knowledge must be conceptualized as an independent but essential component of human inquiry.

As in the case of the empirical-analytical sciences, Habermas is also sharply critical of the monopolistic tendencies of the historical-hermeneutic disciplines to claim that they provide the most fundamental knowledge of man and the world. The self-understandings of both these methodological orientations mistake the parts for the whole. Basically, they fail to recognize that there is a nonreducible plurality of fundamental cognitive interests. As he puts it, the verification of lawlike hypotheses in the empirical-analytic sciences has its counterpart in the historical-hermeneutic disciplines in the interpretation of textual meaning, concerned with clarifying the conditions of communication and intersubjectivity.[43] At the epistemological level, the theory of cognitive interests is capable of distinguishing a technical orientation toward prediction and scientific control of objectified processes from a practical orientation in pursuing the question of "what is to be done?" In methodological terms, it clarifies the distinctions between naturalistic modes of causal explanation pursued by "the empirical-analytic sciences" and the interpretively oriented disciplines, such as *verstehende* (or phenomenological) sociology, history, and the humanities. The implication is that the technically oriented subsystems of action must be distinguished analytically from the sociocultural framework in which they are situated.

Here Habermas has recast the methodological issues that underlay the debate in the social sciences in the late 1960s. Instead of taking sides with the empiricists (arguing the case for causal explanation) or the phenomenologists and philosophers (advocating interpretive understanding), Habermas accepts both modes of knowing. Neither explanation nor understanding is to be denigrated. The task of his project, as a middle course between natural and idealist epistemology, is to demonstrate that a more comprehensive concept of rationality must incorporate both types of knowledge.[44]

The Emancipatory Interest

The third cognitive interest, the emancipatory interest, is more difficult to grasp than the technical and practical interests. The emancipatory interest is concerned with freedom and the problem of self-liberation from pseudonaturalistic constraints. Its purpose is to epistemologically ground the goal of a critical social science, defined as a radical critique of society aimed at furthering human emancipation. Under the rubric of this interest, Habermas wants to accommodate both the tradition of philosophical critique and critical self-reflection.[45]

Part of the difficulty involved in understanding the emancipatory cognitive interest is owed to its derivative character. The first two interests—technical and practical—relate to formal conditions of distinct types of knowledge, hypothetico-deductive systems and interpretive hermeneutic methods, respectively. These two cognitive interests are designated as "fundamental" orientations toward knowledge about work and communication necessary for social existence. The emancipatory interest, on the other hand, is *derived* from the practical sphere of interaction. Unlike the technical and practical interests, which are organized as "formal" knowledge, it is concerned with the basic moral pursuit of human emancipation. As a mode of inquiry (oriented toward what "ought to be"), it is directed at a critique of power and ideology in existing social arrangements that distort moral relations within the sphere of social interaction.

Because of its derivative character, the emancipatory interest has a different anthropological status than the two more basic interests of work and communicative interaction. Aimed at a critique of unnecessary and nontransparent constraints on human freedom, the emancipatory interest, as Habermas explains, "can only develop to the degree to which the repressive force, in the form of the normative exercise of power, presents itself permanently in structures of distorted communication—that is, to the extent that domination is institutionalized."[46] In this respect, it is concerned with the power relationships that establish the connections between theoretical knowledge and an objective domain of practical social life (which comes into existence as a result of systematically distorted communication and thinly legitimated repression). That is, it focuses on the power and ideology that fix work and interaction into specific historical forms of social existence. Such forms cannot be identified as invariant constituent categories of life, as can work and social interaction. Habermas explains it this way:

> The systematic *sciences of action*, that is economics, sociology and political science, have the goal, as do the empirical-analytic sciences, of producing nomological knowledge. A critical social science, however, will not remain satisfied with this. It is concerned with going beyond this goal to determine when theoretical statements grasp invariant regularities of social action as such and when they express ideologically frozen relations of dependence that can in principle be transformed. To the extent that this is the case, the *critique of ideology* . . . take[s] into account [the fact] that information about lawlike connections sets off a process of reflection in

the consciousness of those whom the laws are about. Thus the level of unreflected consciousness, which is one of the initial conditions of such laws, can be transformed.[47]

Although the emancipatory interest is concerned with the explication of "latent potentials" lodged in variant historical forms, there is another sense in which it is itself invariant. Even though the emancipatory interest is derived from the basic categories of social life, Habermas identifies it as primary interest that establishes the very possibility of rational normative standards.[48] His contention is this: If, at the level of philosophical reflection, we examine the forms of knowledge and rationality guided by the technical and practical interest, we can locate in reason itself an internal demand for the conditions of free and open communication. Following Peirce, he maintains that an adequate epistemological understanding of the empirical-analytical sciences must include the existence of an open community of self-critical inquirers.[49] Such open and nondistortive communication is promoted by the emancipatory interest embedded in the historical-hermeneutic disciplines. Thus implicit in the knowledge guided by the technical and practical interests is the demand for the intellectual and material conditions for emancipation (i.e., the ideal state of affairs in which nonalienating work and free interaction can be manifested).

The way in which Habermas formulates what he means by the "emancipatory interest" clearly reveals his debt both to the classical Aristotelian conception of politics as the pursuit of the good life and to the tradition of German Idealism. He has remained faithful to the classical idea that the validity of the truth of a statement is in the final analysis determined by its relationship to the "good life." In terms of German Idealism, Habermas maintains, with Kant and Hegel, that reason can only be properly understood as embodying a primary interest or demand to become fully self-actualized. Through transcendental speculation, it is possible to locate in reason itself an interest in autonomy and responsibility that provides basic normative standards. The emancipatory interest aims at the pursuit of such reflection.

But Habermas also agrees with Marx's critique of German Idealism. Contending that an emancipatory interest cannot be realized by a solitary ego, or Absolute Spirit, he argues that it can be manifested only in and through the concrete social and political lives of men and women. The free and open communication that is the aim of the practical and emancipatory interests requires the existence of determinate social institutions and practices, which exert a powerful *causal* influence on the nature and quality of symbolic interaction. On this point Habermas is in essential agreement with Marx. While he is deeply suspicious of the tendency to think that there are historical material conditions that will automatically bring about the realm of freedom, he nonetheless maintains that free symbolic interaction (or unconstrained communication) cannot concretely exist unless nonalienating and nonexploitative material conditions exist. As he puts it, "A critically mediated knowledge of laws cannot through reflection alone render a law itself inoperative, but it can render it inapplicable."[50]

In subsequent work, Habermas has further elaborated his theory of comprehensive rationality by incorporating the knowledge-constituting categories of theoretical (empirical) and practical (normative) reason in a theory of "communicative competence."[51] Basic to the theory is a distinction between ordinary language communication and theoretical and practical discourses. This distinction is developed to differentiate between the attitude of everyday life (i.e., unreflected, uncritical common sense and opinion) and the theoretical attitude (i.e., scientific inquiry and critical thought based on reflection). In contrast to the everyday context of ordinary "communicative action," discourses are called into play when the truth or correctness of background validity claims become subject to dispute by speakers.

In normal communicative interaction these basic validity claims do not necessarily come into question. Remaining part of the "background consensus" that makes communication possible, the validity of claims (resting on underlying beliefs and norms) are more or less uncritically accepted by speakers. But "it is possible for situations to arise in which one or more of them becomes problematical in a fundamental way, that is, in a way which cannot be dealt with by simply requesting information, clearing up misunderstandings and the like, within the accepted framework of opinions and norms."[52] To eliminate a disturbance in the background consensus, either by restoring the original consensus or establishing a new one, a specific form of problem solving appropriate to the validity claim in question must be called into play. For example, when the truth or legitimacy of a claim comes into question, it can only be redeemed through the logics of theoretical and practical discourse, respectively. In McCarthy's words, "the validity of problematic truth claims or of problematic norms . . . can be redeemed discursively only, that is by entering into a discourse, which has the sole purpose of judging the truth of the problematic opinion or the correctness of the problematic norm."[53]

As a break in ordinary communicative interaction, the speech situation of discourse requires that judgment about certain states of affairs or norms be treated as hypothetical and subjected to systematic argumentation motivated only by the desire to achieve a rationally grounded agreement. Each speaker must have the goal of an ultimate consensus that terminates in intersubjective understanding, shared knowledge, and mutual trust among one another. "Such a consensus is achieved solely through the force of the better argument, determined by the formal properties of the specific mode and level of discourse."[54] There are no absolutely fixed decision procedures or methodologies that differentiate a rational from a nonrational consensus. Here, Habermas relies on a consensus theory of knowledge. Differences of fact or opinion are always subject to further argumentation and reflection at higher levels of theoretical and practical discourse.

Concluding Remarks

As a first step toward the reconstruction of policy science methodology, we have demonstrated here the systematic links between the components of Habermas's theory of comprehensive rationality and the methodological arguments in the social sciences that emerged in the late 1960s and early 1970s. His epistemological categories were seen to speak directly to the issues raised in the mainstream debates—especially those concerning the technocratic thrust of the social sciences—and to provide important clues as to what a theory of comprehensive rationality might look like.

Of particular significance for present purposes is the theory's ability to clarify both the boundaries and the interrelationships of technical and normative reason. As we saw at the outset, the essential epistemological problem underlying the widespread commitment to technical reason is its over-extension into the nontechnical sphere, namely, the social lifeworld governed by intersubjective communication (or communicative interaction). Habermas's analysis accepts the importance of technical reason but carefully situates it within a framework of competing interests. It takes the form of a coordinated system of interrelated cognitive interests (technical, practical, and emancipatory), social media (work, social interaction, and power), and sciences (empirical-analytic, historical-hermeneutic, and critical).

By all standards, the project is enormously ambitious and much remains to be clarified and elaborated. For the discussion here, however, it helpfully enables us to begin rethinking the basic epistemological problem posed by technical reason. Not only does it show how normative discourse is inherently related to technical discourse, it also establishes clear parameters for the applications of technical rationality. These insights are of critical importance to the task of reconstructing expertise generally. Only within a methodological framework of established rules governing the permissibility and priority of technical rationality can professional expertise confront the task of analytically integrating the normative and valuative orientations fundamental to a more participatory concept of expert practices. Toward this end, Habermas's theory of comprehensive rationality is an unparalleled contribution to contemporary social theory.

Finally, we conclude with a disclaimer. While Habermas advances his theoretical framework as a unifying structure designed to connect knowledge and social action with a theory of ideology and socialization, the purpose here is only to borrow specific epistemological elements to assist in the reconstruction of a practically oriented social science methodology. For this reason, the discussion can sidestep the contemporary critiques of Habermas's project as a whole, particularly those of the "postmodernists."[55] At this point, we can turn to the objective of translating the epistemological requirements of comprehensive rationality into a systematic methodology for the assessment of policy arguments. As the task of the next chapter, it is approached in the context of a case study.

Notes

1. The terms *positivism* and *neopositivism* are employed here as Thomas McCarthy uses them. "Positivism now functions more as a polemical epithet than as a designation for a distinct philosophical movement." Because of numerous embellishments, there is no longer a single "positivistic" perspective. The term is used to refer to the "'legacy of logical positivism'—a legacy of convictions and attitudes, problems and techniques, concepts and theories,—[that] pervades contemporary thought. Methodological positions are most easily identified, because they so identify themselves, with respect to this legacy, pro or con." Thomas McCarthy, *The Critical Theory of Jürgen Habermas* (Cambridge: MIT Press, 1978), pp. 137–38. To capture the variety of approaches subsumed under positivism, writers today typically employ the term *neopositivism*. Also, see Bruce Caldwell, *Beyond Positivism* (London: George Allen & Unwin, 1982), pp. 1–96.

2. On the postpositivist critique, see M. E. Hawkesworth, *Theoretical Issues in Policy Analysis* (Albany: State University of New York Press, 1988), pp. 49–71.

3. This particular conception of postpositivism is taken from McCarthy. He explains it as follows: "The outstanding task for a postpositivist methodology of social inquiry [is] to somehow to combine the access to practice of classical theory with the methodological rigor" of modern science. "In other words, what is called for [is] a marriage of the scientific and empirical with the practical and critical." Thomas McCarthy, *The Critical Theory of Jürgen Habermas* (Cambridge: MIT Press, 1978), pp. 126–27; also see Richard J. Bernstein, *The Restructuring of Social and Political Theory* (New York: Harcourt Brace Jovanovich, 1976), pp. 206–7.

4. A comprehensive theory of rationality is, as Bernstein explains, "a topic that is increasingly central for different lines of philosophical, social, and political inquiry. . . . Whatever one's final judgment about the current dispute in the postempiricist philosophy and history of science—disputes among Kuhnians, Popperians, and mavericks like Paul Feyerabend, Imre Lakatos, and Stephen Toulmin, as well as Dudley Shapere, Peter Achinstein, Mary Hesse, and Ernan McMullin—there is rational agreement about the inadequacy of the original positivist understanding of science, knowledge and meaning. But if positivism is fundamentally mistaken, then what is a proper account of science and knowledge?" The answer to this question is the objective of postpositivism or postempiricism. Bernstein, *The Restructuring*, pp. 206–7.

5. Ibid., p. xiv. In his assessment of the search for a postpositivist or post empiricist methodology, Bernstein writes that a comprehensive theory and method "must be at once empirical, interpretive and critical."

6. John Forester, "The Policy Analysis-Critical Theory Affair: Wildavsky and Habermas as Bedfellows?" in *Critical Theory and Public Life*, ed. John Forester (Cambridge: MIT Press, 1985), pp. 258–80.

7. Jürgen Habermas, *Theory and Practice* (New York: Beacon, 1972); Stephen Toulmin, *The Uses of Argument* (Cambridge: Cambridge University Press, 1958); and Paul Taylor, *Normative Discourse* (Englewood Cliffs, NJ: Prentice-Hall, 1961).

8. For a discussion of this distinction between epistemology and methodology, see Abraham Kaplan, *The Conduct of Inquiry: Methodology for Behavioral Science* (Scranton, PA: Chandler, 1964), pp. 3–33.

9. See, for example, Robert A. Scott and Arnold R. Shore, *Why Sociology Does Not Apply? A Study of the Use of Sociology in Public Policy* (New York: Elsevier, 1979); and Henry J. Aaron, *Politics and the Professors* (Washington, DC: Brookings Institution, 1978).

10. Karl Mannheim, *Ideology and Utopia* (New York: Harcourt, Brace and World, 1936), pp. 13–54.

11. Wolf V. Heydebrand, "Technocratic Corporatism," in *Organization Theory and Public Policy*, ed. Richard Hall and Robert Quinn (Beverly Hills, CA: Sage, 1983), pp. 93–114.

12. Jürgen Habermas, *Knowledge and Human Interests* (Boston: Beacon, 1972), p. 67.

13. George J. Graham, Jr., and George W. Carey, eds., *The Post-Behavioral Era: Perspectives on Political Science* (New York: David McKay, 1972).

14. For a guide to the literature on this point, see Frank Fischer, *Politics, Values, and Public Policy: The Problem of Methodology* (Boulder, CO: Westview, 1980), 19–63.

15. Alfred Schutz, *The Phenomenology of the Social World* (Evanston, IL: Northwestern University Press, 1967). In political science, see Robert A. Isaak and Ralph Hummel, *Politics for Human Beings* (North Scituate, MA: Duxbury, 1975).

16. Leo Strauss, *What Is Political Philosophy* (Glencoe, IL: Free Press, 1959); and Sheldon S. Wolin, "Political Theory as a Vocation," *American Political Science Review* 63 (December 1969): 1073–74.

17. See Martin Jay, *The Dialectical Imagination* (Boston: Little, Brown, 1973).

18. Jürgen Habermas, *Theory and Practice* (Boston: Beacon, 1973).

19. Bernstein, *The Restructuring*, p. 173.

20. David Easton, "Commentary on Lane's Paper," in *Integration of the Social Sciences Through Policy Analysis*, ed. James C. Charlesworth (Philadelphia: American Academy of Political and Social Science, 1972), p. 92.

21. Ibid.

22. George J. Graham, Jr., "The Concept of 'Political Evaluation' and the Levels of Theory," (mimeo; Nashville: Vanderbilt University, 1977); and George J. Graham, Jr., and Scarlett G. Graham, "Evaluating Drift in Policy Systems," in *Problems of Theory in Policy Analysis*, ed. Phillip M. Gregg (Lexington, MA: D. C. Heath, 1976), pp. 77–87. Macro evaluation, Graham explains, "links the determinants of the consequences of social policy, including comparative investigation of the relationship between policy processes and such system characterizing variables as the social structure (political pluralism, group, parties), governmental policy making and policy executing structures, and constitutional and ideological constraints." The systems level of evaluation is introduced to establish "parameters and clarify the limitations that will invariably constrain and reduce available courses of public action." As a macro-evaluative framework, the systems perspective provides a methodological basis for a more informed assessment of value goals than the standard conception of means-ends analysis.

23. See, for example, Michael Haas and Theodore L. Becker, "The Behavioral Revolution and After," in *Approaches to the Study of Political Science*, ed. Michael Haas and Henry S. Kariel (Scranton, PA: Chandler, 1970), pp. 479–510. Haas and Becker call for a "multimethodological" approach.

24. See Ian I. Mitroff and Louis Pondy, "On the Organization of Inquiry: A Comparison of Some Radically Different Approaches to Policy Analysis," *Public Administration Review* 34 (September–October 1974): 513.

25. Martin Rein, *Social Science and Public Policy* (New York: Penguin, 1976), pp. 37–95.

26. Rolf-Richard Grauhan and Wendelin Strubelt, "Political Rationality Reconsidered: Notes on an Integrated Scheme for Policy Choice," *Policy Sciences* 2 (Summer 1971): 270.

27. Bernstein, *The Restructuring*, p. 207.

28. Ibid.

29. Ibid.

30. For a general introduction to Habermas's work, see Thomas McCarthy, *The Critical Theory of Jürgen Habermas*, op. cit.; or David Held, *Introduction to Critical Theory: Horkheimer to Habermas* (Berkeley: University of California Press, 1980).

31. Bernstein, *The Restructuring*, p. 205.

32. McCarthy, *The Critical Theory*, p. 126.

33. George Lichtheim, *From Marx to Hegel* (New York: Seabury, 1971), p. 175.

238 POLICY SCIENCE AND THE POSTPOSITIVIST CHALLENGE

34. Trent Schroyer, *The Critique of Domination* (Boston: Beacon, 1973).

35. See Garbris Kortian, *Metacritique: The Philosophical Argument of Jürgen Habermas* (New York: Cambridge University Press, 1980).

36. Jürgen Habermas, "Technology and Science as 'Ideology,'" in *Toward a Rational Society* (Boston: Beacon, 1970), p. 87. Habermas is responding to theorists, such as Herbert Marcuse, who have argued that science itself will be transformed in a politically liberated society. See Marcuse, *One-Dimensional Man* (Boston: Beacon, 1964). Essentially Habermas argues that the specific sociohistorical form of science and technology that is at issue has its origins in particular institutional arrangements, not in the logic of science itself. While these institutional forms are subject to change, the logical structure of science is not. This point, he maintains, can be demonstrated by showing that, as a mode of inquiry, the logic of science and technology is rooted in social self-preservation and material necessity. As long as human societies have to seek their own material self-preservation, achieved through labor and work organizations, there can be no "more humane" substitute for scientific and technical knowledge. Rather than something that can be historically surpassed, technology is part of the human project as a whole. The real difficulty, according to Habermas, is not technical reason as such but rather its overextension into other spheres of social life.

37. See Ludwig von Mises, *Epistemological Problems of Economics* (Princeton, NJ: D. Van Nostrand, 1960), p. 148. Today the perspective in economics and political science that most typifies this emphasis on efficient action is "public choice theory." For a guide to this literature, see Davis B. Bobrow and John S. Dryzek, *Policy Analysis by Design* (Pittsburgh: University of Pittsburgh Press, 1987), chap. 3.

38. Jürgen Habermas, *Knowledge and Human Interests* (Boston: Beacon, 1971), pp. 43–63; and Habermas, *The Theory of Communicative Action: Reason and the Rationalization of Society* (Boston: Beacon, 1984).

39. McCarthy, *The Restructuring*, p. 25.

40. Ibid., pp. 68–75.

41. Ibid., pp. 137–62.

42. Habermas, *Knowledge and Human Interests*.

43. Ibid., p. 309.

44. McCarthy, *The Restructuring*, pp. 75–91. To assert that the knowledge-constitutive interests, and the types of inquiry guided by these interests, are autonomous and not reducible to each other poses a danger of which Habermas is acutely aware. The risk is in making the mistake of assuming that the nonreducible media of social life—work and communicative interaction—operate in mutual isolation from each other. The central problem in his effort, in fact, is to reconstruct the traditional Marxist theory of historical materialism. According to Habermas, positivistic historical materialism is forced to misconceive its own critique of capitalism by virtue of its categorical framework. By restricting the materialistic concept of the synthesis of man and nature to the categorical framework of the mode of production, scientific Marxism has undercut the critical impulse in Marxist analysis by inappropriately subordinating it to the logic of the technical interest. Habermas's argument for the justification of his effort to reconstruct the categorical framework of historical materialism is derived from his contention that Marx recognized the role of ideology and communication in his own material investigations. The problem, according to Habermas, is that Marx never got around to clarifying this category of analysis in a

methodological treatise, a task that fell to Engels and other positivistic followers. See Tony Flood, "Jürgen Habermas's Critique of Marxism," *Science and Society* 41 (Winter 1978): 448–64.

45. Ibid., p. 86.

46. Habermas, *Theory and Practice*, p. 22.

47. Habermas, *Knowledge and Human Interests*, p. 310.

48. McCarthy, *The Restructuring*, pp. 75–91.

49. Habermas, *Knowledge and Human Interests*, pp. 91–112.

50. Ibid., p. 310.

51. Habermas's terms "theoretical" and "practical" discourse are synonymous with "empirical" and "normative" discourse, respectively.

52. Thomas A. McCarthy, "A Theory of Communicative Competence," in *Critical Sociology*, ed. Paul Connerton (New York: Penguin, 1976), p. 476.

53. Ibid.

54. McCarthy, *The Critical Theory of Jürgen Habermas,* pp. 291–333.

55. Because of the emphasis on action-oriented social science, the discussion does not deal with the "postmodern" critique. Postmodernists are correct in arguing that Habermas's effort to reconstruct the Enlightenment concept of reason leaves many questions unanswered. His categories, in fact, raise problematic questions at the level of society. Postmodernists have themselves yet to offer a systematic conceptualization of "post-Enlightenment" reason, but it may well be true that we await a new form of social reason. Should this prove to be the case, it is nonetheless difficult to imagine how, at the levels of organizational action, decision making and political strategy could proceed without the analytical categories of rational discourse and consensus-formation. Habermas's efforts to normatively rescue the concepts of rational action from positivist interpretations represent an unprecedented epistemological advance for those interested in the reconstruction of the organizational and policy sciences. In this respect, the issue appears to be more a matter of how to relate the concepts of rational action to a more encompassing form of reason than one of discarding it altogether.

10

Critical Discourse and
Policy Expertise:
A Methodological Case Study†

In this chapter we examine the relevance of Habermas's theory of comprehensive rationality for the practical questions that arise in public policy.[1] Although Habermas has always emphasized the relationship of theory to practice, it is often quite difficult to grasp this connection in his work. In his own writings the link could hardly be stated more abstractly, a point amply demonstrated in the preceding chapter. For this reason, many social scientists have questioned the relevance of Habermas's scheme for more practical concerns such as those that arise in public policy and organizational analysis. Often writers in these fields have dismissed Habermas's critical theory as a philosophical project with little direct bearing on their immediate concerns. It is to this issue that we now turn. Specifically, the purpose is to clarify the relevance of his theory of comprehensive rationality in the context of a public policy issue.

One of the central themes in Habermas's project is an attempt to reconstruct the logic of the technocratically oriented social sciences. Fundamentally, his purpose is to rescue the social sciences from the

†SOURCE: This chapter is a revised version of "Critical Evaluation of Public Policy: A Methodological Case Study," in *Critical Theory and Public Life,* edited by John Forester (Cambridge: MIT Press, 1985), pp. 231–57; used by permission.

technocratic norms that now generally govern their orientation to practice (i.e., the norms governing the kinds of information that can be brought to bear on questions of social and political action). The function of his theory of rationality is to show the relationship of technical information (usually expressed as a measure of efficiency or effectiveness) to a more comprehensive conceptualization of knowledge itself. Thus, unlike many of the social sciences' critics, Habermas does not altogether dismiss the contribution of technical analysis; rather he has only sought to limit the more exaggerated claims made on its behalf. Instead of being identified as the *essence* of rationality itself, technical rationality (as the object of the empirical-analytic sciences) emerges as only *one* component of a full or comprehensive evaluation. Its implications for action are, therefore, wholly dependent on its relationship to the interpretive (historical-hermeneutic) and the critical (emancipatory) forms of reason. In short, a comprehensive evaluation requires that all three types of knowledge be brought to bear on an evaluation decision.

This chapter approaches the task through a methodological case study of Project Head Start, a compensatory educational program for disadvantaged children. The first step is to show the way in which the three types of knowledge that constitute the theory of comprehensive rationality bear directly on the evaluation of the Head Start program. Second, the chapter offers a methodological framework designed to organize these types of knowledge for a critical evaluation of the program. Drawing on Toulmin's model of substantial arguments and Taylor's logic of evaluation, the empirical, interpretive, and critical modes of reason are translated into a logic of practical questions for policy discourse.[2]

The second step is particularly important for the larger epistemological discussion that continues to ensue in the social sciences. A very large part of the success of the dominant empiricists can be attributed to their ability to say what their method is—indeed, to say it with considerable exactitude. The fact the empirical social scientists frequently violate their own methodological prinicples should not blind us to the strategic value of their textbook precision. It has permitted them to present their adversaries with an uncompromising demand. To those who argue for other types of knowledge, they insist on an account of their methodological procedures.[3] The methodological framework presented here is offered as a suggestive beginning in the attempt to address their challenge.

The Politics of Methodology:
The Case of Head Start

The practical relevance of the empirical, interpretive, and critical forms of knowledge can be illustrated by showing the ways in which they have emerged in specific policy debates. For this ·purpose, we employ the arguments that arose in response to the findings reported in the Westinghouse Learning Corporation's evaluation study of Project Head Start.[4]

As a compensatory educational program for disadvantaged children, Head Start was a prototype of the Johnson administration's War on Poverty. To the leaders of the Democratic party, it appeared as a panacea, "a quick, easy solution for the embarrassing, ever dangerous, problems of poverty, hunger, malnutrition, and explosive political alienations" that found expression in the urban riots of the 1960s.[5] Not only was the program essentially noncontroversial, and thus relatively safe in traditional political terms, it was also a reasonably inexpensive major social program. Opening in 1965, Head Start listed the following among its objectives:

Improving the perceptual, conceptual, and verbal skills of disadvantaged children

Developing cultural and educational curiosity

Providing better medical and dental care to poor children

Assisting in improving the self-discipline of disadvantaged children

Enlarging the sense of personal dignity and self-worth

Developing a socially responsible attitude toward the community and the larger society in both the children and their parents

Initial expectations were high. Educational psychologists spoke in glowing terms of the anticipated outcomes. (Some seemed to believe that several years of educational neglect might be compensated for in the short space of several summer sessions.) This interest and excitement was reflected in the early enrollment figures; in the first summer, more than five times the number of children initially anticipated were enrolled.

Three and a half years after the program opened its doors, negative reports began to appear. The first evaluation studies of the educational effects of the program failed to confirm the initial expectations. As Harrell Rodgers put it, "The studies showed that the ... educational gains tended to be small, especially for children who had not participated in year-round programs."[6] The most significant of these studies was commissioned by the federal government. Conducted by the Westinghouse Learning Corporation of Ohio University, a policy research organization specializing in educational affairs, the study became the subject of a major political controversy.

The controversy was instigated by Richard Nixon, who had based his presidential campaign in part on the "failures" of the War on Poverty. In 1969 as part of his continuing emphasis of this theme, Nixon presented the negative findings of the Westinghouse Report in his economic opportunity message to the Congress on national television. Proclaiming the program "a proven failure," he triggered an intense debate that ricocheted through Congress, the executive branch, educational circles, and the communities of the poor. Had the research organization in fact demonstrated the failure of the program? Did the evidence really show that participation in Head Start had no long-term results? Many leading social scientists were skeptical. Steeped in the empirical techniques of mainstream social science, they questioned whether the evaluators had used proper methodological procedures. Were the statistical samples properly chosen? Did the empirical instruments accurately measure reading achievement? Was the ex post facto research design inherently faulty?[7]

Equally interesting was another group of social scientists who raised a different kind of question.[8] Supported by many leaders of poor communities, they argued that the evaluation study employed the wrong criteria. In basing their conclusions on a measurement of reading scores alone, the Westinghouse evaluators showed that they had failed to understand the nature and purpose of Head Start. The legislation, they argued, had posited improved reading scores as only one of the program's objectives. Equally important was the provision of socially relevant experiences for ghetto children, such as an enlargement of their sense of personal dignity and self-worth and the development of socially responsible attitudes. Many sociologists and psychologists argued that these social experiences were critical for the transition from poverty to the middle class. Only through the experiential assimilation of mainstream social values could these disadvantaged children successfully function in middle-class institutions. Thus to judge the Head Start program a failure based on narrowly conceived empirical measurements of individual reading scores was a methodological error. Instead of objectively amassing empirical data from test scores, evaluators must develop subjectively relevant measures of social progress derived from firsthand experience with the disadvantaged community and its children; they must, in short, assume a phenomenological orientation.

There was a third type of argument that pertained more to the development of socially responsibile attitudes toward the larger society.[9] Concerned about theoretical and ideological principles, these critics maintained that, regardless of outcomes or consequences, (whether based on objective reading scores or on community-related standards), empirical measurement was an insufficient ground for judging Head Start a failure. In this view, Head Start had been designed to facilitate a basic value that must extend to all citizens in a democratic system: the right to equal opportunity. Thus the final evaluation of such a program must rest on a normative commitment to the equal opportunity principle, regardless of its secondary or indirect consequences for other dimensions of the social system. Compensatory programs like Head Start are designed to nurture long-term harmony and stability in the social order and must be judged accordingly.

Because of the ideological foundations of this argument, in the pragmatic realm of public policy it was sometimes advanced through implicit assumptions rather than stated premises.[10] We can, however, more or less reconstruct it as follows. Equal opportunity is one of the basic legitimating principles of liberalism. In this system educational institutions (designed for social mobility through the principle of merit) are the primary vehicles for the realization of equal opportunity. Thus, in a society marked by growing social inequalities, educational programs for disadvantaged children are of critical importance. Without programs such as Head Start, explicitly designed to give material meaning to the opportunity principle, the social system is left vulnerable to what Habermas calls a "legitimation crisis." To avert the social and political turmoil that can result from a general collapse of belief systems, compensatory programs must ensure adequate socialization of disadvantaged children, the potentially problematic citizens of the future generation. At this level of analysis reading scores are of secondary importance; the program's primary contribution must be measured in terms of its basic contribution to social legitimacy. Indeed, one of the primary factors that confers this legitimacy is the very existence of the program.

The foregoing arguments shared two common assumptions, one political and one methodological. All three—the empirical probe, the phenomenological concern about social relevance, and the ideological justification of equal opportunity—reflected a political concern that the

Westinghouse study would be used to eliminate Head Start. As one source put it, they "feared that Congress or the Administration [would] seize upon the report's generally negative conclusion as an excuse to downgrade or discard the Head Start program." [11] These fears were justified. While the Nixon administration was never able to eliminate the Head Start program entirely, the program budget was continuously cut. As Harrell Rodgers puts it, the Westinghouse Report's "negative findings were basically accepted at face value and cost Head Start much of its support in Congress." [12]

In the social sciences the phenomenologically and philosophically oriented arguments also shared a methodological concern. For these positions the issue was how to fit the Westinghouse data into alternative theoretical and normative frameworks. No longer could empirical data based on objective criteria be offered as value-neutral evidence. Evaluators would have to recognize that criteria such as reading scores are indicators drawn from a particular conception of social life.

Comprehensive Rationality

What does one make of these competing perspectives? On the surface of the matter, they would appear to have little in common with one another. Such arguments make it difficult for the trained observer, let alone the average editorial page reader, to form an intelligent opinion about Head Start. How to make sense of the situation became a prominent part of the public debate.

In the face of this turmoil, it is not surprising that the issue in methodological circles began to shift away from the question of "Which methodological orientation is right?" to "What is the relationship among them?" It is at this point that Habermas's theory of comprehensive rationality began to attract considerable attention in the United States. Some of the most important reconceptualizations can, in fact, be attributed to his influence.

In the previous chapter, we examined Habermas's theory of comprehensive rationality in some detail. It was seen to emerge from an analysis of the relationship between various types of knowledge and the needs and interests of particular social and political institutions. [13] Specifically, the component parts of the methodological debate in the social sciences—empirical, phenomenological, and philosophical—were conceptualized as "cognitive strategies" required for maintaining a stable, enduring social system. In turn Habermas linked these modes of discourse to the structure of ordinary language and the process of argumentation. Drawing on the work of Stephen Toulmin, he showed that "substantial arguments" are "pragmatic unities" that situate ordinary language sentences in relation to the basic social categories of reality (work, social interaction, and power) and their respective cognitive strategies (empirical, phenomenological, and philosophical methodologies).[14]

Fundamentally, then, a comprehensive system of rationality is a multimethodological system. As a postempirical model, it not only incorporates but also transcends its empirical data by interpreting their meaning both in the specific phenomenological context of action and as a fundamental critique of society's normative principles and axioms. In these terms a critical evaluation is one that explicates (for the purposes of discourse) the full range of empirical and normative assumptions that contribute to a particular judgment, from manifest to latent, from concrete to abstract.

While the theory of cognitive interests provides a rational basis for relating the competing methodologies to one another, we must still explore how these cognitive orientations might be employed as an integrated assessment procedure at the practical level of argumentation and evaluation. Beyond the demonstration that all three modes of rationality are component parts of a comprehensive theory of rationality, the viability of the contribution for the practice of policy evaluation will ultimately depend on our ability to specify the logical connections that integrate these cognitive strategies within the framework of a specific discourse, such as the Head Start debate. What is needed is a method of logic designed to clarify the structures and functions of the different propositions that constitute a comprehensive evaluation argument.

The objective is to translate the epistemological requirements of the three modes of inquiry into a unified framework for the discursive assessment of policy arguments. As a meta-structure such a framework would provide a logical basis for judging the soundness, strength, or conclusiveness of an argument. By clarifying the nature of an evaluation's propositions, it would guide an assessment of the relevance of the different types of objections that might be validly offered as criticisms in the various phases of a discourse.

Although Habermas does not explore this more practical level of the problem, he again provides an initial insight. Pointing to Toulmin's work on "substantial arguments," Habermas maintains that the progress of knowledge takes place through explanations or justifications based on a nonpositivistic (nondeductive) "informal" logic.[15] This suggests that the place to begin the search for a logic of a unified methodology capable of interconnecting validity claims of the basic cognitive strategies is in the structural form of the substantial argument.

Toulmin's study of arguments is addressed to the problems that arise from an overreliance on the classical syllogism as a mode of inference.[16] Where positivists argue that explanations that fail to approximate the ideals of the formal syllogism are imperfect or incomplete, Toulmin has shown that such a model rests on a limited conception of logic appropriate only to various stages of inquiry, both scientific and normative. An argument in a particular "substantial" context that fails to fulfill the requirements of the formal syllogism need not be judged incomplete or irrational. Its rationality can be properly judged only by the rules of inquiry appropriate to its own context (or "knowledge domain" in Habermas's terms).

Toulmin provides a six-element representation of the logical structure of a substantial argument (Figure 10.1). As a scheme for mapping out arguments, the elements D, W, and C parallel the model of the formal syllogism. The principal difference between the classical form and the substantial model is based on the introduction of Q, R, and B. Q and R express the tentative and contextual character of substantial arguments; Q expresses the degree of cogency or force attributed to a claim, while R specifies the contextual conditions under which the acceptability of the claim can be challenged. B reflects the demand for discursive redemption of the warrant. While in the classical syllogism the warrant (as major premise) tautologically establishes universal proof of the claim,

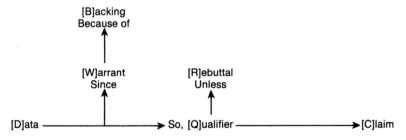

Figure 10.1   The structure of arguments.

in the substantial argument good reasons must be given to back a warrant. This opens the possibility of a second form of argument required to justify the use of the warrant.[17]

This second form of argument differentiates a comprehensive methodology from the conventional approach in the social sciences. Where rationality in the positivist's assessment of social action culminates with evidence on the technical efficiency of means, a comprehensive evaluation includes the justification of the warrant. But what does this form of argument look like? Beyond the pursuit of B, Toulmin has not schematically worked out this line of the model. For this purpose we can turn to the work of Paul Taylor, also writing in the informal logic tradition.[18] Taylor has sketched out the informal logic of a complete evaluation argument, that is, the way in which we give good reasons to justify a particular judgment. The remainder of this chapter will present this logic of evaluation and use it to demonstrate two essential points. First, it provides a more comprehensive, multimethodological model of rationality, which pursues the reasons given to support a judgment from the empirical evidence on technical efficiency, through the norms of the situation, to the abstract philosophical principles that back the warrant. Second, and more important for our present purposes, the method can be applied in practice for policy evaluation, as I shall illustrate with the Head Start arguments.

A Logic for Critical Evaluation

The logic of evaluation is concerned with two questions: What does it mean to evaluate something? How can such evaluations be justified? Specifically this logic focuses on the rules implicitly or explicitly followed in an attempt to judge a rule or standard to be good, to justify a goal as right, or to show that a decision to take an action ought to be made.[19]

A critical evaluation is one that systematically examines the full range of empirical and normative assumptions that contribute to a particular judgment. In this section I show how the probe of the logic of evaluation extends from concrete empirical questions to abstract normative issues concerning the subject's way of life. Specifically, this range of questions is structured around four phases that interrelate two fundamental levels of evaluation. First-order discourse, consisting of verification and validation, involves decision making based on principles fixed in the value system governing the particular decision-making process in question. In second-order discourse, composed of vindication and rational social choice, evaluation turns to questions about the acceptability of the value system itself. Each of the four phases has specific requirements that must be fulfilled in making a complete justification of a value judgment. For a reason to be considered a "good reason" it must meet all of the requirements of the four-phased probe.[20]

It is also important to note that evaluative discourse can be initiated by a problem emerging in any of the four phases of inquiry. For the purposes of systematic presentation, however, it is helpful to examine them in a formal order ranging from first- to second-order discourse.

Technical Verification of Program Objectives

Verification is the most familiar of the four phases. It is addressed to the basic empirical questions that have monopolized the attention of social and policy scientists. At this level an evaluator must seek answers to problems revolving around the three following types of questions:

Does the evaluatum (program) empirically fulfill its stated objective(s)?

Does the empirical analysis uncover secondary effects that offset the program objectives?

Does the program fulfill the objectives more efficiently than alternative means available?

The questions of technical verification (specifically concerned with measuring the efficiency of consequences) are quite familiar in policy evaluation methodology. They rest on the problems of observation, experimentation, measurement, and hypothesis testing. In Habermas's terminology, they are "empirical-analytic" questions that are organized and pursued through the analytic logic of the formal syllogism (D, W, and C) in Toulmin's model.

We recognize these concerns to be the ones that triggered the Head Start debate. The initial question raised about the Westinghouse evaluation involved empirical methodology: Was the control group adequate? Was sufficient attention paid to program variations? Was the sample random? The correspondence between technical verification in the logic of evaluation and this issue in the Head Start debate is direct and requires little further elaboration. Before passing to the next phase of the logic, however, I should add an interesting political footnote to the debate about the Westinghouse evaluation.

Even though the Westinghouse Report was widely criticized, Congress and the president basically accepted its findings and proceeded to cut the Head Start budget. At least this was the case until the advent of the Carter administration. Although it received much less fanfare than the Westinghouse study, further academic research now began to reveal different conclusions. In fact, new studies showed that participation in Head Start did improve reading and other cognitive skills. As an expert in the Office of Child Development explained, new evaluations offered "compelling evidence that early intervention works, [and] that the adverse impact of a poverty environment on children can be overcome by appropriate treatment."[21]

Most important, the new findings reflected the development of more sophisticated methodologies for measuring program outcomes. The early critics of the findings were thus correct in their initial judgments: the Westinghouse study had not adequately measured the program. This point was not lost on Democratic party politicians. Touting the legacy of Great Society programs, the Carter administration used these new results to restore part of the Head Start budget. Methodological research thus bore directly on the political outcome.

Situational Validation of Policy Goals

Criticisms directed at the technocratic conception of policy evaluation largely derive from a failure to extend evaluation beyond the verification of program objectives. From technical verification the logic of evaluation leads to questions of validation, concerned with whether the particular goals (from which the objectives are derived) are relevant to the situation. At this level, evaluation turns from the methodological principles of empirical verification to the logical rules of first-order normative discourse. As a process of reasoning that takes place within an adopted value system, the focus of discussion here centers on the following questions:

Is the objective or goal (standard or rule) relevant? Can it be justified or grounded by an appeal to principles or to established causal knowledge?
Are there circumstances in the situation that require an exception to be made to the goal?
Are two or more goals equally relevant to the situation?
Does the value system governing the evaluation place higher precedence on one of the conflicting goals? Or does it make contradictory prescriptions in such a situation?

Because they are concerned with relevance and situational circumstances, the questions of validation share a number of central concerns with the phenomenological conception of social science. Here we shall simply indicate the key connecting points. The phenomenologist's concepts of social relevance and the logic of the situation are the life-world counterparts to validation's questions about relevant standards and the circumstances of the situation. Being concerned with the social actor's cognitive reality (constructed from subjective experience), the phenomenologist's task is to explicate the actor's relevant rules and standards as employed in social decisions. Where the good-reasons approach focuses on the logical structures of everyday arguments, the phenomenological social scientist pursues an empirical description of the specific logics utilized by particular actors to shape the meaning and purpose of the situation under observation.[22]

Pursuing the Head Start illustration in the context of situational validation, we can begin with the recognition that those who criticized the Westinghouse conclusions for failing to employ socially relevant criteria in their study addressed issues at the level of situational validation. Countering the conclusion that Head Start failed, minority leaders and academic researchers raised two types of criticisms. The first concerned the use of multiple criteria. Minority leaders argued that the Head Start study was too narrowly conceived. They questioned the validity of reading scores as the sole criterion for judging the overall success of a program designed to improve the life opportunities of socially deprived children. Head Start was also designed to teach other types of socially relevant knowledge, such as personal health, self-discipline, and socially responsible attitudes toward the community.

Others, particularly academic researchers, focused on the methodological issues raised by the particular learning situation. Often drawing on the holistic techniques of phenomenological social scientists, they argued for the use of experience-related criteria for the contextual and longitudinal measurement of cognitive skills. If the general purpose of the program is to provide children with both the cognitive and the social skills necessary to function successfully in mainstream middle-class institutions, an evaluation must follow their life situation from Head Start into those institutions. In short, the educational development of these children must be monitored contextually through a progression of institutional situations.[23]

These turned out to be much more than partisan criticisms, as had often been suggested during the initial Head Start debate. Indeed, educational experts have attributed most of the new findings to the introduction of just these methodological improvements. Especially important was the use of new experience-related teaching techniques and their socially based measurement criteria. Even more impressive were the results achieved through longitudinal measurement:

> The studies showed that Head Start is very successful in cutting down in the rate of school failure, in improving IQ scores and reading achievement, and in helping children gain self-confidence. . . . The earlier and the more exposure children had to Head Start, the greater the gains they tended to make and maintain.[24]

Systems Vindication of Value Orientations

At this point, we shift from first- to second-order discourse. The systems vindication of a value subsystem requires that the evaluation process step outside the value orientation from which the standards and rules are drawn in the course of validation and examine their overall implications for the larger social system.

In systems vindication reasoning shifts from the logical mode of argumentation back to empirical inquiry. By requiring justification of the adoption of the value system as a whole, this phase of the logic asks whether the consequences of this commitment further specific ideals and whether living in accordance with the system is consistent with the desired way of life. Systems vindication is principally a "pragmatic test." A value system is demonstrated to have instrumental value when it is shown to be pragmatically successful in furthering certain ends of the larger system; it has contributive value if it is an essential component of the system as a whole. Deliberation here revolves around two basic questions:

> Do the practical consequences resulting from a commitment to the value system facilitate the realization of the ideals of the accepted order?
>
> Do other value systems, which reflect interests and needs in the social system as a whole, judge the consequences (as benefits and costs) to be distributed equitably?

Vindication is an empirical evaluation. Scientific knowledge and techniques are required for valid predictions of the instrumental or contributive role of a value system in realizing the ideals of a given social order. In the mainstream methodological debate, vindication reflects the concerns advanced by the advocates of the systems perspective. As a shift from the micro to the macro levels of evaluation, Habermas refers to the systems approach as "second-order technical knowledge." His purpose is to designate the relation of the more comprehensive systems framework to the first-order technical analysis of means to ends. At this level the kinds of issues examined include the physical, social, and psychological consequences that result from a specific way of life and the relevance of specific value systems to particular social situations or circumstances.

Although the empirical complexity of the questions raised in vindication are often beyond the capabilities of existing social science methodologies, it is nonetheless possible to locate the concerns of this level of evaluation in policy debates. In the case of Head Start the most salient issue at this level has been the controversy about the culture of poverty. Essentially an extension of the issue raised in situational validation, it has often taken the following form: If social researchers can empirically demonstrate that ghetto children are socialized into value systems that lack instrumentality for the American way of life, it can be argued that socially relevant experiences must be the primary criteria for the evaluation of compensatory educational programs such as Head Start.

The culture of poverty, as defined by Oscar Lewis, refers to a lower-class value system that denigrates hard work, discipline, and ambition and sacrifices future rewards for immediate gratification. The outcome is poverty resulting from slothfulness. Passed from parent to child, this value system perpetuates a "cycle" of poverty. Unable to participate in the dominant achievement-oriented culture of U.S. society, these lower social classes are incapable of pulling themselves out of their predicament.[25]

Much of the policy justification for compensatory programs such as Head Start can be traced to the argument that a culture—or more precisely a subculture—of poverty blocks the life chances of disadvantaged children. In the case of the Head Start debate, however, few of the program's critics raised empirical questions about the validity of the phenomenon per se. More typically the critics of such compensatory programs took a different line of attack. For example, Edward Banfield, a leading social scientist who supported the attack on Great Society programs, not only accepted the culture of poverty thesis but argued that the very severity of the problem put it beyond reach of government programs such as Head Start.[26] A primary source of governmental policy

failures in this area, according to Banfield, was located in the unwillingness and inability of liberal reformers to address the deeper cultural
differences that entrench urban poverty. Solutions effectively designed
to penetrate the problem at this level would have to be massive in scope.
Anything short of total intervention amounts to mere situational change,
with only temporary ameliorative effects. Massive intervention, Banfield
argued, is politically unacceptable to the power structure. Given existing
political structures and decision rules, particularly interest-group politics and incrementalism, such policy intervention would not only be too
costly, it would also rest on values outside the political culture. Banfield
thus rejected government antipoverty programs because they cannot be
vindicated by the dominant political values of the system. At this point,
he rested his case. In the urban literature this view has been identified as
a new realism based on the hard facts of the political system.

Banfield's position has been attacked from numerous liberal quarters.
One such assault criticized Banfield's treatment of existing political institutions as frozen. Timothy Hennessey and Richard Feen attributed this
treatment to his underlying political philosophy. Banfield, they argued,

> rejects out of hand the possibility that the opinion makers' propensity to
> imagine a future may lead them to a view of the facts decidedly different
> from [his]—namely an alarming deterioration in the social and political
> climate in American cities which in turn impels them to use considerable
> skill to design realistic programs to alleviate the problem.[27]

This argument opens the way for a different line of discourse. Fundamental to the logic of evaluation is the possiblity of an alternative
vision of political culture. Evaluation halts at vindication only if all parties agree on the answer to the question, "Do you accept this political
way of life?" It is, indeed, on this point that Banfield's most truculent
critics have launched their objections. This recognition of alternative
visions of a political way of life moves the argument from vindication to
the next and final phase of the evaluation process, rational social choice.
At this stage evaluation shifts attention from the existing or "real" culture
to the pursuit of an ideal culture.

Social Choice

Disparities between the standards of equity and the empirical consequences of a particular social system encountered in vindication trigger

political debate about the social system itself, which ultimately leads to the philosophical concerns of the fourth level of evaluation. The transition from systems vindication to rational social choice raises the following types of questions:

> Do the fundamental ideals that organize the accepted social order provide a basis for an equitable resolution of conflicting judgments?
>
> To what extent can an unequal distribution of benefits be shown to be advantageous to all needs and interests?
>
> If the social order is unable to resolve value system conflicts, do other social orders equitably prescribe for the relevant interests and needs that the conflicts reflect?
>
> What is the empirical or speculative evidence that supports the justification of an alternative social order?

At the level of rational social choice, an attempt is made to establish a basis for the choice of one way of life over another. Rational choice, as employed here, is not to be confused with the decisionistic rational choice theories that have proliferated in the managerially oriented social sciences in recent years. Here it refers to the task of the classical conception of political philosophy: the construction of models of the rational way of life. Based on the identification and organization of specific values—such as equality, freedom, or community—these models can serve as a basis for the adoption of evaluative standards and norms.

The notion of rational choice in the selection of a way of life is a conceptual ideal. In describing the ideal, we must state the conditions for any person to render a fully rational choice. For this purpose we must include at least three primary conditions: freedom, impartiality, and enlightenment. To the extent that a model of a way of life is chosen in a manner that approximates these conditions, it can be legitimately employed as a basis for criteria utilized in justifying value judgments.

Each of these conditions only sets up an ideal toward which the processes of choice must be oriented. No actual choice can ever be completely free, fully enlightened, or altogether impartial; hence no choice made among alternative ways of life can be fully rational. In the real world of political conflict, argumentation at this level of evaluation characteristically takes the form of ideological debate.

Questions of rational social choice are part of the traditional concern of the philosopher. The work of John Rawls, for example, has revived general interest in the classical problems of rational social choice and in the process has become a source of heated controversy in political as well as scholarly journals.[28] Rawls is concerned with developing a method for determining the type of social order a "rational person" would choose and the reasons that would be given for that decision. To uncover the nature of such an order, he establishes a fundamental situation called the "original position." Free of distracting circumstances, the original position is a methodological device designed to assist social actors in making rational choices about values. Like Habermas's "public sphere," the device permits the participants to establish hypothetically a social order in which each person agrees to certain basic rights and principles. In turn, these values and principles can be used as a basis for the critique of the extant social system. As Habermas explains, such critique is aimed at explicating both manifest and latent ideologies and domination in the exercise of social and political power.[29]

During the period of the Head Start debate, political philosophers, influenced by Rawls's theory of justice, focused on a number of issues that bear directly on the evaluation of compensatory educational programs. Of particular importance were the principles of equal opportunity and the nature of an egalitarian society.[30]

Those in the Head Start controversy who argued that evaluation must ultimately rest on ideological principles were essentially arguing at this level. More specifically, the exchanges regarding the relative importance of reading scores and socially relevant standards had a second-order counterpart in a debate that focused on the nature of the good society. One group contended that the good society emerges from the long-term social benefits of a meritocratic system based on the values of individual competition and native skill (generally measured as IQ). Another group stressed the advantages of pursuing an egalitarian social order founded on the values of community and fraternity. While to many observers these arguments seemed to have little practical import for the immediate issues in the debate arising from the Westinghouse evaluation, on closer examination they are essentially the theoretical counterparts of the more practical concerns surrounding the project. In short, those advocating a meritocratic social order were presenting second-order philosophical reasons for emphasizing the importance of reading scores as the primary measure of progress. Those representing the egalitarian cause were offering a second-order justification for the first-order emphasis on socially relevant standards.

One of the most interesting studies that illustrates the nature of argumentation at this level was conducted by Samuel Bowles and Herbert Gintis. In *Schooling in Capitalist America*, Bowles and Gintis sought to show that the principle of equal opportunity cannot be realized through compensatory education programs in a capitalist social order.[31] At the level of systems vindication they provided an impressive array of historical data to demonstrate that commitment to the equal opportunity principle has not led to greater equality in capitalist societies. The primary function of this principle is not, they assert, social justice but rather the facilitation of social control. By blurring the class divisions that constitute the basic realities of the educational system, belief in the principle serves as a powerful stabilizing force in capitalist societies.

Where others (such as Banfield) reject equal opportunity as an idealistic principle, Bowles and Gintis use it at the level of rational social choice to call for alternative egalitarian institutions. Rather than rejecting the equal opportunity principle because it clashes with extant political values, they employ the principle as the basis for a critique of the real values of capitalism. For them, equal opportunity can be achieved only by a radical change brought about by the adoption of socialist value principles. In short, they call for a new way of life.

Integrating Themes

I have attempted to weave together three themes: the arguments of the Head Start debate, their methodological counterparts in the mainstream social sciences, and a multimethodological logic of critical evaluation. One way to emphasize these comparisons is to use a diagram. Following Toulmin's model, I have sketched the logical framework of a comprehensive-critical evaluation in Figure 10.2.

A critical judgment as presented here is one that has been pursued progressively through the four phases of evaluation. The formal logic of an empirical assertion moves from D (data) to C (conclusion), mediated by a warrant backed by normative and empirical assumptions. In normal discussion these assumptions generally serve as a background consensus and are called into question only during disputes. The task of a comprehensive-critical evaluation is to make explicit these assumptions through a progressive critique extending from validation to rational social choice (or from rational social choice to validation).[32] It is here that we can understand Habermas's classical Aristotelian contention that in the last instance an empirical statement must be judged by its inten-

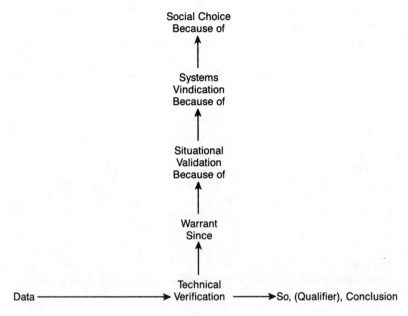

Figure 10.2   The logical structure of critical evaluation.

tions for the good and true life. As reflected through the logical link of an empirical assertion to the level of rational social choice, a full delineation of the logic of an evaluative argument discloses its meaning and implications for the pursuit of a particular conception of the ideal society.

We can also show the relationship of the Head Start policy arguments and their methodological counterparts in Figure 10.2. In the case of the policy arguments, the purpose is to illustrate how the seemingly disparate criticisms that emerged in response to the Westinghouse evaluation are in fact different aspects of a comprehensive evaluation.

In actual debate, most critics appear to be talking past one another. Each has chosen a specific dimension of the Head Start program as the crucial issue on which the debate is seen to turn. But as the logic of evaluation makes clear, each of these orientations is only part of a full assessment of the question. From the perspective of the methodology presented here, evaluators would present not only their empirical findings but also the full range of assumptions on which their criteria (norms and standards) were based. This would provide the basis for a systematic critical debate that would explore the full range of issues, from evidence to principles. In Table 10.1, the issues at each level of the Head Start debate are related to their level of evaluation. The table also shows the relationship of their respective methodological orientations to the logic of evaluation.

Concluding Comments

The nature of the critical evaluation method offered here is bound to generate controversy, especially among critical theorists. Some have argued that an effort to pin down the logic of a critical social science is a violation of its basic objective, an emancipatory discourse for political self-determination. In this view, the very attempt to say what the rules of such a method are is to introduce intellectual constraints. For this reason it is important to be clear about what I have attempted here. While such criticisms are indeed relevant to the processes of critical reflection, the task has not been to offer specific methodological procedures for this level of evaluation. Instead, the purpose has been to clarify the logic of the relationship between critical reflection and the phenomenological and empirical modes of inquiry in evaluative discourse. In the context of a struggle to supplant the dominant technocratic patterns in the social

Table 10.1 Head Start Arguments and Methodological Issues

Head Start Arguments	Methodology of Critical Evaluation	Methodological Debate
Principle of equal opportunity	Social choice	Political philosophy
Culture of poverty	Systems vindication	Systems perspective
Socially relevant experiences	Situational validation	Phenomenological approach
Measuring reading scores	Technical verification	Empirical analysis

and policy sciences, the ability to specify the logical connections between empirical and normative discourse in specific policy arguments is essential to open and expand the scope of the mainstream dialogue.

Few political science and sociology departments teach critical theory, let alone integrate its components into their methodology courses. In the absence of methodological specification, critical social science will continue to be relegated to the softer side of the curriculum—philosophy and the history of ideas. For some, especially philosophers and intellectual historians, this will present no particular problem. But for those engaged in the trenches of mainstream social science—teaching subjects such as policy evaluation, urban planning, or research methodology—much depends on the attempt to bring the concepts of critical theory into the disciplines. If we are to train a new generation of social scientists to reject positivism and technocracy, we must be able to provide alternative methodologies for science and decision making.

The effort here has been designed to address this need. In this regard one of its most important advantages for a methodological politics is its ability to undermine the technocratic conception of knowledge on its own terms. By systematically relating the normative questions of phenomenology and political philosophy to the deductive syllogism of the empirical sciences, technical-instrumental knowledge is reduced to a component of a larger inferential process. Moreover, its relationship to questions about the good life is schematically portrayed.

Empiricists typically dismiss phenomenological and philosophical analyses by suggesting that they are concerned with other types of questions and concerns. By implication, empirical and normative theories can, therefore, be developed in relative isolation, a reality reflected in the departmental character of the modern curriculum. The methodological error behind this separation is clarified, however, by a full delineation of the logic of evaluation. The modes of inquiry—empirical science, phenomenology, and political philosophy—are shown to be interrelated components of a comprehensive-critical judgment. Each has its own type of data and internal logic, but none can stand entirely alone. As coexisting perspectives on the same social reality, they are the components of a larger inferential process. Integrating the range of normative and empirical perspectives, the methodological framework suggests the dimensions of a postpositivist theory of rationality.

At this stage the method is advanced more as a project than as a finished product. As an exploration of relatively uncharted territories, it is designed to open a new direction and to expand the contemporary academic dialogue. Ultimately, of course, the value of the method will depend on its usefulness as an alternative tool for the critical assessment and evaluation of policy arguments. In the interim, its discussion is aimed at encouraging others to join in and take up the methodological challenge.

Notes

1. The term *public policy evaluation* is used here in the most generic sense of the phrase. It does not refer to a particular technique of policy analysis but to the field as a whole.

2. The methodological framework presented here is based on insights drawn from Jürgen Habermas's critical theory. He established the agenda and developed the direction. But the proposed method is in no way the product of explicit textual exegesis. As a suggestive beginning, it is a synthesis of interrelated contributions by Habermas, Stephen Toulmin, and Paul Taylor.

3. For a general discussion, see Frank Fischer, *Politics, Values, and Public Policy: The Problem of Methodology* (Boulder, CO: Westview, 1980), pp. 1–64; and Richard J. Bernstein, *The Restructuring of Social and Political Theory* (New York: Harcourt Brace Jovanovich, 1976).

4. *The Impact of Head Start: An Evaluation of the Effects of Head Start on Children's Cognitive and Affective Development*, Study by the Westinghouse Learning Corporation (Athens: Ohio University, July 12, 1969).

5. Harrell Rodgers, "Head Start—Where Are the Headlines Now?" *Dissent*, Spring 1979, p. 234.

6. Ibid., p. 235.

7. Walter Williams and John W. Evans, "The Politics of Evaluation: The Case of Head Start," in *Evaluating Social Programs*, ed. Peter Rossi and Walter Williams (New York: Seminar, 1972), pp.249–64. Also, see M. S. Smith and J. S. Bissell, "Report Analysis: The Impact of Head Start," *Harvard Educational Review 40* (Winter 1970): 51–105.

8. Ibid.

9. See Edmund W. Gordon, "Guidance in the Urban Setting," in *Opening Opportunities for Disadvantaged Learners*, ed. Harry Passow (New York: Teachers College Press, 1972), p. 213.

10. The best guide to the general outline of this argument is Samual Bowles and Herbert Gintis, *Schooling in Capitalist America* (New York: Basic Books, 1976). For a guide to the political arguments in support of the initiation of the Head Start program, see "Head Start—A Retrospective View: The Founders," in *Project Head Start*, ed. Edward Zigler and Jeanette Valentine (New York: Free Press, 1979), pp. 43–134. As president, Lyndon Johnson announced plans to extend the project with these words: "We have reached a landmark not just in education, but in the maturity of our

democracy. The success of this year's Head Start program—and our plans for the years to come—are symbols of this nation's commitment to the goal that no American child shall be condemned to failure by the accident of his birth."

11. *New York Times*, cited by Williams and Evans, "The Politics of Evaluation," p. 263; and Walter Williams, *Social Policy Research and Analysis* (New York: American Elsevier, 1971), pp. 103–30.

12. Rodgers, "Head Start," p. 235.

13. Jürgen Habermas, *Knowledge and Human Interest* (Boston: Beacon, 1971), pp. 301–17; also see Thomas McCarthy, *The Critical Theory of Jürgen Habermas* (Cambridge: MIT Press, 1978), for the best methodological explication and interpretation of Habermas's project.

14. In reference to "substantial arguments," see Jürgen Habermas, *Legitimation Crisis* (Boston: Beacon, 1975), p. 107; also see Habermas, *The Theory of Communicative Action*, vol. 1 (Boston: Beacon, 1984), pp. 24–27.

15. Ibid.

16. Stephen Toulmin, *The Uses of Argument* (Cambridge: Cambridge University Press, 1958).

17. Ibid.

18. Paul W. Taylor, *Normative Discourse* (Englewood Cliffs, NJ: Prentice-Hall, 1961).

19. Ibid.

20. For a detailed guide to these phases of evaluation, see Fischer, *Politics, Values, and Public Policy*.

21. Bernard Brown, "Long-Term Gains from Early Intervention: An Overview of Current Research" (Paper delivered at the 1977 annual meeting of the American Association for the Advancement of Science, Denver, February 23, 1977).

22. See Fischer, *Politics, Values, and Public Policy*.

23. Barbara Dillion Goodson and Robert D. Hess, "The Effects of Parent Training Programs on Child Performance and Parent Behavior" (Paper delivered at the 1977 annual meeting of the American Association for the Advancement of Science, Denver, February 23, 1977).

24. Rodgers, "Head Start," p. 235.

25. Oscar Lewis, *Five Families: Mexican Case Studies in the Culture of Poverty* (New York: Basic Books, 1959). The debate over this hypothesis triggered the publication of a number of controversial studies, including the Moynihan Report and Banfield's *Unheavenly City*—U.S. Department of Labor, Office of Policy Planning and Research, *The Negro Family*, prepared by Daniel Patrick Moynihan (Washington, DC: Government Printing Office, 1965); and Edward C. Banfield, *The Unheavenly City: The Nature and Future of Our Urban Crisis* (Boston: Little, Brown, 1970).

26. Banfield, *Unheavenly City*.

27. Timothy M. Hennessey and Richard H. Feen, "Social Science as Social Philosophy: Edward C. Banfield and the 'New Realism' in Urban Politics," in *Varieties of Political Conservatism*, ed. Matthew Holden, Jr. (Beverly Hills, CA: Sage, 1974), p. 29.

28. John Rawls, *A Theory of Justice* (Cambridge, MA: Belknap, 1971).

29. Habermas, *Knowledge and Human Interest*, p. 310.

30. See, for example, James Fishkin, *Justice, Equal Opportunity and the Family*

(New Haven, CT: Yale University Press, 1983). On compensatory education and Head Start, see pp. 68-74.

31. Bowles and Gintis, *Schooling in Capitalist America*.

32. In Figure 10.2, the arrows connecting Technical Verification to Social Choice point upward. This is because the discussion here focuses on the reconstruction of the empirical sciences and thus begins at the bottom of the diagram with D and C. In general, however, the arrows move in either direction, up or down, depending on the particular issues in question.

PART VI

RECONSTRUCTING ORGANIZATION THEORY: FROM TECHNICAL TO POLITICAL RATIONALITY

The main advantage of the "technostructure" is its specialized knowledge, training and familiarity with modern, exact methods of management. However, its fatal weakness is the lack of any goal, other than the increase of production. . . . Thus we are flooded with information about the incredibly high standard of living of the "postindustrial society," about new materials, new instruments and machines . . . and new methods of controlling people. But we are told little or nothing about human relationships, social structures, new social institutions, and the distribution of political power.
—MIHAILO MARKOVIC

Let him give us the manual (which explains how it works), let him put it on the table so that each may go through it, let him allow us to draw out, pick apart, know the details and together, yes together, ignoring the prejudices of collar and rank, let us initiate ourselves into the mystery and functioning. . . . Let them leave us to plunge wholly into the dominating of the [new machine] instead of letting us leave in the evening as we came, as deprived of knowledge, as ignorant of what crushes us.
—SEMISKILLED FRENCH FACTORY WORKER

We turn in this section to the issue of organization. In the context of technocracy, it is directly related to the critique of neopositivism, the epistemological foundation of technocratic knowledge. The connection is established in the fact that different types of knowledge are generated by different types of organizational inquiring systems.

Concerned with the translation of knowledge into political and administrative action, the technocratic task is dependent on particular forms of organization for problem solving, policy formulation, and implementation. For this reason, an attempt to replace the neopositivist conception of knowledge and problem solving with postpositivist understanding requires that we also turn our attention to the issues of organizational change that it entails.

Already we have seen that neopositivist knowledge is based on an objective conception of rationality—that is, knowledge is "out there" in the world. Objective knowledge is said to be theoretically and empirically independent of the interests of social actors (those pursuing the knowledge as well as those it purports to explain). Max Weber was the first to recognize the integral link between this concept of objective/positive knowledge and the emergence of rationally structured bureaucratic organizations; Frederick Taylor subsequently laid the groundwork for the positivist/technical conception of the workplace in his principles of scientific management; and Herbert Simon, perhaps more succinctly than anyone else, spelled out the basic prescriptive propositions for the managerial design of such organizations as a whole. Structured as a hierarchical chain of authority, as Simon made clear, bureaucratic organizations are designed to facilitate the upward flow of relevant "value-free" (or "context-free") information from different subunits of the organization to the top of the structure. At this level, top management is to use the information to lay out "the best" course of action (primarily defined as the most efficient action) based on empirically established prescriptive principles. The job is seen to be technical in nature.

Postpositive knowledge, by contrast, is inherently linked to the normative world and is in part "socially constructed"—that is, knowledge is dependent in essential ways on the subjective interpretations of the social actors themselves. While postpositivism does not turn its back to empirical knowledge, it does substitute positivism's stress on empirical investigation with an emphasis on normative analysis and argumentation. Reality, most assuredly, has an empirical dimension but the determination of what constitutes it depends on the discursive weighing of both empirical and normative considerations. Rejecting the concept of a value-neutral science, knowledge for postpositivists is understood to be an outcome of dialectical interactions between interpretive understandings of social reality.

In organizational terms, a postpositivist orientation emphasizes the presence of competing interests struggling to interpret reality. The departments of an organization are conceptualized as social contexts with varying goals and interests, as well as differing interpretations of the situations they confront. For this reason, postpositivist organization theory is fundamentally grounded in a political rather than a technical understanding of organizational processes. The two chapters that follow focus on the development of a political interpretation of organizational structures and processes and the implications that follow from it.

The first of the two chapters, "Organizations as Political Systems: The Managerial Bias in Critical Perspective," examines the "crisis" in organization theory and shows it to result in large part from an overreliance on managerially biased technical models of organization. As an alternative, the chapter presents a political model of organizational behavior and draws out its implications for policy decision making and management. Of particular importance are its implications for workplace participation. The possibility of developing a less technocratic workplace is shown to depend on a political reconceptualization of labor-management practices. Most fundamental is the need for managers to relinquish their rigid adherence to hierarchical and technical forms of control. Alternatively, they must join with other organizational members to build internal political coalitions among workers, supervisors, and technicians based on consensually derived decisions about mutual obligations and benefits.

The formation of political coalitions is seen to be of special importance in the high-tech workplace, the topic of Chapter 12, "Technological Politics in the Postindustrial Workplace: The Problem of Expertise," which turns to the computerization of work and examines the political role of expertise in the high-tech organization. Focusing in particular on the design and use of computerized technologies to control, deskill, or replace workers, the development of more equitable and democratic high-tech work organizations is seen to depend on the introduction of participatory systems of expertise and knowledge formation, both technological and managerial. To illustrate the nature of such participatory expertise, the chapter concludes with a description of an innovative Swedish project in which computer experts, graphics workers, labor leaders, and social scientists joined together to design and implement participatory computerized graphics technologies for the Scandinavian newspaper industry.

11

Organizations as Political Systems:
The Managerial Bias in Critical Perspective†

This chapter examines the emerging empirical-analytic models of organizational politics and attempts to draw out their implications for a critical dialogue in organization theory. The first step is to show that the political model of organizations makes a substantial contribution to the demystification of the dominant technocratic approach to organization theory. The second step is to show that, beyond this contribution, the empirical-analytic approach, wittingly or unwittingly, harbors the kernel of a much more critical organization theory and practice and that, for the purposes of theoretical strategy, critical organization theorists can profitably build upon this contribution by extending its implications.

The chapter proceeds in four sections. First, it presents the "crisis" of modern organization theory and shows the current interest in organizational politics to be a response to this organizational malaise. In particular, it is seen to represent a theoretical challenge to the rational (technocratic) model of organization, widely viewed as the source of the contemporary problem. In the second section, the chapter presents the emerging political theory of organizations. Here the discussion focuses

†SOURCE: Part of this chapter originally appeared as "Reforming Bureaucratic Theory: Toward a Political Model," in *Bureaucratic and Governmental Reform*, edited by Donald J. Calista (Greenwich, CT: JAI Press, 1986), pp. 35–53; used by permission.

on a selection of the more influential studies that have appeared. Next, the analysis turns to a critique of the political model. The purpose in the third section is to show that, while the political perspective demystifies the political ideology of the technocratic model, it nonetheless remains anchored to an uncritical acceptance of managerial power. Employing a more critical conceptualization of power, the discussion draws out the hidden dimensions of managerial power that latently prestructure the play of organizational politics.

Finally, the chapter turns to the issue of praxis. Building upon the critique of the political model, the analysis seeks to illustrate the ways in which political theory and research can be used to develop effective oppositional strategies for challenging bureaucratic domination. Some of the potential uses of such strategies are then briefly outlined for both the workplace and the management classroom.

The Crisis of Theory

There is growing recognition that organizational science is in trouble. Whether one turns to the scholarly literature on public or private sector organizations, steady reference is found to an "organizational gap" between theory and practice. Ostrom, for example, refers to this gap as the "intellectual crisis" of modern organization theory; Denhardt calls it a "crisis of legitimacy"; and Susman and Evered portray it as a "crisis in organizational science."[1] Susman and Evered put it this way:

> Many of the findings in our scholarly management journals are only remotely related to the real world of practicing managers and to the actual issues with which members of organizations are concerned, especially when the research has been carried out by the most rigorous methods of the prevailing conception of science.[2]

Beyond the confines of academe, talk of organizational failures has begun to attract attention in the press as well. For instance, concern about the country's falling rate of productivity has called attention to the provocative thesis of two Harvard Business School professors, Robert Haynes and William Abernathy.[3] Instead of blaming our economic problems on the standard scapegoats (unionization and worker apathy), they attribute them to bad *management* practices. For them, our difficulties are rooted in management's failure to set the conditions conducive to innovation and productivity. Moreover, such arguments have generated interest in the success of worker-oriented managerial styles used in Japanese companies, our leading industrial competitors.

Economists Bowles, Gordon, and Weisskopf point to the same problem but offer a much more scathing indictment.[4] For these writers, the decline of the U.S. economy is not a result of bad management per se. They attribute the situation to corporate management's *political* motives. According to them, faced with breakdown in the postwar system, management has sacrificed efficiency and innovation in a struggle to maintain tight control over its power. Such techniques as excessive supervision, underemployment, antiunionism, induced recessions, and corporate flight have resulted in increasing inefficiency, falling productivity, and corporate waste. The solution, in their view, is to be found in a radical turn to industrial democracy and worker self-management.

These issues have generated a new wave of interest in organizational theory. The result has been a proliferation of competing theoretical approaches: political economy, phenomenology, ecological perspectives, and Marxism, to name just a few. While a fully adequate alternative has yet to emerge, the competing theories tend to share a common concern: all seek to offset or replace the traditional conception of organizational action, namely, the rational model and its modern technocratic variants.[5] For these theorists, the failure of mainstream theory to shed its emphasis on technical rationality in explanation and decision making is responsible for the current gap between theory and practice. They seek to overcome this gap by locating theory and practice in a wider set of social and political variables.

It is difficult to list all of the criticisms that have been leveled at the rational paradigm.[6] For present purposes, we shall single out only those that bear most directly on the failures of administrative practice. These include the paradigm's overemphasis on efficient goal attainment, its enduring dedication to technical models of decision making, and its failure to confront the diversity of motives and interests in the organization as a whole.

The Rational Model

In the rational model of organization, the purpose of an organization is relatively nonproblematic: organizations are defined as instruments for efficient goal attainment. For the most part, goals and objectives are treated as if they belong to the organization rather than to individuals, groups, or other interested parties. Thus it is largely assumed that everybody involved in the organization's activities is in reasonable agreement with the overall goals and purposes of the organization. Disagreements will exist; many individuals may possess varying ambitions and motives, but these differences are all based on a common set of norms and values that belong within the basic framework of organizational consensus. (Many of those beyond the pale of consensus are unlikely to join the organization in the first place; others will be resocialized; and the remainder will be asked to work elsewhere.)

The existence of such consensus makes possible the adoption of a particular conception of rational action. In view of the presumed agreement on goals, rationality can be defined in narrow instrumental terms. Organizational analysis can thus focus on the issues that principally concern the organization's managers: how to increase achievement of the goals already taken for granted. Because such a perspective so rigorously emphasizes *efficiency*, this orientation has often been criticized as an overly mechanistic approach to administration.

Gouldner has captured the technical orientation of this model in these terms: "It views the organization as a structure of manipulable parts, each of which is separately modified with a view toward enhancing the efficiency of the whole."[7] Modifications of the organization can thus be introduced through "rational" planning based on scientific analysis. It is assumed that, by applying the established propositions of organizational science, administrative planners (usually top-level elites) will design a cooperative setting for the harmonious fulfillment of the various organizational interests and goals. Such a model articulates a form of "technocratic" governance, or "technocracy," a system in which those with knowledge and position make decisions for the entire organization.

Knowledge, in this approach, is based largely on the principles of positivism and its modern variants. Such knowledge is judged to be "value-free" in character (i.e., purged of contamination by human interests and values). Administrative scientists and managerial decision makers are directed to focus their attention on verifiable "factual propositions" about means for achieving mandated ends. Organizational analysts thus function largely to calculate the costs and benefits of alternative means for achieving the organization's goals. The goals themselves, specified by the organization's owners or derived form legislative policy, are ruled to be beyond the purview of organizational science. As a result, the substantive or value-laden dimensions of organizational decision making are largely denigrated. In the end, such significant realities as competing motivations, differing interpretations of administrative situations, or conflicting goals and objectives are reduced to irrational interruptions that impede the methodological requirements of "efficient" decision making.[8]

It would be wrong to portray the development of this modern technocratic model as a steady progression from the initial assumptions of the rational paradigm. In many ways, the model has continued to undergo change and reformulation. Much of this has been prompted by the growth of literature on the dysfunctions and inefficiencies of the rational model. In the face of this stream of problems, administrative theorists and practitioners have proceeded from a modified version of the original premise: If modern organizations cannot be ideally rational in the rigorous scientific sense of the term, they can nonetheless be *reasonably* rational. In this regard, the influential work of decision theorists, human resource psychologists, and systems and contingency theorists can all be properly described as "neorationalistic" in character.[9] In these theories (implicitly and explicitly), the function of the manager and the organization theorist is to replace "irrationality" with technically rational actions. Moreover, such a perspective takes for granted the belief that better managers and better organizational science will keep *less* irrationality from creeping in.

This persistent quest for technical rationality is clearly reflected in modern administrative practices. It is seen in the contemporary emphasis on social engineering and "crisis management." The tools of the trade include increasing rationalization of decision processes through automation (extended by computers and data processing); more systematic quantification of inputs and outputs for long-range planning; objective decision making through cost-benefit and risk-benefit analyses; the pursuit of administrative flexibility through contingency strategies; increased use of technology for innovation, such as the introduction of robotics; and the use of behavioral modification techniques and organizational development strategies, including the redesign of organizational cultures.[10]

Under the guise of value-neutral methodology, these modern administrative techniques direct attention away from both the social origins and the political implications of an organization's goals. For example, systems modeling and computer simulations downgrade the importance of human values and social goals by treating them as variables and assumptions in a technical analysis. In this way, as Goldman explains, organizational science narrows the field of inquiry, and thus offers an incomplete picture of organizational reality.[11] Mainstream organization theory, as a result, provides ideological support for the elite administrative planners at the expense of other existing interests and needs in the organization. In this respect, theory programmatically embodies the interests, values, and objectives of the professional managerial stratum and the corporate economic form that it serves.

One of the classic illustrations of this administrative bias can be seen in the standard managerial interpretation of unionization. Instead of recognizing unionization as a response to basic interests and needs, work behavior that fails to conform to the administrative conception of rationality is commonly judged to be dysfunctional or even deviant. Indeed, the rationality of efficient *administrative* behavior becomes confused with other modes of rationality in organizations. Thus the administrative perspective itself determines *the* definition of organization. Denhardt captures the implications of this in these words: "As the values of the organization replace those of the individual, it becomes apparent that one's contributions will be most helpful if they are consistent with the vision of the organization held by those who control it."[12] It is inevitable that "obedience to the demands of those in authority is not merely efficient, it is rational."

Toward a Political Model

The search for an empirical alternative to the rational model and its modern variants has its roots largely in the natural systems perspective and the emergence of the open systems model.[13] These approaches, each in its own way, have sought to widen the scope of social and political criteria to be incorporated into organizational analysis. As these models have matured, political criteria have become more and more important. Indeed, by the late 1970s, numerous writers influenced by these traditions began to reformulate organizational behavior in explicitly political terms. This section offers a brief sketch of the resulting political model, emphasizing its points of contrast with the rational model.

The primary purpose of the political model is to transcend the rational model's restricted normative focus. That is, its aim is to bring the full array of competing interests into organizational theory. As depicted here a political model does not altogether discard the main feature of the rational approach, namely, an instrumental perspective. Instead, its purpose is to situate such an orientation within a political context. Organizations remain instruments, but the questions of "organization for whom and what?" come to the fore. In this respect, organizations also become arenas of political conflict about value preferences and desired consequences of action.

Power in a Political Perspective

People in organizations customarily speak of politics and "power plays," but these concepts have largely been relegated to a secondary status in the predominantly technical approach to organization theory. For the most part, the analysis of power has been limited to a formal discussion of authority and influence as they relate to privileges and rights attached to the offices of the hierarchy. These include such powers as the ability to hire and fire employees, the power to regulate remuneration, the ability to control the vertical flow of information, the power to manipulate normative symbols, and the potential for coercion in some cases.

Institutionalized as executive authority, these powers largely govern the one-way, top-down relationships between superiors and subordinates. Beyond this static emphasis on the vertical structure of power, most investigation has largely been relegated to a narrow focus on individual discretion and conflict resolution, especially in small groups. Power has been treated as something to be minimized and contained, except perhaps in some cases where competition is needed to generate innovation. And even then, theorists have emphasized a limited exercise of power, carefully restricted within the framework of managerial objectives.

The political model seeks to examine power on its own terms. Rather than interpreting power from an administrative perspective, the objective of the political approach is to uncover the patterns of power that underlie both the formal and the informal structures of the organization and to reveal the ways in which these power relations shape the actual operations of the organization as a whole. Power is identified as the commodity of a pervasive and systematic pattern of intraorganizational politics. Although there have been many disagreements over the conceptualization of power, it is understood here in traditional political terms, namely, as a relation among participants in which one is able to get another to do something the latter would not otherwise have done.[14]

Toward this end, Pfeffer defines organizational politics as the activity undertaken by individuals and groups "within organizations to acquire, develop, and use power . . . to obtain . . . preferred outcomes in a situation in which there is uncertainty or dissensus about choice."[15]

In sharp contrast to the rational mode, the political perspective begins with the assumption that organizations embody a wide range of conflicting preferences.[16] These conflicts can stem from basic value differences, or they can result from disagreements over which means best achieve desired goals. Such differences can arise from a variety of sources: "from different socialization and training prior to joining the organization, from the development of subunit identification and loyalty after joining the organization, from differences in information and from being imbedded in different social networks both on and off the job."[17] Where the rational model too quickly assumes goal consensus, the political model takes consensus to be the exception to the rule.

This is not to lose sight of the fact that organizations are initiated and designed by specific groups to further their own interests. Indeed, they introduce hierarchical control structures with the explicit purpose of keeping employees from substituting for the pursuit of these interests the pursuit of their own. But such control is always imperfect, especially in the presence of significant goal disagreements. Such slippage gives rise to an internal competition over goals and means. It takes the form of an internal political system.

As a political system, an organization is governed by the chief executive and managed by the administrative system. In this view, the executive functions as a political broker mediating among the participants' competing demands. These demands, as March writes, "are essentially the price required for the participation in the coalition." Various members participate in the coalition on the expectation of receiving rewards. These can take the direct form of promotion and higher wages, or can be less tangible, such as an opportunity to advance a particular set of interests in the organization.[18]

To say that many different interests compete for the executive's attention is not to say that everyone competes. Not all individuals or groups in the organization take an interest in its governance; not all who do participate care about every decision concerning the organization. For this reason, Weick conceptualizes organizations as "loosely coupled" systems.[19] Such systems are politically segmented rather than monolithic. The connections among segments vary in strength; stable segments tend to be small in size.

To study these internal patterns of organizational politics, it is essential to shift attention away from formal authority and to focus on the role of *influence*.[20] In contrast to the static, one-dimensional nature of authority based on hierarchy, political influence is a dynamic, multidimensional phenomenon; it moves both vertically and horizontally. Where the office-based authority governing the superior-subordinate relationship tends to be zero-sum, influence is actually zero-*non*-sum. It can be exercised formally or informally; it can be used in the name of a wide range of competing values, including resistance to formal authority. In this way, formal and informal systems of influence open the possibility of competing power networks that move at once in different directions. Influence is thus the dynamic, tactical aspect of power relationships. It is the currency of organizational change.

This emphasis on influence permits us to more easily identify a wider range of activities that must be included in the study of power. For example, information and expertise become much more than top-down phenomena. Regardless of formal position in the organizational structure, actors with expertise are seen to have numerous political opportunities to exercise power on particular issues or problems at specific times in the organization. In some cases, mere proximity to those in power can provide critical opportunities to exercise power.

In contrast to the rational model, then, power in the political model is not just the preserve of top management and its chain of command. It is a phenomenon exercised at *many* points throughout the organizational system. Indeed, the system itself is a politically negotiated order held together by political bargains and agreements. Thus, to understand organizational politics, the first step is to look beyond the formal structures of authority to the networks of political influence and the patterns of negotiated agreements that give operational content to internal structures and processes.

Power as a Structural Phenomenon

The structures of an organization, especially the formal structures managed by the administrative system, are critically important determinants of the shape of internal political patterns. Power in organizations is acquired and exercised by individuals and groups, but their behavior is shaped by organizational structures, both formal and informal. Essentially, structures establish the terrain upon which the struggle for power takes place. In organizational terms, power is thus a structural

phenomenon shaped by the division of labor. By constituting an interdependence among the organizational subunits, the division of labor
sets the conditions that give rise to interest groups, the agents of
organizational politics.[21]

To carry out their goals, organizational subsystems must have a mini-
mum level of interconnection. For this reason, the essence of organization is a limitation of autonomy among subgroups. To achieve
interdependence, each subgroup is partially subordinated to the power
of the others. Unlike individuals who are relatively free to decide
whether to cooperate, organizational subgroups literally exist to engage
in joint action. Such shared action is required more out of necessity than
out of concern for principles of participation. Emerson has conceptualized this sharing of power in the following proposition: "The dependence of actor A upon actor B is (1) directly proportional to A's
motivational investment in goals mediated by B, and (2) inversely
proportional to the availability of those to A outside the A-B relationship." Thus, if B were to have the ability to carry out requirements essential to A's tasks, B's power as a subunit would increase. If B should have
a monopoly on these requirements, leaving A with no alternative, B
would dominate A. The specific configuration of power in an organization will, of course, depend upon its particular structural characteristics
that affect the nature of the A-B relationships.[22]

The pressure to cooperate is one of the principal sources of organizational politics. By its very nature, the division of tasks between departments gives rise to two potentially conflicting processes. On the one
hand, to achieve cooperation under a division of labor, there must be a
high degree of contact across subunit boundaries. On the other hand,
the existence of many discrete subunits promotes the development of
differing points of view. Focusing mainly on their own specific tasks and
responsibilities, subunits invariably shape their own preferences, needs,
and interests. Abell identifies four factors that play a primary role in shaping the subunit's outlook: differing estimates concerning future streams
of costs and benefits, unclear options, the cognitive limits of rationality,
and self-regarding behavior.[23] Each of these factors introduces uncertainties for subunits; each opens a stream of problems and issues that
widen a subunit's discretion to interpret events according to the dictates
of its own goals and interests.

Given these variations in interpretation across the system of subunits,
the need for cooperative contact among them breeds the potential for
conflict. Organizational politics is thus a response to conflicts over these

competing interpretations. Inevitably such politics takes the form of one subunit, as an interest group, angling to influence decisions that affect its own position vis-à-vis other organizational subunits. All organizations experience such conflict; in some it is endemic.

One of the most important structural features of the division of labor affecting the nature of power in organizations is the degree of centralization or decentralization. While politics is an important dynamic in all organizations, its forms and pervasiveness are determined by the structural dispersion of power. In highly centralized systems, the exercise of power usually takes the form of hierarchical authority. Decision processes are carefully guarded by the dominant managerial coalition; influence is often difficult to observe. Conflicts over goals and technologies are generally resolved by the top-down imposition of managerial preferences on the other subunits of the organization. In the name of central authority, this lends an apolitical quality to the organizational processes. Such processes will overtly appear to be orderly and rational, but this is only because goal disagreements and technological uncertainty have been submerged in the premises of the choice processes through the centralization of authority and influence. Under centralized power, participants have less opportunity or motivation to engage in the contests for control that provoke *visible* conflict and political behavior. The potential for political conflict remains, but it is constrained by internal structural controls. Political activity thus tends to be more *covert*. It becomes manifest around specific issues but remains latent or hidden around others.

As organizations grow, they tend to move away from the basic centralized model.[24] Large-scale organizations, which now dominate the landscape, are distinguished by complexity and decentralization. Some feature elaborate combinations of centralization and decentralization. These sometimes take the form of multiple hierarchies within the same organization. In such organizations, the political activities of interest groups and bargaining coalitions are much more overt than in the standard hierarchy of authority. Because the subunits of such organizations structurally provide more points of access to power, the interplay of political interest groups struggling to gain power in the decision-making process is a salient organizational process.

Interest Groups and Coalition Politics

Interest groups in organizations are formed by people with common objectives, goals, and values. In significant part, they are political responses to various barriers imposed by organizational structures. As institutional structures evolve to meet the pressures of change, political opportunities for competing groups are necessarily opened and closed. To fend against these shifting patterns of power, interest groups emerge to protect existing resources and to exploit new access to power. Their formation is "structurally staged," but never directly determined. Empirically, the shape and content of such groups is always dependent on a mix of situational factors.[25]

For the most part, interest groups are based around similar professional or occupational categories. One of the classic divisions of interest discussed in the literature is that between staff and line groups. Staff units are the niche of professional groups with power based on expertise. These groups include engineers, budget analysts, personnel managers, lawyers, and the like. Line groups orient around the organization's production processes. These include foremen and supervisory personnel, shop floor operators, maintenance men, and so on. In his famous study of staff and line relations, Gouldner illustrated how these different positions give rise to conflicting values and views. For example, he identified the professional outlook as that of the "cosmopolitan." Cosmopolitans were found to lack basic loyalties to the organization, to be highly committed to expertise (specialized techniques and skill), and to be likely to seek political support from interest groups external to the organization. Locals, by contrast, are individuals and groups in the line organization who tend to be very loyal to the organization, less committed to special techniques or skills, and most likely to form internal coalitions for political support.[26] As competing value orientations in the division of labor, line and staff interest groups often are the source of political tension and conflict in organizational processes.

Bacharach and Lawler argue that all hierarchies of authority, centralized or decentralized, unleash tendencies toward the formation of coalitions. A coalition is an alliance for joint political action by two or more interest groups against another group or coalition.[27] Coalitions may involve both internal and external alliances (with groups in the organization's environment). Much of the study of organizational politics focuses on the analysis of the factors that lead to the development of coalitions. One of the most important is the role of scarce resources.

Decisions about scarce resources are likely to give rise to both internal and external coalition building. Such coalitions are formed to protect existing resource allocations and to seek a more favorable share of the future stream of resources. Because interest groups with ample resources have the greatest potential influence in decision-making processes, interest groups with unfavorable resource allocations are usually the most likely to seek coalitions.

In organizational politics, where groups must continue to work together long after a particular decision has been made, there is an inducement for those with power to make internal coalitions as large as possible. Often exploiting the organizational "myth" about the common goals and purposes of the various subsystems, coalition leaders frequently continue the discussion and debate of an issue long after sufficient support has been formed behind a particular position. As Pfeffer puts it, the need "for a widely shared consensus at times means that making the decision rapidly or as soon as it is politically possible to do so is sacrificed in the interests of getting as many organizational interests as possible behind a decision."[28] One of the important implications of this is that it encourages small "nonwinning" interest groups to engage in coalition politics. In organizational situations where there is pressure to enlarge the coalition, winning is often more a matter of degree of influence than a finite outcome.

Interest groups also seek external relationships to help with support in internal affairs. This is especially common among specialized or profession-based groups. Evidence shows that in many contexts subunits attempt "to develop relationships with external groups as a way of enhancing their powers within the organization and increasing the likelihood of getting their way in organizational decisions."[29] To mobilize support for internal subunits, such outside groups or organizations must have interdependent relationships with the organization. For example, a purchasing agent can mobilize support through an alliance with the company's suppliers; social workers in a welfare department can rally their clients in support of a particular program; and so on.

External constituencies have both advantages and disadvantages. A primary advantage is that an external ally is less likely to be in direct competition for resources and power with a particular subunit than are the other internal units. For this reason, such relationships tend to be more symbiotic than competitive. On the other hand, an external ally will generally lack direct involvement in the internal decision processes. It can apply pressure on the internal system but, unlike internal subunits, it has much more difficulty advocating specific positions. Thus, while an external coalition can be of considerable help at times, its role is usually more uncertain than that of an internal ally. Over time, an internal ally tends to be more valuable in influencing decision outcomes.

It is also important to note that external coalitions tend to be formed

282 RECONSTRUCTING ORGANIZATION THEORY

more circumspectly than internal alliances. Because of the ideology of shared goals that characterizes most organizations, building external alliances can be viewed as an act of disloyalty to the organization and its goals. As Pfeffer puts it, "To build alliances with external groups suggests a rejection of the organization's interests for selfish interests of the subunit, a view which is likely to be seen as going against the norms of internal cooperation and goal sharing."[30]

Decision Making as Political Bargaining

In large part, "organizational politics involves the efforts of actors to mobilize interest groups and coalitions for the sake of influencing the decisions of those in authority."[31] Decision structures, for this reason, are the primary points of access to power; they are the basic arenas for political conflict and bargaining. Abell suggests that the structure of an organization should be conceptualized as an interrelated set of political bargaining zones rather than as a technically based decision structure.[32]

It is around the spheres of decision that one of the most important implications of the political model of organization theory can be found.[33] The result is a very different picture of the decision process from the one derived from the rational model and its technical variables. In contrast to a well-ordered hierarchy of efficient decision making, the political model presents a disorderly picture of conflict and struggle among competing interest groups.

Decisions in the political model are not presumed to result from an overarching intention or premise. In descriptive terms, organizational decision points tend to emerge as opportunities around which various problems, participants, and solutions tend to converge. Decisions result from competing interpretations of relatively independent streams of interest. These streams consist of problems, solutions, participants, and choice opportunities. As one writer puts it, "streams of problems entering or leaving the organization" are like flows "independent of other streams of choices, solutions, and energies." Presuming no internally or externally imposed deadlines, problems are merely worked on until they are solved or disappear. Such problems move with relative autonomy among competing choice opportunities "in search for a choice process in which [they] can be resolved."[34]

Cohen, March, and Olsen emphasize the problematic nature of participation in these decision processes.[35] Such processes are frequently so overloaded with problems and solutions that participants will be able to attend only to certain decisions. In some cases, the problems will actually dominate the decision makers. Unlike the rational model of decision, where outcomes are seen to be shaped by basic preferences, the political model acknowledges that actual preferences are often determined by outcomes. Indeed, Weick argues that most organizations appear to be running backward. It is not that individuals or groups abandon their goals or preferences, they simply must consider the possibilities made available by existing bargaining options and the necessity to compromise.[36]

Thus the political model conceptualizes the decision process as a pluralistic clash of intentions advanced by competing interest groups and subcultures. Confronted with conflicting preferences, interest groups and coalitions will bargain politically to shape the flow of problems, solutions, and choice opportunities. The political model hypothesizes that the bargaining participants with the greatest authority and influence will receive the greatest rewards from the interplay of organizational politics. Because the outcomes will result from political bargaining, the process will always be characterized by uncertainty and risk. Decisions will seldom reflect the preferences of any one interest group or subunit within the organization. Thus outcomes *cannot* be predicted with the high degree of confidence sought by the rational model theorists. Indeed, it is fair to say that a growing percentage of their predictions are only remotely related to the real-world outcomes that confront managers.[37] For writers like Susman and Evered, it is this failure that truly constitutes the "crisis in organizational science."

Organizational Change as a Political Process

Of the organizational processes discussed here, none better illustrates the role of politics than the process of organizational change. In fact, one can argue persuasively that organizational politics (at least as understood in mainstream theory) is largely a process that emerges in the context of organizational change. Even though power is everywhere in organizations, not everything in organizations is political. This is not to deny that all things in organizations are at all times potentially political; it is only to suggest that it is the activation of the processes of change that generally makes something political.

To illustrate the political dynamics of organizational change we return to the issue of the productivity crisis in modern organizations. The productivity crisis can be defined as the inability of organizations to innovate in rapidly changing environments.[38] Innovation in organization theory is understood as a process of organizational change. It can be defined as "the adoption of change which is new to an organization and to the relevant environment."[39] In traditional theory, where change is largely discussed within the framework of the dominant managerial goals, such an adoption is mainly viewed in terms of passive support or reaction to an intervention from the top. The political model, by contrast, directs attention to the underlying patterns of interest-group consensus and conflict that potentially initiate or block adaptation and change. In a complex and uncertain environment, the political perspective emphasizes the differential impact innovation has on the various subunits of the organizational system. It is alert to the fact that innovation threatens the existing equilibrium of power and resource sharing; it focuses on the political processes that are activated by such efforts to introduce change. Where the technical conception of innovation obscures the multiplicity of conflicting goals in the path of change, the political model not only anticipates competing goals, it also offers strategies for dealing with the realities of this conflict. Instead of suppressing conflict and influence (generally through increased centralization and technical decision making), this alternative perspective confronts these issues head-on. For the political model, coalition building and the political management of influence not only describe the realities of change, they also articulate the keys to successful innovation and change.[40] Essentially the model directs those concerned with innovation to the task of forging a coalition of interest groups with a vested interest in the outcome of change. Based on an assessment of influence differentials in the power distribution, managers and informal leaders must develop tactics that address the political requirements of the situation. Organizational politics is thus the lever that facilitates change. It comes about when a configuration of interest groups is "able to articulate a new set of strategies which are more consonant with the present environmental contingencies and [is] able to generate sufficient support for implementation within the organization."[41]

Reich concretely captures this point in his much-touted analysis of the organizational productivity crisis. For him, the identification and support of such a "new set of strategies" must be "the Next Frontier" in American industrial policy. The problem is clear: "Employees who doubt that the burdens and benefits of rapid adaptation will be shared equitably resist change outright or resort to subtle forms of sabotage."

Blue-collar employees "cling to work rules and rigid job classifications and fight against new technologies and productivity improvements; technical specialists steal company assets and make off with company secrets; managers earn as much money for themselves as they can before deserting the company for more lucrative positions elsewhere."[42] The solution, according to Reich, is to reconceptualize the organization as a political entity. Managers must relinquish their rigid adherence to hierarchical control and join with other organizational members to build an internal political coalition of workers, supervisors, and technicians based on a consensually derived network of mutual obligations and benefits. Often this will require the introduction of new concepts of equity, power, and participation in the workplace. To forge alternative relationships based on new ideas about mutual obligations and rights is political work; most managers are unprepared for the job.

Beyond the Managerial Bias

In terms of mainstream theory, the political model is an important advance over the technocratic model. Throughout the discussion in the preceding sections, the political perspective revealed a deep-reaching capacity to invalidate the assumptions technocratic organizations advance to explain and legitimate themselves. By illustrating the underlying political patterns that establish and maintain organizations, the model necessarily demystifies the technocratic model. To the degree that the technocratic approach exists to obscure the political realities of organizational life, the political model threatens technocracy at its core.

Having said this, however, it is important to recognize that much of this challenge to technocracy has thus far been largely reformist in nature. While the political model deserves credit for having opened the door to a wider range of competing organizational interests, it still has yet to fully transcend a managerial perspective. The discussion in the second section draws almost exclusively on theory and research couched in the concerns of managerial reform. In short, the emerging political model remains fundamentally anchored to the "managerial bias" and is itself subject to a more radical normative critique.

If the purpose is to fully understand the play of organizational politics, it is ultimately essential to employ a more critical conceptualization of power, the fundamental commodity of politics. Basically, this involves the development of a model that can grasp bureaucratic politics from the bottom up as well as from the top down. The place to begin is with a critique of the empirical-analytic model's conceptualization of power. Most of the theoretical perspectives surveyed in the foregoing section rely on the pluralist theory of politics and power (frequently that of Robert Dahl, widely recognized as one of the pioneers of pluralist political science). In this view, A has power over B to the extent that he or she can get B to do something that B would not otherwise do. Adapted to the study of organizational politics, such power is taken to reflect one subunit's ability to influence other organizational units to produce desired outcomes.

Absent from this work is any attention to the criticisms that have been leveled at modern pluralist theory. It is now widely recognized that the standard pluralist model is based on an anemic conception of power. Fundamental to the criticisms of this model is its emphasis on the more overt, objective aspects of power. Focusing primarily on empirically measurable phenomenon, particularly the behavior of interest groups and coalitions, pluralist theory underplays the hidden institutional dimensions of power that prestructure the terrain of political conflict. It is not that pluralists misrepresent the phenomenon that they describe so much as they tend to obfuscate the less accessible dimensions of power that are critical to its interpretation.

In the pluralist approach to organizational politics, power is seen to be relatively diffused throughout the organization. In this model the organization is conceptualized as a series of interrelated power centers, none of which can be wholly sovereign. Interest groups and coalitions, the political agents of these power centers, are seen to act relatively freely on an issue-by-issue basis. Pfeffer and Salancik, for instance, define a bureaucracy as a "coalition of groups and interests, each attempting to obtain something from the collectivity by interacting with others, and each with its own preferences and objectives."[43] Using the language of the pluralist power model, Rosen typifies their position this way:

> If A has power over B with respect to the issue X, this does not influence A's relationship with B with respect to issue Y. Political action is a process in which a plurality of interest groups align, misalign and realign over subsequent issues of concern. There is no power elite.[44]

Missing from the pluralist model of organizational politics is an account of the asymmetrical nature of bureaucratic power. In Rosen's words, the coalition model of organizational politics must be "superceded with a model of organization as a stratified, non-neutral terrain of conflict among competing groups." By focusing on

> the objective . . . largely observable—dimensions of power and politics, pluralism has failed to incorporate the hidden institutional factors—often latent and subjective—that pre-shaped interest group behavior. To interpret the meaning of individual, interest group, or coalition politics by merely charting their objective moves is to misrepresent the nature of such activity.[45]

Stewart Clegg likens it to examining the positions of the pieces on a chessboard without knowledge of the rules of the game. He puts it this way:

> To the extent that all pieces were able to negotiate their positions, more or less, then in a game with a fixed number of pieces, that piece which ended up ruling over the greatest number of pieces, serving its *interests* in preference to theirs, would be the most powerful. But obviously, in an ongoing game, then a piece like the Queen would start in a more privileged position than a pawn, simply because the extant rules . . . enable her to begin with more potential moves to make.[46]

To fully grasp the nature of this underlying power, it is essential to recognize the ways in which power is embedded in the very structures and practices of the bureaucratic system. Toward this end, it is necessary to examine the nature of institutionalized power.

Institutional power is a subtle and evasive phenomenon. Writing of political systems generally, Bachrach and Baratz describe the institutionalization of power in this way: It is a process in which "a set of predominant values, beliefs, and institutional practices operate to the benefit of certain persons and groups at the expense of others."[47] The process in bureaucracies is nearly synonymous with organizational design. In the very construction of a bureaucracy the goals and values of its masters (owners, managers, or political leaders) are built into the organizational structures and practices. For example, as Edwards explains, "hierarchical relations are transformed from relations between (unequally powerful) people to relations between jobholders or relations between jobs themselves, abstracted from the specific people or the concrete work tasks involved."[48] The effect is to obscure the fact that power belongs to specific individuals or groups, particularly those at the top. Instead, it appears to emanate from the formal organization itself.

Much of organization theory has traditionally involved an attempt to institutionalize managerial power. While the literature scarcely speaks about these political purposes of the process, its critics have clearly illustrated the ways in which it has helped to design and reinforce barriers that block workers' abilities to effectively voice grievances against specific policies and practices.[49] One of the most fascinating statements of this intention is found in Herbert Simon's now-classic statement on organizational design. For Simon, the key to design lies in translating substantive decisions about goals and values into technical decisions about efficiency. Substantive goals are structured at each level of the organization to be "rationally" approached as "value-neutral" premises in decisions about means to managerially established ends. The result is a hierarchical chain of technical decisions. At any point in the hierarchy, the substantive value premise of one level is presented as a factual premise to the level below. Because each level in a hierarchy is subordinate to a higher level, the entire structure is experienced in practical terms as a vertical chain of technical decisions, at least until one reaches the top level of the organization. The result is a top-down system of institutional control. By supplying participants at each level with factual premises to shape and channel their behavior, the designers structurally bias the organization to move in the direction desired by its mandators. In short, organizational behavior is rigged from the top.

Thus, in contrast to the pluralists' limited focus on overt exchanges between interest groups (negotiations, argumentation, protests, and so on), power is also exercised when one group devotes its energies to shaping the terms of the exchanges. In this respect, the dominant managerial group's ability to determine the official organizational agenda is one of its most important sources of institutional power. By creating or reinforcing political values and practices that limit the scope of the political process to official consideration of those issues that are comparatively innocuous to the dominant group, the strategy can successfully prevent other groups from bringing to the fore issues and problems that are potentially detrimental to the dominant preferences.

Understanding this hidden dimension of organizational power is essential for exploring the kinds of research issues raised by a critical perspective.[50] Because formal bureaucratic structures and practices are designed to thwart and punish organizational workers who challenge managerial authority, such politics invariably goes underground, only making itself visible at critical moments in the course of organizational events.

Writers such as Deena Weinstein and Martin and Carol Needleman have already explored the nature of this hidden politics.[51] Weinstein, for example, sets out the idea that organizations are special kinds of political systems. Because they seek to deny the existence of dissent, and thus provide no institutional mechanisms for its expression, bureaucracies can be likened to authoritarian political regimes. Opposition in such regimes, particularly opposition to managerial interests and values imposed from the top, takes special forms, usually indirect and covert. One strategy is to camouflage the purposes and goals in the "official" organizational rhetoric. On other occasions, the opposition actions take the form of inaction (they might, for instance, withhold their participation as a form of a silent disagreement or protest). In such situations, it is difficult to distinguish between an interest group's immediate strategy and its basic motives and goals.

To say that politics in authoritarian regimes goes underground is basically to say that it is conducted through a series of informal networks. For this reason, many of an organization's most important political rules are informal in nature. Often they are based on *tacit* agreements forged and accepted by competing groups. Thus to get at these hidden dimensions of power researchers often must enter the organizational situation as participant-observers. Only as insiders can researchers become party to these informal political understandings. This, of course, poses a problematic barrier to the development of a critical organization theory. There are, however, some promising signs of progress in this area, particularly as an anthropological perspective emerges as a research focus in organizational theory.[52]

Organizational Praxis:
Exploiting the Political Model

As a reform strategy, the political model largely emphasizes the processes of adaptation and change. Managers are encouraged to learn to assess the power distribution in their organizations and to use such information to forge alliances with interest groups and coalitions that have a vested interest in the desired forms of change. Toward this end, political skills training is advocated as an important component of managerial expertise.[53]

Rather than exploit the distribution of power, the goal from a critical

RECONSTRUCTING ORGANIZATION THEORY

perspective is to change it. If political research can be employed to uncover useful strategies for managerial change, by extension the same theoretical approach can be used to develop effective oppositional strategies. Clegg and Higgens, for instance, argue that the goal from a critical perspective is to develop a theory that can assist the political struggle against bureaucratic modes of governance and to provide guidance in establishing democratic or self-managed organizations.[54]

Such empirical work is especially important for the design of democratic organizations. If the development of political skills has become a requirement for management generally, it is even more essential for democratically managed organizations, where politics is institutionalized as the primary mode of decision making. Here research must provide direction for the development and teaching of special skills necessary for democratic decision making. In this respect, researchers must begin to study the politics of the democratic workplace.[55]

Political Participation as a Structural Reform

One way to approach this task is through Andre Gorz's concept of a "structural reform."[56] According to Gorz, a structural reform is designed to transform organizational power relations from within. As a theoretical construct, it is based on two interrelated analyses. The first is an identification of existing weaknesses in the organizational system; the second is an analysis of how these weaknesses might be exploited to move the organization in the direction of a more fundamental form of change. By supplying oppositional groups with a theoretical strategy designed to increase their political leverage, structural reform can guide action toward the breakdown and reconstruction of the organizational system.

The idea of a structural reform rests on the argument that a continuous series of small-scale reforms can gradually subvert the fundamental structures that perpetuate existing patterns of workplace power.[57] Where managers can be pressed to extend such reforms, they unwittingly run the risk of triggering a basic transformation in the relations of power and decision making. For example, the piecemeal but progressive introduction of workplace participation schemes can be used to illustrate this point.

Workplace participation schemes, or participatory management techniques, are usually put forward as administrative reforms and, as such, are not designed to challenge the basic structures of managerial governance. In the brief analysis of organizational innovation, for instance, political participation was seen as necessary to make technocratic organizations more flexible in the face of complexity. In such organizations this has meant an increasing delegation of authority to specific task units and the use of various forms of participatory management.[58]

From the perspective of a structural reform, these new forms of political behavior open up access to power. Thus those who introduce such reforms must attempt to carefully delineate the nature and degree of the participation they seek to promote. Participation must make decision processes more flexible without, at the same time, challenging the *fundamental* managerial structures that control and direct the organization as a whole. By identifying these new forms of participation as sources of power, and fostering the development of worker strategies for exploiting access to this power, the political model can be used to undercut efforts to limit participation to specific areas of decision making. In politics it is a long-established fact that meaningful political involvement tends to unleash the desire for more participation. Indeed, Pfeffer has noted that once an organization becomes *overtly* political it is extremely difficult to return it to a depoliticized mode of decision making.[59] Participatory reforms thus run a substantial risk of setting off such a demand for more participation (to use Habermas's phrase, a demand for the elimination of "unnecessary domination"). As more and more questions about the governance of the organization are subjected to a wider range of participatory decision making, the deliberative processes systematically progress toward basic issues about who governs and why. Pushed to its logical extreme, this necessarily poses a serious threat to managerial and technocratic authority. Insofar as political participation introduces processes that are ultimately alien to technocratic management, such practices necessarily probe the weaknesses and limits of such a system. For this reason, the strategic introduction of participatory models of decision making and political skills training can bring about structural reforms.

Academic praxis. The political model can play a similar role in the sphere of management education. As noted above, an important implication drawn from the mainstream approach to organizational politics is that managers need to develop political skills. Indeed, a number of writers have already begun to formulate models and techniques for political skills training.[60] In some cases, researchers have approached model building by attempting to identify the specific political tactics employed by managers.[61] Another approach has been to focus on the role of negotiations in organizations.[62] One such effort had involved the study of negotiation processes that help to achieve effective agreements.

The work of Lax and Sebenius represents an example of the effort to translate this work on negotiations into practical classroom skills.[63] Beginning with the basic elements of negotiation analysis and an examination of the various roles of the manager as negotiator, they take up a number of theoretical and practical bargaining situations, such as budgetary negotiations, policy-making strategies, and coalition building for organizational change. They emphasize the ways in which negotiations deal with parties, issues, and alternatives. In the process, they draw out the critical tensions that arise in negotiations. For example, one theme centers on the question of how negotiators differentiate between cooperative moves needed to create joint value and cooperative moves that parties make to claim value for themselves.

Such questions can be more problematic than they first appear. To fully grasp the nature of the potential problem, it is important to appreciate the context in which such political discussions occur, namely, the school of management. Consider the underlying social role of the management school. Essentially, it is the institutional site for the reproduction of the dominant technocratic ideology of modern capitalist institutions and the middle-class careers that the ideology supports. Management schools produce—on the whole—sound and reliable functionaries for the ruling elites, both economic and political. They do this by instilling knowledge and competencies (e.g., strategic planning, financial analysis, and organizational design). As Clegg and Dunkerley point out, these schools, in a sense, produce functionaries who have "complex technocratic rules built into" their thought processes.[64]

The reproduction of any ideology is always fraught with risks. Because technocratic ideology in management education is designed either to obscure or to legitimate certain basic realities of power in the workplace, such education must be carefully managed. Inasmuch as important aspects of the management curriculum require students to keep abreast of developments in the social sciences, there is a possibility at times that such knowledge will raise basic contradictions in the technocratic ideology itself. In fact, in the face of an escalation of educational "credentialism" in the professional-managerial strata, some writers have argued that the extension of education can be a "Trojan Horse" in modern organizational life.[65]

In this context, the political model of organization theory can be something of a problem. As a critical social scientific perspective on the management process, its very existence in the curriculum is bound to create tensions. At the most obvious level, the political model exposes the technocratic effort to repress the political groupings that constitute the "real" organization. In more political terms, the effort to introduce political skills training can stir up sensitive issues that have to be carefully managed. For example, political exercises are likely to reveal the ideology of cooperation to be a cover for the harsher underlying reality of self-interested groups vying for power.

Political skills, in face of the skewed distribution of power, are usually employed in organizations to advance the particular interest of a few at the expense of many. For this reason, the study of specific political strategies can potentially generate a dissonant response among students. In a course titled "Power and Negotiations in Organizations," for instance, one management professor reports that students say the exercises make them feel too aggressive and self-interested. Although they generally agree that such behavior is essential for getting ahead in modern organizations, the students are uncomfortable personally participating in these political realities. Many simply believe that such activities are morally wrong. Because the strategies are built as much on manipulation as on the cold logic of modern organizational design, troublesome contradictions that underlie managerial authority come to the surface of analysis. Once in the open, it is difficult to avoid discussing the implications of these realities. While such discussions fall far short of major transformations, they indeed constitute important opportunities for critical dialogue.

Even those pushing the political model as a managerial reform recognize the implications of raising awkward political issues. Pfeffer notes a steady resistance to the use of political terminology in the management curriculum and attributes it in part to the high stakes involved.[66] As long as the political model remains only a *theoretical* challenge to technocracy, the stakes are largely relegated to the intellectual realm. Once it is introduced as a central theory in the education and training of aspiring managers, however, it begins to take the form of a challenge to existing organizational relations themselves. To open up the issues of organizational power is to court the ire of corporate management itself. Not only might it jeopardize the corporate financial contributions upon which most prestigious management schools depend, it could also threaten the career channels that lead directly from these schools into the corporate world.

Against these stakes, the political model can be much more than an alternative description of organizational reality. For those interested in raising consciousness about inequality and political domination in modern organizational arrangements, the political model is also a strategic resource for pursuing such dialogue in a citadel of corporate capitalism itrself, the school of management.

Conclusion

This chapter has covered a good deal of ground. It began with a discussion of the "crisis" in modern organization theory and suggested that its implications are significantly related to one of our most pressing problems, namely, the productivity "crisis" of the national economy. Against this background the political model was introduced as an alternative theory that addresses the primary failure of mainstream theory, its adherence to a rational technocratic model. On its own terms, it was seen as a welcome attempt to incorporate a wider range of social and political interests into organization theory.

Beyond a description of the political model and its implications for the current theoretical crisis, this chapter sought to extend the contribution in a more radical direction. Toward this end, the third section showed the seeds of a critical organization theory to be inherent in the mainstream political perspective itself. Indeed, given the political bias of technocratic theory, the political model was seen to offer one of the rare instances in which empirical description is itself virtually tantamount to normative critique. The development of a critical approach to organizational politics thus essentially involves a deeper analysis of the basic issues opened by the pluralists.

In the context of the current theoretical malaise, it is clear that the political perspective provides a powerful and exciting way of rethinking organization theory. Like any theory that speaks to reality, it will continue to gain credibility. For this reason, there can be little doubt that the political perspective will play an increasingly important role in the theoretical debates that shape the future of organization theory.

For critical social scientists the emergence of the political model can open a unique opportunity to engage the discipline in a more radical discussion of organizational realities. Most conventional theorists have treated the critical perspective as an alien point of view. Typically, it has been dismissed as a radical critique that has little to do with running a firm. At the same time, however, conventional theorists have hidden behind the technical model, often presented as the product of a natural (or universal) logic of organizations. The growing legitimacy of the mainstream political model helps to break down this dichotomy. By shifting the terms of the theoretical debate to a vocabulary that bridges mainstream and the critical perspectives, the political model establishes an avenue capable of extending the discourse to both a critique of bureaucratic domination and the development of the workplace democracy. Given the growing interest in critical organization theory, as well as a political theory of organizations, it seems fair to conclude that the theoretical linkages are ultimately inevitable. In large part, it is a matter of taking up the challenge.

Notes

1. Vincent Ostrom, *The Intellectual Crisis in American Public Administration* (University of Alabama: University of Alabama Press, 1974); Robert Denhardt, *Theories of Public Organizations* (Monterey, CA: Brooks/Cole, 1984); Gerald Susman and R. Evered, "An Assessment of the Scientific Merits of Action Research, *Administrative Science Quarterly* 23 (1978): 582–608.

2. Susman and Evered, p. 582.

3. Robert Haynes and William Abernathy, "Managing Our Way to Economic Decline," *Harvard Business Review*, July–August 1980, pp. 66–77.

4. Samuel Bowles, David Gordon, and Thomas Weisskopf, *Beyond the Wasteland: A Democratic Alternative to Economic Decline* (New York: Doubleday, 1983).

5. Frank Fischer and Carmen Sirianni, eds., *Critical Studies in Organization and Bureaucracy* (Philadelphia: Temple University Press, 1984).

6. Mary Zey-Ferrell and Michael Aiken, eds., *Complex Organizations: Critical Perspectives* (Glenview IL: Scott, Foresman, 1981).

7. Alvin W. Gouldner, "Organizational Analysis," in *Sociology Today*, ed. Robert K. Merton et al. (New York: Basic Books, 1959), pp. 404–5.

8. See Mats Alvesson, *Organization Theory and Technocratic Consciousness* (Berlin: Walter de Guyter, 1987), for a critical discussion of the positivistic approach to organization theory and design.

9. Charles Perrow, *Complex Organizations* (Glenview, IL: Scott, Foresman, 1972), p. 145.

10. See Wolf V. Heydebrand, "Technocratic Corporatism: Toward a Theory of Occupational and Organizational Transformation," in *Organizational Theory and Public Policy*, ed. Richard Hall and Robert Quinn (Beverly Hills, CA: Sage, 1983), pp. 93–114.

11. Paul Goldman, "Sociologists and the Study of Bureaucracy: A Critique of Ideology and Practice," *The Insurgent Sociologist* 3 (1978): 21–30.

12. Denhardt, *Theories of Public Organizations*, p. 79.

13. Richard W. Scott, "Developments in Organization Theory," in *The State of Sociology*, ed. J. F. Short (Beverly Hills, CA: Sage, 1981), pp. 199–214.

14. Robert A. Dahl, "The Concept of Power," *Behavioral Science* 2 (1957): 201–15; and Dennis Wrong, *Power* (New York: Harper and Row, 1979).

15. Jeffrey Pfeffer, *Power in Organizations* (Boston: Pitman, 1981), p. 7.

16. Henry Mintzberg, *Power in and Around Organizations,* (Englewood Cliffs, NJ: Prentice-Hall, 1983).

17. Jeffrey Pfeffer, "The Micropolitics of Organizations," in *Environments and Organizations*, ed. Marshall M. Meyer et al. (San Francisco: Jossey-Bass, 1978), p. 37.

18. James G. March, "The Business Firm as a Political Coalition," *Journal of Politics* 24 (1962): 662–78; and Douglas Yates, *Bureaucratic Democracy* (Cambridge, MA: Harvard University Press, 1982).

19. Karl E. Weick, "Educational Organizations as Loosely Coupled Systems," *Administrative Science Quarterly* 21 (1976): 1–19.

20. Samuel B. Bacharach and Edward J. Lawler, *Power and Politics in Organizations* (San Francisco: Jossey-Bass, 1980), pp. 22–44.

21. See Pfeffer, *Power in Organizations,* p. 4; and Richard Edwards, *Contested Terrain* (New York: Basic Books, 1979).

22. R. M. Emerson, "Power-Dependence Relations," *American Sociological Review* 27 (1962): 31–40. On the limitation of autonomy among subgroups, see D. J. Hickson et al., "A Strategic Contingency Theory of Interorganizational Power," in *Organizational Influence Processes*, ed. R. W. Allen and L. W. Porter (Glenview, IL: Scott, Foresman, 1983), pp. 33–51.

23. P. Abell, "Organizations as Bargaining and Influence Systems: Measuring Intra-Organizational Power and Influence," in *Organizations as Bargaining and Influence Systems* (London: Halsted, 1975), p. 12.

24. L. E. Greiner, "Evolution and Revolution as Organizations Grow," *Harvard Business Review,* July–August 1972, pp. 37–46.

25. Mintzberg, *Power in and Around Organizations.*

26. Alvin W. Gouldner, "Cosmopolitans and Locals," in *Organizations,* vol. 1, ed. Joseph A. Litterer (New York: John Wiley, 1969).

27. Bacharach and Lawler, *Power and Politics.*

28. Jeffrey Pfeffer, "Coalitions," in *Organizational Influence Processes,* p. 314.

29. Ibid., p. 316.

30. Ibid.

31. Bacharach and Lawler, *Power and Politics,* p. 213.

32. Abell, *Organizations as Bargaining,* p. 16.

33. Andrew M. Pettigrew, *The Politics of Organizational Decision-Making* (London: Tavistock, 1973).

34. S. S. Weiner, "Participation, Deadlines, and Choices," in *Ambiguity and Choice in Organizations*, ed. James G. March and Johan P. Olsen (Bergen, Norway: Universitetsforlaget, 1976), p. 243.

35. Michael D. Cohen, James G. March, and Johan P. Olsen, "People, Problems, Solutions, and the Ambiguity of Relevance," in *Ambiguity and Choice in Organizations,* pp. 24–37.

36. Karl E. Weick, *The Social Psychology of Organizing* (Reading, MA: Addison-Wesley, 1969).

37. Charles Perrow, "Demystifying Organizations," in *The Management of*

Human Services, ed. R. C. Sarri and Y. Hasenfeld (New York: Columbia University Press, 1978), pp. 105–20.

38. Michael Piore and Charles Sabel, *The Second Industrial Divide* (New York: Basic Books, 1984).

39. K. E. Knight, "A Descriptive Model of the Intra-Firm Innovation Process," *Journal of Business* 40, no. 4 (1964), p. 478.

40. See, for example, Harvey M. Sapolsky, *The Polaris System Development* (Cambridge: MIT Press, 1972).

41. Pfeffer, *Power in Organizations*, p. 339.

42. Robert Reich, *The Next American Frontier* (New York: Times Books, 1983).

43. Jeffrey Pfeffer and Gerald R. Salancik, *The External Control of Organizations* (New York: Harper & Row, 1978), p. 36.

44. Michael Rosen, "Culture and Power in Formal Organization" (Unpublished paper, 1986), pp. 70–71.

45. Ibid.

46. Steward Clegg, *Power, Rule and Domination* (London: Routledge & Kegan Paul, 1975), p. 49.

47. Peter Bachrach and Morton S. Baritz, "Two Faces of Power," *American Political Science Review* 56 (1971): 947–52.

48. Edwards, *Contested Terrain,* p. 145.

49. Ibid.; Dan Clawson, *Bureaucracy and the Labor Process* (New York: Monthly Review Press, 1980).

50. B. D. Steffy and A. J. Grimes, "A Critical Theory of Organization Science," *Academy of Management Review* 11, no. 2 (1986): 332–36.

51. Deena Weinstein, *Bureaucratic Opposition* (New York: Pergamon, 1979); and Martin L. and Carolyn E. Needleman, *Guerillas in the Bureaucracy* (New York: John Wiley, 1974).

52. Michael Rosen, "Breakfast at Spiro's: Dramaturgy and Dominance," *Journal of Management* 11, no. 2 (1985): 31–48; and Michael Burawoy, *Manufacturing Consent* (Chicago: University of Chicago Press, 1979).

53. John P. Kotter, *Power and Management* (New York: Amacon, 1979).

54. Stewart Clegg and Winton Higgens, "From Critical Theory to Routine Practices in Organizational Analysis" (Paper prepared for the International Conference on Perspectives in Organizational Analysis, Baruch College, New York, September 5–7, 1985).

55. Paul Bernstein, *Workplace Democratization* (New Brunswick, NJ: Transaction, 1976); and Jane J. Mansbridge, *Beyond Adversary* (New York: Basic Books, 1980).

56. Andre Gorz, *Strategy for Labor* (Boston: Beacon, 1964).

57. Ibid.

58. On this point I am indebted to Wolf Heydebrand.

59. Pfeffer, *Power in Organizations*.

60. D. Kipnis and S. M. Schmidt, "An Influence Perspective on Bargaining Within Organizations," in *Negotiating in Organizations*, ed. M. H. Bazerman and R. J. Lewicki (Beverly Hills, CA: Sage, 1983), pp. 303–19.

61. R. W. Allen et al., "Organizational Politics: Tactics and Characteristics of Its

Actors," in *Organizational Influence Processes*, ed. R. W. Allen and L. W. Porter (Glenview, IL: Scott, Foresman, 1983), pp. 475–83; Kipnis and Schmidt, "An Influence Perspective."

62. Bazerman and Lewicki, *Negotiating in Organizations*.

63. David A. Lax and James K. Sebenius, *The Manager as Negotiator* (New York: Free Press, 1986).

64. Stewart Clegg and David Dunkerley, *Organization, Class and Control* (London: Routledge & Kegan Paul), p. 539.

65. Ernest Mandell, *Late Capitalism* (London: New Left Books, 1975), p. 584.

66. Pfeffer, *Power in Organizations*.

12

Technological Politics in the
Postindustrial Workplace:
The Problem of Expertise

In the preceding chapter, we raised the issue of the "productivity crisis." We argued that the decline of organizational productivity can in important ways be attributed to the dominant technical conceptualization of organizational structures and processes. The solution, it was maintained, depends on a reconceptualization of the organization as a political entity. Managers must relinquish their rigid adherence to hierarchical control and join with other organizational members to mutually build an internal coalition of workers, supervisors, and technicians based on consensually derived obligations and benefits. This, it was argued, requires the acceptance of new ideas about equity, power, and participation in the workplace.

Nowhere are these issues of power and participation more important than in the computerized workplace of the emerging postindustrial economy. In this chapter, we examine the implications of new computer technologies for worker participation. Specifically, the focus is on the role of expertise in the development of participatory work systems.

Why focus on expertise? Traditionally, expertise—managerial expertise in particular—has been a barrier to worker participation. Numerous explanations have been given for this phenomenon. The most conventional one focuses on the problem of efficiency. In a complex technical world it is difficult—many would say impossible—to turn decisions over to those who lack a sophisticated grasp of the organizational machinery.[1] Indeed, plenty of evidence can be marshaled to demonstrate inefficiencies resulting from participation, particularly participation for its own sake.

More recent explanations have stressed the use of expertise as a tool for social control.[2] Technocratic rhetoric aside, one of the key functions of managerial expertise has been to ensure the control of organizational elites. Toward this end, managerial theory and practice have evolved in significant part as a strategy to block the participation of a wider range of organizational interests. Most typically, expertise has been used to limit access to power through a technocratic system of organizational stratification. In such systems, organizational position and status are purportedly distributed from the top down according to knowledge and expertise.

Managerial expertise has thus long been deeply involved—albeit covertly—in shaping the political contours of the workplace. This suggests, correctly as we will argue here, that the struggle to reshape the postindustrial workplace must necessarily involve a direct political challenge to established managerial—largely technocratic—approaches to organizations.

In the high-technology workplace, the problem of expertise is magnified dramatically. Even the well-educated professional worker is seldom equipped to deal with all of the technical complexities of the computerized workplace. Our fate would seem to be hopelessly tied to the mercies of a relatively new breed of experts—computer specialists and engineers. But recent studies of computerization show the issue to harbor a number of subtle dilemmas, if not contradictions. More and more it is argued that effective long-run utilization of these computer technologies requires new systems of worker power and participation. How, though, can ordinary workers be expected to participate in the sophisticated decisions pertaining to computer technologies? The answer, we contend here, is to be found in the development of new modes of participatory expertise.

In the postindustrial workplace, then, the struggle for organizational democracy cannot be limited to a confrontation with standard managerial practices. For democratic reforms to be taken seriously we must begin to develop and implement new participatory models of expertise. It is difficult to be highly specific about the nature of such models, as the task of rethinking the expert's role has only begun. Some things, however, are clear. The expert in a democratic setting will have to assume the role of a political facilitator and, as such, will necessarily become much more involved in the internal political development of the workplace. In the process, expertise itself will become a political issue, thus opening the way to what Winner has called "technological politics."[3] It is to these issues that the present discussion is primarily addressed.

The discussion will proceed in four parts. First, we shall examine the role of managerial expertise. The purpose is to draw out both its technical and its ideological dimensions. Management, it is shown, has traditionally served to secure and sustain the power of the dominant organizational elites. The second part of the chapter turns to the uses of new automated technologies in the modern factory and office. The focus here is on the nature of these computerized work systems and their implications for a dramatic increase in managerial control of the labor process. Computerized work is shown to be evolving as a modern Tayloristic form of managerial control. In the third part, we discuss the need for a political strategy to confront the serious threat posed by current trends in automation. In particular, emphasis is placed on the need to forge an alliance between labor and expertise. Finally, in the fourth part, we examine an alternative technology project developed by the Swedish labor movement in conjunction with workplace and technology experts at the Arbetslivscentrum in Stockholm. The purpose is to illustrate an innovative alternative that such a coalition can make possible.

Managerial Expertise: Technical and Ideological Roles

Until the past decade, organizational theorists on both ends of the political spectrum largely ignored the politics of workplace expertise. Underlying this neglect has been the widely accepted view that the technological development of productive forces—whether under capitalism or socialism—is intrinsically positive.[4] In this view, a form of technological determinism, technology is understood as a politically neutral force of production available for the development of very different social systems. The choice of the social system is largely a matter of political ideology; the development of the technological forces themselves is purely technical. In the realm of production, the use of technology involves little more than the efficient organization of these forces. This, as we have seen, is the special function of the management profession.

While the practice of management is as old as organized work itself, the concept of management as a specialized function is basically a twentieth-century phenomenon. In broad outline, its development must be attributed to the seminal work of Frederick Winslow Taylor. It was Taylor and his *Principles of Scientific Management* (published in 1911) that established the basic framework of the industrial workplace in this century.[5]

Taylor is often depicted as an eccentric engineer with a fanatic devotion to the science of measurement. As a mechanical engineer, he focused almost exclusively on the measurement of industrial efficiency. His expressed purpose was to find the "one best way" of restructuring the industrial workplace. Defined in terms of efficiency, the "one best way" was to be determined through the scientific analysis of the division of labor. This included the following:

1. The introduction of a planning department to design, monitor, and improve all phases of production. The job of the department began with the breakdown of operations into individual tasks and in turn specific motions. The motions of each task were timed with a stopwatch to determine and eliminate superfluous and inefficient motions.

2. Each worker was assigned a fixed and limited task. An ideal time was determined for completing the task and instructions for each worker were printed on cards.

3. Equipment and purchasing practices were standardized and inventory controls were introduced.

4. Foremen were assigned to oversee individual tasks and superior performances were rewarded.[6]

Scientific management's impact has been far-reaching. What emerged initially as a narrow technical focus on efficient work relations was literally to evolve into the dominant theory of labor-management relations. Because efficiency would lead to greater output and hence the possibility of a larger dividend for both management and labor, scientific management was touted as the basis for a new harmony of interests.[7] (Indeed, Taylor claimed scientific management to be the basis for "a true democracy.") Capturing the attention of leading industrialists and politicians, both nationally and internationally, Taylor's *Scientific Management* became the bible of an enormously popular movement.[8] As the purported solution to the pressing problem of industrial strife, this "efficiency craze" held sway over the public mind for at least two decades.

Scientific management also became a leading American export. No case better illustrates the power of the technique's appeal than its introduction into the socialist factory system by Lenin in the 1920s. In what was later to be judged a colossal error by many Marxist theoreticians, Lenin promoted the techniques of Taylorism as part of the Soviet Union's industrial leap forward. For Lenin the task was simply a matter of detaching scientific management from the profit mechanism and hooking it up to the Soviet theory of social justice, namely, communism. In his essay, "The Immediate Tasks of Soviet Government," he wrote that "the Soviet Republic must at all costs adopt all that is valuable in the achievement of science and technology."[9] Specifically, he referred to the need to "organize in Russia the study and teaching of the Taylor system." Lenin described the Taylor system this way:

> The Taylor system, the last word of capitalism in this respect, like all capitalist progress, is a combination of the refined brutality of bourgeois exploitation and a number of the greatest scientific achievements in the field of analyzing mechanical motions during work, the elimination of superfluous and awkward motions, the elaboration of correct methods of work, [and] the introduction of the best system of accounting and control.[10]

Taylorism has continued to have a long, enduring history. Although most of Taylorism's specific techniques have long been discredited, the philosophy of Taylorism still underlies much of workplace organization, both in the office and in the factory. Indeed, this has given rise to one of the fascinating questions addressed by contemporary workplace historians: Why has the philosophy of Taylorism hung on long after its specific practices have disappeared? To explain this paradox, it is necessary to examine the history of Taylorism itself.

Contrary to the conventional wisdom, labor historians have shown that as a "science" and a "movement," the "craze" over Taylorism had faded by 1930. Scientific management, at least as a formally specified set of techniques, appeared to have failed. Judged against Taylor's original forecasts, his science significantly spurred neither efficiency nor productivity. Many of Taylor's followers in the industrial world thus abandoned his techniques.[11]

The Hawthorne experiments of the 1920s identified the root cause of

Taylorism's problem. Giving rise to the "human relations movement," these studies brought to the fore scientific management's failure to recognize the significance of the social and psychological aspects of workplace behavior.[12] Stated in the simplest terms, human relations psychology showed that workers seldom work for economic rewards alone. The result was a fundamental shift in the focus of workplace investigations, namely, from the workers' tasks to the workers *themselves*. For scientific management, anchored to the idea that workers would embrace the techniques of efficiency to maximize their rewards, this discovery was profoundly problematic. What is more, workers were found to deeply resent the strict workplace regimentation introduced by Taylor's methods. Far from eliminating labor conflict, Taylorism often generated it.

Experiments, from Hawthorne forward, show that productivity can be increased by enlarging the worker's role. It is now an established premise that dramatic gains in output can be achieved through various forms of job enlargement and teamwork. Although such schemes seldom involve worker participation in managerial matters (which opens them to the critique leveled at human relations techniques in Chapter 5), they do permit decentralized work teams to organize important aspects of the production process as they see fit. Through a reduction in the division of labor, along with the elimination of highly repetitive tasks, workers are invited to learn and display a spectrum of skills and to take on the coordination, planning, timing, and even testing of their products. To be sure, companies organized in this manner have their difficulties, but, by and large, many of them have proven to be very successful.[13]

Such productivity schemes stand Taylorism on its head. And, in doing so, they raise critically important questions: If research and experimentation show that participation and teamwork systems increase productivity, why is work seldom organized this way? Why is the modern workplace still dominated by a breakdown of tasks into smaller units? Why the continued reliance on hierarchical structures of authority? Why the separation of manual and intellectual training?

Answers to these questions can be found in the research on American management practices carried out in recent years by contemporary Marxist sociologists and historians.[14] Beginning with the landmark work of Harry Braverman, Marxist scholars have demonstrated conventional organization theory's failure to grasp the critically important element of Taylorism. For these writers, the real contribution of scientific management lies not so much in the introduction of efficient workplace practices but in managerial control of the organization. In sum, the hierarchical division of labor is designed to ensure the transfer of workplace control from workers to managers.

The main thesis of Braverman's book, *Labor and Monopoly Capital,* can be stated fairly simply: In the interest of lowering the costs of labor and securing control over workers, managers in capitalist systems deliberately design the labor process to deskill workers.[15] The book identifies and describes actual deskilling practices in many workplaces, both blue and white collar, and it dramatically underscores the need to focus on power and control in organizational and labor process research.

One can cite an impressive array of studies that have elaborated Braverman's thesis.[16] For present purposes the work of Dan Clawson is particularly illustrative. Focusing on the development of scientific management, Clawson reveals the way in which Taylorism was a specific response to the divided workplace authority that characterized industry in the latter half of nineteenth-century America. Taylor's objective was essentially the design of a management strategy for gaining greater control of the work processes during a period of chronic labor struggles that accompanied rapid industrialization, especially from 1880 to 1920.[17] Clawson documents in detail the way scientific management was used to build capitalist control into workplace technologies themselves (see Table 12.1).

While in the textbooks Taylorism is relegated to the historical origins of organization theory, its contribution is nonetheless still deeply embedded in the organization of the American workplace, in both private and public sectors. Rather than scientific techniques for measuring work, its real impact has been on the basic mode of authority governing work processes. As Clawson puts it,

> What for Taylor was a clearly conscious process, and at one important level remains a conscious process, is now at the same time unconscious in that it is accepted . . . by both management and workers . . . as the self-evident way to organize work processes and is seen as "natural," "inevitable," or simply "most efficient."[18]

Essentially, then, what Taylor introduced into the industry of his day, and what has continued to prevail in work organizations today, is managerial domination. In the modern discussion of management, the fact that management dominates the internal political structure of the organization is usually disguised—more or less—by the emphasis on the "value-

Table 12.1 Scientific Management as Political Strategy

Scientific management emerged as an early twentieth-century strategy to wrest workplace control away from labor and to reestablish it in the hands of a new group called "management."[19] The function of scientific management, as conceived by Taylor, was to enter the workplace and learn what workers already knew—how to plan and direct the details of the work process. Once in possession of this knowledge, managers could use it to develop and issue detailed instructions to each worker. Taylor insisted that taking charge of the work organization and restructuring it to suit managerial objectives was the only way for capitalists to control the speed of production, the key workplace controversy at that time.

Basic to the strategy was the removal of planning and decision making from the shop floor. Its most obvious manifestation was the vast expansion of employees on the managerial side, or what Taylor interestingly enough called "nonproductive" labor. Approximately 25% of the employees in Taylor's ideal workplace (the engineers, managers, and clerks) were "nonproductive" bureaucrats, an unprecedented number for his day. The crux of their work—planning—was to establish the sequence of tasks and to set the speed of production, thus eliminating the worker's ability to intentionally resist the rate of output.[20]

On the shop floor, the division of labor was increased by giving workers more specialized, less complex tasks. As a cost-saving device, it permitted the substitution of cheaper, less skilled workers with skilled workers. Work was less interesting and more repetitive for the worker, but it was more profitable for management. To foil resistance, Taylor's strategy also introduced a number of technical changes. For example, work was designed to make the production process *incomprehensible* to workers.[21]

The principal instrument for determining the proper steps and speed of the work process was the time and motion study. According to Taylor, it was the time and motion study that gave his system the right to be called "scientific management." While the same sort of knowledge had previously existed in an unorganized fashion in the workers' heads, scientific management's claim rested upon its systematic classification of this knowledge. However, one of the very interesting aspects of the time and motion study is that Taylor was never able to explain adequately how these estimates were determined.[22]

neutral" science of management. Technique rather than management appears to provide the basis for determining a day's fair pay and a day's fair work. In reality, it is management's power to dominate the workplace that decides such issues.

Clawson's work, in addition to that of Noble, Shaiken, Zimbalist, Greenbaum, and others, has given rise to a widespread reversal of the left's traditional faith in the inevitable progress of technology.[23] For many Marxists, in fact, technological change under capitalist arrangements has come to be seen as the enemy of the working class. Adler has identified four basic arguments that underlie this position:

> (1) Technological change in capitalist societies is a major cause of economic dislocation and unemployment; that it usually leads to a reduction in skill requirements; that only organized worker resistance can limit this change; and that only fundamental social change can turn the potential offered by technological change to good purpose.[24]

The argument has received substantial support in recent years from a number of studies concerned with the impact of modern-day computer technologies on unemployment and deskilling. This work has illustrated the ways in which contemporary computer-based machine technology designs are extending the standard Tayloristic logic of managerial control—indeed, advancing it a major step forward. Beyond the narrow definition of jobs, the impetus is to eliminate the worker altogether. The logical extension of Taylorism turns out to be robotics. We turn next to a discussion of these new developments.

Toward the "Factory of the Future"

The computerization of work can be understood as the modern corporation's response to postindustrialism. In the coming decades, as Robert Howard explains, the new "technologies of the computer and telecommunications will constitute the central nervous system of the postindustrial workplace."[25]

Computerization is already described as the most dramatic revolution in the workplace since the introduction of the assembly line 75 years ago.[26] It is a transformation fueled by a $50-billion annual investment in new workplace technologies, for both the office and the shop floor. In American offices, the result has been the installation of approximately

1.5 million "electronic work stations" by the mid-1980s, a figure expected to multiply tenfold by 1990.[27] Equally dramatic has been the development of computer-controlled machine tools and industrial robotics in the factory. In the automobile industry, for example, it is estimated that by 1985 more than 250 auto plants had been rebuilt with the latest in computer technology, and billions of dollars more were spent to convert thousands of the industry's supplier factories.[28]

Nothing better symbolizes these new forms of automation than the robot. As Shaiken puts it, "When *Time* magazine gave an award for the 'Man of the Year' to the computer in 1982, the robot surely must have been the runner up."[29] During the past decade, robotics has been the cutting edge of automation. Its growth, moreover, has been dramatic. Analysts estimate that the market for robots could climb to $2 billion per year by 1990, up from about $150 million in 1981. (If related equipment is included, the market could be as high as $4 billion per year.)[30]

In mechanical terms, it would be wrong to describe the robot as a dramatic departure from standard machine technologies. Fundamentally, a robot is a multijointed arm used for moving production pieces to specifically designated points in the manufacturing process. The basic difference between the robot and the conventional machine lies in the fact that the movement of the robot's arm can be varied through an almost limitless range of programmed instructions. Through computerized programming, the robot becomes a general-purpose machine with enormous flexibility. It is this flexibility that gives the robot its power to transform the workplace.

To focus on the robot, however, is to miss the essence of modern automation. Although robots never cease to reveal new capabilities, their full significance is only realized after they have been linked to a larger network of computerized manufacturing technologies. It is this linking process that makes automation truly revolutionary. Robotics, in short, is just one element in an "integrated manufacturing system," or, more commonly, the "computerized factory."

The computerization of the factory—or workplace generally—has largely proceeded piece by piece. In pursuit of complete automation, the primary strategy has been to link together as many computerized processes as technically possible. The process started with the automation of production machines but now has shifted as well to the linking of support services to accompany them. These processes include such things as the scheduling of production, the loading and unloading of production pieces and parts, the transferring of parts between machines, quality control, and maintenance. The ultimate goal is a hierarchy of computers directing the entire production process. Such a supercomputer system will define, collect, and control the processing of information pertinent to the manufacturing process. Indeed, factory management itself increasingly becomes the management of information.

The linking of these automated devices gives rise to a sophisticated management information system. The hierarchical interlocking of computer systems creates "an electronic model of the factory in which management is provided with up-to-the-minute information about what is happening and a data base for longer term analysis and planning." Moreover, when new directives have been issued, "the way they are carried out can be instantly observed, evaluated from countless different angles, and the results made a matter of easily accessible computerized records."[31]

In these factories production machinery is guided through a system of digital devices that transmit data about machine operation to other electronic controlling devices, which, in turn, relay it to a central computer. The central computer is the foundation of a management information system that reaches throughout the entire organization.[32] Writing about the Ford Motor plant in Batavia, Ohio, Shaiken describes the functions of the plant's management information system in these words:

> The computer network, linked by "data highways," is made up of five separate systems: first a machine monitoring and downtime network that tracks production flow and dispatches maintenance workers; second, a time and attendance system that monitors personnel data such as tardiness and absenteeism; third, a stock status system that locates purchased parts, raw stock, and tooling; fourth, an Automated Manufacturing and Planning Engineering system (AMPLE) that combines engineering information with production data; and finally, an energy management system that, among other things, is capable of lowering the heat and turning on the lights.[33]

Managers throughout the plant tap into this data through more than 70 computer terminals.

> These terminals—a TV-like screen and keyboard—are in the offices of each production foreman on the shop floor, in the offices of maintenance supervisors, in the six zone offices that are responsible for the major sections of the plant, in the tool-room, in the warehouse areas, and in the key departments in the administration building.[34]

The system makes available a staggering amount of information.

> AMPLE, for example, provides a data base for the entire manufacturing operation. It already includes entries for all 106 production processes in the plant, 22,000 items in the general warehouses and tool cribs, 4,000 gauges, and 3,000 manufacturing drawings. . . . Moreover, [the] system provides . . . managers and engineers with some unique capabilities for using this information. Production information is always current. If an engineer alters a production process at 11:00 A.M., the change is available throughout the plant at 11:02 A.M.[35]

There are, in addition, plans to include other forms of critical information in the system.

> In the future, plans call for including critical information about machine operation and maintenance and, ultimately, for taking in personnel records, material control data and financial information.

These automation processes are generally justified in the name of scientific progress. General Electric, for example, has used the words of Lestor Colwell of the University of Michigan to lend scientific authority to the automation of factories. In his words,

> The most important objectives in the implementation of computer-aided-manufacture are to convert the "know-how" of manufacturing from an "experience-based" technology to a "science-based" technology, and to recognize and integrate the "information structure" so that computers can be used to implement this "know-how" in product design, in manufacturing planning, and for control of the shop floor.[36]

Such language, to borrow a phrase from Peter Keen, reflects the dominant "technocentric approach" to the computerization of work.[37] The orientation is essentially a modern "systems" approach to scientific management. As such, the exploitation of new computer technologies in the workplace is conceived primarily as a technical issue. The goal of workplace technological change is to increase efficiency by mechanizing production and reducing costs. (Stated simply, the goal is "less direct labor for a given volume of work.") The design and implementation of new technical systems is the special responsibility of technical experts in "systems design" and often grouped in special "electronic data processing" or "information resources management" departments. Worker involvement in the process is considered a potentially disruptive activity and is thus avoided.

The systems perspective dominates both the design and the construction of new computer technologies. Computer design is viewed as a process that takes place at the top of the organization. The organization itself is viewed as a formally specified "structure" in which jobs are reduced to "algorithmic procedures." Computers and workers together are conceptualized as "information processing systems" across which problem-solving capabilities are distributed. In practice, the result is greater specialization and an increase in the division of labor. While a few workers require increased skills, overall there is a general reduction in the need for experienced and skilled workers. Moreover, for those who remain, there is less need to possess a broad understanding of the production process as a whole.

Although corporate executives often publicly assert that automation will upgrade workers to more creative and satisfying jobs, thus far much of the process appears to involve the replacement of people. Professor Richard Wysk, director of Virginia Polytechnic Institute's Automation Laboratory, explains the process in these works: "When you focus on automation generally you're trying to have a more dependable mechanism than a human performing these activities . . . so we've done many things to make the process automated and tried to take the person out, except to fulfill certain obligations."[38] Robotics, to be sure, is the most dramatic step in this direction.

The overall purpose of these efforts is to gain greater control over workers and unions. A 1981 survey of metalwork industry executives clearly captured this point. The findings were summarized in these words: "Workers and their unions have too much to say in manufacturers' destiny, many metalworking executives feel, and large sophisticated . . . [Flexible Manufacturing Systems] can wrest some of the control away from labor and put it back in the hands of management where it belongs."[39] Computerized technologies, in short, are the latest technocratic strategy in management's continuing struggle to dominate the workplace.

For those workers who manage to hang on to their jobs, skilled or deskilled, the new workplace imposes many "hidden" personal costs. Often it means a decline in the quality of working conditions, particularly those concerned with health and safety. Many of the health and safety problems associated with computerized work occur because of an increased pace of production and the loss of authority to make task-related decisions. These lead to a number of hazardous situations, particularly the rise of fatigue, stress, and boredom. For instance, in an examination of the effects of video display terminals on clerical workers' health, the National Institute of Occupational Safety and Health has found that workers who used computer terminals full-time exhibited the highest levels of stress ever reported in a NIOSH study.[40]

Much of the development of these new technologies has been sponsored by the federal government, mainly the Department of Defense. Most important has been the air force's Integrated Computer-Aided Manufacturing project (ICAM). From 1979 to 1984 alone, the air force, through its "Partners in Preparedness" program, spent $100 million to advance the much publicized and long-awaited "factory of the future." By sponsoring a new generation of computerized manufacturing systems, the air force has sought to encourage the development of these new technologies and to promote their dissemination and transfer (just as the military has done with earlier workplace technologies). Initially designed for the aerospace industry, the program has involved the participation of approximately 70 industrial and academic contractors. Basically, it has provided them with risk capital to facilitate innovations that would otherwise be considered too broad in scope and too long-term for manufacturers to initiate on their own. Using public tax dollars, the air force has nurtured a joint effort between industry and selected universities (particularly their engineering schools) to shape both the technical and the political dynamics of the industrial workplace.[41]

The directors of the program have never been circumspect about the political goals of the project. As one director of ICAM explained, the project addresses the fact that "many factories today appear unmanageable, labor forces are seen to be out of control and costs are all but unknown." Another described it as "an effort to try to reduce the enormous indirect costs and remove power and judgment from the shop floor." Thus, in addition to automation and robotics at the point of production, the program promotes the integrated development of computer-aided techniques for managerial decision making, production planning, inventory control, maintenance scheduling, and the like. Management control is described by the project managers as "the system's greatest payoff."[42]

Nothing better signifies the emphasis on management control than the exclusion of labor participation in the program. The unions involved with the companies participating in the program have been deliberately denied a role in the decision processes. Repeatedly the air force has rejected the requests of the machinists' to participate in the design of the new workplace. The reason for the rejection is apparent: There are no unions in the computerized factory of the future.

Labor and Expertise:
Politicizing Technology

The social impact of this transformation has powerful implications both inside and outside the workplace.[43] At present it is difficult to describe the impact as a positive one. While computer technologies clearly hold out a great number of promises, there currently appears to be a large gap between the promise and the present reality. For example, proponents of computerized work usually argue that it will stimulate new job development. In fact, these technologies are now often being used to eliminate existing jobs. Similarly, it is argued that computers will bring more creative and satisfying jobs to the workplace. Although computerization does lead to new skills for some, for many more it appears to be laying the foundation for a general deskilling and degradation of work. Others maintain that automation will make the domestic economy more productive, but numerous studies show that it is now frequently helping American corporations to operate independently *outside* the country. The state, some contend, will help offset the impact of automation on jobs through new job training and social service programs, but one could scarcely infer this from projects such as the air force's "factory of the future." There the goal is clearly to help corporations rid themselves of labor unions. In short, many fear that the humanistic, participatory possibilities offered by these new technologies is fading from consideration.[44]

The problematic consequences of current computerized work portend many of the most critical political issues in the coming decades. Taken together, they raise important issues about the role of corporate control of workplace technology. In capitalist systems, work and technology are shaped—almost exclusively—by the interests of private corporations and the managers who run them. Under this arrangement the corporation's logic of profit competitiveness—success at almost any expense—defines the ends according to which technology is designed and used in the workplace. The reduction of costs and the expansion of profits are thus the prime determinants of technology's impact on workers and society.

The legitimacy of this practice is deeply embedded in a basic premise of the American political economy: That which is considered good for the corporation is good for society. However, in the case of an issue like automation, which has disruptive effects on the lives of enormous numbers of people, many have begun to ask questions about the acceptability of the corporation's unquestioned authority in technological development.[45] Automation, it is argued, raises fundamental policy issues that transcend the concerns of the corporation and its managers. Increasingly, workers and citizens have begun to ask the state to introduce basic protections against this menacing threat.

Underlying this challenge are two basic questions: Can the current trends in computerized work be reversed? And, if so, can these technologies serve more humanistic ends? At present, there is a rather strident debate surrounding the first question. Many of the harshest critics of American capitalism are quite pessimistic about the possibility of turning back this new corporate thrust. Often drawing on the work of Braverman, they point to the power and prescience capitalists have shown in structuring the labor process to maintain their control over workplace issues. For most of these theorists, organized worker resistance can at best hope to limit the damages caused by such changes. Many of them contend that only a fundamental social transformation can turn the potential offered by technological change to good purpose.[46]

Others take exception to this position. They argue that it is easy to underestimate the degree to which workers have historically shaped the labor processes. Moreover, they see automation as holding out a number of strategic possibilities for labor in its ongoing workplace struggles. They point to a growing realization that the genuine cost-effectiveness of these new technologies depends on higher degrees of worker skill, commitment, attention, responsibility, and learning. The emerging postindustrial workplace is seen to require—in the interest of efficiency and effectiveness—the introduction of a less hierarchical, debureaucratized participatory system.[47] In short, the "new Taylorism" of the postindustrial workplace also confronts the human factor.

It is at this juncture that workers and their organizations may well be able to take advantage of a critical opportunity. If managers come to realize that the effective operation of their new technologies depends on the cooperation of a skilled work force, a well-organized workers' movement can place itself in a strategic bargaining position with regard to the shaping of these technologies. The question is whether or not the workers will be able to take up the challenge.

It is difficult to take sides in this debate. From different angles both positions have a corner on important truths. For example, even if it proves possible for labor to shape the use of computerized technologies, this in no way necessarily undercuts management's fundamental control of the workplace. In this respect, there is good reason to accept Athanasiou's admonishment: namely, that we should not forget management's historic commitment to mechanization. As he puts it, "It seems fairly clear that, while advancing technology does lead to reskilling, deskilling nevertheless continues." Indeed, much evidence suggests that it is today the dominant tendency in specific sectors of the economy. The problem is that "systems far more automated than . . . rationally justified can be made to work, if enough effort is expended on doing so."[48] The computerized factory would certainly seem to be a case in point.

When we turn to the second question, however, we find some general agreement between these two positions. Whether through social transformation or progressive reform, writers on both sides of the issue agree that new technological designs must be guided by a democratic vision. As Howard puts it, the construction of such designs can no longer be seen "as the products of some ineluctable technological development, autonomous and pure, but as a sometimes very messy act of social construction, built upon a foundation of myriad interests and goals."[49] The design must include all institutions and groups:

> The workers who actually use technology in the workplace and the unions that represent them; the designers whose technical expertise and talents are so crucial to the proper functioning of new technical systems, but who have little to say about the ends to which the technology they create are put; citizens who must live with technology's impact . . . ; and finally, government officials who approve the vast amounts of public money supporting technological research and development and, more important, are the ultimate representatives of the public good.[50]

In light of the diversity of interests involved, the question of who controls the direction of research and development necessarily comes to the fore. It takes little investigation to discover that the fundamental financial and managerial decisions governing technological research are in the

316 RECONSTRUCTING ORGANIZATION THEORY

hands of a small number of large corporate firms and investment banks. Nor is it difficult to discover that these same institutions have vast influence over the research agendas of major technical universities. The corporate community, in short, has an enormous voice in questions of research and development.

To open technological decision making to a wider range of interests, an essential step must be the establishment of a national research policy, that is, a consensually derived political agenda of research priorities and the financial commitments required to meet them. Only through the open debate of research goals in public forums can the kind of broad-based consensus needed to legitimate technological development be established.[51] The question as to whether this will happen depends on many political factors; two of the most important are the labor movement and the scientific community.

For all of its problems, the labor movement still remains the single most powerful voice of workers, both in the workplace and in the political arena. The future of a viable technological politics will doubtless depend on labor's willingness to take a vigorous interest in technology policy at the national level. Fundamentally, the challenge for labor is "to translate workers' interests into concrete organizational principles for technology, work and social life."[52] At the outset, this involves an articulation of and struggle for workers' rights to participate in the design and use of new computer technologies. Most important, this requires reopening the issue of "management prerogatives." Of all the issues that have traditionally been considered an exclusive prerogative of corporate management, none is more important for the postindustrial era than the design and development of workplace technology.

Although labor unions in the United States are far behind their European counterparts on these issues, there are at least a few positive signs that some unions are awakening to the issue. For example, the International Association of Machinists has articulated a "New Technology Bill of Rights." This document, conceived as a proposed amendment to U.S. labor law, states that workers, "through their trade union bargaining units," should have an "absolute right" to participate in all phases of management planning on decisions "that lead to the introduction of a new technology or the changing of the workplace systems design, work processes, and procedures of doing work, including the shutdown or transfer of work, capital and equipment."[53] The document's ten points appear in Table 12.2.

Table 12.2 International Association of Machinists: A New Technology
Bill of Rights

I

New technology shall be used in a way that creates jobs and promotes
community-wide and national full employment.

II

Unit labor cost savings and labor productivity gains resulting from the use of
new technology shall be shared with workers at the local enterprise level and
shall not be permitted to accrue excessively or exclusively for the gain of capital,
management, and shareholders.

Reduced work hours and increased leisure time made possible by new technology shall result in no loss of real income or decline in living standards for
workers affected at the local enterprise level.

III

. Local communities, the states, and the nation have a right to require employers
to pay a replacement tax on all machinery, equipment, robots, and production
systems that displace workers, cause unemployment and thereby decrease local,
state, and federal revenues.

IV

New technology shall improve the conditions of work and shall enhance and
expand the opportunities for knowledge, skills and compensation of workers.
Displaced workers shall be entitled to training, retraining, and subsequent job
placement or reemployment.

V

New technology shall be used to develop and strengthen the U.S. industrial base,
consistent with the Full Employment goal and national security requirements,
before it is licensed or otherwise exported abroad.

VI

New technology shall be evaluated in terms of worker safety and health and shall
not be destructive of the workplace environment, nor shall it be used at the
expense of the community's natural environment.

(continued)

Table 12.2 continued

VII

Workers, through their trade unions and bargaining units, shall have an absolute right to participate in all phases of management deliberations and decisions that lead or could lead to the introduction of new technology or the changing of the workplace system design, work processes, and procedures for doing work, including the shutdown or transfer of work, capital, plant, and equipment.

VIII

Workers shall have the right to monitor control room centers and control stations and the new technology shall not be used to monitor, measure or otherwise control the work practices and work standards of individual workers, at the point of work.

IX

Storage of an individual worker's personal data and information file by the employer shall be tightly controlled and the collection and/or release and dissemination of information with respect to race, religious, or political activities and beliefs, records of physical and mental health disorders and treatments, records of arrests and felony charges or convictions, information concerning sexual preferences and conduct, information concerning internal and private family matters, and information regarding an individual's financial condition or credit worthiness shall not be permitted, except in rare circumstances related to health, and then only after consultation with a family- or union-appointed physician, psychiatrist, or member of the clergy. The right of an individual worker to inspect his or her personal data file shall at all times be absolute and open.

X

When the new technology is employed in the production of military goods and services, workers, through their trade union and bargaining agent, have a right to bargain with management over the establishment of Alternative Production Committees, which shall design ways to adopt that technology to socially useful production and products in the civilian sector of the economy.

Entering the realm of technology development poses difficult problems for labor. Not only do unions have to confront political opposition from their traditional foes—industrial leaders, conservative politicians, and investment bankers, among others—they must also face their own internal limitations concerning expertise. Indeed, these new tasks require very different skills than the ones they have traditionally utilized. Primarily oriented toward collective bargaining over wages and work conditions, as well as providing protection against the arbitrary exercise of managerial power, unions have relied on the skills of organizing and negotiating. The source of such skills, moreover, has generally been their own membership, especially in the case of organizing skills. (Other skills, particularly legal skills pertinent to the negotiation process, have been largely provided by full-time union staffs.) Such resources do not equip union leaders to engage in the scientific/technical decisions required of technology development. Technical expertise is not typically found on the union staff.

To further complicate the matter, scientific and technical expertise is generally available to management in ample supply, especially in technically intensive industries. In large part, this is a result of the traditional structure of control in the capitalist firm. Management, in short, defines the standards for technological development and has long-established connections to the kinds of expertise needed for the purpose. Such advantages can only be offset by unions through independent access to expertise. However, under current institutional arrangements (particularly those concerned with the financing of technology research and development), unions experience great difficulties getting the kinds of scientific and technological resources they need to be taken seriously in the technology development.

It is for this reason that the scientific community constitutes the other critically important group for the future of an alternative technology movement. If current trends in the computerization of work are to be reversed, scientific and technical experts must begin to take a more active interest in the political and ethical implications of their work.

Seldom has management given the technical experts who develop workplace technologies much say about how they will be used. Moreover, as we saw in Chapter 5, management has often employed technical experts more to legitimate and rationalize its own authority and control of the organization than to encourage technological advances per se. Technical expertise has thus long been controlled by management to serve its own interests.

For this reason, many radical theorists have in more recent years begun to recognize expertise as a strategic issue in the struggle between labor and management. Revolutionaries, anarchists, and radical democrats, for example, have long argued that the solution is to defuse the political role of expertise by distributing it to workers throughout the organization. In this way, expertise cannot become the province of any one group or interest. No longer would it be a resource that one group can use to manipulate another. In modern times, the Chinese Cultural Revolution represents the classic attempt to effectuate such a policy.[54] Unfortunately, many of its dramatic failures stand more as lessons of what not to do than as practices to emulate.

A survey of these experiences only illustrates the complexity of such a project. Given a suitable political and cultural climate, the diffusion of expertise might be made to work in the early states of industrialization. At the very least, the possibility remains debatable. In the postindustrial setting, however, such diffusion is clearly an impossibility. The kinds of technologies that constitute the computerized workplace are *vastly* more sophisticated than, say, the time and motion studies of scientific management. If scientific management mystifies the workers, the new computer technologies mystify just about everybody.

This is not to overlook the fact that workers can in many cases learn enough about computer programs to strategically manipulate them in the struggle for workplace control. (Many examples of such skills have been reported in the chemical and tool and dye industries, both of which are highly computerized.) Rather, at issue here is the more fundamental kind of expertise required to program the computerized factory in the first place. Such knowledge includes the ability to continually reprogram the workplace in response to worker strategies.

This more basic knowledge of computer technologies, it is fair to say, would be impossible to distribute throughout the workplace. For one thing, everyone does not have the intellectual wherewithal to grasp the kinds of complex technical intricacies involved in computer design. For others, it simply would not be their "cup of tea"; they would prefer to devote their time and energies to other interests. There is, in short, no way to dispose of the experts. For radical reformers the implications can be profound; many have had trouble accepting them.

How then to proceed? Do workplace reformers face a managerial fait accompli, or is there another political strategy better suited to these contemporary realities? One strategy is surely to seek a different kind of expertise. Instead of attempting to do away with experts, perhaps workplace expertise can be reconstructed according to more humanistic criteria. It is, of course, too early to speculate on the success of such a project, but it is possible to outline some of the steps that would have to be taken.

The first step is to recognize that, while expertise and politics are always linked together in practice, expertise itself involves a complex set of technical concerns governed by its own logic (as we saw in Chapter 9). In analytical terms, the rationality of technical decisions can be logically separated from political rationality. This fact permits a reformulation of the issue. Instead of accepting the standard relationship between expertise and management, as many progressive reformers have in the past, it is possible to explore the ways political and technical components can be recombined with other workplace interests (a point clarified by Zuboff). Indeed, it was the recognition of this possibility that led Lenin to argue that the technical aspects of Taylorism could be recombined with Soviet communism.

But Lenin made the mistake of believing the task to be straightforward and unproblematic. The fact that technical data are a nonpolitical form of knowledge governed by the laws of cause and effect does not mean they can be neutrally "plugged into" different organizational systems without concern for the social and political consequences. Technical criteria must be carefully adapted to the social dimensions of each system. Lenin was right to applaud the search for efficient industrial techniques but, as many socialists have subsequently argued, it was wrong to think that Taylor's scientific management could merely be plugged into the communist factory. In short, he failed to fully grasp the ways in which the causal foundations of scientific management had been built upon capitalist workplace relationships. Instead of adopting techniques designed to facilitate a capitalist system of managerial control, Soviets needed efficient procedures uniquely organized to facilitate their own theories of worker control.

If the development of alternative forms of technology is to succeed, a segment of the scientific/technical community must take up this challenge. Those who accept it must proceed on two fronts. They must first conceptualize a positive, alternative vision of the possible. For Winner, the challenge ultimately requires the development of a new discipline of "political ergonomics." (*Ergonomics* is an engineering term that refers to the process by which the shape of a technology is designed to fit the human form; the study of political ergonomics would be concerned with the relationship of technology to social and political life.) As he puts it, "If different forms or designs of technology are suited to qualitatively different forms of social and political existence, then the science of politics must include an ergonomics able to specify a suitable fit between a good society and its instruments." The new science would be organized around questions such as Which machines and systems are distinctly compatible with conditions of freedom and social justice? How can we design the instrument systems to be responsible to these ends?[55]

Scientists and technical experts must also join with progressive forces to help carry out the alternative vision. In large part, this means assisting the labor movement. Together with labor, workplace experts must develop a programmatic strategy aimed at integrating new technologies with human and societal development.

It is, to be sure, far easier to call for such cooperation than to specify with any precision the specific aims toward which it is to be devoted. On the most fundamental level, such cooperation is a call for extensive research and experimentation in technology design and worker participation. In the context of the high-technology workplace, where knowledge and expertise are critical determinants of power relations, it must focus in particular on the ways in which expertise and participation can be integrated.

Basic to this research agenda is the cooperation of at least four groups: technical experts (scientists, engineers, computer specialists, and the like); social scientists (particularly sociologists, psychologists, and political scientists); labor union leaders and workers; and, last but not least, company managers and supervisory personnel. Obtaining such cooperation is not an easy accomplishment, as these groups have a long history of misunderstanding and distrust. Technical experts and social scientists often line up against one another when the topic turns to technology policy. And, of course, labor and management remain committed to two very different philosophies of workplace control.

Such cooperation might be structured in various ways. One possibility is for labor unions to hire their own experts to negotiate with those employed by management. Another is to set up publicly financed institutes designed to assist both labor and management in solving technology-related problems. In Europe there have been a number of interesting experiments along these lines. For example, in Holland the government has mandated that research universities set up "science shops" to supply technical information and research to individuals and representatives of interest groups who request it.[56] It is also increasingly common in Europe to find consulting firms that specialize in providing labor with technical assistance and advice. For both labor leaders and technical experts in the United States who begin grappling with the formation of new cooperative relationships, such models provide interesting insights.

At this point, it should be clear that nothing is easy or obvious about the development of more participatory workplace technologies. Howard and Schneider identify a number of barriers that can "threaten to constrain either the interests subject to participation, the degree of influence that workers actually have, or the scope of the issues open to participation."[57] Perhaps most important are four variables.

First, if a company faces a disadvantageous market position, broad-based participation can be difficult to maintain. Howard and Schneider put it this way: "When near-term competitive pressures are overwhelming, the short-term costs that participation can entail become too expensive."[58] In such cases, worker participation is often "relegated to the back burner of both managerial and union priorities."

The state of technology itself can also be a barrier to worker participation in technological change. In the early stages of a technological application, both the technology and its uses are not well understood. In these circumstances, technology experts tend to dominate the decision-making processes, as narrow technical problems press for attention. Broad participation in such situations typically proves problematic if not altogether unworkable.

A third potential barrier is more organizational than technological. It pertains to "the ingrained practices and habits of thinking and working that influence (and, often, inhibit) what can be described as the organizational learning process." The effective introduction of new technologies (as we saw in the previous chapter) requires new ways of thinking that are seldom easy for an organization to come by. As such, technology management must be conceived as a dimension of the larger processes of organizational development, that is, the dynamics essential "to the realization of the goals and values of the organization as a social institution." Finally, the absence of formal institutions to represent worker interests in the organization is also a substantial barrier. "When participation is managed entirely by management, there is a tendency in situations of conflict to revert to narrow business interests or to do away with participation altogether."[59]

For such reasons, participatory technology projects must be approached cautiously. There are, however, important precedents from which we can learn. A number of labor unions in other countries, particularly Norway, Sweden, Australia, and West Germany, have begun to come to grips with the issues of participation and expertise.[60] Cooperative undertakings in these countries provide a rich source of information and experience upon which other labor unions and researchers can draw. To illustrate the nature of these activities, we turn in the next section to a Swedish example.

Lessons from Sweden

While the issue of labor technology policy is a new idea in the United States, Swedish trade unions have for more than a decade been devising technology development strategies. In Sweden, this concern has in large part emerged as a result of efforts to deal with quality of work life issues, particularly those concerned with health and safety. Swedish trade unions found that existing technologies can impose constraints that significantly limit the possibility of improving the quality of work life. As a result, labor leaders gradually came to recognize the need to seek a voice in the selection and development of technologies themselves.

In general, Swedish labor technology development policies have emerged as an extension of traditional trade union concerns, namely, full employment, manpower development, and the improvement of working conditions. As advanced capitalist economies have increasingly turned to high-technology production strategies, labor's traditional concerns have inevitably become enmeshed in technology-related issues. Indeed, for some time now many unions have bargained with management over issues related to the impact of newly introduced technologies. What is new in Sweden is labor's effort to get involved in the very *design* of such technologies *before* they are introduced. It is to these activities that we devote attention in this section of the chapter. What follows is drawn from a variety of sources. Particularly helpful has been the insightful research of Andrew Martin, as well as discussions with members of the Swedish Center for Working Life (Arbetslivscentrum or ALC).[61]

A labor research policy. To deal with the new technological realities of the workplace—particularly the computerized workplace—Sweden's major trade union confederations began to take an interest in the pre-design phases of technological development. Increasingly, these groups began to advance the argument that unions must not only get involved in the development of new workplace technologies from their inception but that this involvement should extend to the R&D processes by which the technological options themselves are shaped. They also recognized that Swedish labor unions, like labor unions in general, were poorly equipped to carry out these new tasks, and thus they initiated this new policy thrust with the development of a research policy designed to build this capacity.

The basic principles of this new research policy are spelled out most precisely in a 1981 report of the Swedish Confederation of Labor (LO), *The Trade Union Movement and Research*. Essentially, the country's oldest and largest trade union federation proposed an R&D policy addressed to both the promises and the dangers of technological development. The report asserted that "it is ... more important than ever that the trade union movement engage itself in research ... by increased union influence and by widened dialogue with researchers." Labor unions "must have the possibility of defining the questions and problems that have to be the object of research in order to be solved."[62]

The critical element in acquiring this new capacity was specified as the ability to act independently in defining research problems and bringing expertise to bear on them. What the unions sought was not simply greater participation with others on research addressing common interests. In the past, much of their participation had been governed by collective bargaining agreements. Such "two-party" common interest research projects limited the scope of the questions the unions were interested in, as it precluded research that employers did not regard to be in their interest. In the words of the report, "It is research on its own terms, from our perspective, and with union problems and goals that the trade union movement wants to get done."[63]

Among the questions the unions wanted to see addressed more fully were the following: To what degree do new technologies necessarily eliminate jobs? Must they inevitably deskill workers? In what ways does management use these technologies to strengthen their control of the workplace? Can they be made to serve the interests of workplace democracy? These were the kinds of questions that unions found themselves asking. They needed a strategy for finding answers.

Guided by these questions and considerations, the report delineated a range of research proposals. It called for a national research policy to direct the financing and development of new technologies. Toward this end, it proposed the appointment of a new cabinet minister with responsibility for coordinating research policy around a wider range of interests, including those of the labor movement. It called for more money and less business bias in university research concerned with industrial policy. It proposed greater funds for interdisciplinary research between the engineering professions and the social sciences, and it called for special emphasis on computer-based work systems.

The UTOPIA Project. Especially important was the first attempt to put the report's principles into practice. This took the form of an experimental project called UTOPIA, a Swedish acronym for "training, technology, and products from a quality of work perspective."[64] It stands as one of the promising examples of how unions can bring technological expertise to bear on the development of alternative technologies.

The UTOPIA project was developed as an attempt to confront the revolutionary changes being brought about in the printing industry by computerization in the 1970s. The project resulted from a convergence of two different sets of concerns. One was the Nordic Graphics Union's worries about the elimination and deskilling of printing jobs in the Swedish newspaper publishing business. Computerization, moreover, was diminishing the quality of both the graphics product and the artists' general working conditions. The other concern was a study conducted at the Swedish Center for Working Life (ALC) on the impact of technological change in general and computerization in particular on the quality of work life. Based on their findings, researchers at the center began to urge greater cooperation between labor and computer engineers in the design of new technologies. Dialogues between the union and the researchers gave rise to the UTOPIA project.

The graphics workers were well suited for the UTOPIA experiment. They have been described as the archetypal craft industry. As Blauner puts it, the combination of "craft technology, favorable economic conditions, and powerful work organization and traditions" provided graphics workers with "the highest levels of freedom and control in the work process among industrial workers."[65] During the past two decades, however, the computerization of typesetting, text-entry, and layout has had a profound impact on the printer's role. The most apparent impact has been a loss of jobs. Jobs for Swedish printers have declined dramatically over the past 15 years. Equally important, those workers who managed to remain employed suffered substantial changes in both their creativity and their autonomy. Howard puts it this way: "The keyboards, terminal screens, and software of computerized systems require altogether new skills. Workers have suddenly found themselves dependent on their employers and computer companies for new training in the tools of what, for generations, they had considered 'their' trade."[66]

Some of the changes are simply the product of new technological capacities. "Reporters," as Howard continues, "can type their stories directly into the computer system, which automatically typesets them and eliminates the need for many skilled typographers."[67] But this is far from the full story. In other situations, "the technology provides a smokescreen to disguise what are really managerial decisions about how to organize work."[68] It was this latter issue that most troubled the graphics workers.

The specific pretext of the UTOPIA project was a technology agreement the graphic unions had negotiated with newspaper publishers in the mid-1970s. The agreement offered workers a number of job guarantees with regard to the introduction of new technologies, rules pertaining to personnel operating new equipment, and rights concerning job retraining for restructured work tasks, among other things. Rather than entering into a defensive strategy aimed at resistance to displacement and deskilling, the union sought an offensive strategy aimed at developing technological alternatives geared to their general work quality demands. To pursue such a strategy, it was necessary for the unions not only to have access to relevant technology and work organization expertise but also to develop methods for bringing expertise to bear on the union's concerns. UTOPIA was conceived as a response to the opportunities opened up by this technology agreement.

The prospectus of the UTOPIA project stated that it was to address difficulties encountered in previous trade union efforts to deal with the quality of work life, particularly those issues pertaining to skill content, good working environment, and democratic organization. Specifically, it sought to develop alternative computer technologies for text and image processing in the makeup of newspapers, along with the work organization and training required to utilize the technology. It was described as both "a technological development project and a social-scientific experiment to understand the conditions for technology development responsive to union goals."[69] To carry out this interdisciplinary project, a 15-member team was assembled. It consisted of social scientists from ALC, skilled print workers from several Nordic newspapers, and computer scientists from two Scandinavian universities. This group reported to a board of representatives drawn from graphics unions in all four Scandinavian countries.

At the foundation of the researchers' efforts was an attempt to facilitate greater democratization in the technological work environment. This goal was built into the basic methodological design of the project.

Specifically, it was manifested in an effort to replace the standard managerial "systems approach" to the technological design with a worker-based "tool perspective." Where the systems (or "technocratic") approach facilitates managerial control from the top down, the tool perspective introduces worker participation from the bottom up.[70]

The first task in the development of the tool perspective involved a careful examination of the evolution of the printer's role. Computerization, in this respect, was perceived as the third and most recent phase of a gradual but long diminution of the printer's role. In the early days of printing—the days of lead type—skilled craft workers "made up an entire page of articles, headlines, photoengravings, and advertisements in metal, according to a rough sketch provided by the editorial department." Because makeup workers could "put their hands on it . . . [they] could easily judge the quality of their design."[71]

Lead was subsequently replaced by paper. In this phase, workers pasted columns of text onto page boards. The pages tended to lose some of the sharpness of detail associated with lead type, but makeup workers could still easily evaluate and rearrange the elements of the page. With the advent of the computer, however, the printers' relationship to the page changed dramatically. As ALC researchers explain, "Early systems made layout extremely abstract, and some still do not show the page on the terminal screen. They require the workers to retain a mental image of the page while they feed codes into the computer that instruct it to create certain shapes and spaces on the page."[72] More recent advances in computerized systems now do show empty boxes on the screen that represent headlines, photographs, and articles. But makeup workers still do not see the actual pictures and texts and continue to have difficulties judging page design. As one Swedish lithographer puts it, "It's almost as if you were working blind."[73]

In the first phase of the alternative design process, the computer scientists and ALC social scientists entered the makeup process "to learn from the graphics workers what the operations were." Similarly, to evaluate the computer scientists' proposals for new design procedures, graphics workers in turn "had to learn from the computer specialists what the possibilities and limits of computer technology were, at its current or near-future state of development."[74] Essential, then, to the development of the project was a mutual learning process between workers with particular graphics skills and scientists with the relevant computer and organizational skills.

UTOPIA formalized the mutual learning process through the development of a "technological laboratory" for exchanges between workers and scientists. The basic laboratory technique was a work-simulation process. Graphics designers and computer specialists "used various simulation methods to be able to work as though the new page make-up and image processing technology already existed." Through cooperative efforts "on the simulation equipment, graphics workers and researchers gained concrete experience which made it possible to define the requirements for computer based make-up and image processing."[75]

The technology laboratory and its participatory tool perspective can be likened to a form of reverse Taylorism. Where Taylorism sought knowledge from workers to better control them, the laboratory provided a method for cooperative worker participation. By taking the skills and knowledge the workers already possess as the point of departure, researchers conceptualized the computer as a tool for enlarging and extending those skills. In this way, the laboratory countered the autocratic methodologies of the technocentric approach. Instead of imposing a "rational" plan from the top of the organization, computer experts and social scientists collaborated with the workers to build new work methods relevant to the realities of the shop floor. Rather than reducing graphics jobs to a set of "algorithmic procedures," computer applications were conceptualized as extensions of the workers' own knowledge and experience. Where management-oriented experts have sought to dominate the design process, the laboratory experts attempted to serve as "facilitators." One of their primary tasks, in the process, is to establish the conditions necessary for the workers' learning and participation. The laboratory, in short, permitted the experts to set up a learning environment in which the workers developed their own conceptions of these new technologies and how they could best assist them in their work.

Some have argued that such facilitation provides the basis for the development of an alternative postindustrial conceptualization of professional expertise. Such a model, of course, has profound implications for organizational management at all levels. In place of the standard top-down conception of management, its ultimate success would depend on the introduction of a thoroughgoing system of organizational democracy. Fundamentally, it would require a well-defined system of worker self-management. Indeed, in this model management expertise itself would have to undergo a transformation. Like technical experts, managers would themselves become facilitators.

Finally, it is also important to concede a number of problems. None of

Table 12.3 The Computerization of Graphic Work: Three Models

The "New Way" of Organizing Work

Star News is published in the Los Angeles suburb of Pasadena. The management of this paper has consciously introduced new technology to get rid of graphic workers. The graphic workstations are placed in the news room where they are operated by editorial staff. The organization does not allow any room for makeup staff, but the journalistic model is still transformed into a graphically designed page.

The problem is that the people who perform the work do not have the necessary graphic competence, which results in a deteriorating product quality. Furthermore, the news staff is not organized in trade unions, they receive lower wages, and they have usually not received a journalistic education.

The "Traditional Way" of Organizing Work

With the introduction of graphic workstations it may seem apt to try to maintain the traditional way of organizing work. The makeup staff in the composition room get powerful computer-based tools. The assistant-editors may get expensive electronic sketch pads. Both professional groups and their respective competences are intact and may even be developed. But the technical possibilities for a more flexible production with a later "deadline" for manuscripts are not exploited.

The instructions from the editorial staff to the composition room are written instructions, primarily rough layout sketches even in situations where oral instructions would have been sufficient. If the assistant-editors have electronic sketch pads, the instructions are communicated electronically in the form of boxes on a display.

These instructions are formal and static. The intentions behind the instructions are not expressed. Assistant-editors and makeup staff do not cooperate closely, even though they work with the same pages. The division between the news room and the composition room obstructs the necessary dialogue in connection with questions, suggestions, changes, follow-up, and exchange of ideas.

The "Scandinavian Way" of Organizing Work

There are, however, work organization alternatives. The newspaper *Østlændingen* is published in Elverum. It is the Norwegian answer to the American challenge. The first steps on the path toward what hopefully may be called the "Scandinavian way" of organizing integrated production have been taken.

Assistant-editors and makeup staff work in the same room—the borderland. The graphic workers have powerful computer-based tools for makeup. The journalists have suitable computer-based facilities for editorial planning and text editing.

Assistant-editors and makeup staff become acquainted with each other's working conditions and prerequisites. Together they can plan and coordinate the work. Instructions are given orally, or as a list of priorities. Oral communication of jounalistic intentions also increases the makeup person's understanding of the assistant-editor's idea for the page. Should the makeup person become uncertain or get ideas for improvements when he makes up the page on the computer-based makeup table, he may easily and quickly discuss it with the assistant-editor. There is also a simple laser printer that makes it easy to take out proof-prints of the page for closer study and correction.

SOURCE: Adapted from "The UTOPIA Project," *Graffiti* no. 7 (May 1985): 29–30.

the foregoing praise of the UTOPIA project should obscure some of the rough sailing that the researchers and workers experienced. At various stages in development, the project leaders had difficulties convincing traditional institutions to lend support, particularly financial support. Even the Swedish government's Office of Technology Development, largely dominated by technocratic engineers and scientists, was often unwilling to provide financial and technical support. Another problem was the unwillingness of other workers to support the graphics workers' effort. In fact, many journalists who often work alongside graphics employees were opposed to participation in the project.[76]

In the final analysis, however, the project has been judged an important success. Martin has summed up its significance in these terms:

> UTOPIA serves as a valuable demonstration project, providing a rich fund of experience on the problems and possibilities of developing a trade union strategy for influencing technological development. On the positive side, its most important contribution has been its demonstration of how workers can participate actively in technological development, incorporating their skills, including tacit knowledge built up through long experience, directly into the design process. This provides a credible countermodel to the conventional approach to technological development that dispenses with workers by relying on experts alone to incorporate operations equivalent or alternative to those carried out by workers into the design process on the basis of theoretical knowledge and formal description.[77]

If space permitted, it would be possible to report on a number of other fascinating attempts on the part of workers and technical experts to come to terms with the technological development process. Among them would have to be included a discussion of the project at the Lucas Aerospace Company in Britain in the mid-1970s. There technical experts and other workers demonstrated that it is possible to produce a plan for transferring their skills from the development of military technologies to civilian products with socially desirable uses.[78]

Summing Up

This chapter evolved as an extension of the attempt in the previous chapter to conceptualize the political dynamics of organizational and work processes. Developed as an alternative to the dominant technocratic paradigm, the political model was advanced as a response to the contemporary "crisis" in organization theory. In this chapter, the focus shifted from the theoretical development of the political perspective to its implications for a practical organizational problem, namely, the problem of expertise in the contemporary workplace.

To set the stage for the discussion, the chapter first examined the development of managerial expertise. Such expertise, typically explained in technical terms, was seen as designed to serve the political interests of the dominant organizational elites, both owners and top-level managers. Technocratic rhetoric aside, managerial expertise—from Taylor forward—evolved as a key component of a long-term struggle to shape the political contours of the industrial workplace. Specifically, the discussion of Taylorism illustrated the way in which managerial "science" was itself imbued with a political purpose. Although purportedly justified as a value-free science, managerial expertise was by its very design conceptualized as a strategy to facilitate capitalist control over the labor process. In short, the expert's "one best way" to organize work was more than just a matter of efficiency: It was *best* because it sought to locate the particular set of efficient arrangements that would reinforce the dominant power relations of the capitalist workplace.

Against this background, the chapter demonstrated the way in which this political interest manifests itself in the modern postindustrial workplace. Although automation is widely heralded as the path to economic revitalization, for workers the realities of these new computerized systems is often quite harsh. For many it has meant the loss of jobs; for those who retained jobs it has often led to less meaningful work and a general degradation of the work environment. Indeed, the computerized workplace appears to be rapidly evolving as the logical conclusion of Taylorism. Where Taylorism used to focus on minimizing the role of workers, it has now literally begun to replace them with robotic machines. Orchestrated initially in the industrial sector, the strategy has become part of a concerted effort organized by dominant institutions of society, including the federal government and the universities. Even though the political motivation behind this managerial alliance is now relatively easy to discern, the engineers, management specialists, and computer experts who continue to pioneer the transformation still—both wittingly and unwittingly—hide behind the standard scientific ideology: that is, an appeal to the inevitable force of technological progress.

For those concerned with labor and the struggle for workplace democracy, the implications of these trends are clear and unmistakable:

If democratic participation is to be taken seriously in the postindustrial workplace, technology and expertise must be transformed into political issues. The politicization of these issues, in fact, must be moved to the top of the reform agenda. Moreover, it must be accompanied by a search for viable alternatives to the standard managerial approach to technological design. The possibility of such an alternative, as we saw, depends on an alliance between labor and progressive experts. It was for this reason that we turned to the Swedish example.

The Swedish project defies the conventional wisdom. To those who say that the idea of a participatory (or democratic) technology is a pipe dream in an age of complexity, the UTOPIAN project puts forward a powerful counterexample. By demonstrating that the "imperatives" of technological design are not as immutable as technocrats would have us believe, the experiment reveals the problem to be ultimately one of political will and commitment. Against the incredulity that the suggestion of a "democratic technology" usually encounters, this is no minor contribution.

The Swedish research has, of course, only scratched the surface of the problem and thus has left many important questions unanswered. Fundamentally, its value has been to open these questions up for further exploration. Most important, from our point of view, was its effort to rethink the role of the expert. By replacing management-oriented experts with those dedicated to the task of setting up a learning environment designed to assist workers in developing their own conceptions of new technologies, the UTOPIA researchers created an innovative, facilitatory model of expertise that provides a foundation for a postindustrial alternative. For this reason, we turn specifically to the concept of "facilitatory" expertise in Part VII.

Notes

1. One of the classic statements of this position is found in Robert Michels, *Political Parties: A Sociological Study of the Oligarchical Tendencies of Modern Democracies* (New York: Dover, 1915).

2. For a review of this literature, see Paul Goldman, "Sociologists and the Study of Bureaucracy: A Critique of Ideology and Practice," *The Insurgent Sociologist* 3, no. 1 (Winter 1978): 21–30.

3. Langdon Winner, *Autonomous Technology* (Cambridge: MIT Press, 1977).

4. See Andre Gorz, "Technical Intelligence and the Capitalist Division of Labor," *Telos* no. 12 (Summer 1972): 25–41.

5. Frederick Winslow Taylor, *Scientific Management* (New York: Harper & Row, 1911).

6. Ibid.

7. Samuel Haber, *Efficiency and Uplift: Scientific Management in the Progressive Era, 1890–1920* (Chicago: University of Chicago Press, 1964).

8. Judith A. Merkle, *Management and Ideology: The Legacy of the International Scientific Management Movement* (Berkeley: University of California Press, 1980).

9. V. I. Lenin, "The Immediate Tasks of the Soviet Government," in *Lenin: Selected Works* (New York: International Publishers, 1971), p. 417.

10. Ibid.

11. See Howard P. Segal, *Technological Utopianism in American Culture* (Chicago: University of Chicago Press, 1985), p. 107.

12. See Chapter 5 in this book.

13. I am indebted to Carmen Sirianni for sharing his investigation of this issue with me.

14. Goldman, *Sociologists and the Study.*

15. Harry Braverman, *Labor and Monopoly Capital* (New York: Monthly Review Press, 1974).

16. Dan Clawson, *Bureaucracy and the Labor Process* (New York: Monthly Review, 1980); Richard Edwards, *Contested Terrain* (New York: Basic Books, 1979); and Joan M. Greenbaum, *In the Name of Efficiency* (Philadelphia: Temple University Press, 1979).

17. Clawson, *Bureaucracy and the Labor Process.* Also, see David Montgomery, *The Fall of the House of Labor: The Workplace, the State and American Labor Activism, 1865–1925* (New York: Cambridge University Press, 1987).

18. Clawson, *Bureaucracy and the Labor Process*, p. 265.

19. Although Taylor threw his lot in with the capitalists, he understood the position of both labor and capital. Largely a result of experiences gained as a machine shop worker, Taylor in fact expressed sympathy for labor's struggles with capital. Both labor and capital, he argued, were rational with respect to their own interests and needs. Driven by the logic of capitalism, owners inevitably pushed for higher profits. Generally this meant increasing production and lowering wages. An increase in production, especially in the early factory system, usually required an increase in the speed of the work process. This, in turn, depended on the owner's ability to control the work process itself. Workers, on the other hand, were rational to resist the owners' efforts. They recognized that the project at best called for more work at the same pay. Moreover, the division of authority between management and labor in the early factory system gave workers sufficient leverage to stifle—if not block—the owners' workplace strategies.

Understanding the division of workplace authority is crucial to grasping Taylor's role. In the early factories the owners held fundamental authority to make decisions about production—what to produce, where to produce it, and so on—but the workers essentially controlled the practical details of how the work was actually carried out. It was to the division of workplace authority that Taylor addressed his strategy. Basically, he realized that capitalists could never win their struggles with labor under the existing system of authority relations. Until owners grappled with the fundamental assumption about who controlled the work organization, they would remain frustrated. As long as capitalists continued to take for granted that workers would retain control of the details of the labor process, they would remain dependent on the voluntary cooperation and active initiatives of the workers. Taylor recognized that capitalists must conceive and implement an alternative organization of production. The solution was the introduction of a new category in the workplace—that is, "management." Clawson, *Bureaucracy and the Labor Process,* pp. 202–53.

20. Because worker resistance was rational in the context of the situation, Taylor saw little point in trying to reason with workers. The only course for management was to displace workers as the group with knowledge of and control over the work process. This was to be carried out by careful study and advanced planning of all work previously done by the workers. Central to this idea was the creation of the planning room, a crucial element of his program. As Taylor put it, "all possible brain work should be removed from the shop and centered in the planning or laying-out department." Clawson, *Bureaucracy and the Labor Process;* and Frederick Winslow Taylor, *Shop Management,* reprinted in Frederick Winslow Taylor, *Scientific Management* (New York: Harper, 1947), p. 98.

21. The work situation was often structured so that workers not only did not need to understand the production process but they also *could not* understand the complicated symbols and directions employed to explain it. Clawson, ibid.

22. According to Clawson, it appears that Taylor and his followers merely asserted that they were "scientific." In reality, he never conducted anything that approximated a scientific experiment to test the possible output of workers with and without the benefit of his methods. So, even if we accept Taylor's account, there is no basis for telling whether he *improved* work procedures or just speeded them up. Clawson, ibid., p. 238.

23. David F. Noble, *Forces of Production* (New York: Knopf, 1984); Harley Shaiken, *Work Transformed: Automation and Labor in the Computer Age* (New York: Holt, Rinehart & Winston, 1984); Andrew Zimbalist, *Case Studies on the Labor Process* (New York: Monthly Review Press, 1979); Greenbaum, *In the Name of Efficiency;* and Philip Kraft, *Programmers and Managers: The Routinization of Computer Programming in the United States* (New York: Springer-Verlag, 1977).

24. Paul Adler, "Technology and Us," *Socialist Review* 16 (January–February 1986), p. 67.

25. Robert Howard, *Brave New Workplace* (New York: Viking, 1985), p. 200.

26. Tom Forester, ed., *The Information Revolution* (Cambridge: MIT Press, 1985); and Paul A. Straussmann, *Information Payoff: The Transformation of Work in the Electronic Age* (New York: Free Press, 1985).

27. In this discussion the focus is primarily on industrial work. For a critical assessment of the automated office, see Howard, *Brave New Workplace,* pp. 105–18; and Shoshana Zuboff, *In the Age of the Smart Machine: The Future of Work and Power* (New York: Basic Books, 1988).

28. Shaiken, *Work Transformed,* pp. 2–3, and "The Automated Factory: The View from the Shop Floor," *Technology Review,* January 1985, pp. 17–24.

29. Ibid., p. 153.

30. Ibid., p. 157.

31. Ibid., p. 175.

32. Robert E. McGrarrah, "Do Computerized Intelligence Systems Cause Artificial Management," *Challenge,* November–December 1985, pp. 38–43.

33. Shaiken, *Work Transformed,* p. 176.

34. Ibid.

35. Ibid.

36. Colwell, cited in Noble, *Forces of Production,* p. 333.

37. Peter Keen, "Editor's Preface," *Office: Technology and People* 1 (1982): 1–11.

38. Wysk, cited in Noble, *Forces of Production,* p. 333.

39. *Iron Age Magazine,* September 1981.

40. Barbara Cohen, "An Overview of NIOSH Research on Clerical Workers," in *Office Automation: Jekyll or Hyde?* ed. Daniel Marshall and Judith Gregory (Cleveland: Working Women Education Fund, 1983), p. 159; Harley Shaiken, "When the Computer Runs the Office," *New York Times,* March 22, 1987, p. F3; and Peter Rachleff, "Machine Technology and Workplace Control: The U.S. Post Office," in *Critical Studies in Organization and Bureaucracy,* ed. Frank Fischer and Carmen Sirianni (Philadelphia: Temple University Press, 1984), pp. 143–56.

41. Noble, *Forces of Production,* pp. 330–32; and Howard, *Brave New Workplace,* pp. 210–12.

42. Noble, *Forces of Production;* also, see Jonathan Schlefer, "Negotiating the Factory of the Future," *Technology Review,* January 1985, pp. 24–27.

43. Michael Dertouzos and Joel Moses, eds., *The Computer Age: A Twenty-Year View* (Cambridge: MIT Press, 1979).

44. See Simon Nora and Alain Minc, *The Computerization of Society* (Cambridge, MIT Press, 1980), for a general assessment of the pros and cons of this issue. See also Herbert I. Schiller, *Information and the Crisis Economy* (Oxford University Press, 1986); and Zuboff, *In the Age of the Smart Machine*; for an interesting discussion of the deskilling issue, see Paul Attewell, "The Deskilling Controversy," *Work and Occupations* 14, no. 3, pp. 323–46.

45. See, for example, David Dickson, *The New Politics of Science,* (Chicago: University of Chicago Press, 1988), and Tom Athanasiou, "High-Tech Politics: Artificial Intelligence," *Socialist Review* 17, no. 2 (March–April 1987): 7–37.

46. Noble, *Forces of Production;* Shaiken, *Work Transformed.*

47. Larry Hirschhorn, *Beyond Mechanization: Work and Technology in a Postindustrial Age* (Cambridge: MIT Press, 1984); Hirschhorn, "The Postindustrial Labor Process," *New Political Science,* no. 7 (Fall 1981): 11–32; Adler, "Technology and Us"; Harold Salzman, "Computer Technology and the Automation of Skill" (Paper delivered at the American Sociological Association Meeting, August 17, 1987); Shaiken, "The Automated Factory," pp. 17–24; David Moberg, "The Robotics Industry Discovers It's Missing Some Key Components," *In These Times,* May 13–19, p. 7.

48. Athanasiou, "High-Tech Politics," p. 27.

49. Howard, *Brave New Workplace,* p. 198.

50. Ibid., p. 199.

51. David Dickson, "Choosing Technology," *Science for the People* 19, no. 5 (September–October 1987): 5–8.

52. Robert Howard, "Toward a Brave New Workplace?" *Dissent,* Winter 1986, p. 94.

53. International Association of Machinists, "Workers' Technology Bill of Rights," *Democracy* 3 (Spring 1983): 25–27. Also, see Shaiken, *Work Transformed,* chap. 8.

54. Rudi Volti, "Organizations and Expertise in China," *Administration and Society* 8 (February 1977): pp. 423–58.

55. Langdon Winner, "Political Ergonomics" (Paper prepared for delivery at the 1987 Annual Meeting of the American Political Science Association, Chicago, September 3–6, 1987).

56. Dorothy Nelkin and Arie Rip, "Distributing Expertise: A Dutch Experiment in Public Interest Science," *Bulletin of Atomic Scientists,* May 1979; and Rolf Zaal and Loet Leydesdorff, "Amsterdam Science Shop and Its Influence on University Research: The Effects of Ten Years of Dealing with Non-Academic Questions," *Science and Public Policy* 14, no. 6 (December 1987): 310–16.

57. Robert Howard and Leslie Schneider, "Worker Participation in Technological Change: Interests, Influence, and Scope," in *Worker Participation and the Politics of Reform,* ed. Carmen Sirianni (Philadelphia: Temple University Press, 1987), pp. 87–90.

58. Ibid.

59. Ibid.

60. For a general guide to these experiments, see Sirianni, *Worker Participation.*

61. Andrew Martin, "Unions, the Quality of Work, and Technological Change in Sweden," in Sirianni, *Worker Participation,* pp. 95–139. Also, I am indebted to Åke Sandburg and Casten von Otter of the Arbetslivscentrum in Stockholm for taking time to discuss the UTOPIA project with me.

62. Martin, "Unions," p. 110.

63. Ibid., p. 111.

64. Ibid., pp. 121–37; and *The UTOPIA Project: An Alternative in Text and Images,* Summary Report (Stockholm: Swedish Center for Working Life, 1985).

65. Robert Blauner, *Alienation and Freedom* (Chicago: University of Chicago, 1964).

66. Robert Howard, "UTOPIA: Where Workers Craft New Technology," *Technology Review* 88 (April 1985), p. 44.

67. Ibid., pp. 44–45.

68. Ibid., p. 45.

69. Martin, "Unions," p. 124.

70. Ibid., p. 127.

71. Howard, "UTOPIA," p. 45.

72. Ibid.

73. Ibid.

74. Martin, "Unions," p. 128.

75. Ibid., pp. 128–32.

76. Ibid., p. 136.

77. Ibid., pp. 133–34.

78. See Mike Cooley, "Drawing up the Corporate Plan at Lucas Aerospace," *Architect or Bee: The Human/Technology Relationship* (Boston: South End Press, 1982), pp. 81–106.

PART VII

EXPERTISE AND EMPOWERMENT: TOWARD AN ALTERNATIVE PRACTICE

The future of what is called modern society depends on how willing, or rationally and effective the intellectual community in general, and the educated and scientific estate in particular, assume responsibility for political action and leadership.

—JOHN KENNETH GALBRAITH

Political action on the side of the oppressed must be pedagogical action in the authentic sense of the word, and, therefore, action *with* the oppressed. . . . [The] real humanist can be identified more by his trust in the people, which engages him in their struggle, than by a thousand actions in their favor without that trust.

—PAULO FREIRE

In the two concluding chapters, we explore the elements of a democratic reconceptualization of managerial and policy practices. The problem is introduced in Chapter 13 through an examination of Lasswell's call for a "policy sciences of democracy." Although policy science is today largely described as "instrumental" and "apolitical," an interest in improving its contribution to democracy is shown to have roots that trace back to the very origins of the policy science movement. As we saw, however, the discipline was shaped, both politically and methodologically, to foster a very narrow and elitist kind of democracy, typically referred to as "democratic elitism." In the process, the chapter examines specific practices that wed policy experts to an elitist bias. Singled out in particular are the

339

discipline's emphasis on a technical conceptualization of rationality and its acceptance of a hierarchical model of expert-client relations.

The last chapter, "Restructuring Practice: The Elements of Participatory Expertise," focuses on a methodological orientation that counters many of the technocratic abuses of the social sciences. The methodology, in large part aligned with the struggles of alternative social movements, is called "participatory research." Fundamentally a *collaborative* research technique, it is designed to "facilitate" the kinds of expert-client interactions basic to such efforts as the UTOPIA project (discussed in Chapter 12). Rather than attempting to mystify workers with expertise (as we saw, for example, in the case of human relations psychology), participatory research seeks to engage workers in an authentic dialogue about their own needs and interests. Toward this end, it confronts not only the task of developing a critical postpositivist methodology but also the need to reorganize expert practices.

Finally, a caveat: The task of democratizing expertise rests on sophisticated epistemological and political issues that cannot be resolved here. Thus the discussion that follows is necessarily tentative and incomplete. It seeks to modestly convey a simple but important point: namely, that a viable nontechnocratic methodology is not only possible but, in fact, the construction of such an alternative has already begun.

13

Democracy and Expertise:
The Case of Policy Science

Managerial and policy expertise are today thriving industries. Paradoxically, however, the place of such expertise in the social sciences remains controversial. Indeed, many political and social theorists portray the managerial and policy sciences as intellectually bankrupt. They are said to represent the near-complete capitulation of the social sciences to the instrumental and rationalizing processes of the modern industrial/ technological system and its state apparatus.[1] Furthering what Weber described as the "disenchantment of the world," modern managerial and policy scientists have been portrayed as the contemporary "specialists without spirit."[2]

Social Science, Expertise, and
Democratic Elitism

There is a major irony underlying the history of this development in public policy analysis. Consider, for example, the work of Harold Lasswell, generally taken to be the father of modern policy science.[3] Lasswell presented his new science as anything but a narrow, technocratic endeavor. Indeed, his stated purpose was the innovation of a new science that would overcome the limitations of the traditionally fragmented social sciences. It would be a broad, interdisciplinary science, drawing on anthropology, physics, psychology, and history as well as economics, organization theory, and political science. It would, furthermore, be grounded in a fundamental moral objective, namely, the protection and furtherance of democracy in America and the world. The policy sciences, as he put it, would be "the policy sciences of democracy." He describes the objectives in these terms:

> It is safe . . . to forecast that the policy-science approach will bring about a series of "special" sciences within the field of the social sciences, much as the desire to cure has developed a science of medicine which is distinct from, though connected with, the general science of biology.[4]

The nature of this new science, Lasswell maintained, can already be seen in the United States.

> The American dominant tradition affirms the dignity of man, not the superiority of one set of men. Hence, it is foreseen that the emphasis will be upon the development of knowledge pertinent to the fuller realization of human dignity. Let us for convenience call this the evolution of the "policy sciences of democracy.". . . It is probable that the policy-science orientation in the United States will be directed toward the knowledge needed to improve the practice of democracy.[5]

The goal of the policy sciences of democracy, then, is the realization of human dignity in both theory and practice. Such a science, to be sure, is as laudatory as it is ambitious. But nearly 40 years later the result is scarcely judged as anything approximating the furtherance of democracy and human dignity. Indeed, as already noted, the policy science orientation is widely accused of fostering a narrowly instrumental and largely managerial orientation. Frequently, it is seen as the antithesis rather than the bulwark of democracy. For instance, after surveying leading textbooks on public policy analysis, Bennett could conclude the following:

> If you open a public policy textbook, particularly one elaborating the rational decision approach to policy analysis . . . you encounter almost complete silence about democracy. Despite the renewed attention to values in public policy analysis, some texts never even utter the word.[6]

The reasons for this very different outcome are complex and cannot be dealt with here in any detail. We limit our observations to only the most essential characteristics of the instrumental, apolitical science that did in fact emerge. We begin with the issue of democracy itself.

Democratic Elitism: Mediating Between
Elite Requirements and Mass Demands

The failure of the policy science movement to fulfill its democratic commitment arises not so much from an abandonment of democracy as from a shift in the definition of democracy that came to inform it. Merelman, for instance, has shown that, while Lasswell and other leading social scientists of the time were genuinely worried about the future of democracy, their concern must be understood in a particular political context.[7] During the postwar period it became increasingly clear that the emergence of a complex technological society, accompanied by the corporate "managerial revolution" and the rise of "big government," posed special problems for the future of democracy in America. Specifically, the traditional role of the citizen, the most essential element in a democratic society, could no longer be taken for granted. How was the individual citizen to grapple with either the complexities of a technological society or the imposing organizational structures of a large-scale corporate state?

The answer was to be found in a new concept of democracy, later to be called "democratic elitism." Rather than challenging the emerging role of technologies and government, typically described as the "engines of economic progress," leading social scientists of the period saw the solution to involve adjusting the principles of democracy to the exigencies of these new realities. The problem was politically defined as trying to mediate between the complexities of these large-scale technological-based institutions and the general citizenry.[8]

Who was to do this mediation and how was it to be carried out? Social scientists sought to play a major role in this process. Both wittingly and unwittingly, they developed techniques to help mediate the tensions between the corporate sector, the state, and mass society.[9] Through the innovation and employment of such behavioral science techniques as survey and marketing research, polling and interviewing techniques, and increasingly sophisticated data processing methods, social scientists began to collect data about citizen interests and demands that could be used in the development of strategies designed to ameliorate social conflicts, particularly those that arose between citizens and corporate-state efforts to translate the "imperatives" of modern technologies into public policy. This latter task, of course, was a central concern of policy science.

Often this new role for the social and policy sciences was both modeled and legitimated along standard professional lines. Its development was typically portrayed as a "consultative" relationship with the clientele groups, if not the society at large.[10] As possessors of scientific knowledge about the functions and processes of complex sociotechnical systems, professional policy experts would accept responsibility to help the individual citizens understand this world and how to adjust to it. Parsons, in fact, saw the advance of this "professional complex" as "the single most important component" in the structure of the modern postwar society.[11] In turn for status and authority, professional social scientists would behave as though there were a formal agreement binding them to carry out the mission responsibly. In part, this professional obligation was purported to be grounded in the "value-neutral" character of scientific and technical knowledge. The essentially political function that organizational and policy-oriented social scientists fashioned for themselves was thus largely legitimated in the name of science.

In policy science the professional/consultative relationship has often been analogized to that of the medical profession.[12] It has been described as intervening in the "body politic" to remedy economic and social problems in much the same way that the medical doctor prescribes medicines to cure the human body. Some theorists have compared the task of policy-making to that of psychotherapy. Lasswell, for instance, spoke of both as trying to relieve the pressures that caused problems for a postwar liberal society (the psychiatrist at the level of the individual psyche, the policymaker at the level of collective goals). Moreover, he suggested a number of strategies for coordinating these endeavors that today, if not then, would raise disturbing ethical questions. Among them was the idea of setting up experimental political/psychological communities "to expunge the anarchic impulses that threaten the liberal polity."[13] (Similarly, organizational psychology and the human relations movement, as we saw in Chapter 5, have sought to mitigate—if not eliminate—the conflictual labor-management tensions that threaten the stability of the corporate workplace.)

Social Science for Prediction and Control

Although Lasswell's specific recommendations were never taken up, the experimental orientation permeated postwar social scientific research. The dominant methodological theme that guided this emergent professional project was that of "behavioralism." As a postwar variant of neopositivism, it sought to rigorously adapt and apply the methodologies of the physical sciences to the study of social life. It thus gave impetus to a social science oriented more to the principles of prediction and control of behavior rather than to the values of human dignity, critical reflection, and democratic participation.[14]

Parenthetically, it is worth noting that Lasswell played an important but ironic role in the development of this new behavioral science orientation. While on the one hand he called for the development of "the policy science of democracy," on the other he was a leading spokesperson for a methodological orientation grounded in a very different set of values.[15] An explanation for these otherwise contradictory objectives can be found in the elitist concept of democracy. Behavioral science, in short, was quite well designed to facilitate the mediating role fashioned for the social sciences in the postwar liberal state. Not only did it hold out the promise of developing a truly "scientific" knowledge about the social world, it also set the behavioral scientists apart from ordinary citizens. As professional experts, these new scientists were deemed to possess special knowledge inaccessible to the larger citizenry. This, in turn, was seen to necessitate, if not legitimate, the development of a professional/consultative relationship to society and its members.

Positivistic methodologies were, moreover, set up as the key to normative policy decision making. Governed by positivism's principle of "value-neutrality," the managerial and policy sciences were in particular designed to supply decision makers with empirical knowledge about efficient courses of action. In ideal form, such action is evaluated in terms of the costs and benefits of alternative means for achieving goals. Such calculations are to be unhampered by the value implications of the particular political goals or organizational goals; these are left, respectively, to the consensual processes of the political system (in the public sector) and the preferences of ownership (in the private sector). The social scientist's role in this scheme is not to determine policy but only to empirically evaluate policy options for duly mandated decision makers.[16]

Behavioralism was also held out as the key to institution building. If the elitist conception of democracy was to function successfully, specific institutional linkages would have to be forged between top-level elite decision makers and the general public (or rank and file in the workplace). Social scientists, in this respect, saw behavioral science as holding out the possibility of developing the "verifiable" and "reliable" knowledge required for this assignment. In the case of the managerial and policy sciences, the objective was to transcend a narrow emphasis on policy outcomes by also investigating the structures and processes of policy decision making itself. Aside from supplying the "intelligence needs of policy," researchers were to seek knowledge about policy decision-making processes as well.[17] Here Simon's behavioral theory of organizational design and administrative decision making became a classic of the period.[18] Such knowledge was seen as an essential ingredient for the building of organizations and institutions.

Thus, in contrast to a broadly conceived social science dedicated to realizing the goals of democracy, what evolved has largely been a set of technocratic research strategies employed for undemocratic ends. This became most apparent during the latter half of the 1960s, when the social and policy sciences— like professional expertise in general—were subjected to sharp criticisms for what came to be seen as the manipulatory, elitist tendencies underlying their consultative role. Indeed, basic to the protest movements of this period were caustic complaints about "the tyranny of the experts."[19] Not only were experts accused of failing to generate solutions relevant to the diverse range of interests in society as a whole, they were also charged with buffering the power elites of modern society from the political challenges from below. What appeared to be a neutral or objective role in mediating system problems was revealed to be deeply rooted in the biases of the system itself. By largely taking their definitions of the system from those at the top, managerial and policy scientists had basically adopted a conception of systems conflicts that rested on an acceptance of the elite power structure. When the power structure itself proved to be at the root of the problem, these applied scientists themselves became part of the problem. Often quite vituperatively, experts were portrayed as perpetuating the social injustices plaguing modern Western societies.[20] Such complaints can still be heard today; in some circles they remain quite obstreperous.

Expertise for Participatory Democracy

To be sure, in the professional disciplines such charges have not been taken lightly. Indeed, it became common to speak of the "crisis of the professions."[21] Such outcries have frequently led to political and epistemological turmoil within the disciplines, including the organizational and policy sciences.[22] Typically, the political strife in the professions has been related to inherent epistemological failures. The critics attribute these failures, by and large, to the professions' overly technical, instrumental conception of rationality. This, as we saw in Chapter 9, has given rise to the demand for social and political relevance, most commonly defined as the pursuit of value-oriented, humanistic, and critical approaches to theory and practice.[23]

While most organizational and policy professionals continue to plod forward with the established technical methodologies, a small but growing number of theorists have begun to rethink the practices of expertise. Much of their work can appropriately be characterized as the search for a more "democratic" or "participatory" concept of professional practice. Rather than facilitating the elitist model, they seek for the practice of expertise a political and methodological orientation appropriate to participatory democracy. Just as earlier behavioral scientists sought to supply democratic elitism with a specific type of policy expertise, these theorists attempt to supply participatory democracy with an expertise appropriate to its own decision processes. Basic to their efforts is an attempt to shift the policy expert's role from that of a "mediator" of power and interests to that of a "facilitator" of dialogue and empowerment. The remainder of this chapter is an effort to pull together some of the basic issues underlying this emerging intellectual project and to examine their implications for a reconstruction of organizational and policy expertise.

For present purposes, we need only specify the most basic premises of participatory democracy. In simple but essential terms, participatory democracy is a political system (governmental or organizational) in which each citizen is able to authentically engage in the political processes of policy decision making.[24] Speech and argumentation are the basic media of these processes; each citizen must, therefore, have a significant voice in them. The outcome of the deliberative process, a democratic decision, must be founded on the most persuasive argument. Waltzer graphically sums up the ideal model in this way: No one can "use force, or pull rank or distribute money"; each participant "must talk about the issues at hand." Citizens arrive at "the forum with nothing but their arguments." They must leave all of their "non-political goods . . . outside: weapon and wallets, titles and degrees."[25]

The discussion of participatory democracy and the political decision structures that best sustain its practices is a complex subject well beyond the scope of the present study. Much theoretical and practical research is required before its theoretical premises can be translated into concrete institutional terms.[26] Here the purpose can only be to grapple with one piece of the problem: the structure of expert practices in a system dedicated to advancing the value of democratic participation. In the remainder of this chapter, and in the next one, we explore the conceptual contours of an expert practice designed to facilitate the principle value upon which democratic political structures must be built, namely, the open and free discussion of competing interests and goals. Indeed, following Lasswell's earlier lead, we take one of the primary tasks of democratic expertise to be the discovery and elaboration of the structural requirements of participatory decision-making processes.

Participatory Democracy and Advocacy Research

The first significant effort to anchor social and policy research in the advancement of participatory democracy emerged as a component of the political struggles of the 1960s. As part of the critique of professional expertise generally, it appeared as a call for an advocacy orientation in social research. Largely promoted by those aligned with progressive political issues (the War on Poverty, the environmental crisis, the antinuclear movement, the women's movement, and so on), "advocacy research" developed as an effort to directly confront the elitist political biases of mainstream research.[27]

In epistemological terms, advocacy research represents an attempt to transcend the "value-neutral ideology" of expertise by explicitly anchoring research in the interests of particular interest groups and the processes of political and policy argumentation in society generally. In doing so, it seeks to offset the disciplines' allegiances to the dominant political and economic elites, especially as they are manifested in a mediating role between elite requirements and mass demands. By making professional expertise available to groups otherwise excluded from the process, advocacy calls attention to the implicit, hidden elitist politics embedded in the ostensibly "consultative" relationship. For this reason, it clearly constitutes an important political and methodological step toward a less elitist, more democratic, practice of expertise.

While advocacy was an important step in the right direction, it nonetheless largely failed to fulfill the promise of a genuinely participatory methodology.[28] In the course of their struggles, many activists came to recognize that advocacy is a useful methodology for *representing* views not otherwise heard in the political process, but not well designed for the *fundamental* requirement of participatory democracy, namely, helping people speak for themselves. The failure is best captured by the words of a frustrated antipoverty advocate:

> [Office of Economic Opportunity] staff members were advocates for the poor as opposed to mere custodians. But too often the focus of their activities was on themselves—on their caring, their righteousness, their willingness to go out on a limb to fight for the interests of the poor.[29]

Seldom did agency workers trouble themselves to determine if they were fighting for the issues that really bothered the poor.

> The mere fact that they were employed by an anti-poverty program seemed to convince them that whatever they were doing was in the best interests of the poor. The fact that participation of the poor was limited to token representation on boards of directors, or to dead-end paraprofessional positions, seemed to elude them. The rhetoric of public participation was its own reward.

The advocate's role was essentially program or issue oriented. Their emphasis tended to be on policy changes, on influencing the behavior and attitudes of public officials, particularly those in old-line government agencies. "They had a genuine desire to assist the poor, but on *their* terms, using *their* methods, and *their* time frame, and in some cases *their* issues." The resolution of the policy issue, rather than the development of an ongoing community process, became the primary goal.

> Consequently, the advocates avoided dealing with the major frustration of poor people, which is not that they do not have enough programs or that no one cares about them, but that they have no control over the decisions affecting their lives.

Moreover, the left's emphasis on advocacy gave rise over time to some unanticipated consequences in the political sphere that proved to be quite problematic. Ironically, advocacy research's failure to grapple with the empowering dimension of participation tended to politically devaluate the process of policy argumentation. Largely introduced by liberal and progressive policy experts, as we saw in Chapter 6, conservative politicians have responded to the politics of advocacy by nurturing their own policy "counterintelligentsia." With liberal advocates pitted against conservative advocates, the result has been to transform policy expertise into a full-blown adversarial process: Each side hires its own experts, touts its own studies, then ignores the research of the other side. Policy experts, as a consequence, are turned at times into something approximating the "hired gun."

The adversarial character of the resulting process intensifies a new kind of politics, what we have called here the "politics of expertise." The result is a politics far removed from the original participatory promise attached to the advocacy approach. What started out as an attempt to bring a wider range of viewpoints into the political processes has been manipulated to serve as an impediment to meaningful citizen participation.[30]

The problem is lodged in advocacy research's failure to deal with the hierarchical character of both expertise and democratic elitism. As became apparent to many activists in the middle 1970s and early 1980s, advocacy has merely been grafted onto a system of hierarchical interest-group organizations, which tend themselves to be oligarchic. The leaders of these organizations are seldom as representative of their constituencies as they purport to be. As much research makes clear, the representation of a group by experts almost always leads to an elitism that impedes the possibility of authentic member participation.[31]

The challenge cuts to the core of professionalism itself. In the standard model of professionalism, practitioners possess authoritative knowledge (largely defined as rigorously tested theory) that clients must deferentially respect. To be sure, practitioners typically engage in consultations with their clients, but the actual decision process is ultimately governed by professional power and authority. Even though it is the client's interests that are at stake, in a particular area of expertise the professional, when all is said and done, is considered to know what is best for the client. Such authority is held to be based on tested "formal" knowledge about techniques, practices and consequences.

The relationship raises difficult issues. Experts, after all, are in possession of a product their clients need, namely, a specific body of knowledge. Indeed, in a technological society deference to expertise is widely touted as the *solution* rather than the impediment to contemporary problem solving. But even here the problem returns in another form. Such optimism is substantially diminished by the growing recognition that professional decision making, regardless of how good the expert's intentions, does not always turn out to be in the best interests of those concerned. There is much evidence showing that professional standards themselves frequently hinder effective problem solving.[32] For writers such as Schön, this reality is what virtually constitutes the "crisis" of the professions.[33] The problem is thus anything but insignificant.

If citizens are to participate in the development of the policy decisions that affect their own lives, the standard practitioner-client model must give way to a more democratic relationship between them. This does not mean that citizens can themselves become experts, although some modern-day utopians occasionally suggest it.[34] More formally, this view has been described as a "participant dominated" model of expertise.[35] Even though it is possible to demonstrate specific circumstances in which such an approach can be workable, as a general model it is problematic. Given the complexity of contemporary society, the participant-dominated model is clearly beyond reach. Much more practical is a "collaborative" or "participatory" model of expertise. It is to this model that we devote our attention in the next and concluding chapter.

Conclusion

It is useful by way of concluding to briefly summarize the argument that brings us to the professional-client relationship. We have seen that the question of the relationship of democracy to policy expertise has deep roots in the history of policy science. Although Lasswell's initial concept of a "policy sciences of democracy" never took hold in the discipline, the question of how to better distribute expertise throughout society has continued to plague the discipline, especially in face of increasing trends toward technocratic governance. During the social turmoil of the 1960s, in fact, the practice of advocacy research emerged as a direct response to political elitism and the turn to technocratic strategies. But advocacy research, giving rise to "counter" experts, led to an unanticipated and ironic consequence—the political neutralization, if not devaluation, of policy research. This led others, particularly intellectuals and activists involved in, or identified with, new social movements, to recognize more fundamental questions about the nature of professional advice. Whereas advocates focus on the client's relationship to the external social and political world, these writers see the problem to penetrate also the very structure of the professional-client relationship itself. For them, the next step must be to open this relationship to a broader participatory dialogue. This concern has given rise to a methodology called "participatory research." We turn to this emerging model in the next chapter.

Notes

1. See, for example, Jürgen Habermas, *Toward a Rational Society* (Boston: Beacon, 1970); and H. T. Wilson, *Political Management* (New York: Walter de Gruyter, 1978).

2. Max Weber, *Max Weber: Selections in Translation,* ed. C. G. Runciman (Cambridge: Cambridge University Press, 1978).

3. Harold D. Lasswell, "The Policy Orientation," in *The Policy Sciences,* ed. Daniel Lerner and Harold D. Lasswell (Stanford, CA: Stanford University Press, 1951), pp. 3–15.

4. Ibid., p. 10.

5. Ibid., pp. 10, 15.

6. Douglas Bennett, "Democracy and Public Policy Analysis," in *Research in Public Policy Analysis and Management,* Vol. 3, ed. Stuart S. Nagel (Greenwich, CT: JAI, 1986), p. 12. Bennett adds: "We can take it that [the authors] would not be more pleased if their text sat on office [shelves] in Sofia as well as Washington, nor if it were adopted for classes in Asuncion as well as Cambridge."

7. Richard M. Merelman, "On Interventionist Behavioralism: An Essay in the Sociology of Knowledge," *Politics and Society* 6, no. 1 (1976): 57–78.

8. For a discussion by a leading social scientist during this period, see Paul F. Lazarsfeld, "An Episode in the History of Social Research: A Memoir," in *The Intellectual Migration: Europe and America, 1930–1960,* ed. Donald Fleming and Bernard Bailyn (Cambridge, MA: Harvard University Press, 1969); and Michael Pollak, "Paul F. Lazarsfeld: A Sociointellectual Biography, " *Knowledge: Creation, Diffusion, and Utilization* no. 2, (1980): 157–77.

9. Merelman, "On Interventionist Behavioralism."

10. On the "consultative relationship," see Heinz Eulau, *Technology and Civility* (Stanford, CA: Hoover Institution, 1977), pp. 66–93; and Guy Benveniste, "Some Functions and Dysfunctions of Using Professional Elites in Public Policy," in *Research in Public Policy Analysis and Management,* ed. Stuart S. Nagel (Greenwich, CT: JAI, 1987), pp. 113–14.

11. Talcott Parsons, "Professions," in *International Encyclopedia of the Social Sciences,* vol. 12, ed. David Sills (New York: Macmillan and Free Press), pp. 536–47.

12. Robert Axelrod, "The Medical Metaphor," *American Journal of Political Science* 31, no. 2 (May 1977): 430–32.

13. Harold D. Lasswell, *The Future of Political Science* (New York: Atherton, 1963), pp. 177–78.

14. See Manfred Stanley, *The Technological Conscience* (Chicago: University of Chicago Press, 1978).

15. Lasswell, *The Future of Political Science.*

16. Frank Fischer, *Politics, Values, and Public Policy: The Problem of Methodology* (Boulder, CO: Westview, 1980), p. 23; and Brian Fay, *Social Theory and Political Practice* (New York: Holmes & Meier, 1976), chap. 2.

17. Lasswell, "The Policy Orientation," p. 4.

18. Herbert A. Simon, *Administrative Behavior* (New York: Free Press, 1945). Simon, it is worth noting, was a disciple of Lasswell and his behavioral approach.

19. Jethro Lieberman, *Tyranny of Expertise* (New York: Walker, 1972) and Magali Sarfatti Larson, "The Production of Expertise and the Constitution of Expert Power," in *The Authority of Experts,* ed. Thomas L. Haskell (Bloomington: Indiana University Press, 1984), pp. 28–80.

20. For illustrations of the harshest criticisms, see Ivan Illich, *A Celebration of Awareness: A Call for Institutional Revolution* (Garden City, NY: Doubleday, 1970), and *Deschooling Society* (New York: Harper & Row, 1970); Magali S. Larson, "Professionalism: Rise and Fall," *International Journal of Health Service* 9, no. 4 (1979); and Steven Wineman, *The Politics of Human Services: A Radical Alternative to the Welfare State* (Boston: South End Press, 1984).

21. Donald A. Schön, *The Reflective Practitioner* (New York: Basic Books, 1983), pp. 1–20; and Ann Withhorn, *Serving the People: Social Services and Social Change* (New York: Columbia University Press, 1984).

22. Fischer, *Politics, Values, and Public Policy.*

23. See, for example, Frank Fischer and John Forester, eds., *Confronting Values in Policy Analysis: The Politics of Criteria* (Newbury Park, CA: Sage, 1987).

24. Daniel C. Kramer, *Participatory Democracy* (Cambridge, MA: Schenkman, 1972).

25. Michael P. Waltzer, *The Spheres of Justice* (New York: Basic Books, 1983), p. 304.

26. No issue is more pertinent to such research than the relationship between participation and equality. See Waltzer, ibid.

27. John L. Foster, "An Advocate Role Model for Policy Analysis," *Policy Studies Journal* 8, no. 6 (Summer 1980): 958–64.

28. Timothy W. Kennedy, "Beyond Advocacy: A Facilitative Approach to Public Participation," *Journal of the University Film and Video Association* 34, no. 3 (Summer 1982): 33–46; and Robert Kraushaar, "Outside the Whale: Progressive Planning and the Dilemmas of Radical Reform," *Journal of the American Planning Association* Vol. 54, No. 1 (Winter 1988) pp. 91–100

29. Kennedy, "Beyond Advocacy," p. 35. For a historical perspective on this problem, see Willard Gaylin et al., *Doing Good: The Limits of Benevolence* (New York: Pantheon, 1978).

30. For a general discussion on citizen participation, as well as strategies to get around the barriers, see Jack DeSario and Stuart Langton, eds., *Citizen Participation in Public Decision-Making* (Westport, CT: Greenwood, 1987).

31. See, for example, Robert Michels, *Political Parties* (New York: Dover, 1915). For a contemporary case study, see Jane Mansbridge, *Why We Lost the ERA* (Chicago: University of Chicago Press, 1986).

32. For a discussion of the failures of professional knowledge in the social and policy sciences, see Charles Lindblom and David K. Cohen, *Usable Knowledge: Social Science and Social Problem Solving* (New Haven, CT: Yale University Press, 1979). For an example in the natural sciences, see Georges Benguigui, "The Scientist, the Fisherman and the Oyster- Farmer," in *The Social Direction of the Public Sciences,* ed. Stuart Blume, Joske Bunders, Loet Leydesdorff, and Richard Whitley (Dordrecht: D. Reidel, 1987), pp. 117–33.

33. Schön, *The Reflective Practitioner.*

34. For a summary of this view, see Paul Halmos, *Professionalism and Social Change* (University of Keele: Sociological Review Monograph, December 1973).

35. Frederick A. Rossini and Alan L. Porter, "Public Participation and Professionalism in Impact Assessment," in *Citizen Participation in Science Policy,* ed. James C. Peterson (Chicago: University of Chicago Press, 1985), pp. 62–74.

14

Restructuring Practice:
The Elements of Participatory Expertise

Finally, we come to the most difficult question: Is there an alternative to technocratic methodology? This concluding chapter outlines the framework of an alternative methodological orientation for managerial and policy expertise. Insofar as the purpose is to draw on work that is already under way, the task is as much descriptive as it is theoretical. Much of the work can be characterized as the search for a more "democratic" or "participatory" concept of expert practice; it seeks for this practice a political and methodological orientation appropriate to participatory democracy.

The beginnings of this alternative model of expertise are in large part found in the work of intellectuals, activists, and progressive professionals identified with the "new social movements" of the past two decades. Social movements, often defined as "populist" movements in the United States, are the principle agents in the contemporary struggle for participatory democracy. The emergence of these movements—ecological and "Green" movements, feminist movements, progressive trade union movements (more typically in Europe and the Third World than in the United States), neighborhood control movements, consumer cooperatives and worker ownership movements, and so on—represent an uncompromising call in contemporary society for democratic participation and self-management.[1] As alternative movements, they have identified the technocratic system and its apolitical decision-making strategies as primary targets of their countercultural opposition. Indeed, numerous influential writers take the confrontation between the democratic thrust of new social movements and the manipulatory policies of state-corporate technocrats as a fundamental political tension shaping the future of Western political systems.[2]

The efforts of these movements to develop a participatory politics and the democratic culture required to sustain it provide a social forum, if not laboratory, for experimentation with new sociocultural models, including models of expertise.[3] The classic tensions between expertise and participation are central to their experimental alternatives, as their existence is often a direct response to the impact of new technologies on modern social life (the ecological and antinuclear movements being prime examples). Such experimentation, largely designed to counter the bureaucratic and elitist tendencies that define contemporary political and organizational processes, have in significant part been geared to social movements' emphasis on empowerment and self-help strategies. The theorists of these movements, or "movement intellectuals," have attempted to step beyond the limits of the advocacy orientation by asking the more fundamental question: Is it possible to restructure the largely undemocratic professional-client relationship?[4] Toward this end, one of the key targets of movement intellectuals has been the hierarchical relationship the professions maintain with their clients. Their direct confrontation with this problem offers interesting and suggestive ideas as to how expertise might be adapted to accommodate democratic organizational practices. For this reason, such alternative cultural movements have stimulated a nascent but insightful discussion on alternative expert practices. It is to the literature generated by this discussion that we turn for guidance as to how the expert's function might be reconstructed in the context of a genuine commitment to participation. We begin with the critique of professional expertise central to the project of these movements.

The Critique of Expertise

Dedicated to the expansion of participation, the efforts of social movements are typically described in the language of "empowerment" and "self-help." Whereas the traditional concept of power that has informed policy decision making (particularly bureaucratic decision making) focuses on how to get people to do things they would not ordinarily or necessarily do (through either appeals to legitimation or coercion), empowerment refers to the political process of providing people with the resources to make their own decisions about what to do and how they might best go about achieving their goals.[5]

The literature of empowerment takes up the question of expertise directly. Typically, it rests on a radical critique of the professions. For the theorists of empowerment, the professions have too often misappropriated their specialized knowledge to serve both their own interests and those of a power elite intent on maintaining its own dominance over the rest of society. They are portrayed as elite functionaries of the establishment. Their mandates, licenses, and autonomy are said to work toward a profoundly unjust distribution of social benefits and thus serve as mechanisms for social control, particularly the control of the have-nots—the poor, the dispossessed, ethnic and racial minorities, women, and the like, by the dominant elites.[6]

But the complaints do not only concern the interests of the minorities and the poor. Professionals have also suffered harsh criticisms from segments of the middle and upper classes as well. Here the complaints tend to have more to do with the overextension of technical strategies into social and cultural realms. Most typically, they concern the acceleration of a technocratic society in which many people prefer not to live. This is especially the case among relatively affluent groups more concerned with the quality of everyday life than the struggle for economic subsistence. Indeed, many of the new social movement members tend to be dropouts from the more affluent strata of society.[7]

The mechanisms through which this social control is manifested are the professional-client relationship and the technical conception of professional practice. Both are primary concerns of social movement intellectuals, activists, and progressive professionals intent on reconstructing expert practices. We consider first the structures of hierarchy and control basic to the professional-client power relationship.

The prototypical examples of the professional-client relationship are taken from medicine and law. The structure of these relationships, with their high degrees of authority, status, and autonomy, provide the model for the professions generally. The less-well-developed professions, or "minor professions" as they have been called, typically seek to emulate these relationships with their clients.[8] Indeed, we have already noted the tendency for policy scientists to seek parallels between medicine and their own practices.

On the professional side of the equation, experts are presumed to deliver their services to the limits of their competence, to respect the confidences granted them by their clients, and not to misuse for their own benefits the special powers given them within the boundaries of the relationship. In return, clients are expected to accept the professional's authority in specific areas of expertise, to submit to the professional's ministrations, and, of course, to pay for the services rendered. One writer likens the relationship to an "informal contract" in which the client agrees not to challenge the professional's judgment or to demand explanations beyond the professional's willingness to give them.[9] In short, clients are expected to behave as though they accept and respect the professional's autonomy as an expert.

Although there is room for discretion on both sides of the relationship, the client has little real control over the professional's behavior. To be sure, nothing compels the professional to betray his or her obligations to the client and clearly many do not. But the essential point is that the client's ability to determine whether or not legitimate expectations have been met is limited. By and large, accountability for the professional's performance is relegated to his or her professional peers. Only the professional's peers are considered intellectually equipped to determine whether he or she has performed satisfactorily.[10]

But even here the possibilities for accountability are limited. First, there is the well-established fact that professionals most typically support one another in matters of malconduct. Confronting another colleague's performance, particularly in a public forum, is frequently countenanced only as a measure of last resort. And even then the task is impeded by a number of problems inherent in the professional-client relationship itself. A big one is the fact that the relationship is usually characterized by privacy, thus making it difficult to establish routine means for peers to assess each other's performance.[11]

What this critique describes, then, is a socially institutionalized relationship that bestows very substantial powers on the professional. Although professionals publicly agree to act in a socially responsible way, the mechanisms for ensuring such control belong to the professions themselves. For some of the harshest critics, this reality represents something of a "conspiracy" against society at large.[12]

But malfeasance per se is not the heart of the matter. While there is plenty of corruption to be rooted out, the more subtle and significant problem is lodged in the professional's acceptance of the system's own definitions of its problems. The difficulty can be traced to the professional's middle-level position in the social hierarchy, or, as radical theorists often put it, their position "between labor and capital." Because most professionals—like most everyone else in the social structure—receive their rewards from those above them, they typically come to see the world from the eyes of the elites who employ them.[13] Thus, as middle-level functionaries of the power elite, the definitions they adopt and impose on their clients are generally those conditioned, more or less, by elite opinion; they are infused with an elite interest in stable social control, if not class domination. This means that experts, through their power to define the client's problems, impose definitions and meanings that speak at least as much or more to the system's "imperatives" as to the needs of their clients. Regardless of the expert's personal or moral intentions, then, he or she—wittingly or unwittingly—buys into a system of explanations designed to accommodate the client's needs and problems to the structures of a larger system of domination. This can be identified as the essence of the mediating relationship between elites and the mass citizenry. If, of course, the system itself is accepted as morally legitimate, there is then perhaps little room for deep concern here. On the other hand, if the system is seen as fundamentally unjust and inequitable, as it is by the members of new social movements, the professional's complicity with the system of domination constitutes a fundamental political problem.

It is from this perspective that the technical conception of professional practice is interpreted as a technique for social control. Through the translation of basic normative questions into technical issues pertaining to instrumental means, technical rationality and its "value-neutral" methodologies disengage decisions from the social and political contexts that give them meaning. By focusing instead on pragmatic systems-related accommodations, they draw attention away from the professions' social control functions. In this way, technical rationality and its methodologies serve to mystify the political dimension of the professional role.[14]

Others, it should be noted, more directly challenge the professions' technical knowledge itself. When exposed to careful scrutiny, they argue, the profession's claims to technical knowledge are often discovered to rest on remarkably shallow empirical foundations.[15] Here, however, it would seem to depend in significant part on the particular profession in question. In the case of medicine, for example, the claim is clearly problematic. Brain surgeons surely possess skills that cannot be written off as mystification. On the other hand, when it comes to the "minor professions," say social work or management, the charge at times has a distinct ring of credibility. In these cases, the function of such professional expertise often appears to serve in large part as legitimation for decisions based on social and political considerations.[16]

It is for these reasons that the radical critics of the professions reject the validity of the professional's claim to authority and the necessity of the client to submit to it. The client, from this point of view, must learn to see the professional as a potential adversary. Not only must the client be given rights to resist such control, the professional-client relationship itself must be replaced with a new model in which more democratic exchanges can occur between the client and the expert. Such concerns are fundamental to the search for an alternative model.

Before turning to the search itself, it is important to concede the contentious nature of the critique. Although critical theorists have amassed an impressive array of evidence to support their polemic against the profession, the nature of the professional role is complicated and remains the subject of much debate. Whether or not social movement theorists overdraw their case, however, in no way vitiates the value of their efforts to innovate a democratic alternative. Such efforts to restructure expertise provide valuable insights for the reconstruction of professional expertise generally.

It is also necessary to situate the managerial and policy professions within the context of this critique. Because these professions, like most "minor professions," are bureaucratized (i.e., their members are employees of organizations rather than practitioners in the free marketplace), their autonomy and authority are restricted. Even though their professional societies strive for greater professional autonomy and authority, as practitioners they are hired (for staff positions by decision makers) to facilitate the organization's goals. As such, the link between their work and the interests of organizational elites is direct and explicit. Their professional autonomy is thus constrained—if not controlled—by those above them. They serve, in this respect, as functionaries. With regard to those below them, however, the standard professional model structures their basic professional-client interactions. In the case of the management profession, professional authority mediates the expert's relationship with other workers; in the case of the policy expert, it shapes the analyst's relationship with external clients and interest groups. It is this mediation of elite interests in the name of expertise and autonomy that constitutes the object of reconstruction in these closing pages.

We turn at this point to the nature of the reconstruction itself. Specifically, we examine the methodological development of an alternative practice that has come to be called "participatory research." We begin by pointing first to several theoretical perspectives on the development of alternative expertise put forward by leading social movement intellectuals; then we turn more specifically to the methodological orientation underlying the development of "participatory research" and the model of expert practices that this research underlies.

Participatory Research: Methodological Foundations

Most of the important theoretically based sociological writing on the development of alternative expertise is found in Europe, where social movements (and movement intellectuals) tend to be strongest. Of special significance is the research strategy developed by the French sociologist Alain Touraine.[17] For Touraine, the task is to develop a research methodology "for the political awakening of society." His "sociologie d'action" focuses directly on social movements, which he takes to be the principal agents of history. Rather than merely reproducing established social arrangements, social movements seek the transformation of society through the creation of new institutions and values. Specifically, Touraine has developed concepts designed to facilitate discussions within social movements. His methodology of "l'intervention sociologie" and its process of "autoanalysis" are employed to enable movement members to give social meaning to their political confrontations with the larger society. It has been applied to the student movement of the 1970s, the antinuclear movement, and the Polish workers' struggles and their "Solidarity" union.[18]

Another important example has been the research methodology, *conricerca,* developed by a group of Italian Marxists identified with a journal called *Quaderni Rossi.*[19] Influenced by Kurt Lewin's collaborative methodology, "action research," *conricerca* was introduced in the 1960s as a means for developing collaborative industrial relations research with shop floor workers. The group sought to redefine collaborative research in political terms. They captured the reorientation in these words: "From being object, the worker makes himself subject; from being mere data, number, statistical phenomenon, he makes himself protagonist." The researcher, at the same time, "turns himself from an antiseptic social engineer into the incarnation of a revolutionary vanguard."[20]

This transformation has two basic objectives. As Wagner explains, it was employed to assess "the development of capitalist work organization and thus [to] help . . . refine the theoretical analysis of the capitalist system." In the process, it was also used to "make the workers aware of the exploitive conditions under which they were living and working, and [to] initiate or advance their reflections about counter strategies."[21] While the actual research projects of the group largely failed to achieve the level of theoretical and methodological sophistication they sought, their project clearly laid important foundations for an alternative research strategy.

In the case of the United States, it is important to mention Friedmann's efforts to spell out a critical planning strategy. Friedmann also seeks a critical approach based on the objectives and struggles of social movements. It is a conception of planning practices that is "to be articulated through the network structures of social movements" and is aimed at the realization of "emancipatory values."[22] Built around a radically democratic conception of society, the basic model of social organization is a network of small task-oriented action groups. Each group is governed by an internal dialogue but is also engaged in a political struggle with the dominant external powers that impede the realization of its political objectives. The model, he contends, "conforms to the actual practices used in major political struggles of recent decades (labor, ethnic group, gender, environmental, anti-nuclear, . . .) and is decidedly nonutopian."[23] It is a highly explicit attempt to link policy planning with the participatory thrust of social movements, emphasizing in particular the problems of work, gender relations, education, and forms of governance.

If much of the theoretical work on the relation of intellectuals and expertise to social movements has been carried out in Europe, the practice itself is particularly prominent in the Third World. Given the disparate character of a dispersed Third World literature, coupled with a base in social movements that typically stand outside of the mainstream of society, it is difficult to present a comprehensive, fully developed picture of "participatory research." The task is further complicated by the fact that much of the work is conducted outside of universities and is seldom published in standard academic journals. Indeed, it is the product of intellectuals and professionals who have turned away from the dominant institutions. One of the richest contributions to participatory research is found in the literature of the alternative educational movement, particularly the literature concerned with adult education. For present purposes, we shall draw most heavily on the publications and projects of a group called the "participatory research network."[24]

Participatory research takes its methodological foundations from a variety of sources. Its most important influences have been the collaborative methodology of action research, especially its emphasis on social learning theory; the work of the Brazilian educational theorist Paulo Freire; trends in anthropological research, particularly applied anthropology; and the emphasis in the social sciences on phenomenology and discourse. Because participatory research can in important respects be defined as a radicalized conceptualization of action research, we begin with the collaborative orientation of action research.

Before doing that, however, we offer a word of caution. The following discussion is largely limited to the theoretical and methodological *foundations* of participatory research. It is not a discussion about how to do participatory research per se. Moreover, it is difficult in the context of a theoretical discussion to adequately capture the dynamic of a participatory methodology. Much of the significance of such a methodology derives from the interpersonal exchanges it promotes and doubtless can only be fully conveyed in the process of actually carrying out such research.

The Collaborative Orientation

This history of the effort to construct a participatory research methodology is in part traceable to the action research methodology pioneered by Lewin in the 1940s. Initially developed as a full-scale effort to facilitate a democratic practitioner-client relationship, Lewin's work was motivated by a desire to fashion a mode of inquiry capable of dealing with the social problems of the postwar period, particularly the problem of fascism. Toward this end, he worked out a collaborative research methodology designed to democratize authoritarian decision cultures.[25] (In this respect, it is interesting to note that Lewin's alternative was developed at about the same time as Lasswell's policy science discipline, largely in response to the same problem—namely, the need to resuscitate democratic practices.)

Collaborative research, as it emerged from action research, is first and foremost a "client-centered" methodology designed to facilitate social learning.[26] Formally, it can be defined as a deliberative, collaborative process in which a practitioner (or practitioners) and a client-system are brought together to solve a problem or to plan a course of action through the processes of collective learning. Emphasizing learning among participants, it proceeds through task-oriented groups, typically involving fewer than a dozen participants. Whereas in the scientific approach "the problem to be studied is identified by the researcher, and, quite frequently . . . framed in such a way as to take advantage of data already assembled in a library, various agency documents, or a computer," collaborative research takes place in the clients' "natural" settings, drawing on their own opinions and resources.[27] Essential to the relationship are the following conditions: (1) a joint effort, growing out of an interaction between practitioners and clients that involves mutual determination of goals; (2) a "spirit of inquiry" based on publicly shared data; (3) equal opportunity for each party to influence the other; and (4) freedom on the part of both practitioners and clients to discontinue their relationship after mutual consultations.[28]

In methodological terms, collaborative research is a "messy," multimethodological approach that both overlaps with and diverges from standard scientific research. Like the scientific tradition, it seeks knowledge that can be empirically generalizable and at the same time is relevant to specific real-life contexts. Like applied research, collaborative research demands that knowledge be useful. But, unlike both basic and applied research, the collaborative orientation requires that the inquiry process speak to the forming of goals and purposes.[29]

When approached properly, collaborative research's emphasis on social learning grapples with two of the most sophisticated epistemological issues facing the organizational and policy sciences, namely, the relationships of theory to practice and of empirical to normative analysis. As a form of knowing intrinsically related to human activity, effective social learning is seen to come from the experience of reality. Social learning research thus focuses as much on social psychological and situational contexts of learning as on cognition per se. Examining problems from the perspective of those engaged in practice, it takes the social environment and the actors' own "ordinary knowledge" to be a primary empirical focus in the analysis of learning situations. Relying on the mediating role of small groups, it stresses the crucial function of dialogue in the formation of collective goals and purposes.[30]

This commitment to connecting theory and practice through collaborative social learning has long been a fundamental tenet of critical theorizing. It links collaborative research to a disparate but influential collection of social theoreticians, including Dewey, Mumford, and Mao

Tse-tung.[31] In recent years, the most significant example has been the theoretical project of Habermas. Indeed, collaborative research's goals and objectives have been likened to those of Habermas's critical social science. One can point to their common emphasis on the linkage of theory and practice, the methodological synthesis of empirical and normative research, and the goal of social learning (a fundamental component of Habermas's attempt to situate his theory of communicative interaction in a historical context).[32] While comparisons with such a much-debated project are necessarily hazardous, it seems fair to concede that something like the collaborative orientation would surely be required to carry out critical social science research.

However, collaborative research, at least in the tradition of action research, has failed to fulfill this critical function. In this context, collaborative techniques have mainly been adapted for use in the bureaucratic context of managerial and organizational research. It is now, in fact, a technique and ideology advanced in significant part by management consultants. In the texts on the subject one can today scarcely find mention of the word *democracy*. Instead, its practitioners speak of "participatory management" and tout its use as a technique for making bureaucratic organizations more responsive to change. In short, the objectives of democratization have disappeared.

If something like the collaborative orientation is required to carry out critical social science research, that something would appear to be "participatory research." Emerging in large part with the new social movements, participatory research's departure from the earlier models of collaborative research is found in the purposes to which it is put rather than the methodology itself. Where action research's collaborative orientation largely developed to assist bureaucratic clients, participatory research has evolved from efforts to deal with the political problems and needs of poor and oppressed peoples.

Phenomenology and Critical Discourse

Participatory research, like action research, is epistemologically grounded in a phenomenological perspective.[33] Both seek to understand the individual and his or her problems within the "logic of the situation." But participatory research, in contrast, attempts to link this logic of the situation to the larger social structure. It is an effort, in short, to interpret the situation in terms of the more fundamental structures of social domination that shape it. As such, participatory research casts its findings in the framework of a larger social critique, an epistemological step that links it to critical theory and the "emancipatory interest."

Especially important from the phenomenological perspective is an emphasis on the actor's own "common sense" or "ordinary knowledge."[34] Collaborative researchers draw a sharp distinction between the formal (abstract) knowledge developed in professional inquiry and the actor's own informal (and contextual) knowledge, often organized in narrative form and told as stories.[35] They accept both as valid types of knowledge but recognize each to be geared to different problems or purposes. As we saw in the UTOPIA project (Chapter 12), the task of the researcher is to bring these two types of knowledge together in a mutually beneficial problem-oriented dialogue.

In this respect, participatory research's emphasis on ordinary-language dialogue and storytelling links up with the emerging turn to discourse and argumentation in the social and policy sciences. This "argumentative turn," as we saw in Chapter 10, is itself largely a response to the political and epistemological limitations of the managerial and policy sciences' technical orientation, particularly their narrow treatment of values.[36] Discourses and narratives permit the integration of a broader selection of social meanings, norms, and values into the analytical process. It constitutes an effort to supplement the standard quantitative analysis of efficient means to given ends with a qualitative discussion of the means themselves. The task is to combine the standard of technical efficiency with goal-oriented criteria (conceptualized by Gordon as the pursuit of "qualitative efficiency"[37]).

The most well-developed discourse models in the managerial and policy sciences draw on Toulmin's "informal logic" of argumentation.[38] In Chapter 10, we illustrated the way in which an informal logic of policy evaluation provides a discursive methodology for both the presentation and the analysis of policy arguments. The logic was also shown to integrate the basic methodological concerns of technical analysis, phenomenological interpretation, and social critique in a single methodological framework. Through a framework of empirical and normative questions, the logic of policy evaluation offered a deliberative guide to problem posing, both empirical and normative. In the next section, we examine more specifically the ways in which these inter-related emphases on the actor's social context, the processes of discourse, and group learning are combined in the participatory expert's role as "facilitator."

Facilitating Empowerment:
The Function of Participatory Expertise

On paper, the basic sequence of methodological steps in the design of a participatory research project can look much like that of the standard empirical research methodology. Eldon, for example, specifies four critical decisions confronting the participatory researcher: (1) Problem definition: What is the research problem? (2) Choice of methods: Which methodologies will best provide the required data? (3) Data analysis: How are the data to be interpreted? (4) Use of findings: How can the outcomes be used? Who learns what from the research findings?[39]

"Research is participatory," Eldon explains, "when those directly affected by it influence each of these four decisions and help to carry them out." Compared with other types of researchers, the participatory researcher "is more dependent on those from whom the data come, has less control over the research process, and has more pressure to work from other people's definition of the situation."[40] This raises unique role demands on the expert, ranging from theoretician and expert to colleague and coproducer of knowledge. In each case the basic determinant of the expert's role choices must be his or her usefulness in "facilitating" the collaborative learning process. In short, the question is this: How can the expert role facilitate the development of a learning process that, once set it motion, can proceed on its own.

As we saw in the UTOPIA project, the process of facilitation is designed to enlarge the clients' abilities to pose the problems and questions that interest and concern them, and to help connect them to the kinds of information and resources needed to help them find answers. Brookfield defines facilitation as the process of "challenging learners with alternative ways of interpreting their experience" and presenting them with "ideas and behaviors that cause them to examine critically their values, ways of acting, and the assumptions by which they live." Teachers and students, experts and clients, "bring to the encounter experiences, attitudinal sets, and alternative ways of looking at their personal, professional, political, and recreational worlds, along with a multitude of differing purposes, orientations, and expectations." The medium of this interaction is a highly complex dialogue "in which the personalities of the individuals involved, the contextual setting for the educational transaction, and the prevailing political climate affect the nature and form of learning." The dialogue is likened to a "transactional drama" in which the philosophies, personalities, and priorities of the "chief players interact continuously to influence the nature, direction, and form of the subsequent learning."[41] Sometimes this dialogue can even take the form of a story or drama, utilizing video equipment and various forms of role-playing.

Hirschhorn's discussion of the professional practices of the alternative human services movement helps to clarify the expert's facilitative role. Taking up the "crisis of the professions," Hirschhorn focuses directly on the social, emotional, and intellectual distance that separates the professional from the client's experiential life-world.[42] Largely concerned with the client's social welfare, the problem is especially significant in human services work. Indeed, distance has become the source of strident disagreements over the definition of the client's social situation as well as who should have the responsibility for determining the issue. Such struggles invariably raise the question of social control, typically leading to acrimonious polemics about the professional's role in the service-delivery process. For Hirschhorn, the solution can only be found in the redesign of the professional-client relationship: The expert, in short, must be remade into a "facilitator" of client learning.

As a facilitator, the expert's task is to assist clients in *their own efforts* to examine *their own interests* and to plan appropriate courses of action. In a human services setting, this means that professionals must be skilled in such processes as "role definition, life-course planning, and the collective definition of mutual responsibilities." The assignment is "to learn the *conditions* for client learning" and to design and facilitate "the environment within which clients develop their own conceptions of satisfactory roles." In short, "professionals must become experts in how clients learn, clarify, and decide."[43] As Hirschhorn puts it:

> In such settings the professional becomes a *facilitator* of group processes. He or she must design the setting for the group (where it takes place, how many members there are, the range of professionals that can be called on) and then function as a *consultant* to it.[44]

The important exchange in this process is the one conducted between group members.

> The emphasis is on establishing the institutional conditions within which clients can draw on their own individual and collective agencies to solve their problems. . . . Methods for self-evaluation and behavior change are

enforced by the group.... [T]he professional acts as a programmer, mobilizer of resources, and consultant to a self-exploration and learning process on the part of group members.

To illustrate the differences between such alternative practices and those of the traditional expert, Hirschhorn turns to the medical analogy. In contrast to the traditional superior-subordinate relationship, alternative health services are designed to promote nonhierarchical, cooperative associations between practitioners and clients. Often such associations have centered on the establishment of "self-help" groups. Women's health clinics are one of the best examples. In these clinics, doctors help their clients (or groups of clients) learn to detect changes in their bodies, to anticipate and manage stress, and to become sensitized to their own limits and capacities, among other things. Within this framework, "the doctor acts as a consultant to people's attempts to develop their own conception of health (of which there can be many, depending on preferences for physical activity, diet, the role of acute stress, etc.)."[45]

Essential to the facilitation of empowerment, then, is the creation of institutional and intellectual conditions that help people pose questions in their own ordinary (or everyday) language and decide which issues are important to them. Theorists interested in developing these concepts have most typically turned to models of social learning and discourse. The central focus of such models is on how to establish "inquiring systems" that assist learners in the "problematization" and exploration of their own problems and interests. In the case of the UTOPIA project, that took the form of a specially designed technology laboratory.

Problem Posing and the Professional-Client Relationship

Freire's work on "problematization" or "problem-posing" is basic to the development of participatory professional-client research.[46] Problem posing, he contends, must supersede the "magister dixit" behind which hide those who regard themselves as the "proprietors," "administrators," or "bearers" of knowledge. Using the techniques of dialogue and problem posing, the educators-professionals and educatees-clients must work out a critical attitude toward their world and its problems.

Problematizing for Freire is the direct antithesis of technocratic problem solving. In the technocratic approach the expert establishes some distance from reality, analyzes the problem into component parts, devises means for resolving difficulties in the most efficient way, and then dictates the strategy or policy. Such problem solving, as Freire makes clear, distorts the totality of human experience by reducing it to those dimensions that are amenable to treatment *as mere difficulties to be solved.* To "problematize," on the other hand, is to help people codify into symbols an integrated picture or story of reality, which, in the course of its development, can generate a critical consciousness capable of empowering them to alter their relations to both the physical and the social worlds.

Consciousness-raising, or what Freire calls "conscientization," is the critical goal or test of problem posing. Conscientization is described as "learning to perceive social, political and economic contradictions and to take action against the oppressive elements of reality." In the conscientization process, "thematic investigation involves participation in an ever-deepening analysis of words or experiences common to their reality in order to question common assumptions and facilitate a better understanding of that reality."[47] Through thematic dialogues and the exchange of stories with others, learners can become the "transforming agents" of their own social reality. They emerge, in the process of such discourse, as the *subjects* rather than the *objects* of their own history. Or, as C. Wright Mills so aptly put it, history is turned into biography.[48]

Problem posing and conscientization pose a fundamental challenge to the traditional teacher-student/professional-client relationship. As Freire puts it, in the context of critical dialogue, "the teacher-of-the-students and the students-of-the-teacher cease to exist and a new term emerges: teacher-students with students-teacher." No longer is the teacher "merely the-one-who-teaches, but also one who is himself taught in dialogue with the students, who in turn are learning to teach. As the coproducers of knowledge, they become "jointly responsible for a process in which all grow."[49]

In the mainstream literature on professional expertise, the writings of Donald Schön come the closest to taking up the issue of problem posing and its implications for the professional-client relationship.[50] Schön is fundamentally concerned about the lack of an open and authentic professional-client interaction in the managerial and policy sciences. For him, it is key to the reconstruction of expert practices.

Like Freire, Schön attributes the failure of professional managerial and policy expertise to an outdated adherence to the technical model of rationality and the superior-subordinate professional-client relationship that it requires. Giving rise to one-dimensional, distorted communications between practitioners and their clients, the relationship impedes the activity most critical to effective practices, what Schön refers to as "problem-setting." The term is used to connote essentially the same intellectual task conceptualized by Freire as "problem-posing."[51]

Problem *setting* is nontechnical in nature and contrasts sharply with problem *solving*. Whereas the latter involves technical knowledge and skills, such as those typically associated with managerial and policy science methodologies (cost-benefit analysis, systems analysis, program evaluation, and so on), problem *setting* is fundamentally normative and qualitative. In technical analysis, values and goals are taken as given; in problem setting, analysis focuses on their identification and discovery. Indeed, at times it involves the consensual shaping of new value orientations. An inherently creative exercise, problem setting can neither be explained nor taught from the technical (positivistic) perspective that informs much of professional practice. In this sense, problem setting is better understood as an art form than a science per se.

In more specific terms, problem setting concerns two interrelated tasks: the determination of the relevant problem situations to be addressed and the theoretical normative frameworks (or simply "frames," to use Schön and Rein's term) that structure and shape our basic understandings of particular policy issues, including the criteria appropriate for their evaluation.[52] (In terms of the logic of evaluation presented in Chapter 10, questions pertaining to problem situations and normative frames can be conceptualized, respectively, as issues confronted at the levels of validation and social choice.)

Analytically preceding technical problem solving, problem setting requires professionals to initiate what Schön calls a "conversation with the situation." Focusing in particular on naming situations and defining the problems that arise in them, "reflection in action" necessitates a new epistemological orientation. The quantitative modes of reason that have shaped policy inquiry must, in short, make room for interpretive modes of qualitative reason. This epistemological reconstruction, as we have seen in Chapter 9, is the project of postpositivism.

Professional Training

Participatory research poses some sophisticated challenges for professional training. One concerns the educational curriculum. Once

we recognize that participatory research is as much a creative art form as
a science, we venture into unknown pedagogical territories. Scientific
methodology texts, perhaps unfortunately, can be organized like cook-
books. But an art form is different. Not only is there no formula, we
know very little about the creative impulse itself. How, for example, do
we educate an analyst to appreciate the range of human folly or the
boundaries of human virtue? How do we train the investigator to intui-
tively sense openings and opportunities in human affairs? If there is an
answer, it no doubt includes greater exposure to the creative arts, novels,
poetry, cultures, and so on. But these are only generalities; the question
remains open.[53]

Beyond the creative dimensions, however, one requirement is relatively straightforward. In more immediate terms, professional-client
collaboration requires the expert to have special knowledge of the
client's needs, interests, and values. Toward this end, there have been
numerous projects designed to *resocialize* professionals to the client's
"natural setting." In the context of community and human services, for
example, Gottlieb and Farquharson state the objective in fairly typical
language:

> Social workers, psychologists, and family physicians must be prepared to
> examine both the limits of their own knowledge base, and the psychologi-
> cal and financial costs to the public of the technologies they practice.
> They also need to develop a deeper appreciation of the nature, scope and
> effects of the support systems and caregiving arrangements that have been
> invented without the advice of experts, but which have capitalized on
> people's experiential knowledge.[54]

Toward this end, they have spelled out the elements of a pedagogical
strategy designed to accommodate the investigator "to the ways that citizens handle their own health and welfare needs." Most important, is "the
need first to undermine the professional's trust and beliefs in the ascendancy of technology, and force a reexamination of a professional enterprise that casts nonprofessionals into the subservient role of client or
patient." Specifically, professionals must gain firsthand knowledge of
encounters with self-help groups and other collective projects. They
must "get acquainted with local residents who have animated and en-
abled others to take into their own hands the responsibility for effecting
change"; they must learn firsthand "the empowering impact of a mutual-
aid group"; and they need "to observe how a collectivist agency's non-

hierarchical organizational structure can mitigate the burnout that attends traditional institutional forms."[55]

In curricular terms, then, alternative professional training means building in educational experiences that bring professionals into closer contact with the client's everyday experiences, language, and culture. Such experiences must be designed to wean professionals away from their faith in technique, their adherence to hierarchy, and their reliance on the ideologies of expertise. In many cases, it will involve building contacts with alternative social and political movements.

Facilitating Participation: Political Implications

It is important also to say a word about the political implications of the facilitator's role in the professional-client relationship. Facilitation and its problem-posing orientation are founded on the long-established but largely ignored assumption that "the acts of teaching and learning— and the creation and alteration of beliefs, values, actions, relationships, and social forms that result from this—are ways in which we realize our humanity." As Brookfield puts it, "The extent to which adults are engaged in a free exchange of ideas, beliefs, and practices is one gauge of whether society is open, democratic, and healthy."[56]

Although clearly political in its import, a commitment to such dialogue is not in and of itself to be confused with a commitment to a specific doctrine or ideology (although Freire's critics tirelessly argue that he uses his methodology to purvey a Marxist view of the world). For participatory researchers firmly committed to democratic values, educational facilitation and political proselytizing are geared to fundamentally different objectives. Political ideologists, accepting their beliefs as the *one true way* of thinking about the world, proselytize with a predetermined definition of the successful outcome; diverging views are simply dismissed as wrong thinking, bad faith, or false consciousness. By contrast, the facilitator may passionately advance ideas about how people should learn and act, but such views must themselves be presented to learners for the same kind of critical scrutiny to which the educator has subjected other views of which he or she is personally critical. The end of the encounter, in other words, is not the acceptance by participants of the facilitator's preordained values and beliefs. Rather, it is to pose problems and questions for critical dialogue and group concensus formation.

In the process, the facilitator must be especially careful not to confuse the general task of enlightenment with that of deciding questions of strategic action. Theoretical discussion and consciousness-raising can never legitimate a fortiori the risky decisions of strategic action. As Habermas puts it, "Decisions for . . . political struggle cannot at the outset be justified theoretically and then be carried out organizationally." The only "possible justification at this level is consensus aimed at in practical discourse, among the participants, who, in the consciousness of their common interests and their knowledge of circumstances, of the predictable consequences and secondary consequences, are the only ones who can know what risks they are willing to undergo, and with what expectations."[57] In short, the facilitator can bring theoretical and empirical knowledge to bear on the participants' circumstances, but it is the participants themselves who must actually decide which courses of action they are willing to undertake.

Concluding Thoughts

Although projects devoted to empowerment and participatory research are only in their nascent stages, the number of experimental efforts continues to grow. Not only do these self-help projects represent an important step toward the creation of a genuine participatory culture, their experiments with facilitative approaches to problem solving offer important insights for the innovation of an alternative model of professional expertise.

This is not to imply that all of the projects to reconstruct the practices of professional expertise have been successful. Many of them have in fact been abysmal failures. As a model for expertise, however, the efforts behind participatory research pose a very interesting and direct challenge to mainstream organizational and policy research. In sharp contrast to the mainstream commitment to the corporate-bureaucratic state, participatory research has emerged from a genuine commitment to social movements and a democratic culture. Whereas the "bureaucratic" sciences focus primarily on techniques for analyzing means to ends, participatory research emphasizes the process of formulating policy ends. It recognizes the importance of means but relegates standard means-ends analysis to a subordinate status.

It is unlikely that participatory research will have a direct and significant impact on the managerial and policy sciences, at least not in the near future. The reason is clear: They serve two very different and antagonistic conceptions of the state: corporate-bureaucratic and participatory. Indeed, participatory research has developed as a direct challenge to the institutional methodologies of the corporate-state bureaucratic system.

Thus bringing empowerment and participation into the managerial and policy sciences must be recognized as the radical project that it is. This, however, doesn't mean that the discussion is only theoretical and utopian. Rather, it means that the project faces formidable political and practical obstacles that must be confronted on their own terms. For those interested in joining the effort, we close with an outline of some of the primary elements of an agenda for praxis. The project must, in this respect, proceed on two interrelated levels, epistemological and political.

On the epistemological level, the task ahead is fairly clear but it poses rigorous intellectual problems. The effort to introduce collaborative research based on the methodologies of problem posing, discourse, and social learning confronts the most interesting and sophisticated epistemological issues in the social sciences. Underlying these methodologies are two critically important epistemological questions: How do we analytically integrate empirical and normative knowledge? How do we combine the professional's scientific knowledge with the citizen/client's ordinary knowledge? Although such work is already under way, largely under the banner of postpositivism, it is still in its emergent stages. Much of it, moreover, remains intellectual and largely unconnected to politics and participatory movements.

In political terms, the task is to take up the cause of participatory democracy. In a country that fancies itself as a democracy, such a commitment surely has virtue in its corner. On the surface of the matter, its legitimacy cannot be questioned. Moreover, the openness of American society provides numerous possibilities for initiating alternative social experiments. Against the dominant elitist practices of American democracy, however, participatory democracy will in reality meet with substantial opposition. Its nonelitist orientation cuts to the most fundamental nerve of the political system. At issue here is a broad-scale transformation of the political culture of contemporary society; bureaucratic and elitist decision-making processes and practices must be replaced by participatory institutions and processes.

Change of this order can only be brought about by political forces outside the dominant institutions. At present, the possibility of such change depends largely on the political strength of alternative social and political movements and the methodological sophistication of their projects. Stated in these terms, one must concede that such a societal transformation is not on the political horizon. Given the deeply entrenched character of the corporate state and its bureaucratic apparatus, it would be misleading to suggest such social transformation to be anything more than a long-term political struggle.

Beyond a broad-scale social transformation, however, there are also more immediate reasons in contemporary society to take seriously the values of participatory democracy. In recent years, for example, there has been in advanced industrial societies a significant increase in "post-materialist" values that has brought growing demands for more participation in the workplace as well as in the political sphere.[58] Indeed, it is not incorrect to interpret many of the social movement projects as political manifestations of this broader postindustrial social demand. Such trends clearly indicate a continuing interest in participation and, as a consequence, in the relevance of new models and practices within the existing structures of modern societies, advanced industrial or postindustrial.

The effort to bring empowerment into the mainstream disciplines can, therefore, be interpreted as an effort to infuse them with new social values that are already emerging in society generally. Such change, of course, never occurs automatically. It depends on the presence of both external and internal political forces. This latter requirement sets out a role for those in the discipline sympathetic to participatory social movements. Their function as social scientists must be to bridge the gap between the movement and the disciplines. As such, it is both political and intellectual.

Even though such activity is largely missing in the managerial and policy sciences, it is possible to identify such projects within various kindred disciplines. Inspired in many cases by social movements, such groups exist in economics (the Union for Radical Political Economy), urban planning (the Planners' Network), law (the Critical Legal Studies movement), public health (Health/PAC), education (the critical pedagogy movement), computer science (Computer Professionals for Social Responsibility), the natural sciences (*Science for the People*, the public interest and critical science movements), and medicine (Physicians for Social Responsibility), among others. Even in the managerial professions one can find a small—and less-well-organized—group of scholars committed to workplace democracy and the various organizations that promote it (the Association for Workplace Democracy).[59] Basic to these groups is an interest in alternative expert practices. For those eager to take up the challenge, they provide important models for an alternative project in the managerial and policy sciences.

In specific procedural terms, it is essential to examine systematically the institutional and intellectual conditions that support the successful use of participatory inquiring systems.[60] In particular, we need to develop systematic rules for structuring collaborative problem posing, expert-client discourse, and social learning. When participatory research projects fail, the problem most commonly stems from a misbegotten belief—namely, that participation assigns equal weight to all opinions and, worse, that everyone can talk at will (if not all at once). Under these conditions, participatory research opens up a cacophony of miscommunication that easily degenerates into vituperative name-calling. In the absence of a well-structured model of expert-client discourse, including rules of evidence and evaluation criteria, participatory research can be a formula for trouble. To avoid its premature failure, and to avert disillusionment among both experts and clients in the process, it is essential that the ground rules of the alternative model, procedural as well as methodological, be carefully worked out.[61] Such procedures must develop alongside the political struggle to democratize the inquiry process. To proceed on the political front without having established procedures for the research process itself is to jeopardize the project from the outset.

With these remarks we can conclude our exploration. The foregoing discussion, of course, is only a sketch of an alternative practice. Nonetheless, it has established the fact that alternatives to the technocratic model are available. While there is much to be done in methodological terms, it is at least clear where the search for professional relevance begins. Far less clear is the question of where the politics will come from. Much will depend on the viability of social movements in the society as a whole. This question emerges as the central issue on the agenda of those concerned with the problem of technocracy and the politics of expertise.

Notes

1. For a guide to this literature, see Claus Offe, "New Social Movements: Challenging the Boundaries of Institutional Politics," *Social Research* 52, no. 4 (1985): 817–68; Tim Luke, "Power and Resistance in Informationalizing Postindustrial Societies," in *Screens of Power* (Urbana: University of Illinois Press, 1989), chap. 8; Carl Boggs,

Social Movements and Political Power: Emerging Forms of Radicalism in the West (Philadelphia: Temple University Press, 1986); Herbert Kitschelt, "New Social Movements in West Germany and the United States," in *Political Power and Social Theory,* vol. 5, ed. Maurice Zeitland (Greenwich, CT: JAI, 1985), pp. 273–324.

2. The tension between technocrats and populists, it is important to note, typically cuts across the lines of established political parties. In the United States, for example, both technocratic and populist tendencies can be found in both parties. This conflict is an important factor presently undercutting the ability of the Democratic and Republican parties to pull together a united constituency around a commonly accepted program.

3. Andreas Knie, "Alternative Wirtschaft = Alternative Technik? Uberlegungen zu einem experimentellen Ansatz Berliner Regional-politik in einem Zentrum für soziale Erfindungen," in *Zukunfstmetropole Berlin: Kritik und Perspektiven wirtschaftspolitischer Leitbilder,* ed. Klaus Burmeister and Weet Canzler (Berlin: Rainer Bohn Verlag, 1988).

4. On "movement intellectuals," see Jacqueline Cramer, Ron Eyerman, and Andrew Jamison, "Intellectuals and the Environmental Movement" (Paper delivered at the Conference on Intellectuals, Culture and Science, University of Amsterdam, Post-Graduate Institute of Sociology, June, 17–19, 1987); and Olga Amsterdamska, "Intellectuals in Social Movements: The Experts of 'Solidarity,' " in *The Social Directions of the Public Sciences* ed. Stuart Blume et al. (Dordrecht: D. Reidel, 1987), pp. 213–45.

5. Empowerment concerns the ability to create, give, and share power. See C. H. Kieffer, "Citizen Empowerment: A Developmental Perspective," *Prevention in Human Service* no. 3, (1984): 8–36; H. Moglen, "Power and Empowerment," *Women's Studies International Forum* 6, no. 2 (1983): 131–34. On empowerment in the workplace, see Charles Derber and William Schwartz, "Toward a Theory of Worker Participation," *Sociological Inquiry,* Winter 1983.

6. Frank Riessmann, "New Directions in Self-Help," *Social Policy* 15, no. 3 (Winter 1985): 2–4.

7. See, for example, Robert Mitchell, "National Environmental Lobbies and the Apparent Illogic of Collective Action," in *Collective Decision Making,* ed. Clifford Russell (Baltimore: Johns Hopkins University Press, 1979); and, more generally, Daniel Bell, *The Cultural Contradictions of Capitalism* (New York: Basic Books, 1976).

8. On the concept of "major" and "minor" professions, see Nathan Glazer, "The Schools of Minor Professions," *Minerva,* 1974, p. 346.

9. Donald A. Schön, *The Reflective Practitioner* (New York: Basic Books, 1983), p. 292.

10. See Eliot Freidson, *Professional Power* (Chicago: University of Chicago Press, 1987); and B. J. Bledstein, *The Culture of Professionalism* (New York: Norton, 1976).

11. To be sure, in the case of flagrant violations it is possible for the client to legally sue the professional, as in the case of a medical malpractice suit. But such actions are often prohibitively expensive and time-consuming and the possibilities for satisfaction are far from certain.

12. Ivan Illich, *A Celebration of Awareness: A Call for Institutional Revolution* (Garden City, NY: Doubleday, 1970).

13. Magali Sarfatti Larson, *The Rise of Professionalism* (Berkeley: University of California Press, 1977).

14. Manfred Stanley, *The Technological Conscience* (Chicago: University of Chicago Press, 1978).

15. The case of psychiatrists voting to determine whether or not homosexuality is an illness is a pertinent example.

16. The classic example is Taylorism, including its contemporary variants. See Chapter 12.

17. Alain Touraine, *Sociologie de l'action* (Paris: Editions du Seuil, 1965), and *The Voice and the Eye* (Cambridge: Cambridge University Press, 1981); and Peter Kivisto, "Contemporary Social Movements in Advanced Industrial Societies and Sociological Intervention: An Appraisal of Alain Touraine's *Pratique*," *Acta Sociologia* 27 , no. 4 (1984): 355–66.

18. Alain Touraine, *Solidarity* (Cambridge: Cambridge University Press, 1983).

19. On *conricerca*, see the journal *Quaderni Rossi*, especially the six issues that appeared between 1961 and 1967. For a programmatic debate, see no. 5 (March 1965). Also, see Angela Zanotti, "Sui rapporti tra sociologia e potere in Italia: Gli auuni '50 e '60," *La Critica Sociologica*, no. 66 (Summer 1983).

20. Quoted in Francesco Apergi, "Sulle origini di una sociologia marxista in Italia: il caso dei 'Quaderni Rossi,' " *Critica Marxista*, no. 1 (1978), p. 118.

21. See Peter Wagner, "Social Sciences and Political Projects: Reform Coalitions Between Social Scientists and Policy-Makers in France, Italy and West Germany," in Blume, *The Social Directions,* pp. 277–306.

22. John Friedmann, *Planning in the Public Domain,* (Princeton, NJ: Princeton University Press, 1987), part III.

23. John Friedmann, *The Good Society* (Cambridge: MIT Press, 1979).

24. I am particularly indebted to Wendy Kohli of the State University of New York at Binghamton for sharing with me both her extensive literature on participatory research and her personal, firsthand observations on the movement. See Peter Reason and John Rowan, eds., *Human Inquiry: A Sourcebook of New Paradigm Research* (New York: John Wiley, 1981); Juliet Merrifield, *Putting the Scientists in Their Place: Participatory Research in Environmental and Occupational Health* (New Market, TN: Highlander Center, 1989); Yusuf Kassam and Kemal Mustafa, eds., *Participatory Research: An Emerging Alternative in Social Science Research* (Nairobi: African Adult Education Association, 1982); and Walter Fernandes and Rajesh Tandon, eds., *Participatory Research and Evaluation: Experiments in Research as a Process of Liberation* (New Delhi: Indian Social Institute, 1981); and Society for Participatory Research in Asia, *Participatory Research: An Introduction,* Participatory Research Network Series no. 3 (Society for Participatory Research in Asia: Rajkamal Electric Press, 4163 Arya Pura, Delhi 110007, 1982). These publications contain bibliographies and discussions of case studies drawn from projects in the United States, Africa, Latin America, India, England, Canada, Indonesia, as well as other information. The last one contains a guide to participatory research network centers. In the United States, the Highlander Center in Tennessee is perhaps the most important ongoing institution engaged in participatory research. Their participatory research on land-use policy in Appalachia serves as a standard reference point in the development of the movement. Also, in North America the "Participatory Research Group" in Toronto is particularly active.

25. Alfred J. Marrow, *The Practical Theorist* (New York: Basic Books, 1969).

26. Chris Argyris et al., *Action Science* (Cambridge, MA: Harvard University Press, 1985); Gerald I. Susman, "Action Research: A Sociotechnical Systems Perspective," in *Beyond Method: Strategies for Social Research*, ed. Gareth Morgan (Beverly Hills, CA: Sage, 1983), pp. 95–113; and Gerald I. Susman and Roger D. Evered, "An Assessment of the Scientific Merits of Action Research," *Administrative Science Quarterly* 23 (December 1978): 582–603.

27. Frank Sherwood, "Action Research and Organizational Learning," *Administration and Society*, December 1978, pp. 21, 38.

28. Warren Bennis, *Changing Organizations* (New York: McGraw-Hill, 1966).

29. See Donald D. Stull and Jean J. Schensul, eds., *Collaborative Research and Social Change* (Boulder, CO: Westview, 1987); and Argyris et al., *Action Science*.

30. Ibid.

31. For discussion on this point, see John Friedmann, *Planning in the Public Domain*, pp. 187–219.

32. Argyris et al., *Action Science*.

33. For a general guide to the phenomenological perspective, particularly from a methodological point of view, see Paul Filmer et al., *New Directions in Sociological Theory* (Cambridge: MIT Press, 1973).

34. On "ordinary knowledge," see Charles Lindblom and David Cohen, *Usable Knowledge* (New Haven, CT: Yale University Press, 1979). They define "ordinary knowledge" as knowledge "that does not owe its origin, testing, degree of verification, truth status, or currency to distinctive . . . professional techniques but rather to common sense, casual empiricism or thoughtful speculation and analysis." Also, see Casten von Otter, "Worker Participation and Working Knowledge" (Discussion paper, Swedish Center for Working Life, 1975).

35. On storytelling, see Martin Krieger, *Advice and Planning* (Philadelphia: Temple University Press, 1981); and Thomas Kaplan, "The Narrative Structure of Policy Analysis," *Journal of Policy Analysis and Management* 5, no. 4 (Summer 1986): 761–78.

36. See John Forester and Frank Fischer, eds., *The Argumentative Turn in Planning and Policy Analysis* (Durham, NC: Duke University, forthcoming).

37. David M. Gordon, "Capitalist Efficiency and Socialist Efficiency," *Monthly Review* 28 (July–August 1979): 19.

38. Stephen Toulmin, *The Uses of Argument* (Cambridge: Cambridge University Press, 1958); C. West Churchman, *The Design of Inquiring Systems* (New York: Basic Books, 1971); Ian Mitroff, "A Communications Model of Dialectical Inquiring Systems: A Strategy for Strategic Planning," *Management Science* 17 (June 1971): B634–48; Richard O. Mason, "A Dialectical Approach to Strategic Planning," *Management Science* 15 (April 1969): B403–14; William Dunn, *Public Policy Analysis* (Englewood Cliffs, NJ: Prentice-Hall, 1981); Robert Hoppe, "Assessing the Quality of Public Policy Discourse: The Case of Ethnic Policy in the Netherlands," in Forester and Fischer, *The Argumentative Turn*; and Chapter 10 of this book.

39. Max Eldon, "Sharing the Research Work: Participative Research and Its Role Demands," in *Human Inquiry: A Sourcebook of New Paradigm Research*, ed. Peter Reason and John Rowan (New York: John Wiley, 1981), pp. 253–66.

40. Ibid.

41. Stephen D. Brookfield, *Understanding and Facilitating Adult Learning* (San Francisco: Jossey-Bass, 1986), pp. 1–24.

42. Larry Hirschhorn, "Alternative Service and the Crisis of Professions," in *Co-ops, Communes and Collectives: Experiments in Social Change in the 1960s and 1970s,* ed. John Case and Rosemary C. R. Taylor (New York: Pantheon, 1979), pp. 153–93. Also, see Julian Rappaport et al., "Collaborative Research with a Mutual Help Organization," *Social Policy,* Winter 1985, p. 15; and Stull and Schensul, *Collaborative Research.*

43. Hirschhorn, "Alternative Service," p. 188.

44. Ibid.

45. Ibid; and Audrey Gartner, "A Typology of Women's Self- Help Groups," *Social Policy,* Winter 1985, pp. 25–30.

46. Paulo Freire, *Pedagogy of the Oppressed* (New York: Seabury, 1979), and *Education for Critical Consciousness* (New York: Seabury, 1973).

47. Society for Participatory Research in Asia, *Participatory Research: An Introduction,* p. 3.

48. C. Wright Mills, *The Sociological Imagination* (New York: Oxford University Press, 1959), pp. 143–64.

49. Freire, *Pedagogy of the Oppressed.*

50. Schön, *The Reflective Practitioner.*

51. This point is recognized by Brookfield, *Understanding and Facilitating,* p. 248.

52. Donald Schön and Martin Rein, "Frame Analysis," in *Social Sciences and Modern States: National Experiences and Theoretical Crossroads,* ed. Björn Wittrock, Carol Weiss, Peter Wagner, and Hellmut Wollmann (Cambridge: Cambridge University Press, forthcoming).

53. On these points I am indebted to the helpful comments of Leslie Pal.

54. Benjamin H. Gottlieb and Andrew Farquharson, "Blueprint for a Curriculum on Social Support," *Social Policy,* Winter 1985, pp. 31–34.

55. Ibid.

56. Brookfield, *Understanding and Facilitating,* p. 1. He adds: "If adults of widely differing class and ethnic groups are actively exploring ideas, beliefs, and practices, then we are likely to have a society in which creativity, diversity, and the continuous re-creation of social structures are the accepted norms. By contrast, societies in which inquiry, reflection, diversity and exploration are the prerogatives of a privileged minority are likely to be static, ossified, and hierarchical."

57. Jürgen Habermas, *Theory and Practice* (Boston: Beacon, 1973), p. 33.

58. Robert Inglehard, "New Social Movements: Cognitive Mobilization and Value Change" (Public Lecture at the Free University of West Berlin, John F. Kennedy Institute for North American Studies, June 30, 1988).

59. For a specific example, see Robert Mangabeira Unger, *The Critical Legal Studies Movement* (Cambridge, MA: Harvard University Press, 1986). On the public interest science movement, see Joel Primack and Frank von Hippel, *Advice and Dissent: Scientists in the Political Arena* (New York: Basic Books, 1974). In the case of management, the potential for such a movement is not to be dismissed. The attendance at the 1985 conference on Critical Perspectives on Organizational Analysis held at Baruch College of the City University of New York clearly demonstrated the existence of a significant interest in alternative perspectives in the discipline of management.

60. For a thought-provoking discussion, see Peter deLeon, "Participatory Policy

Analysis: Prescriptions and Precautions" (Paper delivered at the meeting of the International Political Science Association, Washington, DC, August 31, 1988).

61. Disillusionment can lead to several unfortunate possibilities. One is that the expert, in the face of despair, gives up his or her commitment to alternative movements and joins the ranks of the corporate-state bureaucracy. The other is the possibility that the expert becomes so close to the membership of a social movement that he or she abandons—wittingly or unwittingly—the objective use of needed methodological techniques. The history of social movements illustrates the dangers of both possibilities. It is especially important for this reason to develop an alternative professional community with guidelines that such experts can fall back on in the course of their practices. I owe these observations to Peter Wagner.

Index

About the Author

FRANK FISCHER is Associate Professor of Political Science at Rutgers University and Director of the Science, Technology and Society Program in Newark. Currently a visiting scholar at the Science Center in West Berlin, he is engaged in research on the role of the state in science and technology policy. Included among his publications are *Politics, Values and Public Policy*; *Critical Studies in Organization and Bureaucracy* (coedited with Carmen Sirianni); and *Confronting Values in Policy Analysis: The Politics of Criteria* (coedited with John Forester). At present, he is completing *Evaluating Public Policy: A Postpositivist Approach* (coauthored with Jerry Mitchell). In addition, he is serving as the guest editor of *Industrial Crisis Quarterly* and is a member of the editorial boards of the *Policy Studies Journal, Administration and Society*, and the *International Journal of Public Administration*.